MW01616479

Essential Ethics for
Social Work Practice

Allan Edward Barsky

Florida Atlantic University

Essential Ethics for Social Work Practice

Allan Edward Barsky, JD, MSW, PhD

Florida Atlantic University

OXFORD
UNIVERSITY PRESS

OXFORD
UNIVERSITY PRESS

Oxford University Press is a department of the University of Oxford.
It furthers the University's objective of excellence in research, scholarship,
and education by publishing worldwide. Oxford is a registered trade mark
of Oxford University Press in the UK and in certain other countries.

Published in the United States of America by Oxford University Press
198 Madison Avenue, New York, NY 10016, United States of America.

© 2023 by Oxford University Press

For titles covered by Section 112 of the US Higher Education Opportunity
Act, please visit www.oup.com/us/he for the latest information about
pricing and alternate formats.

All rights reserved. No part of this publication may be reproduced,
stored in a retrieval system, or transmitted, in any form or by any means,
without the prior permission in writing of Oxford University Press,
or as expressly permitted by law, by license or under terms agreed with
the appropriate reprographics rights organization. Inquiries concerning
reproduction outside the scope of the above should be sent to the Rights
Department, Oxford University Press, at the address above.

You must not circulate this work in any other form
and you must impose this same condition on any acquirer.

CIP data is on file at the Library of Congress.
ISBN: 978-0-19-758513-9
Library of Congress Control Number: 2022937020

Printing number: 9 8 7 6 5 4 3 2 1
Printed by Sheridan Books, Inc.,
United States of America

PREFACE

A MESSAGE FOR STUDENTS

Ethics and values are fundamental components of social work education and practice. The first core competency in the Council on Social Work Education's (CSWE, 2022) Educational Policies and Accreditation standards is "Demonstrate Ethical and Professional Behavior." The materials in this textbook have been designed to help you develop knowledge and skills identified in this competency, including the abilities to

- make ethical decisions by applying the standards of the NASW Code of Ethics (2021), relevant laws and regulations, models for ethical decision-making, ethical conduct of research, and additional codes of ethics as appropriate to the context;
- demonstrate professional demeanor in behavior, appearance, and oral, written, and electronic communication;
- manage personal and professional value conflicts and affective reactions;
- use technology ethically and appropriately to facilitate practice outcomes; and
- use supervision and consultation to guide professional judgment and behavior (CSWE, 2022, pp. 4–5).

As you work through this textbook, you will learn how to integrate social work values and ethics in all aspects of practice with clients, colleagues, research participants, and communities. Rote memorization of rules and laws is neither sufficient nor interesting. Instead, this textbook invites you to engage personally in a range of learning experiences: reflecting on your own values, analyzing practice situations, role-playing social worker-client interviews, and pondering challenging ethical issues. Challenge yourself to think through situations from other people's perspectives. Do not be afraid to play the devil's advocate, stating positions or asking questions that others may not have considered. By having good ethical conversations with our classmates and role-play partners, we can practice the skills of managing ethical conflicts and promoting outcomes consistent with our core professional values. At his trial for impiety and corrupting youth, Greek philosopher Socrates suggested that an unexplored life is not worth living. Throughout your readings and class discussions, you will have the opportunity to make your life worth living by questioning, examining, and thinking through a broad array of situations raising ethical and moral issues.

As you ponder each case example, be creative in your thinking. Take risks during role-plays. Classroom exercises give you an opportunity to test different ideas, skills, and strategies without posing risks to real clients. The first time I counseled a client with suicidal ideation, I had no prior experience with the ethical and clinical issues that arose—not even in a role-play. I knew suicide intervention from a theoretical perspective, but I had little understanding of suicide intervention from an experiential one. Use the scenarios in this textbook to practice application of various strategies and skills for managing ethical issues. Raise your own questions to help bridge the gap between theory and practice.

Ethical practice is not simply a critical thinking process conducted as if we are objective third parties. As the tenets of virtue ethics (described in Chapter 2) suggest, ethics is embedded in our ongoing interactions and relationships with clients and others. Ethical practice involves emotional presence, reflection, analysis, conversation, problem-solving, and action. In a departure from the third-person objective style of many textbooks, I use first-person ("I") and second-person ("you") language in many of the case illustrations. By referring to you, me, or us in the examples, I am hoping that we immerse ourselves in the scenarios. Rather than talking about ethical issues as if they are happening to other people, I encourage you to reflect on how you would feel, think, and respond if you were directly involved in each situation. By immersing ourselves in the case examples, we can raise self-awareness and prepare ourselves for responding to actual ethical issues that we are bound to experience in our professional lives.

If you are looking to this textbook for simple, definitive answers for handling difficult ethical issues, you may be disappointed—at least initially. Although we have a range of laws, agency policies, and ethical codes as guides for ethical practice, in many situations, the best response to an ethical problem is not clear. In some cases, there may be conflicting ethical and legal obligations. In other cases, there may be no way to accurately predict which course of action will lead to the greater good— or avoid the greater harm. Being able to manage uncertainty and the stress caused by uncertainty is crucial. This textbook does not necessarily provide you with specific answers to complex ethical problems; it does provide a range of tools and strategies that can guide you toward solution. As you work with clients and colleagues to manage challenging issues, remember to keep an open mind and an open heart.

A NOTE FOR INSTRUCTORS

Thank you for considering this textbook for your course. As the title of this textbook suggests, the following materials focus on the essential knowledge and skills that students will need to promote social work values and conduct themselves in an ethical manner. Whereas my prior textbook, "Ethics and Values in Social Work: An Integrated Approach for a Comprehensive Curriculum," included materials allied with both generalist and specialist areas of social work, this textbook is geared toward generalist practice. Although this volume includes certain information from the prior textbook, it is presented in a more concise manner so the material may be covered in a single course rather than across an entire BSW or MSW curriculum. This volume is organized according to specific sets of values and ethical principles, including social justice and anti-oppression, autonomy and self-determination, privacy and informed consent, and honesty and integrity. Throughout each chapter, students will have an opportunity to learn how each set of values and ethical principles apply to practice and research with individuals, families, groups, and communities. They will also have opportunities to apply the "Framework for Managing Ethical Issues" for situations in which social workers, clients, and colleagues are faced with conflicting values or ethics. (The Framework appears in Box 2.1 and also on the inside back cover of the text for easy reference.) You may support student autonomy and proficiency by encouraging students to work through the ethical issues, presenting their own professional judgments and reasoning. For many situations, there is not a single correct answer. Still, it is important for students to use critical thinking skills and to be able to justify how they would respond to challenging ethical situations. Foster a class culture that embraces diverse perspectives, open and respectful expression of ideas, empathic listening, and a commitment to learning rather than simply debating.

The study of values and ethics often involves analysis of complex laws, policies, values, and ethical standards. In writing this book, I have tried to be careful with the accuracy of information that I provide and my choice of words to explain key concepts. As you work through this textbook with your students, you may question certain information or statements. I welcome your questions and feedback. I may be able to clarify information or provide support for what I have written. If I have provided misinformation, I will provide corrections online and in future editions. Feel free to email me at barsky@barsky.org or view my website at https://www.barsky.org. For additional teaching resources and learning activities, please consult the ancillary materials posted on the Oxford University Press website for this textbook (http://www.oup.edu). The password-protected ancillary materials include a test bank of 140 multiple-choice questions, PowerPoint slides for each chapter, a sample course syllabus, textbook updates, and other suggestions for teaching and learning activities.

ABOUT THE AUTHOR

Dr. Barsky has a background in social work, law, ethics, and mediation. He has taught at a university level since 1989 in four schools of social work (University of Toronto, Ryerson University, University of Calgary, and Florida Atlantic University, where he is a full professor). He chaired the National Ethics Committee of the National Association of Social Workers and was awarded the NASW's "Excellence in Ethics Award" in 2015. From 2015 to 2017, Dr. Barsky served on the National Task Force on Social Work and Technology. He also chaired the NASW's Code of Ethics Revision Task Force, leading to the 2018 revisions to the Code. Dr. Barsky's other book authorships include *Conflict Resolution for the Helping Professions* (Oxford University Press), *Interdisciplinary Practice with Diverse Populations* (Greenwood, co-edited), and *Clinicians in Court* (Guilford). He was named "Scholar of the Year" at Florida Atlantic University in 2020. For further information and publications, please see https://barsky.org

ACKNOWLEDGMENTS

The past few years have been marked by the COVID-19 pandemic, political turmoil, horrific wars, a flood of misinformation disseminated through social media, and a social reckoning over racism and systemic discrimination. Throughout these challenges, I continue to be inspired by the commitment, vision, and creativity of our social work students as they learn how to put social work values and ethics into practice. I thank the wonderful students in my ethics and practice classes for their energy, compassion, and insights. I am extremely grateful to Dr. Heather Thompson and the Sandler School of Social Work at Florida Atlantic University for their ongoing support of my aspirations as a social work academic and advocate for social justice. I truly appreciate Dana Bliss, Sherith Pankratz, Alyssa Palazzo, Emma Stens, and the other staff at Oxford University Press for their tremendous support, ideas, feedback, and editing throughout the publication process. Many thanks to Ann Borman and her colleagues at Straive for their kind service and attention to detail during the production process. Thank you, also, to Sabrina Clark, Christopher A. Mallett, Consoler Teboh, Mark Bonacci, Susan Radzilowski, Thelma Rodriguez, Rose Marie Lichtenfels, Frann Franklin, David C. Barry, Michaela Rinkel, Catherine Earley, Amanda Hill, Elise Reed, Cheryl Hyde, Lisa Adams-Qualls, Kim Boland-Prom, Jeannie Lawrence, Theresa Maher, Randy Hoffpauir, Carolyn D. Haney, Jina Sang, Stephanie Hicks-Pass, and April Jones, for your thorough reviews and exceptional feedback on earlier drafts of this volume. To my husband Greg and daughter Adelle, I love you and thank you for all your kindness, moral support, understanding, and good humor. And finally, I wish to dedicate this book to my dog, Tippy II, my constant companion—at my side or under my feet for many hours as I worked on this book. Tippy II is a fantastic model for unconditional positive regard and maintaining confidentiality. In terms of learning goals, he still has some work to do on maintaining appropriate boundaries and embracing cultural humility.

COVER IMAGE

The cover image, Savage Innocence #2, is provided courtesy of Canadian Ojibway artist Doris Cyrette. The image of two wolves chasing one another is open to different interpretations. Are they playing (innocently) or are they fighting (savagely)? As you ponder ethical issues throughout this volume, consider what is ethical or unethical from the perspectives of various people affected by the situation. Our first impressions can be deceiving and may not take the full context of the situation into account.

CONTENTS

1

Introduction to Social Work
Values and Ethics

LEARNING OBJECTIVES

Upon successful completion of this introduction, you will be able to

- define the following concepts: ethics, values, laws, agency policies, morals, professional ethics, personal ethics, ethical issues, ethical breaches, ethical dilemmas, moral distress, principles, standards, rules, beliefs, convictions, and feelings;
- identify how each of these concepts apply in social work practice situations; and
- reflect on your own values and clarify how they relate to the core values of social work.

When social work students meet with their first clients, they often wonder, what do I say? How do I know whether I am helping the client? How do I know that I am not doing anything harmful? As students proceed through their practice courses, they learn about particular stages and processes for working with clients. They learn to engage and assess before helping clients determine their goals and preferred methods of help. Within each stage of the helping process, social workers can choose relevant strategies and skills; for instance, active listening to engage clients and open-ended questions to help clients share their stories and concerns. In theory classes, students learn how to interpret the information shared by clients in order to conceptualize the client's needs, strengths, and concerns, and develop intervention plans based on theory and research. When determining what is the right thing to say, the right way to engage with clients, and the right way to help them achieve their goals, social workers also need to consider their values and ethics. Values and ethics provide overarching guidance for all stages of the helping process (Hepworth et al., 2023). They encourage social workers to act with honesty, respect, and compassion. In addition, values and ethics offer guidance on how to reduce risks of harm, protect vulnerable people, make good choices when faced with competing ethical concerns, and promote individual and social wellbeing.

Learning social work ethics does not mean simply memorizing specific rules and standards of practice for every situation that may arise. Ethical practice requires **professional** self-awareness, critical thinking, and the ability to manage complex information, values, and principles from a variety of sources (Barsky, 2019a). This textbook is designed to provide you with a practical understanding of the ethical principles and standards that guide social work practice, as well as frameworks for raising awareness of your own values and biases, for thinking through challenging ethical issues, and for working with others to decide how to respond to such issues.

The present chapter provides an orientation to social work values and ethics, including definitions of key concepts that we will be using throughout this textbook. This chapter also includes an introduction to the National Association of Social Workers (NASW) Code of Ethics. Chapter 2 offers theory and practical strategies for managing ethical issues, including how to respond to ethical breaches and how to make good decisions when challenging dilemmas arise. Chapters 3 illuminates social, environmental, economic, and technological justice as overarching principles for social work practice. Chapters 4 to 8 explore our ethical obligations toward clients in relation to the following ethical principles: self-determination and informed consent, confidentiality, professional competence, cultural competence, and professional boundaries. These chapters highlight different applications of these principles depending on whether social workers are practicing with individuals, families, groups, organizations, or communities. Chapters 9 to 11 explore broader ethical issues including obligations to practice settings (employers), access to services, and honesty and integrity. Chapter 12 delves into social work regulation, including ways that we may be held accountable for breaches of ethical and legal standards. Chapter 13 presents a benefit-risk approach to managing ethical issues. Essentially, this approach puts the ethical principles of beneficence (doing good) and non-maleficence (avoiding harm) into practice. The final chapter summarizes various approaches to ethical practice, highlighting the importance of being able to explore ethical issues through different lenses. This chapter also explores the future of social work ethics, including how we may approach emerging issues in social work practice.

Before delving into the specifics of ethical decision making and promoting ethical practice, let's explore the meanings of key concepts. Throughout this volume, you will find case examples that are designed to help you think critically and apply what you are learning to various social work situations. As an introduction to the use of case situations, please read Box 1.1 and respond to the questions. Write down your answers to help reinforce your learning and to prepare yourself for class discussions.

BOX 1.1

EMALYN

Let's use the following situation to gauge what you already know about social work ethics. As you read Emalyn's story, identify specific examples of how she acts in an ethical manner and how she acts in an unethical manner. For each example, write a brief explanation about why the particular behavior is ethical or unethical. If you are unsure whether a particular behavior is unethical, explain what the possible concerns about the behavior might be.

Emalyn has recently been hired as a community outreach social worker. She works for a program that identifies students at risk of dropping out of school due to absenteeism, low academic performance, or a history of school suspensions due to behavioral problems. Emalyn's supervisor hands her a file on a student, Neil Bassem. Emalyn decides not to read the file so that she will not be biased by it. She wants to formulate her own assessment of Neal's situation. Without making an appointment, Emalyn goes to the Bassem's apartment and knocks on the door. Due to a current pandemic, she is wearing a mask over her mouth and nose. Mr. Bassem answers the door and Emalyn explains, "Hello, I am a therapist from the school district. I've come to speak with you about your son, Neal, who has been missing a lot of school recently." Mr. Bassem is shocked and says that he does not want to speak with her. Emalyn explains that they need to speak with her or she will be required to report them to the police or child protection authorities for educational neglect. Mr. Bassem reluctantly agrees to allow Emalyn into the apartment, but asks her to remove her mask. Emalyn removes her mask and her shoes and enters the apartment. Mr. Bassem invites Emalyn into the kitchen so that Neal, Emalyn, and Mr. Bassem can sit together at the table. Mr. Bassem asks Emalyn if she would like anything to drink. Emalyn says, "Coffee, please." To open the discussion with some friendly chitchat, Emalyn says to Mr. Bassem, "You don't look like you're from around here. Where are you from?" In a somewhat frustrated tone, Mr. Bassem says he was born in Virginia. Emalyn shares that she was born in Virginia, too. Emalyn then explains her role, "I'm here from the school district. My job is to find out what's wrong with the family so I can help you make sure that Neal is successful at school this year." Neal explains that his father lost his job due to the pandemic and Neal has been working online to help support the family. Emalyn responds, "It's not your job to support the family. It's your job to go to school. Your mother and father are supposed to support you." Mr. Bassem clarifies that Neal's mother left them two years ago and he does not know where she is. Emalyn responds, "That's so sad. I feel very sorry for you." Emalyn asks Mr. Bassem if he would like assistance finding a job. Mr. Bassem responds that he certainly would like help. Neal asks if there is any way that he can continue to work and perhaps participate in an alternative school program with more flexible hours. Emalyn validates Neal's desire to work and go to school. She agrees to research some options and work with him to determine what is viable.

ETHICS VERSUS VALUES

Although some people use the terms *ethics* and *values* interchangeably, we will be using them as distinct but related terms. **Values** *are ideals to which an individual, family, group, organization, or community aspires.*[1] Values identify ideals that people believe are good, worthy, or valuable (Cottone et al., 2022). They reflect a priority of moral preferences or aspirations. Values can motivate us to action. If you value fairness, for instance, you may be motivated to respond to situations of discrimination or inequity (Schroeder et al., 2019).

All people have values; however, different people may have different selections or ordering of values. You might place a high value on privacy, whereas a client might value openness and transparency. Values do not declare specific ways of behaving. Although you value privacy, this information alone does not tell us how you will put privacy into practice when working with clients or when dealing with your personal affairs. Values are relative; that is, when we consider a value such as privacy, we should consider how important it is in relation to other values. Assume that you also value life, freedom, and authority. Where does privacy fit in relation to these other values? For instance, you might say that life is your highest value, followed by freedom, privacy, and authority. This set of interconnected values may be called your *value system*.

Ethics *refers to a system of guidelines defining what types of behavior are appropriate and inappropriate.* Different individuals, families, groups, organizations, or communities may declare or abide by different ethics. Social work ethics suggest that social workers should honor a client's right to self-determination, that is, they should allow clients to make decisions over matters affecting their lives. In contrast, law enforcement officers are ethically obliged to restrict self-determination to protect potential victims and society from criminal activity.

Whereas *values* identify a person's sense of "what is good," *ethics* identify a person's sense of "what is right" (Dolgoff et al., 2012). According to the NASW Code of Ethics,[2] the profession of social work embraces six core values: service, social justice, dignity and worth of the person, importance of human relationships, integrity, and competence. This list represents a consensus among the NASW membership concerning social work's highest moral preferences. Each ethical standard in the NASW Code is based on one or more of these values. For instance, because social workers value service, they have ethical responsibilities to ensure that clients have access to services and they should not abandon clients in need (s.1.17[b]). Because social workers value professional competence, they have ethical responsibilities to

---

1. For ease of reference, I may refer to "individuals, families, groups, organizations, or communities" collectively as "people." Given that social workers practice with all types of client systems, specific cases used throughout this textbook will demonstrate how values and ethics apply with each of them.

2. Throughout this volume, references to the NASW Code will refer to the 2021 edition.

work only within their areas of competence and to use supervision, continuing education, and other methods to enhance their competence (s.1.04[a]). Social work values and ethics are not just minimum standards to which practitioners are held accountable but ideals to which all social workers should strive. In essence, ethics are "the application of values to human relationships and transactions" (Levy, 1993, p. 1).

ETHICS VERSUS LAWS, AGENCY POLICIES, OR MORALS

Ethics refer to behavioral guidelines indicating what types of conduct are appropriate or inappropriate. Ideally, people should follow good ethical guidelines regardless of whether there are explicit mechanisms to enforce those guidelines. For instance, people should be honest even if there are no punishments for being dishonest. When ethical guidelines are formalized into a code of ethics, the authorizing organization typically provides a method of enforcing its ethical guidelines. The NASW, for instance, has a process for professional review of complaints made about social workers who are alleged to have violated its code of ethics.

Laws *are behavioral guidelines enacted by the state and enforced by the state* (e.g., by local, state, or national governments, courts, police, and public justice systems). Many laws are based on ethics (Janebová, 2012). For instance, criminal laws that prohibit murder, theft, rape, and other acts of violence are based on the ethical principle of *preventing harm*. Divorce laws that establish parental rights and responsibilities toward their children are based on the **ethic** of *ensuring that children's needs are fulfilled*. Mental health laws that allow the state to commit people with suicidal ideation to psychiatric facilities are based on the ethic of *preserving life*.

The consequences for violating laws vary depending on the specific law that has been broken. Consequences range from imprisonment to fines, community service, probation, terminating parental rights, or public censure. These consequences are intended to deter people from certain types of behavior, ideally promoting ethical behavior. Not all laws are ethical (Johns, 2016). For instance, consider laws that discriminate against Latin Americans, immigrants, Witches, gay men and lesbians, or any other group. In some situations, a particular law may be viewed as ethical by one segment of the population but unethical by another. Consider laws that allow for medical aid in dying; although some social workers consider these laws to be ethical, others do not. Unethical laws, such as those authorizing slavery, may be challenged and changed over time. In fact, challenging unethical laws is a key aspect of a social worker's obligation to promote social justice (NASW Code, Part 6).

As Table 1.1 indicates, not every law is ethical and not every ethic is reflected in the law (Koocher & Keith-Spiegel, 2016). Quadrant A describes behaviors that are legal and ethical. For instance, it is legal to offer case management services to

Table 1.1. Ethical vs. Legal Behavior

	Legal	**Illegal**
Ethical	*A. Ethical and Legal*	*B. Ethical but Illegal*
Unethical	*C. Unethical but Legal*	*D. Unethical and Illegal*

clients and it is also ethical to do so. Quadrant B depicts behaviors that are ethical but illegal. In a state that prohibits providing services to undocumented people from other countries, for instance, a social worker could argue that it is ethical to do so based on the ethical principles of **justice** and respect for the dignity of all people. Quadrant C describes behaviors that are unethical but legal. Standard 1.13(b) of the NASW Code says social workers should not accept gifts from clients; if there is no law specifically prohibiting receipt of gifts, then it could be unethical for a social worker to accept a gift, but still be legal to do so. Quadrant D indicates behaviors that are both unethical and illegal. For instance, it is both illegal and unethical to physically assault a client. When laws and ethics align (under quadrants A and D), social workers have consistent guidance on how to behave. When there are conflicts between laws and ethics, social workers are faced with ethical dilemmas.

For the purposes of this volume, an agency is any organization, partnership, or group of people that provides social work services. **Agency policies** *are behavioral guidelines created by an agency and enforced by an agency.* In some situations, agency policies can be enforced through court proceedings.[3] Although many agency policies are not specifically intended to formalize ethical rules, other agency policies are specifically intended to do so. For instance, an agency policy may require employees to maintain client confidentiality. If an employee breaches client confidentiality, the agency may establish processes for the client to issue a complaint and for the agency to determine appropriate consequences. For lesser breaches, agencies may require greater supervision or further training to ensure that the employee does not commit further violations. For more serious offences, the agency could suspend or terminate employment. As with laws, agency polices may or may not reflect the ethics of particular individuals or groups. Consider agency policies requiring workers to use personal phones and computers for work purposes; these policies could pose ethical issues for social workers, as social workers are supposed to maintain professional boundaries with clients.

Morals *are first-order primary convictions about what types of behavior are right or wrong.* Similar to ethics, laws, and agency policies, morals are guidelines that distinguish between appropriate and inappropriate behavior. Unlike laws and agency policies, morals are not legislated by an external body and they are not limited to a specific professional role (such as social work). People learn morals from their

---

3. Agency policies may establish the terms of the contractual relationship between the agency and its employees. If this contract is breached, the party hurt by the breach can go to court to sue for damages.

social context, including family, religious or spiritual community, cultural group, neighbors, and close friends (Cottone et al., 2022). *Universal morality* refers to moral systems that are common to all people, religions, cultures, and social institutions (e.g., the notion that murder is wrong). *Particular morality* refers to moral systems that are specific to certain cultures or social groups (e.g., the belief among Christians that salvation is achieved by accepting Jesus Christ; Beauchamp & Childress, 2019). Although some people use the terms 'values' and 'morals' interchangeably, remember that values refer to ideals (what inspires us as good or valuable) whereas morals provide guidance on the rightness or wrongness of particular behaviors (what behaviors we hold to be appropriate or inappropriate).

Morals are considered "first-order convictions" because they are central to the person, guiding understandings about good and evil without requiring the person to make conscious attempts to reflect upon why certain behaviors are right or wrong (Frunză & Sandu, 2016). In contrast, ethics are considered "second-order convictions" because they require the person to reflect on her[4] values and morals in order to determine what types of behavior are considered right or wrong (Hinman, n.d.). We speak of "social work ethics" rather than "social work morals" because social workers should use second-order convictions, taking their professional role and context into account. Consider parents who believe that it is appropriate for a 10-year-old to be left home unattended for long periods of time. They are operating on the moral principle that says children should be self-reliant. Self-reliance is something they learned from their upbringing, rather than something they follow because it is a law or official policy. Self-reliance is a way of life for them, not a choice that they deliberated over before reaching their conclusion.

From a broader perspective, the study of ethics and values is a process of moral inquiry and curiosity (Churchill, 2020). If we are to live good moral lives and behave ethically, we need to face ethical questions with an open mind and a caring heart. We do not simply follow laws, agency guidelines, or codes of ethics. We use critical thinking to question the bases for these guidelines and to determine whether and how they apply to our current choices and situation. We also use reflection to raise self-awareness, helping us to be more conscious of our biases and to make more deliberate choices.

PROFESSIONAL ETHICS VERSUS PERSONAL ETHICS

Professional ethics guide social workers or other professionals in the choices that they make in their professional capacities (Cottone et al., 2022). *Personal ethics guide people in their private lives, in their roles as parents, family members, friends, neighbors, citizens,*

---

4. To manage the issue of how to use gender-specific pronouns, I have rotated the use of "he/his" and "she/her" throughout the text. I have also used "they/their" to refer to individuals who identify as nonbinary or genderfluid. Case examples will include people of different genders in various roles, including social worker, client, supervisor, and other professionals.

and so forth. As a social worker, you will find that many of your personal ethics fit well with your professional ethics. For instance, if you believe in your personal life that it is important to confront racism and oppression, your ethical obligation as a professional social worker to promote social justice will simply be an extension of your personal ethics. In some situations, however, you will find that your personal and professional obligations are different. As a private person, for instance, you may provide friends with whatever advice you want, regardless of whether you have professional training to provide advice (e.g., "You should get married before you have a child"). As a social worker, however, you should not provide advice to clients unless that type of advice is within your specific training and areas of competence. Rather than providing clients with advice about getting married, social workers help clients make their own decisions, honoring their right to self-determination.

Consider also the interplay between religious morals and professional ethics. Eva identifies as an evangelical Christian. She believes the teachings of Christ are good. In her private life, Eva reaches out to friends and acquaintances to teach them the gospel of Christ, as per Matthew 28:19, "Go forth and make disciples of all nations." In her social work role, however, she is bound by a social work ethic that prohibits evangelizing clients. According to the NASW Code of Ethics (Ss.1.06[b] & [c]), for instance, social workers should avoid exploiting vulnerable clients for their own religious purposes and they should maintain appropriate boundaries with clients. Thus, what may be ethically appropriate in Eva's private life is not ethically appropriate in her professional role (Valutis & Rubin, 2016). Further, social workers should not re-interpret their professional ethics through the lenses of their personal morals or religious beliefs (Chechak, 2015). Rather, they should be aware of their personal morals, religious beliefs, and professional ethics, as well as any differences between them. Consider court clerk, Kim Davis, who refused to assist same-gender couples file for marriage licenses despite a court order requiring her to do so. She prioritized her religious beliefs over her professional and legal obligations (Chechak, 2015). As a result, she lost her job.

ETHICAL ISSUES, ETHICAL DILEMMAS, ETHICAL BREACHES, AND MORAL DISTRESS

Ethical issues *refer to questions related to the rightness or wrongness of behavioral choices.* Three types of ethical issues are ethical dilemmas, ethical breaches, and moral distress. **Ethical dilemmas** *arise when people need to choose between two or more conflicting ethical obligations* (Beauchamp & Childress, 2019). When someone is faced with an ethical dilemma, there is no clear, singular response that satisfies all the relevant ethical, legal, agency, and moral obligations. Consider a social worker facilitating a mutual-aid group for people mourning the loss of a spouse. One group member tells the worker, in confidence, that she did not lose a spouse and that she is attending the group to meet men who she might date. How should the worker balance his obligations to honor the member's confidentiality with his obligation to be open and honest with other group members? Ethical dilemmas are defined from an objective perspective: Could reasonable people differ on the appropriate behavioral response to the particular situation? Consider the issue of same-gender marriage and religious freedom. Some social workers might say that they believe the correct response is clear and unambiguous—social workers have an ethical obligation to serve same-gender couples even if they believe that homosexuality goes against their religious beliefs. Although subjectively these workers do not view this situation as a dilemma, it is a dilemma if other people can reasonably disagree with their conclusion.

Whereas an ethical dilemma has no clearcut or universally acceptable answer about right and wrong conduct, an **ethical breach** *is a clear violation of a specific ethical rule.* Consider a social worker who continues to work with clients despite experiencing severe anxiety. If anxiety is impairing the worker's ability to serve clients, then the worker is breaching standard 4.05(a) of the NASW Code. Two types of ethical questions may arise in relation to ethical breaches. The first question is retrospective (looking back): Did the worker's actions breach a particular ethical standard? For instance, did the worker's anxiety issues "interfere with [his] professional judgment and performance" or "jeopardize the best interests" of the clients (as per standard 4.05[a])? The second type of question about ethical breaches is prospective (looking forward): Given that the social worker breached [a particular ethical standard], what should be done now to address the situation? This question relates to the adage, "If you make a mess, you should clean it up." Thus, if a social worker's impairment has affected client services, what should the worker, agency, and other relevant stakeholders do to address the situation? If clients have suffered harm, they could be compensated financially. If the clients continue to need help, they could be connected with appropriate professionals. If the worker needs help with anxiety, the worker could be referred to appropriate services and could discontinue serving clients until the worker is well enough to serve them. Of course, each situation depends on the particular circumstances, needs, and wishes of the people involved. Whereas questions about dilemmas involve conflicting ethical standards, laws, or morals, question about breaches involve questions about the violation of one particular obligation.

Situations of **moral distress** *arise when we know our ethical obligations, but current circumstances make it difficult or impossible to fulfill those obligations.* Assume your boss asks you to modify your intake assessment so that it will appear that the client meets your agency's eligibility criteria. You know that modifying your assessment is dishonest; however, you are concerned about losing your job should you act against your boss's wishes. If you report your boss to the agency's executive director, you may be ostracized or rejected by coworkers who support the boss and do not like "snitches." This situation is not a true ethical dilemma because the right thing to do is to document client information honestly and accurately. Still, it is important to be able to identify and discuss situations of moral distress because they do arise and we do need to think about the best ways that we can respond to them. Later in this volume, we will consider **moral courage**, the strength or ability to do what is right even when it is difficult to do so (Papouli, 2019).

VALUES VERSUS BELIEFS, CONVICTIONS, AND FEELINGS

A belief is an understanding of a particular phenomenon. Beliefs may be based on fact or fiction, accurate perception or misperception, and sound reasoning or faulty reasoning. Beliefs may also be based on faith, such as faith in a higher power, a trusted friend, or parents. Alexa believes that corporal punishment should not be used to discipline children. She may have acquired this belief from various sources: her experience growing up in a family that used corporal punishment, her practice as a social worker in a child protection agency, research on the effects of corporal punishment on children, or an article that she read on social media. Her belief may also reflect her values, including respect for the dignity and worth of all people, including children.

Convictions are deeply held beliefs. People may hold tightly onto convictions for various reasons. In some situations, convictions are based on religious faith. In other situations, convictions are based on information indoctrinated into people by parents, teachers, media, or other important influences in their lives. Amnah identifies as a Muslim social worker who believes in *divine will,* meaning that everything that happens–good or bad–has been preordained by God. Amnah operates on this conviction in her personal life, for instance, when a family member celebrates graduation or finds out he has cancer. As a professional social worker, however, she ensures that she does not impose this conviction on her clients.

A feeling is an emotion or affective response such as fear, anger, excitement, eagerness, or hurt. When Amnah finds out her relative has cancer she feels shaken. Sometimes, people use the word *feel* when they mean *think* or *believe.* Believing and thinking are primarily cognitive processes. If a social worker tells a client, "I *feel* you have made remarkable progress," the worker probably means "I *think* you have made remarkable progress." In this case,[5] it would be more precise to say "think" rather than "feel." Feelings affect and are affected by values and beliefs. If Amnah believes that God will protect her relative, she may feel calm and hopeful even though he has cancer. Similarly, if a client values privacy, she may feel particularly infuriated when someone invades her privacy.

---

5. The term *case* refers to a situation involving a social worker and people with whom the social worker is interacting (clients, coworkers, others in the community). I use cases throughout the book to explore how values and ethics apply to various scenarios that a social worker may experience.

Social workers should be keenly aware of their values, beliefs, convictions, and feelings so they can act in a deliberate and ethical manner (Churchill, 2020). Consider, Shelley, a social worker who is angry at the nursing staff for treating a homeless patient with disrespect. If Shelley lacked awareness of her anger, she might respond to the nurses in an aggressive manner. Instead, she takes a moment to reflect. She values respect and acknowledges her ethical responsibility to promote respect for the people she serves. She speaks to her clinical supervisor who allows Shelley to vent her feelings about how the nurses treated the patient. The supervisor helps Shelley channel her energy in a positive manner, encouraging her to communicate with the nurses with respect. Shelley understands that the nurses may have different understandings about what transpired between the nurses and the patient, so she invites them to share their views about what happened. By listening to one another and by being open to hearing each other, they are in a better position to work toward a positive solution for the concerns raised by the patient.

RULES, STANDARDS, AND PRINCIPLES

Ethical **rules**, ethical **standards**, and ethical **principles** are guides for professional behavior. Although these terms are related, there are significant differences. *Rules and standards tend to be more specific guides for professional conduct, whereas principles tend to be more general* (Beauchamp & Childress, 2019). Consider the ethical principle, "Social workers behave in a trustworthy manner" (NASW, 2021). Acting in a trustworthy manner is a very broad guideline that could be interpreted in many ways. Various standards in the NASW Code operationalize this standard by giving more specific guidance; for instance, Standard 4.06 states, "Social workers who speak on behalf of professional social work organizations should accurately represent the official and authorized positions of the organizations." The advantage of general principles is that they can be applied across a broad range of situations. The advantage of specific rules or standards of conduct is that they provide more detailed directions about how to respond, provided that the rules or standards cover the specific situation under consideration. Similarly, laws and agency policies may utilize a combination of specific rules and standards, as well as broad principles in order to balance the needs for clear directions and coverage of a wide range of situations. If you are faced with an ethical issue and can find a specific standard that covers that issue, then you may use the standard for guidance. If there are no ethical standards that cover the issue, then you may use ethical principles for guidance.

The primary difference between rules and standards is that rules prescribe universal and **mandatory** *expectations about conduct, whereas standards state the customary or ordinarily accepted ways that professionals should conduct themselves.* In other words, rules state specifically what social workers *must or must not do*, without leaving room for exceptions or professional discretion. In contrast, standards explain how social workers *should or should not* conduct themselves, based on general consensus of the profession (Schroeder et al., 2019). Social workers may deviate from the expected norms or standards of the profession as long as they can provide appropriate ethical justification. Consider, for instance, a rule prohibiting social workers from having sex with clients (S.1.09(a)). This rule is not a general expectation but a firm directive. As a rule, it does not leave social workers room to argue that sex with clients is justified in certain circumstances. In contrast, a professional standard that says social workers should respect a client's right to self-determination suggests that self-determination is a general expectation, not a rule that applies steadfastly in all cases or social contexts. There are many exceptions to self-determination, for instance, when working with clients planning suicide. In this situation, social workers may justify deviating from the general standard of self-determination because the principle of protecting life supersedes the principle of respecting client autonomy.[6] Standards suggest that social workers should ordinarily behave in a particular way, but there may be situations in which other responses could be ethically justified. Codes of ethics often state professional expectations in terms of standards rather than rules. Using standards balances the need to state the usual expectations for conduct while providing some room to deviate from the standards based on appropriate ethical justification. Federal and state statutes generally provide expectations in terms of rules rather than standards. For instance, many states have laws requiring social workers to have clinical licensure in order to practice psychotherapy or provide psychological diagnoses. Because rules are stated as directives, they are easier to enforce than general expectations or standards.

To practice applying these concepts, please see Box 1.2. What ethical principles, standards, and rules should Bhatia, the social worker, consider as she evaluates whether she acted ethically in serving Mrs. Powell? How have Bhatia's feelings and beliefs affected the way that she responded to Mrs. Powell?

SELF-AWARENESS AND DELIBERATE USE OF SELF

Self-awareness *refers to being conscious of our values, beliefs, convictions, feelings, and behaviors.* Aristotle and other early Greek philosophers viewed self-discovery as a means of moral self-improvement, even suggesting that "knowing thyself" is a necessary precondition for wisdom and moral well-being (Mackenzie, 2018). Self-awareness helps us understand our own motivations. Although focusing on ourselves may sound narcissistic or self-absorbed, self-awareness helps us empathize, connect with, and care for others.

---

6. I say that the worker "may be able to justify" rather than make a definitive statement about being able to justify because some people might argue that clients have a right to terminate their lives, in certain circumstances (e.g., clients who specify in their living wills that they would like life supports to be withdrawn if they experience a persistent vegetative state).

BOX 1.2

BHATIA

Bhatia, a BSW intern, provides discharge planning services in a hospital. One of her patients, Mrs. Powell (87 years old), recently fell and broke her hip. As part of the hospital's discharge protocols, social workers are required to ask elderly patients whether they have living wills or advance directives. These documents indicate how health and personal care decisions will be made when people become mentally incapacitated and unable to make decisions on their own behalf. Initially, Mrs. Powell says she does not have and does not want to have any legal documents about end-of-life decision making. Bhatia explains that living wills and advance directives can ensure that family members and health care providers treat her as she would like to be treated. She explains that although these documents are not legally required, they can help family members make good decisions and avoid conflicts between them. Mrs. Powell asks Bhatia what she would put in her own living will. Initially, Bhatia feels embarrassed and unsure about how to answer. She hesitates, but then responds, "As a Hindu, I believe that preserving life is important. I also believe that when a person is close to death and in a lot of pain, removing life supports can relieve patients and family from pain and suffering. Still, I think that each person needs to decide what is best for their situation." Mrs. Powell says that she agrees with Bhatia and decides to sign a living will explaining how she would like life supports to be removed under certain circumstance. She appoints her eldest daughter as her healthcare power of attorney to make decisions on her behalf. Bhatia is glad that Mrs. Powell agreed to sign these documents before going home. When Bhatia reviews her meeting in supervision, her field instructor asks whether she honored Mrs. Powell's right to self-determination as per Standard 1.02 of the NASW Code of Ethics.

We can enhance self-awareness through a variety of processes including reflection, value clarification, engaging in conversations with supervisors or consultants, meditating, and journaling. As social workers, we use self-awareness to ensure that our interactions with clients are deliberate and ethical. We do not respond to clients based on impulsive reactions, personal preferences, or biases. We do not impose our worldviews or spiritual beliefs on the people we serve. We make decisions about what to say and how to interact with clients based on theory, research, the client's wishes, and the client's needs. Self-awareness is a critical component of ethical practice, ensuring that we respect the dignity and worth of all people, focus on the needs of our clients, and create safe environments to work in partnership with our clients.

Reflection is a process of consciously paying attention to our values, beliefs, convictions, feelings, and behaviors. Thus, before I meet with a client, I may take a few moments to gather my thoughts and feelings. How do I feel about meeting with this client? If I feel scared or apprehensive, what can I do to ensure that I maintain professional presence, attentiveness, and responsiveness with the client (Rogers & Jacobowitz, 2015)? During the session when the client asks whether I have children, I pause to reflect before I answer. Is the client simply asking me out of curiosity or is the client concerned about whether I—as a person without children—can provide well-informed help. After the session, I reflect on how I responded to the client. When I chose not to self-disclose, was I acting out of my own defensiveness or was I truly focusing on the client's interests? At each reflection point, I check myself, I consider my professional obligations, and I consider what is the most effective, ethical way to proceed with the client. If I make any mistakes, I consider what I need to do to make up for them. If I have acted appropriately, I consider how to build on what has gone well in my interactions with the client.

I also check in with my supervisor. My supervisor acts as a mirror, helping me reflect on my interactions with the client, including how my thoughts, feelings, and unconscious processes may have affected how I responded to the client. I have a trusting relationship with my supervisor so that I can be open about my thoughts, feelings, and potential biases. My supervisor asks me insight-oriented questions so I can reflect more effectively. "You said that you hesitated before you provided your answer. As you hesitated, what were you thinking?" Although I am responsible for ensuring my practice is ethical, my supervisor is also responsible for monitoring my practice and helping identify any ethical concerns. If I stray from my ethical obligations, my supervisor helps me correct mistakes and ensure ethical conduct moving forward. "When the client asked about whether you had children, you may have crossed professional boundaries by sharing too much about your personal situation and how you feel about not having children. In the future, please be aware of your own feelings so that you focus on the client's needs and do not over-disclose your personal feelings."

Values clarification refers to an ongoing process of raising self-awareness by reflecting critically on deeply held preferences, giving names to them, and examining the meaning of each of these values or preferences and how they fit together as a system. Although you can reflect by thinking quietly to yourself, reflection can be enhanced through discussions with others, completing values clarification surveys, or through journaling—writing down thoughts and experiences in order to examine them more fully (Kirschenbaum, 2013). Values clarification will not tell you what your values should be, but rather, what your values are. As a developing social worker, you can use values clarification to gain a clearer and more specific understanding of your moral preferences. Ethical social work requires the disciplined use of self (Kaushik, 2017). If and when you find that your values are inconsistent with those of your clients or the social work profession, you will be in a better position to make conscious and deliberate decisions about how to resolve these value conflicts. Social work ethics tells us not to impose our values on clients. To avoid imposing values on clients, it is vital to be aware of our values.

Consider the value of social justice. What does social justice mean to you? Some people define social justice as treating people in a fair or equitable manner. Others define it as ensuring fundamental human rights, addressing discrimination and oppression, or treating others as we want to be treated (Nicotera, 2019). How do these definitions fit with your own understanding of social justice? Further, how important is it to you as compared to values such as honesty and privacy? If you had to choose between these three values, which one would you prioritize and why? By reflecting on the meaning of social justice and how it fits within your value system, you are fostering self-awareness and putting yourself in a better position for making ethical decisions in a thoughtful manner. For a brief exercise in values clarification, please see Box 1.3.

Meditation refers to a process of training our minds to focus on particular thoughts, feelings, sensations, or experiences. People may train their minds by taking meditation classes, practicing yoga, using meditation apps, and engaging in breathing, mind, and body awareness exercises. Practicing meditation on a regular basis builds higher levels of concentration, compassion, calmness, clarity, and self-awareness (Buddhist Centre, n.d.; Whitaker & Smith, 2018). By training the mind, meditation helps us with emotional regulation, allowing us to be more conscious of the effects of stress and various emotions (Strait et al., 2020). In social work practice, we may use meditation to prepare ourselves emotionally for specific interactions with clients or coworkers, calming our minds and attending to the needs of those we will be serving. In the context of ethical decision making, meditation enhances our self-awareness so that we can make more deliberate, prudent choices about our interactions in professional practice (Rogers & Jacobowitz, 2015).

* * * * * * *

This chapter has provided an overview of key concepts that we will be using throughout this volume. Please also refer to the glossary for definitions of

---

BOX 1.3

VALUES CLARIFICATION SITUATION

Due to a recent pandemic, the government has announced that everyone must stay home and maintain physical distance from people outside of their immediate households. Only people who have jobs designated as *essential* may go to work. This policy is intended to reduce the number of people who contract the virus, to keep hospitals from being overwhelmed with patients, and to preserve life. Unfortunately, this policy also means that many people will be unemployed and financially stressed. Some people are also concerned that the government's policy is an affront to their freedom and autonomy. What are your definitions of each of the relevant values in this situation: preservation of life, quality of life, autonomy, and freedom? How do you prioritize each of these values? How would you respond to a clients who say that they are defying the laws and going back to work? What role do your values play in this situation?

---

additional terms that you may encounter. As this chapter suggests, when thinking about ethical issues, the first place to start is with ourselves. We need to be mindful of our values, beliefs, feelings, convictions, and behaviors as we interact with clients and coworkers. Self-awareness and deliberate use of self are ongoing processes that may be enhanced through reflection, supervision, values clarification, and meditation. Self-awareness and deliberate use of self provide the foundation for the next chapter, which provides a framework for analyzing and managing ethical issues.

NASW CODE OF ETHICS

The primary purpose of a code of ethics is to provide practitioners with guidance about how to conduct themselves in a professional and ethical manner. A code educates practitioners about the mission, values, and principles of the profession, while also offering guidelines for managing ethical conflicts and other challenging ethical decisions. A code also provides a set of standards to which clients and members of the public may hold social workers accountable (NASW Code, Preamble). This section provides a brief history of the NASW Code, including key changes in its formats and provisions.

The NASW was established in 1955. It is currently the largest association of social workers, with over 120,000 members. The NASW enacted its first code of ethics in 1960, a one-page document comprising 14 I-statements of professional responsibility (e.g., "I respect the privacy of the people I serve."). The statements acknowledged social worker's general obligations to promote the welfare of individuals and groups, to improve social conditions, to respect the privacy of the people they serve, to practice within the recognized knowledge and competence of the profession, and to prioritize professional responsibility over personal interests. In 1967, the NASW Code was amended to include provisions for nondiscrimination (NASW, n.d.-a).

The second version of the NASW Code was enacted in 1979, expanding to 82 principles that were divided into six sections. Five sections focused on responsibilities to different stakeholders, including ethical obligations to clients, colleagues, employing organizations, the profession, and society. The other section included five principles related to general comportment of social workers. These principles included obligations to maintain the standards of propriety, competence, service, **integrity**, and scholarly research (NASW, n.d-a). In 1993, the NASW Code was amended to include provisions regarding social worker impairment (conditions affecting ability to practice) and dual relationships (avoiding situations that put clients at risk due to conflicts of interest).

In 1996, the NASW Code underwent a major revision, providing the structure that continues to be the basis for the current code. For the first time, the NASW Code defines social work, stating that its mission is "to enhance human well-being and help meet the basic human needs of all people, with particular attention to the

Table 1.2. Values and Ethical Principles

Values	Principles
Service	Social workers' primary goal is to help people in need and to address social problems.
Social Justice	Social workers challenge social injustice.
Dignity and Worth of the Person	Social workers respect the inherent dignity and worth of the person.
Importance of Human Relationships	Social workers recognize the central importance of human relationships.
Integrity	Social workers behave in a trustworthy manner.
Competence	Social workers practice within their areas of competence and develop and enhance their professional expertise.

needs and empowerment of people who are vulnerable, oppressed, and living in poverty." Also, for the first time, the NASW Code identifies the six core values of social work and translates them into ethical principles as per Table 1.2.

The NASW Code builds on these values and principles with more specific standards for professional conduct under six parts: (1) ethical responsibilities to clients, (2) ethical responsibilities to colleagues, (3) ethical responsibilities in practice settings, (4) ethical responsibilities as professionals, (5) ethical responsibilities to the social work profession, and (6) ethical responsibilities to the broader society (NASW, 2021). The Preamble explains that the NASW Code does not prioritize which values, principles, or standards take precedence over one another. When ethical dilemmas arise, social workers need to consider relevant ethical theory, values, principles, standards, laws, regulations, and agency policies. Chapter 2 provides further guidance on how to manage challenging ethical issues.

The 1996 NASW Code provided much more specific ethical guidance than the prior versions. Some modifications reflected changes in statutory and **case law** pertaining to documentation, as well as exceptions to confidentiality to protect people from risks of serious, imminent, and foreseeable harm. A minor revision in 1997 clarified under which circumstances social workers could disclose information to protect the client or others from harm. In 2008, the NASW Code's nondiscrimination standards were expanded to cover discrimination based on sexual orientation, gender identity, and immigration status (NASW, n.d.-a).

In 2018, the NASW Code was revised primarily to update provisions related to the use of videoconferencing, social media, text messaging, electronic **records**, and other technology in practice. The revision built on the 51 existing standards, adding 19 new subsections and 19 revised subsections. The new provisions provide guidance on how to take technology into account when engaging clients in informed consent, when safeguarding client confidentiality, and when considering how to manage professional boundaries with clients (NASW, n.d.-a).

In 2021, the NASW Code was amended to include provisions for self-care and for cultural humility. The NASW Code's purpose section now notes that self-care is an important aspect of professional integrity. For us to be able to take care of the people we serve, we should also take care of our own physical, psychological, social, and spiritual well-being. Revisions to Standard 1.05 suggest that cultural competence includes the concept of cultural humility. As Chapter 7 explains in further detail, cultural humility encourages us to critically reflect on our own values, beliefs, and cultures, so that we may learn from clients as experts in their own cultures and avoid imposing our values and beliefs on them.

Clearly, the NASW Code is an evolving document. Every three years, the NASW conducts a delegate assembly of over 200 people, including the National Board of Directors and member delegates from across the United States. The NASW authorizes various committees to consider policy decisions, conduct research, consult members, and make recommendations about proposed policy changes to the delegate assembly. When the NASW executive determines that it may be useful to update the NASW Code, it authorizes a task force to propose revisions. Although the NASW Code is the primary document on social work ethics, the NASW also develops practice standards covering particular areas of practice, for instance, practice standards for child welfare, cultural competence, technology, end-of-life care, substance use disorders, and supervision (see https://www.socialworkers.org/Practice/Practice-Standards-Guidelines). These practice standards build on the ethical standards in the NASW Code by providing more specific guidance about how to implement social work ethics in particular practice situations.

As you analyze various case situations and ethical questions, please read the relevant sections of the NASW Code, available at https://www.socialworkers.org/About/Ethics/Code-of-Ethics/Code-of-Ethics-English. Use the section headings to guide you to the relevant parts of the code; for instance, Part 1 for responsibilities to clients. You may also conduct word searches within the electronic document, for instance, honesty, impairment, or conflict of interest. Although the NASW Code is not the only source for ethical guidance, it is often a good place to start when ethical issues arise in practice.

CONCLUSION

In basic terms, applying ethics in in social work practice means asking ourselves, our clients, and our colleagues four basic questions: what are we doing; why are we doing it; what should we be doing that would be better; and why would that alternative be better (Schur, 2022). When we are considering what is *better*, we should consider various sources of duties or moral obligations: values, personal convictions, professional ethics, agency policies, and laws. When different sources of obligations provide us with similar guidance about how to behave, our decisions about the best way to act are relatively straightforward. When we have conflicting obligations or when different people affected by the decision have different views about the best way to proceed, then decision making becomes more complex. To help us manage challenging ethical issues, we may benefit from a strategic process for analyzing, discussing, and building consensus around how to respond to the issues. Not coincidentally, Chapter 2 provides such a process.

DISCUSSION QUESTIONS AND EXERCISES

1. *Understanding*: Describe each of the following terms in your own words and provide examples of each: ethics, values, laws, morals, and beliefs.
2. *Distinguishing*: Compare and contrast the terms within each of the following sets:
   a. Values, ethics, and morals
   b. Ethics, laws, and agency policies
   c. Ethical issues, ethical dilemmas, ethical breaches, and situations of moral distress.
   d. Professional ethics and personal ethics
   e. Values, feelings, beliefs, and convictions
3. *Applying*: Review the cases in Boxes 1.2 and 1.3. Briefly state the ethical issues raised by each of these cases. Identify whether each of these cases involves an ethical breach, an ethical dilemma, or a situation of moral distress for the social worker. Provide your reasoning by linking your conclusions with the definitions in this chapter.
4. *Law, Standard, Feeling, and Belief*: Theo (21 years) was convicted for theft and placed on probation. As part of the probation order, Theo is required to see Patty for social work counseling. Theo tells Patty he returned to the store where he was initially caught stealing. Entering the store is a breach of probation. Patty thinks Theo is a good kid who has had a tough life. She is sorry for him and wants to give him a second chance. For Patty, respecting the individual is more important than respecting property. Theo's court order says Patty must report any breaches to Theo's probation officer. If she reports this breach, however, she thinks he could go to jail.

   Review this case and identify one example of each of the following: a law, an ethical standard, a value, a feeling, and a belief. Explain how each example relates to that specific concept. For instance, "Theo's probation order is an example of a *law* because it is a rule that was enacted by the court—an agency of the state—and enforced by the criminal justice system—also an agency of the state."
5. *Professional Ethic, Personal Ethic, Belief, and Conviction*: Felicity facilitates a psychoeducational group for family caretakers of people with dementia. Felicity personally feels that society should take primary

responsibility for taking care of people with dementia. Her parents always told her, "Blood is thicker than water. Families take care of their own." This is a credo that she has come to live by. As a social worker, Felicity understands that families often provide the primary support for individuals in need. She knows that one of her responsibilities as a social worker is to help people take care of their own family members. She feels sad when she sees elders being neglected or mistreated by family members.

Review Felicity's case and identify one example of each of the following: professional ethic, personal ethic, belief, and conviction. Explain how each example relates to that specific concept.

6. *Mindful Ethics*: Ponder the following scenario. What ethical issues does this scenario raise? What could you have done differently to raise your awareness and respond in a more ethical manner?

It is Monday morning. You did not sleep well. Your hair is a mess, so you need to wash it. You are running late. To complicate matters, traffic is horrible and you arrive 20 minutes late to your field placement in a community development agency. Your field instructor says, in an angry tone, "All the community members are waiting for you." When you enter the meeting room, a community leader says, "We didn't think you were going to show up today." You respond, "I'm sorry. I'm having a rough day." Your face starts to blush and you feel your heart racing.

7. *Values Clarification*: For each of the following situations, identify which value you would prioritize, explain how you are defining that value and why you would prioritize it, and describe which aspects of your background may have influenced why you prioritize that particular value (e.g., culture, race, ethnicity, spirituality or religion, education, family of origin).

   a. A city council is debating whether to take money from the budget of police to provide additional mental health and social services. Relevant values include community safety, respect for the dignity and worth of all people, social justice, and psychosocial well-being.

   b. Corinne (58 years and with full mental capacity) has late-stage cancer. She wants assistance to end her life in a time and manner of her choice. Corinne's adult children do not want anyone to provide Corinne with the help she seeks. Relevant values include autonomy of the person, protection of life, freedom from pain, and family responsibility.

   c. Ahmad is wants to conduct qualitative research interviews with teenagers who are nonbinary and have experienced gender-related discrimination and harassment. The Institutional Review Board (which reviews research proposals for ethical and legal compliance) understands the value of the research and also has concerns about the risks of retraumatizing the research participants. Relevant values include generating knowledge, giving voice to vulnerable groups, and protecting people from harm.

d. A social agency that lacks diversity among its professional staff plans to hire three social workers. The agency considers whether to use an affirmative action to ensure the new hires better reflect the diversity of the community it serves. Relevant values include diversity, social justice, fairness, competence, and merit.

8. *Standard Hunt*: To help you become more familiar with the NASW Code of Ethics, identify which specific standard in the NASW Code that the social worker should consider for each of the following situations:

a. A social worker, nurse, and doctor are arguing about who is responsible for what in serving the needs of a particular patient.

b. A community organizer is not sure whether it is ethical to use her work computer and worktime to advocate on social media for her preferred candidate in a presidential election.

c. A group facilitator thinks his cofacilitator has an addiction issue that is impairing her ability to run the group.

d. An employer asks a social work counselor to falsify a client's records in order for services to the client to be reimbursable through health insurance.

e. A case manager does not want to write notes for each client contact because it would take too much time away from providing services to clients.

f. A BSW student has not been provided with criteria for evaluating her field education experience.

g. A social worker wants to conduct research comparing the effectiveness of two interventions. She wants to assign clients randomly, meaning that research participants cannot choose which intervention they receive.

2

Managing Ethical Issues

LEARNING OBJECTIVES

Upon successful completion of this introduction, you will be able to

- accurately identify ethical issues, including ethical breaches, ethical dilemmas, and situations of moral distress;
- access appropriate help for managing ethical issues;
- think critically by applying legalism, teleology, deontology, ethics of care, virtue ethics, and narrative ethics to analyze ethical issues;
- use conflict resolution skills to manage ethical conflicts with clients, coworkers, and others;
- plan and implement strategies for managing ethical issues; and
- evaluate implementation of plans to manage ethical issues and provide follow-up as needed.

When we practice social work, we can expect ethical issues to arise. There is no way to avoid ethical issues. There is also no need to panic when ethical concerns arise. We need to be aware of ethical issues so we can respond deliberately and ethically. When we are proactive, we can do greater good for our clients, our practice organizations, our communities, and ourselves. When we ignore or avoid ethical issues, we are more likely to cause harm and get into trouble. And if we do panic or feel distressed, we need to be aware of our feelings and make use of our professional support systems to work through our feelings.

This chapter is designed to teach you how to recognize and respond to various types of ethical issues. Throughout this chapter, we will discuss various ethical theories, including virtue ethics, deontology, teleology, and narrative ethics. Although the new terminology and theories may seem daunting at first, this chapter provides specific questions to guide our application of these theories. In subsequent chapters, we will continue to use these theories and questions as we consider our core ethical duties in greater depth.

BOX 2.1

FRAMEWORK FOR MANAGING ETHICAL ISSUES

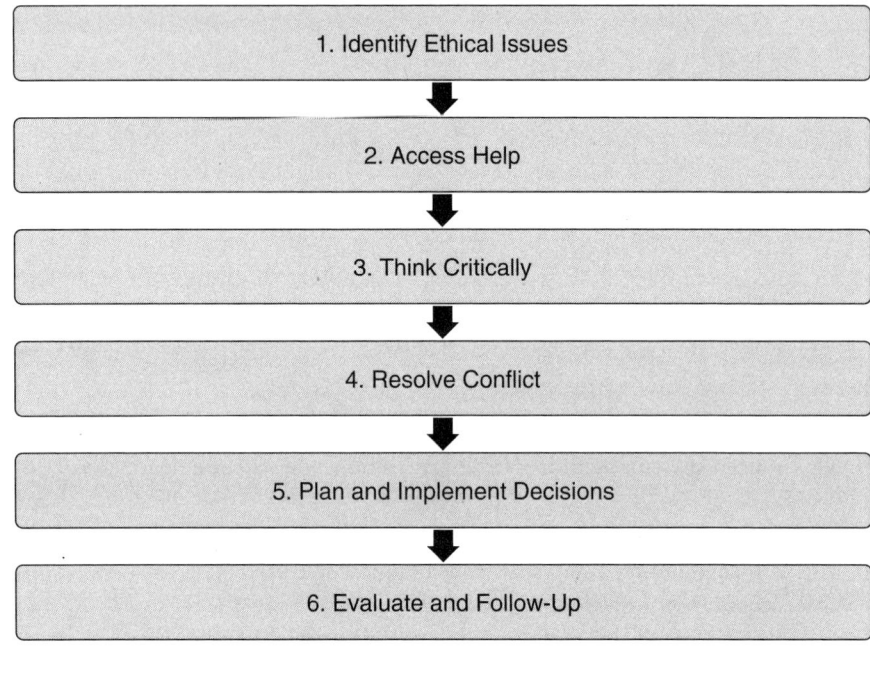

* **Loop back to earlier stages as needed**.

The following sections are based on the six steps from the Framework for Managing Ethical Issues (see Box 2.1 and inside back cover). This Framework provides strategies to guide you, your clients, your colleagues, and other stakeholders as you strive to work together an ethical manner.

1. IDENTIFY ETHICAL ISSUES

When **ethical issues** arise, we need to be able to recognize and describe them in a concise, accurate manner. A client offers you a gift as thanks for your services. Does this situation raise an ethical issue? And if so, what exactly is the issue? Before we can determine the best way to respond to ethical issues, we need to understand the nature of the issues and factors contributing to them. The following provide a useful structure for describing an ethical issue.

     a. What are the relevant facts giving rise to the ethical issue?
     b. What are the relevant ethical, legal, and agency obligations?

  c. What additional information would be helpful to know?
  d. What is the specific ethical question to be considered?

a. Key Facts

The first of the four "ethical description questions" asks you to identify the relevant facts. When you state the key facts, you are providing a context in which the ethical issues are arising. Identify which people are affected, what actions they have already taken, and any additional information that may help you, your supervisor, or others to understand the situation giving rise to the issues. If you ask your supervisor, "May I accept a gift from a client?" you have not provided sufficient information to warrant a specific answer. Consider what additional facts would your supervisor need to know. What was the nature and value of the gift? What was the context in which the client offered the gift? And how might the client's decision to offer the gift be affected by cultural issues? If a young child offered you a drawing to thank you for your services, accepting the gift may present no major ethical issues. If an adult client offered you a $10,000 gift certificate, hoping that you would provide preferential treatment, then more significant ethical issues arise.

b. Relevant Obligations

To identify ethical issues, we need to know which particular **laws, ethical standards**, and **agency policies** apply to our area of practice. Thus, if you work in child protection, you need to know which child protection laws apply. If you work with an interprofessional hospital team, then you should consider not only the NASW Code, but also the ethical codes of physicians, nurses, and other professionals on your team. When reviewing agency policies, consider policies that apply directly to you, as well as policies that apply to your clients or others affected by the decision to be made.

   Consider the gift situation. If you work as an aide for a state legislator, state conflict-of-interest laws may prohibit you from accepting any gifts. In other roles, there may no specific prohibitions against receiving gifts. Note that the NASW Code does not specifically mention gifts. However, Standard 1.06(c) says social workers should avoid dual relationships and should maintain culturally sensitive boundaries with clients. To apply this standard, we need further information about the nature of the gift, the cultural context in which it was offered, and potential harm to the client or others. Some agency policies provide guidance on receiving gifts, for instance, allowing gifts under a certain value or prohibiting all gifts. For the purposes of this discussion, assume that agency policy does not mention gifts but includes language similar to the NASW Code in terms of maintaining culturally appropriate boundaries.

c. Additional Information

When we first become aware of an ethical issue, we may not know all the relevant information. As we formulate our ethical question, we should identify what additional facts would be helpful to make a well-informed decision. In the gift situation, it may be helpful to know the client's financial situation. A $40 gift from a person with financial abundance has different implications than the same gift from someone with limited financial means. It may also be helpful to know how the client might react if the worker declined the gift. If the client is likely to feel angry or rejected, then the social worker would need to take these responses into account when deciding how to respond.

d. Specific Ethical Question

The way that we frame our ethical questions affects the way that we analyze and respond to them. We should frame questions in an open, unbiased manner. If I were to ask, "Should I accept the client's gift certificate even though my agency might see this as a bribe?" I have biased my question by framing the gift as a bribe. Also, I have asked a yes/no question. When we want to explore how to respond to ethical issues, we should ask open questions. Whereas yes/no questions give us a choice between two options, open questions invite consideration of many different options, including creative responses that may not initially be obvious.

There are four types of ethical questions that we may articulate: questions about whether someone breached an ethical **duty**, questions about what do to in response to committing a breach, questions about how to respond to an ethical dilemma, and questions about how to respond to a situation of moral distress. Questions about *whether someone breached an ethical duty* are retrospective (looking back). They ask whether someone violated a specific ethical obligation. For this type of issue, we can use a yes/no question. "Did I breach my obligations to avoid conflicts of interest when I accepted this gift?" Accepting gifts could be seen as a conflict of interest because it may bias our professional decisions. Further, if we accept gifts from clients, some clients may feel that they have to provide gifts in order to receive services. Questions about breaches invite us to explore what happened and to consider how relevant ethical standards, laws, and agency policies apply.

Questions about *responding to a breach* are prospective (looking forward). They invite us to consider what we should do "to make things right" after we have acted in an unethical manner. Elementary school teachers often teach young children, "If you make a mess, please clean it up." Accordingly, we need to ask an open question. "By accepting this gift, I breached my ethical duty to avoid conflicts of interest. Given this breach, what should I do to make things right for my client and my agency?" Note that the question is not, "Should I return the gift to the client?"

Returning the gift is one option, but not the only option. By asking an open question, you might consider additional possibilities; for instance, giving the gift to the agency rather than keeping it yourself, apologizing to the client, or speaking to the client about the conflict-of-interest concerns and coming up with a joint decision about how to deal with the gift. Sometimes, the primary issue is not *what* you do to make up for the breach, but rather, *how* you do it. In this situation, having an honest, respectful conversation with the client may be more important than simply returning the gift.

Questions about **ethical dilemmas** are prospective. When faced with ethical dilemmas, we have two or more conflicting duties and we need to decide which course of action is most ethical—or at least, which course of action will minimize the ethical risks (Reamer, 2022). In the gift situation, one ethical duty is to avoid conflicts of interest. Other relevant ethical duties are to honor client self-determination and respect clients, including their cultures. Arguably, these latter duties could conflict with the duty to avoid conflicts of interest. Assume the client comes from a culture in which gift-giving for professional services is a norm and rejecting a gift may be viewed as disrespectful. The ethical issue arising from this situation could be stated as,

> A client offered me a $100 gift certificate as an expression of gratitude for my service. I let her know that agency policy and my code of ethics prohibit me from accepting gifts. The client asked me to reconsider because, in her culture, gifts are a token of respect and she would feel rejected if I refused the gift. How should I manage my duty to avoid conflicts of interest with my duties to honor client self-determination and respect the client's culture?

This open question invites a full discussion of the relevant ethical issues and options for managing them.

The fourth type of ethical question is responding to a situation of **moral distress**. In a situation of moral distress, you know what your ethical duty is, but you are experiencing pressure or constraints that make it difficult to fulfill your ethical duty (Lavoie, 2021; McMillan, 2020). Consider a prospective client who offers your agency a gift of $100,000 if you bump her to the top of a waiting list for inpatient services. You know that, ethically, you should treat all clients equally and should not accept gifts for preferential treatment. However, your agency director says you should accept the gift and put the client at the top of the waiting list. You may feel pressure to follow the director's wishes, fearing retaliation—including the possibility of being fired—if you do otherwise. Using the four-question format, you might state the ethical issue as,

> A prospective client is on our waiting list. He may need to wait over 6 weeks until a bed is available. He offered our agency $100,000 on condition that I move him to the top of the waiting list. Our director advised me to accept the gift and admit the client immediately. I know it is unethical to accept the

gift because it is showing favoritism and it is unfair to other clients. I am concerned, however, that I could lose my job or face other retaliation if I do not accept the gift and admit the client right away. What should I do?

Note how this statement of the issue does not indicate whether you should accept the gift or not. Further, it opens the discussion to a broad range of options, as will be discussed in the third step of the ethical framework, below. Regardless of whether you are asking about a past breach, how to respond to a breach, how to manage an ethical dilemma, or how to deal with a situation of moral distress, it is important to formulate clear, unbiased questions.

Refer to the situations in Boxes 2.2 and 2.3. For each situation, use the following questions to identify and describe the main ethical issue: (a) What are the relevant

---

BOX 2.2

ORIANA'S STI CONCERNS

Oriana facilitates confidential support groups for clients with sexually transmitted infections (STIs). One of her clients, Jade, has genital herpes. Unbeknown to Oriana, Jade is dating one of Oriana's friends, Floyd. Four weeks into the support group, Floyd tells Oriana he is dating Jade. Oriana does not tell Floyd that Jade is her client. Oriana is concerned about Floyd being exposed to herpes, but she also knows she has certain ethical duties to Jade. She wonders how Floyd would feel if he contracted herpes and found out that Oriana kept this a secret from him. Oriana teaches clients to inform their sexual partners about their STI status. She also teaches them to use condoms and other safer sex practices. She does not know whether Jade is following her suggestions to prevent transmission of STIs.

BOX 2.3

RASHAWN'S RESEARCH QUESTION

Rashawn is conducting a qualitative study of the experiences of refugees who received social work services while awaiting decisions about their refugee status. For this study, Rashawn interviews refugees through a secured videoconferencing program. After conducting 12 interviews, he discovers that he forgot to save copies of the digitally signed informed consent forms. He originally told the research participants that he would only contact them one time, so he is reluctant to contact them again to obtain another informed consent form. He may also have difficulty contacting them because some of them may have been deported or moved to unknown locations. Rashawn wants to use the interviews even though he does not have the consent forms. He thinks that he may not need signed inform consent forms because the risks of the research are low and he did not include identifying information in the data that he collected.

---

facts giving rise to the ethical issue? (b) What are the relevant ethical, legal, and agency obligations? (c) What additional information would be helpful to know? (d) What is the specific ethical question to be considered?

2. ACCESS APPROPRIATE HELP

Once we have formulated our statement of the ethical issue, we can seek help from others to manage the issue. Even the most seasoned ethicists can benefit from conversations with others. When we try to resolve ethical issues in isolation, we may miss important perspectives. Conversations allow us to test ideas, build on each other's knowledge and perceptions, and gain a better understanding of the reasons behind our reasoning. When we voice our ethical concerns and choices with others, they can act as a mirror, helping us reflect and raise our awareness about our initial thoughts and biases. They can ask "why" questions, helping us deliberate over our choices and moral reasoning (Churchill, 2020). In the situation described in Box 2.3, Oriana might tell her supervisor that she must maintain Jade's confidentiality and cannot inform anyone of her STI status. Oriana's supervisor may ask her why she needs to maintain confidentiality. If Oriana says she has to maintain confidentiality because it is an agency policy, the supervisor may ask why the agency has a policy of confidentiality. Oriana responds that the purpose of confidentiality is to build a safe and trusting relationship with her clients. Rather than simply following rules because they are rules, Oriana learns that she needs to understand the rationale for the rules. By helping Oriana express the reasons underlying her thinking, the supervisor enhances Oriana's ability to make good ethical decisions.

The type of people that we seek for help depends on the type of help we need. One of the most common sources of support for managing ethical issues is social work supervision. Supervisors are responsible for overseeing the work of supervisees, including how they follow agency policy and conduct themselves in an ethical manner (Hafford-Letchfield & Engelbrecht, 2020). Supervisors can offer guidance, support, insight, and, in appropriate situations, direction. Supervisors may possess greater experience and training. They may also have greater professional distance and objectivity. In the gift situation, your supervisor could help you explore the agency's policies and consider various options for responding to the client's offer. When working closely with the clients, you may have developed feelings toward the client—perhaps care, concern, sympathy, distrust, or even dislike (Broadley, 2021). Because your supervisor is not working directly with the client, she may help you view the ethical situation from a more objective perspective.

In some situations, you may be required to share ethical issues with specific people in your agencies. Some agencies have ethics committees, risk managers, attorneys, privacy managers, or others that are responsible for assisting with ethical and legal issues. Find out who you need to contact for various types of issues, as well as who else could be helpful due to their ethics training and expertise.

Consulting with people outside your agency may be complicated by your duty to maintain client confidentiality. In some circumstances, you can ask for consultation without providing identifying information about the client. If you have concerns about a potential elder abuse situation, for instance, you might contact adult protective services to determine whether the situation is reportable or whether they have other suggestions about how to respond to such concerns. If you are not sure how the NASW Code applies to a particular situation and you are an NASW member, you may contact NASW's consultation service to help you explore which ethical standards are most relevant. NASW does not provide legal advice. If you want specific legal advice, you may hire your own attorney. Remember, an agency attorney acts on behalf of the agency. Hire your own attorney if you want someone to represent your specific interests. Consider a client who sues for malpractice, alleging that you provided services in an incompetent manner. The agency attorney will not necessarily defend you, for instance, if the agency believes that you acted outside the scope of your agency role. As you will see in the chapter on risk management, it is useful to have professional liability insurance that covers legal costs, including costs of consulting an attorney for information and advice.

Be cautious about consulting with family and friends. Even if you do not share identifying client information, they might be able to identify the client. If a case goes to court, for instance, news about your relationship with the client may go public and people will know who you were discussing. In some situations, family and friends may provide moral support. Consider, for instance, a situation in which your agency is pressuring you to falsify client records so the agency can claim higher reimbursement from health insurance companies. You are concerned that if you confront administration or blow the whistle on the agency, you could lose your job. You may want to speak with your spouse or partner to discuss how to handle this situation. Because you can discuss the issue without disclosing client information, you are not risking any breaches of confidentiality.

Refer back to Oriana's and Rashawn's situations. In each situation, what type of help could the social worker use? Who should they consult for assistance in managing the ethical issue?

3.THINK CRITICALLY

Thinking critically refers to assessing situations or problems in a purposeful manner, taking relevant factors and sound arguments into account (Paul & Elder, 2016). During this stage of the ethical management process, social workers use of a variety of strategies to deliberate over ethical issues in a rational manner. Successful resolution of this stage may or may not result in reaching a definitive decision. In some situations, critical thinking may lead workers to decide upon a particular course of action as the best way to resolve the ethical issues. In such cases, workers may implement their decisions (Stage 5) without needing to consult others. In other situations, critical thinking does not lead workers to a particular decision, but rather prepares them for Stage 4, conflict resolution. When workers cannot resolve the issues on their own, they need to engage others to determine how to proceed. Consider, for instance, an agency creating a policy on whether to use physical restraints for potentially violent clients. An individual social worker could use critical thinking to assess the relevant legal and ethical considerations; however, the worker may not be able to determine agency policy without consulting and building agreement with other agency staff. By using critical thinking, the worker enters the conflict resolution process with a better understanding of the issues and relevant considerations. Even if the worker has a sense of what she believes is the most ethical policy response, she can keep her decision tentative, ensuring that she is open to hearing the concerns, contentions, and arguments of the others. None of us is infallible. Even if we have gone through the critical thinking process in a comprehensive manner, we can still learn from our colleagues and clients.

You may use the following critical thinking questions to guide your analysis. You may not need to use all six questions for analyzing a particular ethical issue. Different questions may be more useful for some issues than for others. The phrases in parentheses indicate which ethical theories are relevant to answering particular questions. You will find explanations of each theory in the following discussion of each question.

a. **Self-Awareness**: What are my own values, beliefs, emotional reactions, virtues, and perspectives, and how do these affect my thinking and responses to the ethical question? (apply **virtue ethics**)
b. **Other Awareness**: What are the values, beliefs, emotional reactions, virtues, and perspectives of others affected by the ethical question? (apply **narrative ethics** and **ethics of care**)
c. **Ethical Goals**: In terms of the ethical management process, what are our goals and potential areas of conflict between these goals?
d. **Obligations:** How should we prioritize our legal, agency-based, ethical, and intrinsic obligations? (apply **legalism** and/or **deontology**)
e. **Consequences:** What options should we consider to address the ethical question? What are the pros and cons of each option? (apply **teleology** or **consequentialism**)
f. **Best Response:** What is the best response to the ethical question and what is our ethical justification for choosing this response?

a. Self-Awareness

It is important to be aware of our values, beliefs, emotional reactions, and virtues so that we do not impose our values and beliefs on clients, and so we can use our feelings and virtues in a purposeful manner. **Self-awareness** allows us to consider our social location, including how our perspectives may be shaped by power, **privilege**, and oppression (Caron et al., 2020). Being aware of our social location and personal perspectives allows us to gain a better understanding about how these perspectives are similar to and different from those of our clients, colleagues, or other stakeholders affected by the ethical issue. Assume that I have a conservative political perspective and believe that government should not interfere in the workings of a free market economy. If I were to advocate for legislative change, being aware of my belief system will help me advocate not only with conservative legislators, but also with progressive legislators. When working with progressive legislators, for instance, I might not appeal on the basis of a free market economy, but rather on the basis of promoting positive social change.

Virtue ethics is a theoretical approach to ethics suggesting that morality is about character. Virtues are moral habits or enduring dispositions that may be learned, cultivated, and expressed. We may nurture our virtues by practicing them regularly and by surrounding ourselves with others who live the virtues to which we aspire (Boyd & Timpe, 2021). If we want to master playing the piano, acquire proficiency in a new language, or develop marvelous gymnastic skills, we need numerous hours of practice over extended periods of time. Similarly, if we want to become fluent in certain virtues, we need to engage in them frequently and throughout our lives (Schur, 2022).

Virtue ethics views people as moral agents who may use wisdom, justice, courage, temperance, and other virtues to guide their conduct and interactions with others (Heydt & Severyn, 2022). Aristotle, Hursthouse, and other proponents of virtue ethics believe that a flourishing or good life is a life lived according to one's virtues (Aristotle, 2013; Higgins, 2021; Shafer-Landau, 2018). A virtuous person acts with good internal motivations rather than simply acting in a way to fulfill legal or moral obligations (Papouli, 2018) or to win praise from others. To employ virtue ethics, we may ask ourselves, "As a social worker, what are my primary moral characteristics?" and "How can I live these virtues in practice?" We may learn virtues by emulating good role models (Banks, 2022). We make deliberate choices, using self-awareness, knowledge, and responsiveness to the situation. We practice our virtues on a continual basis, engraining them conscious habits. In the gift situation, two virtues that we could reflect upon are **honesty** and respect. As honest and respectful social workers, we would not exploit our client for personal gain. We would strive to respect our wishes, while also assessing whether the client is feeling pressured into providing a gift. As honest workers, we would be open with our supervisor and agency. When considering whether to accept a gift, we would consult with our supervisor, discussing what it means to be honest and respectful in this situation.

To engage in critical thinking, we should strive to be kind, open-minded, impartial, honest, compassionate, and honorable. We should guard against vices such as being spiteful, oppressive, egocentric, callous, deceitful, hypocritical, uncaring, or disingenuous (Paul & Elder, 2019). We should not rely on assumptions, stereotypes, intuition, automatic thinking, or blind adherence to stated laws, agency rules, social norms, or ethical directives (Assor & Goodman, 2020; Kahneman, 2011). Self-awareness, humility, and critical thinking not only help us make better decisions (Higgins, 2021); they also help us provide well-reasoned arguments for the decisions we make. When ethical issues arise, there may not be one pat answer for the best way to respond. Thus, we should be able to explain why we took a particular course of action, particularly if harm to a client or others arises. We are not expected to be perfect in our management of ethical risks and benefits; rather, we are expected to act honestly and prudently, based on self-awareness and critical thinking. Being able to provide a sound rationale for ethical decisions facilitates our professional accountability for actions taken in response to ethical issues (Osmo & Landau, 2006).

Consider the situation in which your boss tells you to accept a client gift and put the client at the top of waiting list. You may feel moral distress because you know it is unethical to allow the client to jump the queue, but you are afraid of losing your job if you do not obey your boss. Which virtues may be helpful in this situation? You may want to draw on your moral fortitude, the strength to do what is right even when it is difficult to do so (Boyd & Timpe, 2021). Focus also on your moral integrity, the desire to be honest and forthright.

b. Other Awareness

To engage in effective critical thinking, we need to consider the values, beliefs, emotional reactions, virtues, and perspectives of clients and others affected by the ethical issue. *Ethics of care*, a branch of virtue ethics, suggests we should strive to be agents of care, attentiveness, and compassion (Nissen & Engen, 2021; Shafer-Landau, 2018; Tronto, 2010). Although many frameworks for analyzing ethical dilemmas focus on rational thinking, when discussing and managing ethical issues with others, we need to recognize that rational thoughts and emotions are intertwined (Caron et al., 2020). When responding to ethical issues, we should do so with ethical empathy, placing ourselves in others' positions and striving to understand their values, beliefs, concerns, and perspectives (Paul & Elder, 2019). We need to be in tune with others, including how we are responding to them (Fine, 2019). The virtue of care is particularly relevant to social work because social workers are inspired by the ideals of helping others and promoting social justice (NASW, 2021).[1] In the gift situation, the virtue of care suggests we should be aware and responsive to the client's needs and welfare. What does gift giving mean from

---

1. Different professions may aspire to different virtues, reflecting the roles and ideals of those professions. For instance, the fundamental virtues of medicine, nursing, and the healing professions are compassion, discernment, trustworthiness, and conscientiousness (Beauchamp & Childress, 2022). Additional social work virtues include fidelity, nonjudgmentalism, benevolence, moral courage, social justice, practice wisdom, and altruism.

the client's perspective? As caring social workers, we would not reject a gift in a callous way. We would attend to the client's preferences and feelings.

Anti-oppressive social work practice suggests that we should be aware of power differences in the social worker-client relationship (Morgaine & Capous-Desyllas, M. (2020). We should ensure that the voices of those with less power are heard, acknowledged, and respected. We also need to be aware of various approaches to ethical analysis, so that we can include the values, beliefs, emotional reactions, virtues, and perspectives of everyone affected by the issues.

Narrative ethics is a theoretical approach that encourages us to listen closely to the stories of clients, coworkers, or others affected by the ethical issue (Barsky, 2019b). Stories help us recognize what others hold to be dear and moral, as well as what they deem contemptible and unethical (Brody & Clark, 2014). When working with people who identify with particular religions, for instance, we may gain better understanding of their morality by engaging in discussions of stories from their religious scriptures (Heydt & Severyn, 2022). Narrative ethics encourages empathy including cross-cultural understanding (Sobočan et al., 2020). Narrative ethics builds on social constructivism, noting that there is no universal truth (Cottone et al., 2022); rather, our truths are shaped by the stories that we tell. If I wanted to learn about a client's interpretation of gift giving, for instance, I could ask the client to share stories of gift giving in his family and culture. Assume the client shares stories about his country of origin, suggesting that in order to receive good treatment from government officials, one was expected to furnish gifts. You could then engage the client in a discussion of what gift giving meant in his country of origin and how expectations around gift giving may be different in this country. By listening to the client's stories, you and the client may gain a better appreciation about the client's intentions and moral expectations.

Consider Rashawn's research situation. Why do you think it might be helpful for Rashawn to consider his research participants' stories, including their experiences as refugees?

c. Ethical Goals

Identifying goals refers to identifying what we hope to achieve through the process of managing an ethical issue. Articulating clear and specific goals helps focus everyone on desired ethical outcomes. For instance, are we trying to honor client self-determination, protect certain people from harm, or promote **social justice**? In ethical dilemma situations, we have more than one ethical goal. At least two of the goals may be in conflict. Consider a client who is planning to end her life. One ethical goal may be to preserve the client's life. Other goals may be to respect the client's self-determination and confidentiality. If the client wants to end her life and says we should not disclose her plans or take any other steps to preserve her life, then our ethical goals conflict. Identifying ethical goals clarifies what we are trying to achieve. In the following steps, weighing obligations and options, we can then discuss whether it is possible to achieve each of the goals. If not, we may need to prioritize the goals.

In the gift situation, our goals may be to show the client respect and to act with integrity (avoiding dishonesty and conflicts of interest). Consider Oriana's case regarding the client with an STI. What are the ethical goals that Oriana should consider?

d. Obligations

Obligations refer to directives and duties that guide the conduct of social workers and others. Obligations may stem from a variety of sources including public laws, agency policies, professional codes of ethics, culture-based systems of morality, spiritual beliefs, and religious convictions. When analyzing ethical issues, we need to identify all the relevant obligations for each person affected by the issue. Although we may be able to identify obligations on our own, it is often prudent to consult with supervisors, ethics committees, attorneys, professional associations, or others to ensure we are not missing any important sources of obligations.

As Chapter 1 describes, we may experience conflicting guidance from laws, agency policies, ethical codes, and other sources of obligations. The purpose section of the NASW Code says that when legal, agency, and ethical obligations conflict, we should "make a responsible effort to resolve the conflict in a manner that is consistent with the values, principles, and standards in this Code." Although the Code does not say that we must prioritize ethics over laws and agency policies, it strongly encourages us to find a resolution that is consistent with social work values, principles, and standards. Consider a court that orders a social worker to testify about a confidential counseling session with a client. The court order is a legally enforceable order. If the worker does not comply, the court could find the worker in contempt of court and order jail time for the worker. If the worker does comply, then the worker may be violating the client's right to confidentiality. As we will see in Chapter 5, the worker will need to weigh these obligations and make a difficult choice about which obligation to prioritize.

Legalism is an approach to ethics suggesting that if there are clear laws, agency policies, or ethical standards guiding us about how to respond to a particular ethical situation, we should follow these laws, policies, or ethical standards. Thus, if the law requires us to obtain written consent from a client before disclosing client information, we should obtain written consent before disclosing client information. When laws, agency policies, ethical standards are clear, consistent, and ethical, then it is certainly prudent practice to follow them. Legalism becomes problematic when laws, policies, or standards are unclear, conflicting, or unethical. If laws or agency policies suggested that we should discriminate against a particular group of people based on the color of their skin or their gender, then it would be unethical to follow these directives.

Deontology is an ethical theory suggesting that all people have certain ethical duties or categorical imperatives that should be followed regardless of the situation (Kant, 1779/1979; Reamer, 2022). Deontologists suggest that we should follow these duties because they are intrinsically good and just, not because they are written into public laws, agency policies, or professional codes of ethics. Some ethicists suggest that deontological duties are so important that we may need to break laws or agency policies in order to fulfill our intrinsic ethical duties. Others suggest that we have a moral duty to follow the law, even when the law conflicts with our other ethical duties (Fine & van Rooij, 2021). When there is a conflict between the law and our other ethical duties, we are faced with a challenging ethical dilemma about which duty to prioritize.

Deontology is sometimes called *duty-based* or *act-based* ethics because the rightness of a decision is based on acting upon a duty rather than the consequences of the act (Schafer-Landau, 2018). Assume that you are working on a public education campaign designed to reduce smoking. You have a duty to act honestly. As you design your campaign, deontology suggests that your message needs to be honest. You might think that your campaign might have a stronger impact if you exaggerated facts and used scare tactics; however, your duty of honesty suggests you should avoid such tactics.

So how do we establish what our intrinsic ethical duties are? Kant, one of the leading contributors to deontology, suggests we should be guided by universal rules or natural laws. He believed that although people have *free will* (the ability to choose to act as they please), they should act out of *good will* (Kant [1785] 1964; Pollock, 2017). Good will suggests that people should use their intelligence, talents, resources, and other attributes with intention to do good.

Kant developed the categorical imperative test as a way to determine what types of behavior are moral: "Act only on the maxim through which you can at the same time will that it should become a universal law" (Kant [1785] 1964, p. 88). According to this test, people should act in a manner that they would wish as a guide for how everyone should act. This test is similar to the biblical maxims, "Do unto others as you would have them do unto you" (Matthew, 7: 120) and "Love your neighbor as yourself" (Leviticus, 19: 34). However, Kant's formulation does not depend on how any particular person defines good or fairness (Morrison, 2016). Categorical imperatives are universal principles. According to Kant, examples of categorical imperatives include never steal, never lie, and never break a promise. The morality of behavior is defined by our duty to others (Kant [1785] 1964).

Dolgoff et al. (2012) identify 7 ethical principles that social workers should follow as universal duties:

   i.   Protect life.
   ii. Promote social justice.

   iii. Respect individual's right to self-determination, autonomy, and freedom.

   iv. Choose actions that are likely to result in the least harm.

   v. Promote quality of life.

   vi. Respect privacy and confidentiality.

   vii. Promote truthfulness and full disclosure.

Consider which of these principles apply in Oriana's STI case. Herpes does not cause death, so the **protect life** principle is not relevant. Because herpes does cause pain, ulcers, itching, and negative effects on psychological and sexual well-being, Oriana should consider her obligation to *promote* **quality of life**. Other relevant principles include promoting *self-determination* and *privacy* for her client Jade and *truthfulness and full disclosure* for her friend Floyd. When faced with conflicting ethical obligations, deontology suggests that we should rank our obligations in order of importance. According to Dolgoff et al. (2012) protecting life is the highest priority. The rest of the principles are presented in descending order of importance. According to this approach, protecting Jade's self-determination and privacy is more important than providing full disclosure to Floyd. However, protecting Floyd's quality of life is more important than protecting Jade's privacy. Ideally, we should strive for a solution that meets all the relevant principles, for instance, working in a collaborative manner with Jade and having her voluntarily disclose her STI status to Floyd so they can both protect their quality of life. If Jade does not agree to disclose her STI status, then Oriana faces an ethical dilemma.

Although Dolgoff et al.'s (2012) ordering of ethical principles offers specific guidance on how to resolve conflicts, their ordering may or may not fit with everyone else's prioritization, including your own. By prioritizing protection of life over autonomy and freedom, for instance, Dolgoff et al. support a *pro-life* stance on issues such as abortion and euthanasia. However, many people support *women's right to choose abortion* and dying patients' *right to determine the time and manner of ending their life*. In other words, they may rank autonomy and freedom over life, at least in the context of abortion or euthanasia decisions.[2] Because different people a have different sense of ethical priorities, it may be prudent to review the relevant ethical principles together before applying them. If people agree on the ordering of the principles, then you may apply them as agreed. If people do not agree on the ordering, then you may need to use conflict resolution strategies (described below) to work through the differences.

In Rashawn's research case, which ethical principles do you think are relevant? How might these principles conflict? If Rashawn and his research participants need to rank the principles, which ones do you think should be prioritized, and why?

---

2. Pro-choice arguments could be argued from another perspective, specifically, that an abortion is not the termination of a life but rather the termination of a potential life.

e. Options

Brainstorming options refers to generating a list of possible solutions. Brainstorming stimulates creative thinking, a vital aspect of assessing and managing difficult ethical issues (Barsky, 2017a). Often, we see just one side of an ethical issue—our own side. We tend to view our own way of doing things as the right way. When others propose contradictory solutions, we may assume they are wrong. Egocentricity locks us into seeing just one possible solution. Brainstorming opens our minds, allowing us to experiment by thinking through various courses of action to see what might happen. To help us remain open to new ideas, we should remind ourselves, our clients, and our coworkers that "An act tried out in imagination is not final or fatal" (Dewey, 1922, cited in Casebeer, 2003, p. 30). Experimenting with different decisions in our imagination helps us consider novel ideas, increasing the chances that we will choose the best course of action.

Brainstorming and thinking through the ends of different courses of action fits with a teleological approach to ethical reasoning. *Teleology*, and **utilitarianism** in particular, suggests that ethical decisions should be guided by which course of action produces the greatest good (Mill, 1863; Johns, 2016, Reamer, 2019c). In other words, what can we do in order to *(a)* maximize benefits such as health, safety, happiness, financial resources, and psychosocial well-being; and *(b)* minimize risks such as illness, physical harm, emotional despair, economic hardship, and psychosocial problems.[3] Some utilitarians suggest that we should strive for consequences that produce the greatest good *for the greatest number* (Bentham, 1823). As social workers, we have a special ethical responsibility to our clients (NASW, S.1.01); accordingly, we may need to advocate for the best consequences *for our clients* rather than the greatest good for the greatest number. Whereas deontology focuses on whether the *act* is ethical, teleology focuses on the *consequences* of the act to determine the most ethical response.

To brainstorm, we refer back to the central ethical issues to be managed. As we think of different options, we write them down. We do not assess or critique the options as we generate them. We do not want to discount any options before fully considering them (Fisher et al., 2011). Even silly or bad options can be used to stimulate imagination and ideas for better solutions. Although we may brainstorm options individually, brainstorming with others allows us to build on each other's ideas.

Consider Rashawn's research. He has conducted research but he has not saved his research participants' consent forms. His options include contacting each participant to request new signatures for consent, using the data he has collected without obtaining new consents, throwing away the data he has collected, and collecting data with new research participants who will be asked to sign consent forms. Once

---

3. Note that according to utilitarianism, individuals may need to act against their own interests in order to benefit the greatest good for the greatest number.

Rashawn has brainstormed the options (perhaps with the assistance of a supervisor or ethics committee), the next step is to weigh the advantages and disadvantages of each option. For instance, one advantage of contacting past research participants is that Rashawn can use the data he already collected. This option could save Rashawn time and allow him to publish his research sooner. One disadvantage is that he promised to contact participants one time and some participants could be upset with Rashawn for contacting them a second time. He may be unable to contact some research participants because they may have been sent back to their countries of origin or they may have different phone numbers and email addresses. The second option, using the data without obtaining new consent forms, has the advantage of being able to use all the data. However, using data without having proper documentation for consents could result in punishment for Rashawn and his agency. Could he be fired? Could the agency lose future research funding? The third option, redoing the research with new participants, ensures that Rashawn has proper documentation of consents. He will avoid possible punishment that could have been imposed if he used the original data without having consent forms. The disadvantages are the additional time and costs of contacting new participants, conducting interviews, and analyzing the data. By considering the options, Rashawn may realize that a combination of approaches could be beneficial. He could try contacting the original research participants to ask for consent. To reduce chances that participants will be upset with him for contacting them a second time, he could apologize and let them know that they are free to decide whether or not to sign the consent. If he is not able to obtain the consents of enough original research participants, he could discard the data from the original research participants who do not provide consent and seek new participants to complete his research. Weighing the pros and cons of various options can become complicated. To assist with the process, we could use the format in Table 2.1 to keep track of the main points.

In many instances, it is difficult to predict the precise benefits and risks of each option with certainty. We should use the best information we have and note the limitations in predicting the outcomes of each option. Weighing benefits and risks is an important aspect of managing ethical issues. We should determine who stands to benefit and who stands to lose from each option. We need to consider the risks and benefits to our clients, agency, and others affected by the decisions. As Chapter 13 demonstrates, we should also consider how to reduce the risk of exposing ourselves to malpractice lawsuits or professional complaints.

Table 2.1. Evaluating Options

Option 1:		Option 2:		Option 3:	
Pros	Cons	Pros	Cons	Pros	Cons

f. Best Response

In some instances, critical thinking leads us to a clear, unambiguous response to an ethical issue. If I asked my supervisor how I should respond to a client who is requesting services that go beyond my professional competence, we may arrive at a clear decision that I should offer my client a referral to another professional. From a deontological perspective, I am following my obligations *to provide services within my area of competence* and *to be honest* with clients about the limitations of my competence. From a teleological perspective, referring the client is more likely to lead to positive consequences for the client and reduce the risk that I will be held **liable** for malpractice. When critical thinking leads everyone to a common understanding about how to respond, we can bypass the fourth stage of the Framework for Managing Ethical issues, conflict resolution, and move to the fifth stage, planning and implementation.

In some situations, we may engage in critical thinking, but there is no ideal or unambiguously correct response to the ethical issue. We may be conflicted in our own minds. We may also reach different conclusions than our clients, supervisors, or other people affected by the issue. Consider Oriana's situation. Upon analyzing the ethical issues with her supervisor, she might conclude that the best option is to inform her friend Floyd that Jade has herpes. She may base this decision on her desire to protect him from harm. Her supervisor might conclude that Oriana's primary duty is to her client and that she should prioritize Jade's confidentiality and privacy. After discussing these conflicting views, the supervisor might use her authority to tell Jade what to do. After all, the supervisor has more education and experience. However, as social workers, we believe in respect for the dignity and worth of all people. Rather than imposing decisions on others, we should try to work together and build consensus. If Oriana and her supervisor are unable to reach consensus, the supervisor may need to use her authority and tell Oriana how to proceed with Jade. However, they should first try a collaborative approach to managing the conflict, as described in the next section.

4. MANAGE CONFLICT

Managing ethical issues is not merely an individual decision-making process. We often need to engage with clients, supervisors, coworkers, professional disciplinary committees, and others in order to reach consensus and put plans into action (Corey et al., 2019). When challenging ethical issues arise, some people may adopt adversarial positions, believing that they are right and that they need to defend their positions. In the gift situation, you might believe that accepting the client's gift is ethical and you might try to persuade your supervisor that you are right. Your supervisor might try to persuade you that accepting the gift is unethical. If both of you take a stand and try to defend it, you will engage in a debate. Debates are competitive processes that lead to one side winning and the other side losing. Typically, the person with greater power wins. Rather than engaging in debates, we can engage in win-win conflict resolution processes by working in a collaborative fashion (Barsky, 2017a). Collaboration and consensus building have a number of advantages over debates:

- Collaboration builds trust, mends strained relationships, and enhances the ability of people to work together.
- By enhancing communication and other interpersonal processes, collaboration and consensus building fit with social work values such as human relationships, autonomy, and respect for the dignity and worth of all people.
- When people work collaboratively, they may develop more creative, individualized solutions.
- People are more likely to follow through on implementation of decisions if they have meaningful input rather than having decisions imposed on them (Moore, 2014).

We can use the following strategies to engage in collaborative **conflict resolution**: enhance communication, focus on interests rather than positions, generate options for mutual gain, and improve relationships (Fisher et al., 2011).

a. Enhance Communication

When discussing ethical issues, we need to express our concerns in clear, nonjudgmental language. Rather than saying, "You're wrong. Accepting a gift is not a problem," you could say, "I think it would be appropriate to accept the gift because the client is offering it as a gesture of appreciation and the value of the gift is nominal." This statement expresses your professional opinion. You are not claiming your opinion to be an indisputable fact. In addition to speaking clearly and respectfully, we should be open to hearing from others. "Please help me understand why you think that accepting the gift is unethical." After hearing your supervisor's views, reflect back what the supervisor has said to show you understand her position and her reasoning. "Let me see if I understand your concerns. You note that we are supposed to maintain appropriate professional boundaries with clients. Accepting the gift may blur those boundaries. Are these your main concerns?" Demonstrating understanding does not mean that you are agreeing or disagreeing. You are validating the other person's concerns, showing that you are open to hearing them. Good communication allows people to hear one another more accurately. We can use clarification questions to ensure we understand one another. "What do you mean by blurring boundaries?" We can also use exploration questions to obtain further details and concrete examples. "What do you think might happen if I accept the gift?" Often, when we show interest and understanding in what the other person is saying, they will show more interest and understanding in what we are saying (Institute for the Study of Conflict Transformation, n.d.).

b. Focus on Interests Rather than Positions

When we state our preferred outcome, we are asserting a position. If Rashawn says, "I should be able to use the data without obtaining additional consent," he is arguing for his position. Interests are the person's underlying concerns. To identify Rashawn's interests, we could ask, "Why do you think you should be able to use the data without additional consent?" He could then explain his concerns about the waste of time if he had to repeat the research and how research participants may be upset if he contacted them again. By focusing on interests rather than positions, we open the discussion to more creative ways of resolving the conflict (Fisher et al., 2011). So, rather than having a debate about whether to obtain additional consents, Rashawn and his ethics committee could talk about various ways to satisfy their concerns. When discussing ethical issues, the interests can often be related to ethical principles, for instance, protection of privacy, respect for the dignity of all people, honesty, and protection from harm. By starting with these general principles we can then explore various options to satisfy them.

In the gift case, what is your original position and what are your underlying interests? What is your supervisor's original position and underlying interests?

c. Generate Options for Mutual Gain

Generating options means identifying many possible solutions to the ethical issue. Rather than debating between the original positions of the parties, we can brainstorm various creative ideas, with the ultimate goal of finding an option that meets everyone's underlying interests. Assume Oriana asks Jade to inform Floyd that she has herpes and Jade says no. Oriana's interests include protecting Floyd's health as well as maintaining Jade's confidentiality. Jade says her confidentiality is important to her. She also feels embarrassed about disclosing her STI status and wants to maintain her relationship with Floyd. Jade and Oriana both say they value honesty. Recognizing these underlying interests, they can brainstorm various options before determining how to proceed. Some ideas include Jade using safer sex practices (e.g., condoms), Oriana speaking with Floyd about the importance of safer sex without disclosing Jade's STI status, and Jade asking a public health nurse to have a joint meeting with Jade and Floyd to discuss Jade's STI status and how they can maintain a healthy intimate relationship. They avoid evaluating the options until they have a comprehensive list of options. They can then jointly evaluate the pros and cons of each option in light of the ethical principles and interests they have identified.

Although none of the options may be perfect, they agree that having the nurse meet with Jade and Floyd will be the best option.

d. Improve Relationships

To collaborate effectively, we can use trust-building measures to enhance our relationships (Barsky, 2017a). When trust breaks down, it is difficult to listen to one another and resolve ethical issues through win-win conflict resolution. To build trust, act in a trustworthy manner. Be open and honest even when the other person is not initially doing the same. Say what you mean and mean what you say. Demonstrate an interest in meeting the other person's needs and wishes. Demonstrate vulnerability by sharing your feelings, your concerns, and your uncertainties (Craig, 2020). Acknowledge that there may not be a single truth about what is happening, or what is right or wrong (Cottone et al., 2022). Validate different perspectives. Separate the person from the problem and remember that the problem is the problem (Fisher et al., 2011). When we judge the person or focus on what we do not like about the person, we make it more difficult to work together. Assume that Rashawn thinks the chair of the ethics committee is arrogant and pushy. Regardless of Rashawn's feelings toward the chair, Rashawn will benefit from a positive relationship with her. Rashawn needs to treat the chair with respect and focus on the ethical issues that they need to address. Trust building may take time and conscious effort, but it is a worthwhile investment.

Remember that ethics belong to everyone (Churchill, 2020). As professional social workers we are not the only ones who are responsible for or equipped to make ethical decisions. When we share **ethical decision making** with our clients, supervisors, colleagues, or others, we may learn from one another and build consensus about how to move forward.

5.PLAN AND IMPLEMENT DECISIONS

Once we have reached consensus on how to manage the ethical issues, we need to plan the details for implementing the decisions. A written plan can be used to ensure that each person knows who is responsible for each implementation task. Careful planning and attention to detail can avert problems and raise the likelihood of successful implementation (Kirst-Ashman & Hull, 2018b). The following questions provide a guide for developing the plan.

  i. What is the specific decision to be implemented?
  ii. What tasks are required to implement the decision, who is responsible for each task, and what is the timeframe for completing each task?

iii. What challenges may arise during implementation and how can they be pre-empted or managed?

iv. How will implementation be monitored to enable prompt responses to any problems?

In Oriana's case, Jade has agreed to invite Floyd to a meeting with the nurse to discuss her STI status and how they can have a safer intimate relationship. Jade agrees that she will make the appointment for next week and speak with Floyd this evening about the appointment. Jade notes that speaking with Floyd will be challenging: what should she say and how should she respond if Floyd becomes angry or defiant? Oriana and Jade role-play the discussion and work through various scenarios so Jade can practice what to say. Jade is not sure that she will follow through on her commitment to speak with Floyd. Oriana and Jade agree to speak tomorrow so they can address any issues that arise, including the possibility that Jade avoids speaking with Floyd. Reaching an agreement is not the end of resolving an ethical issue. We need to implement the decisions and monitor the implementation process.

In Rashawn's case, assume that everyone agreed Rashawn should contact each of the original research participants to request their written consent for the research. How should the required tasks be allocated in the implementation plan? What challenges may arise during implementation? What could Rashawn and the ethics committee do to pre-empt or address these challenges?

6.EVALUATE AND FOLLOW-UP

The final stages of managing ethical issues are evaluation and follow-up. Once we implement the decision, we need to gather information to determine whether the ethical issues have been managed successfully and whether any additional steps need to be taken. Sometimes, a supervisor, program director, or ethics committee oversees the evaluation and follow-up. Other times, frontline social workers, clients, and others may be responsible for all or part of these processes. In the gift situation, assume that you and your supervisor agree to accept the client's gift card on behalf of the agency and use the money for the benefit of clients (e.g., to buy refreshments for clients attending group sessions). To evaluate the effectiveness of the plan, the supervisor meets with you and your client. The supervisor asks questions related to the ethical goals determined in step 3, specifically, how well did you show the client respect and to act with integrity. If the client reports that you acted honestly and with respect, no further follow-up is needed. If the client reports feeling manipulated or insulted, then the supervisor could work with both of you to determine how to rectify the situation. If necessary, you could go through the various stages of the framework to manage any new or continuing ethical issues.

When managing ethical dilemmas, we may have conflicting goals. Thus, it would not be unusual for an evaluation to find success in meeting some goals, but problems in achieving others. In a case involving suicidal ideation, for instance, we might find success in achieving the goal of saving a life, but problems in completely fulfilling the goal of honoring client self-determination. Evaluation gives us an opportunity to re-assess an ethical situation and determine what additional steps, if any, should be taken to address outstanding issues. A review of the suicide situation, for instance, might lead us to offer the client alternate services as part of a follow-up effort to enhance client choice and self-determination.

Follow-up may include dealing with specific issues raised by the particular case, as just described. Follow-up may also include dealing with broader organizational or policy issues. For instance, how can our organization pre-empt similar ethical issues form arising in the future? In the gift situation, the agency may want to provide frontline workers with additional training on boundaries, conflicts of interest, and responding to gift offers from clients. The agency could also update its policies to ensure that it provides better guidance to workers on how to manage these situations.

In Oriana's situation, what factors should she consider when evaluating the effectiveness of her plan to redress the issues with Floyd and Jade? What should Oriana do if Jade decides not to disclose her STI status to Floyd? What could Oriana's agency do to help workers manage similar issues more effectively?

CONCLUSION

When identifying and managing ethical issues it is useful to have a strategic framework for analyzing the issues and working toward a collaborative solution. Box 2.4 provides a worksheet that you may use to implement each of the 6 steps in the framework for managing ethical issues. Remember, it is important to start with a clear description of the situation, the nature of the ethical issue, and the ethical issue that you are trying to manage. Managing ethical issues can be complex and stressful. Do not stress alone. Consider whether to access help from a supervisor, professional association, attorney, or others to help you analyze the situation and consider various options. As you and your colleagues analyze the situation, make use of various approaches to critical thinking. Ideally, work toward an agreement that satisfies everyone's underlying interests. Demonstrate empathy, honesty, and respect to build trust and collaboration. Once you have reached an agreement, make sure you develop a detailed plan for implementing the decision. If you do not reach consensus, then you may need additional assistance from a supervisor, attorney, or other professional. After implementing a decision, evaluate how well you have addressed the ethical issues. For any ongoing issues or concerns, you may need to repeat certain steps of the framework to ensure proper follow-up.

BOX 2.4

WORKSHEET FOR MANAGING ETHICAL ISSUES

1. Identify the ethical issue	a. What are the key facts?	
	b. What are the relevant ethical, legal, and agency obligations?	
	c. What additional information would be helpful to know?	
	d. What is the specific ethical question to be considered?	
2. Determine appropriate help	a. What type(s) of help do I need?	b. For each type of help, who should I ask?
3. Think critically	a. What are my own values, beliefs, emotional reactions, virtues, and perspectives, and how do these affect my thinking and responses to the ethical question?	
	b. What are the values, beliefs, emotional reactions, virtues, and perspectives of others affected by the ethical question?	
	c. In terms of the ethical management process, what are our goals and what are the potential areas of conflict between these goals?	
	d. How should we prioritize our ethical, legal, and agency obligations? (apply legalism and/or deontology)	

	e. What options should we consider to address the ethical question? What are the pros and cons of each option? (apply teleology/consequentialism)
	f. What is the best response to the ethical question and what is our ethical justification for choosing this response?
4. Manage conflict	a. What are the challenges in communication between me and others affected by the ethical issue? How can I improve the communication?
	b. What are the positions of each of the people affected by the ethical issue (including my own)? What are our underlying interests, needs, concerns, or ethical principles?
	c. What alternative conflict resolution processes should we consider for addressing the ethical issue? Which is the most appropriate one for the current situation, and why?
	d. What strategies can we use to enhance our relationship so we can collaborate more effectively?
5. Plan and Implement Decisions	a. What is the specific decision to be implemented?
	b. What tasks are required to implement the decision, who is responsible for each task, and what is the timeframe for completing each task?

(Continued)

	c. What challenges may arise during implementation and how can they be pre-empted or managed?
	d. How will implementation be monitored to enable early responses to any problems?
6. Evaluate and follow-up	a. How will the extent to which the ethical goals are met be evaluated?
	b. What type of follow-up is needed to improve upon the outcomes or correct for any problems in the current situation?
	c. What types of policies, procedures, or training could be implemented to improve handling of similar ethical issues in the future?

This chapter introduces the framework managing ethical issues. If you feel some-what uncertain or overwhelmed by the range of strategies presented above, such feelings would not be unusual for this stage of your learning. The following chapters offer further experience in applying these strategies. As you work through various exercises, refer back to specific strategies listed in this chapter. These strategies offer a range of different approaches and factors to consider. Remember, different ethical issues may require different approaches. Although identifying relevant laws and policies may be the most helpful strategy in some cases, self-reflection or brainstorming options may be most helpful in others. Applying ethical theories such as deontology and virtue ethics is not easy, even for seasoned practitioners. As you practice applying them, however, you will gain confidence and competence in how they may be utilized. Do not discount certain approaches to ethical analysis just because they are difficult. Do ask for help—from supervisors, instructors, ethics experts, or others. Regardless of our level of experience in social work practice and ethics education, consultation is a vital component of analyzing and managing ethical issues.

DISCUSSION QUESTIONS AND EXERCISES

1. *Comparing Concepts*: What are the similarities and differences between each of the following pairs of concepts:
   a. Deontology (duty-based ethics) versus teleology (consequentialism)
   b. Virtue ethics versus ethics of care
   c. Positions versus interests (in conflict resolution)
   d. Ethics consultation versus legal advice
2. *Identify Ethical Issues*: Refer to the Worksheet for Managing Ethical Issues in Box 2.4. For each of the following scenarios, use the questions for step 1 of this worksheet to formulate a clear and balanced statement of the primary ethical issues raised in your chosen scenario. Identify whether the issue relates to determining whether a breach has occurred, determining how to respond to a breach, determining how to respond to an ethical dilemma, or determining how to respond to a situation of moral distress.
   a. Bridget is a social worker at a foodbank that serves an ethnically diverse community. A wealthy person from the community, Dr. XYZ, offers the foodbank $1,000,000 to build a new facility that would enable it to serve many more people. Dr. XYZ wants the foodbank's name to be changed to the XYZ Foodbank, with his name prominently displayed on the new building. The foodbank's executive director, Dolores, wants help deciding whether to accept what she calls "a tainted donation." During a staff meeting, Dolores says that Dr. XYZ is racist. He earned his fortune by investing in private prisons. These prisons have a record of treating inmates poorly, including overcrowding, lack of proper sanitation, corporal punishment, and discrimination against prisoners by prison staff. Bridget shares concerns about the donor's prisons but believes that the foodbank should accept the donation. The foodbank could do a lot of good with the money. Bridget is not sure how people in the community will react to the foodbank's new name, but she thinks that providing people with food is the most important consideration for the agency and community. Bridget believes Dolores wants the agency to accept the donation.
   b. Max provides social work services for people with physical disabilities. A client, Zena, asks Max for a referral to an occupational therapist (OT). Max has Zena sign a consent to release information form so he can send Zena's records to the OT. A week later, Zena says she did not want an OT. She calls Max a "stupid twit." She wanted a physical therapist (PT). Max says, "You're wrong. You specifically asked for an OT. It's in my notes." Zena raises her voice, threatening to sue Max for malpractice because he referred her to the wrong type of professional. She says, "Because of you, I lost a day of work. I was so

embarrassed when the OT said I was at the wrong place." Max says he did nothing wrong.

c. Shireen is a social worker who developed an online psychoeducational group for university students. The group offers information and support around dating issues, including safety strategies for meeting people online, identifying scams and risky situations, and accessing the university's services to help with concerns about sexual harassment or other forms of mistreatment. Shireen informs group members that the group is closed and confidential (as per the NASW, S.1.07). She informs members that they will need passwords to gain access to the group. Unfortunately, when Shireen sets up the group, she forgets to require a password. She learns that people outside the group have accessed the group's discussions on the site. She does not know who they are or what they did with the information. She decides to add the password requirement. She is afraid to tell anyone that she messed up. She wonders what she else she should do, if anything.

d. Jiro (SW) is working on a program evaluation that explores the effectiveness of services for families going through separation or divorce. In the first draft of Jiro's evaluation report, he suggests that services are having negative impacts (e.g., increased stress among family members). Jiro's supervisor, Wanda, asks Jiro to delete the negative findings and focus on the program's positive effects. She is worried that a negative report may lead to a loss of funding and staff may lose their jobs. Jiro values honesty. He also understands Wanda's concerns for the agency. With a family of his own to support, Jiro cannot afford to lose his job.

3. *Determine Appropriate Help*: Select one of the scenarios in exercise 2. Which of the following people, if any, should the social worker turn to for help with the ethical issues: supervisor, coworker, ethics committee, attorney, family member, insurance company, NASW, professional licensing body, or the clients? Provide your reasoning.

4. *Think Critically—Self-Awareness*: Assume you are Bridget in exercise 2(a). How would you feel about the agency accepting the donation from Dr. XYZ? What personal values, experiences, or beliefs may be affecting how you feel toward Dr. XYZ and the proposed donation? As a professional social worker in this role, which values in the NASW Code are most relevant to managing the ethical issues raised by this case? What conflicts do you have (if any) between your professional values and your personal values as they apply to this situation? If you disagreed with your boss's preference to accept the donation, how difficult would it be to advocate against accepting the donation? How does ethical fortitude apply in this situation?

5. *Think Critically—Other Awareness*: Review the facts in exercise 2(c). Assume you are Shireen's supervisor. How do you think Shireen may be feeling about forgetting to password protect the online group? Why might Shireen be concerned about telling group members about the confidentiality breach? How do you think group members would feel about people outside the group having access to their online discussions? When helping Shireen decide her next steps, what virtues could you help her consider?

6. *Think Critically—Goals*: If you were Jiro in exercise 2(d), what ethical goals would you establish? In other words, if you could achieve a perfect solution, what ethical consequences would your preferred outcome include?

7. *Think Critically—Obligations*: In exercise 2(b), which specific laws, agency policies, or ethical standards should Max consider? If Max is having trouble identifying relevant laws, agency policies, or ethical standards, who should he consult? Which of the following intrinsic ethical duties are most relevant to this situation: protect life, promote social justice, respect autonomy, do least harm, promote quality of life, promote honesty and full disclosure, or be accountable. Explain why you have identified certain duties as most relevant (i.e., explain how they apply to the situation).

8. *Think Critically: Options and Consequences*: Review exercise 2(a). Identify at least eight options for responding to Dr. XYZ's offer to donate money. Be creative, including options that you may initially think are ludicrous or unfeasible. Identify the potential benefits and risks of each option. Which option do you think will lead to the greatest good? How does your answer depend on whose perspective you are using to define what is the "greatest good" (e.g., from the perspective of Bridget, Dolores, Dr. XYZ, people who use the food bank, people in prisons, or broader society)? Why might social workers focus on the "good for the most vulnerable people" rather than the "greatest good for all people?"

9. *Manage Conflict*: In exercise 2(b), what conflict resolution strategies could Max use to improve communication with Zena? Provide specific examples of what Max could say to foster trust and collaboration. What was Zena's original position? What are her underlying interests? What options could Max and Zena consider to satisfy her interests?

10. *Plan and Implement*: Kayla (SW) tells her supervisor, Steve, "As you may already know, I am transgender and I am planning a social transition. My name will be Kyle and I will be using male pronouns." Kyle wants to be open and honest with clients. He also knows that he needs to maintain appropriate boundaries. Steve and Kyle agree that Kyle should speak with each of his clients about the transition. He will share some personal information and allow clients to respond, and he will limit self-disclosure to maintain appropriate boundaries. To implement this plan, what

specific details should Steve and Kyle consider? What types of challenges may arise in implementing the plan? How could they pre-empt or address each of these challenges?

11. *Evaluate and Follow-Up*: In exercise 10, how should Steve and Kyle evaluate the effectiveness of their approach to informing clients about Kyle's transition? What ethical goals should they measure? What is the best way to gather information related to these goals? If some clients say that they do not want to continue working with Kyle, what plans could they use for following up?

12. *Moderation*: According to virtue ethics, we should act in moderation. Aristotle suggested that we should strive toward the "golden mean" (or middle state) between two extreme qualities, deficiency and excess (Boyd & Timpe, 2021; Broadley, 2021). For instance, we should not be stingy or extravagant, but rather, moderately generous. For each of the following pairs of extreme virtues, identify a golden mean. Provide examples of how you, as a social worker, can put each golden mean into practice.
    a. Cowardly and reckless
    b. Self-effacing and arrogant
    c. Apathetic and irritable
    d. Competitive (self-interested) and accommodating (other-interested)
    e. Impulsive and restrained

3

Social Justice

___

LEARNING OBJECTIVES

Upon successful completion of this introduction, you will be able to

- define social justice according to specific ideological perspectives: egalitarianism, libertarianism, capabilities, and restorative justice;
- assess social justice issues in relation to economic, environmental, and technological concerns;
- identify methods of promoting social justice and acting to eliminate social injustice through practice and research with individuals, families, groups, organizations, and communities; and
- critically analyze social justice issues using the Framework for Managing Ethical Issues.

Social work is a profession anchored in **social justice** (Caron et al., 2020). As a core **value** of social work, social justice inspires us to promote fairness and **equity** in how wealth, opportunities, rights, responsibilities, privileges, and hardships are allocated among individuals and groups in society. Part 6 of the NASW Code of Ethics (2021) defines our ethical responsibilities to society, including the duty to promote social justice and to act to eliminate social injustices. We have a positive duty to work toward the eradication of racism, homophobia, poverty, sexism, ableism, and other forms of oppression and discrimination (Bragg, 2022). Although societal responsibilities are not defined until the final section of the NASW Code, our duty to promote social justice provides us with an overarching framework for practice. As the preamble to the NASW Code states, we may pursue social justice through various social work activities, including "direct practice, community organizing, supervision, consultation, administration, advocacy, social and political action, policy development and implementation, education, and research and evaluation."

Social work's commitment to social justice distinguishes our profession from psychology, counseling, and other helping professions, emphasizing our ethical responsibilities to our organizations, communities, and broader society in addition to our ethical duties to specific clients. Regardless of our primary professional roles—as counselors, community organizers, advocates, case managers, educators, brokers, policy developers, researchers, and so on—we have an ethical duty to foster social justice. Social work has an historic alliance with vulnerable and alienated populations, including people experiencing poverty, violence, discrimination, and oppression. We do not simply help individuals cope with these concerns; we work to eliminate the systemic causes of poverty, violence, discrimination, and oppression, promoting social justice for all (Bragg, 2022; Reisch & Garvin, 2016).

In the first section of this chapter we will consider contrasting definitions of social justice, demonstrating how our understandings of social justice may depend on our philosophical or ideological perspectives. In the second section we will explore how social justice applies in various contexts, including economic, environmental, and technological justice. Although the NASW Code does not refer specifically to economic, environmental, and technological justice, various academics and practitioners have recognized the importance of addressing these issues and augmenting the scope of social workers' duty to promote social justice. In the third section we will study methods of putting social justice into practice. Throughout the chapter, we will consider how to apply the concept of social justice in practice situations. To begin the process of integrating social justice theory and practice, refer to Box 3.1, a situation in which a social work agency is making decisions that have social justice implications.

BOX 3.1

ONLINE SERVICES

EFG Services is a state-funded agency that provides counseling and case management services to older adults experiencing challenges in performing activities of daily living. Some clients have physical challenges such as arthritis, chronic pain, heart disease, visual loss, or hearing impairment. Some have psychosocial challenges such as depression, memory loss, or social isolation.

The government recently cut EFG's budget by 15 percent. To provide services in a more efficient manner, EFG considers reducing in-person services and replacing them with online services (e.g., videoconferencing and text-based communication through a secure email platform). They can reduce office space and expenses by having social workers provide services from their own homes. EFG's social workers note that some clients have computers, tablets, or cellphones that they could use to communicate with clients; however, others do not have such devices or have challenges using them. Some of the clients with the greatest need may not have access to technology. Some workers suggest that the move to online services is unfair and unethical. EFG's administrators say that they have no other viable options.

CONTRASTING DEFINITIONS

One of the most basic definitions of social justice is that it is a situation of fairness or equity (Bragg, 2022). Although this definition sheds some light on the meaning of social justice, it begs the question, "Fairness or equity from whose perspective?" What I might perceive as fair and equitable may be different from what you perceive as fair and equitable. Consider a sanitation department with a regulation requiring that applicants for trash collection jobs pass an English literacy test. I might see this rule as just and necessary; however, I may be viewing this from a biased lens because I am a native English speaker and I may not understand how immigrants from other countries might experience this regulation. As someone without reading disabilities, I may also fail to see how this law discriminates against people with reading disabilities. What purpose does the literacy test serve for this particular job, other than to screen out potential applicants from other countries or people with reading disabilities?

Given our ethical duty to promote social justice, it is important to consider theory-based definitions of social justice. Social justice cannot simply be what each individual social worker thinks is fair. In this section we will examine various definitions of social justice according to contrasting moral philosophies. Note that this exploration is not merely an academic endeavor. How we define social justice will determine what we as practitioners will pursue for our clients, communities, and society. The following sections introduce four theories of social justice: libertarianism, egalitarianism, capabilities, and restorative justice.

Libertarianism

Libertarianism is a moral philosophy emphasizing the importance of individual rights and freedoms. Libertarians believe the state should not exercise control over an individual's life, but rather support the rights of each individual to exercise full control over his or her life (Johns, 2016; Locke, 1689). The U.S. Declaration of Independence (1776) invokes libertarian principles in its statement that all people have inalienable rights, including the rights to "Life, Liberty, and the pursuit of Happiness." Likewise, the 14th Amendment to the U.S. Constitution (1868) suggests that government shall not "deprive any person of life, liberty, or property, without due process of the law." Other basic liberties include freedom of thought, freedom of religion, freedom of speech, and freedom of assembly (Reisch & Garvin, 2016). Libertarianism is the basis for capitalism, an economic system in which most goods and services are owned, produced, and distributed by private corporations and individuals. The government should not use taxes to redistribute wealth or create welfare or health care systems for the needy (Beauchamp & Childress, 2019). Government has a limited role in this type of economy, that of supporting a free market economy in which private producers and consumers determine what types of goods and services will be produced, and at what cost (Boaz, 2015; Nozick, 1974). Libertarians believe that welfare and government assistance programs undermine personal responsibility (Reisch & Garvin, 2016) and promote sloth and dependence (Reamer, 2018b).

Libertarianism is similar to *classic liberalism*, in that both emphasize the freedom from control of others. Current uses of the term *liberalism*, however, suggest that liberals support a larger government role, for instance, promoting equality, nondiscrimination, and justice. Libertarianism is related to the concepts of social Darwinism, conservatism, free market economies, and market justice, which all emphasize individual freedom and autonomy.

In terms of social policy and the distribution of resources, libertarianism offers three essential principles:

1. *Autonomy:* Individuals should be permitted to behave as they wish (freely, rather than controlled by government or others).
2. *Ability to Pay:* The distribution of goods and access to services should be according to each individual's ability to pay.
3. *Social Merit:* Social merit is an acceptable criterion for allocating resources within a society, community, or organization.[1]

One critique of libertarianism is that it is *egoistic*, that is, it encourages people to focus on their own interests and neglect the interests of others (Pollock, 2017). Although social workers support client rights to self-determination, they recognize the importance of human relationships and social environments (NASW Code, S.6.01). Social workers believe there is a role for people to be caring and supportive of one another, within families, communities, and society. Whereas libertarians believe that government should play a minimal role in helping people with their problems, social workers believe that communities should be supportive of individuals and families. Community support, however, does not need to come only from government. Support could come from the private sector, including nongovernmental and charitable organizations.

In terms of the ability to pay principle, the NASW Code seems to reject distribution of resources based solely on the ability to pay. Social workers value access to resources and have a positive ethical duty to promote equal access to resources

---

1. One reason for rewarding social merit is to encourage positive behavior, for instance, participating in the military or civil service. Many social workers and helping professionals reject the notion of making services and resources accessible on the basis of whether the person is deserving, believing that all people have the right to health, mental health, education, housing, and other resources (DePergola, 2018). Further, who gets to decide who is deserving, and on what basis? Should we deprive people of help simply because they have committed a crime, used drugs, or do not follow a particular religious tradition?

needed to fulfill basic human needs and to allow people to develop fully (S.6.04[a]). Social workers tend to support a significant role for government in redistributing resources in support of the needy, including through further development of the welfare state (Johns, 2016).

The libertarian principle of social merit conflicts with the social work value of respect for the dignity and worth of all people. Social work rejects the idea that some people are more deserving of respect (and resources) than others. Rather, social workers advocate for social justice based on the principle of equal opportunity and access to resources, with special regard for vulnerable, disadvantaged, oppressed, and exploited individuals and groups (S.6.04[b]).

Refer back to the online services case and consider how a libertarian approach to justice might apply. Note that EFG Services is state funded. Libertarians might argue that people should be free to use EFG's service, but they are not entitled to service. Anyone who want services should pay for them. Under the social merit principle, libertarians might suggest that older adults have a special status in society (due to their age and lifelong contributions), so they deserve certain state-funded services. Whether those services should be in-person or online would be debatable. According to the ability to pay principle, EFG could provide online services but have clients pay for any technology that they need to access online services. People who cannot afford the technology could be denied services.

Egalitarianism

Egalitarianism is a social philosophy emphasizing legal, social, and economic equality. *Legal equality* refers to having laws that treat people equally, forbidding discrimination on the basis of race, ethnicity, sex, gender, nationality, sexual orientation, religion, disability, and so on. *Social equality* refers to the ways in which government and people actually treat one another; for instance, regardless of what the laws say, what is happening in practice? Are some people denied housing, health care, employment, or other needs due to discrimination? *Economic equality* refers to a relatively equal distribution of resources, including income and wealth, among a community or nation. Consider the Americans with Disabilities Act (ADA, 1990), which prohibits discrimination in employment against people with disabilities. The ADA provides legal equality. Although it is intended to promote social and economic equality, we would need to know the actual experiences of people with disabilities. For example, how do unemployment rates, average pay, and workplace experiences compare between people with disabilities and the rest of the population?

The U.S. Declaration of Independence (1776) incorporates egalitarian thought in its statement that "all men [sic] are created equal." True legal, social, and economic equality have remained elusive goals, though legal equality for African

American and women has been fostered by the abolition of slavery in 1865 (U.S. Constitution, 14th Amendment), granting women the right to vote in 1920 (U.S. Constitution, 19th Amendment), and enactment of the Civil Rights Act in 1964 (ending the Jim Crow laws that legalized racial segregation and discrimination in the southern United States). At an international level, the United Nations (1948) Universal Declaration of Human Rights promotes equality by recognizing that human rights are universal rights and by rejecting classism, sexism, and other forms of discrimination. Social work acknowledges that legal, social, and economic disparities continue to exist, as promoting social justice and access to resources remain core components of social work's values and ethical duties (International Federation of Social Workers, 2018, P.3; NASW Code, Ss.6.01 and 6.04).

One method of promoting egalitarianism is to ensure representation from diverse communities in key decision-making bodies such as the judicial and legislative branches of government, the boards of directors of for-profit and nonprofit organizations, and regulatory bodies. By having diverse representation, these systems are more likely to be responsive to the needs of various ethnic, racial, gender, and socioeconomic groups (Elässer et al., 2020). Consider, for instance, how a legislative body consisting solely of rich white men may think differently about tax reforms than a body that has greater diversity in relation to wealth, race, and gender.

Egalitarianism is based on rights theory and virtue theory (Sen, 2010). *Rights theory* suggests that all people have certain entitlements, for instance, rights to housing, food, health care, and work (Reamer, 2018b). Rights theory takes an objective assessment to ethical issues and behavior. It suggests we should *treat people equally* in order to fulfill their rights. In contrast, *virtue theory* suggests that morality is about character; we must *be moral* rather than simply *act morally* (Aristotle, 2013; Shafer-Landau, 2018). A virtuous person acts with good motivations rather than simply acting in a way to fulfill legal or moral obligations (Papouli, 2018). Thus, egalitarianism is a human trait that people live, rather than something they do.

When putting egalitarianism into practice, social workers should consider

- Does egalitarianism require treating everyone the *same way* or treating people *differently* in order to take differences into account?
- What combination of legal, social, and economic reforms is needed to promote egalitarianism?

Treating everybody equally does not necessarily mean treating everybody in exactly the same way. Egalitarians not only consider *equal treatment*, but also *equal opportunity* and *equality of results* (Johns, 2016). Consider a policy that says anyone who becomes pregnant may be fired. Women might argue this policy is blatantly sexist. On its face, this policy treats men and women the same. If a woman becomes pregnant, she may be fired. Likewise, if a man becomes pregnant, he may be fired. The effect of this policy, however, is sexist. Men do not become pregnant, so the policy has much different effects for men than for women.

Rather than talking about a principle of equality, some ethicists frame social justice in terms of **"equality and inequality"** (Dolgoff et al., 2012). When people are in like circumstances, they should be treated alike. When people are in different circumstances, then equity and fairness may require differential treatment (Rawls, 1971; Pollock, 2017). If a person is blind, should society expect that person to function in exactly the same way as everyone else, or should society make accommodations, such as providing education in the use of Braille and access to computers with text-reading capacity? As the fable about a giraffe and an elephant suggests, a tall and slender house built for a giraffe might not be very accommodating for his friend, the elephant (Thomas, 1999). We can foster equality of results by treating people differentially to rectify disparities, removing disadvantages, and providing equal opportunities for all (Banks, 2021). To promote justice, society may devote resources to empowering people, enhancing the capabilities of people for the benefit of the most vulnerable, as well as for society as a whole (Sen, 2010). Essentially, the principle of equality and inequality directs us to treat people equitably or fairly, rather than simply treating everybody in exactly the same manner (Puschel et al., 2017).

Some people believe that differential treatment violates the principles of equality and egalitarianism. They focus on how people are treated rather than the effects of such treatment. From this perspective, affirmative action is a form of discrimination because it does not treat everyone in the same manner. As advocates for vulnerable populations, the profession of social work tends to consider the *impact* of social policy, not just the *intent* or *manner* of treatment. Thus, Standard 6.04(b) of the NASW Code asks social workers to "expand choice and opportunity for all people, *with special regard for vulnerable, disadvantaged, oppressed, and exploited people and groups*" (emphasis added). Do you believe affirmative action is ethical? Consider a community with high rates of unemployment. Would the government be supporting egalitarianism or discrimination if it allocated extra resources to that community to promote job creation at the expense of taking away resources from communities with low unemployment?

One way to promote egalitarianism is to use the principle of **proportionality** to guide policy decisions. Given limited resources, it may be impossible to provide every single person with the same treatment and resources. The principle of proportionality suggests that policy makers should strike a balance between the benefits, costs, and risks experienced by different groups (Torda, 2006). Consider the online services case. Some older adults may benefit from online services, while others may not be able to use them. An egalitarian approach might suggest that certain resources should be allocated to those who do cannot afford technology and those who would benefit most from in-person services. When considering how to allocate funding and other resources to in-person versus online programs, EFG Services should consider the relative benefits and costs of each type of services. For instance, it may allocate a higher proportion of resources to clients with the greatest need, including those who will benefit most from the services.

The International Federation of Social Workers (2016) supports a *universal right to social protection*, meaning that countries should ensure a minimum level of well-being and social support for all citizens. The right to social protection helps people survive and maintain a certain level of well-being even when they are experiencing significant problems such as death, illness, unemployment, or displacement due to wars or environmental disasters. This approach to egalitarianism guarantees people's basic needs (e.g., food, housing, and health care). However, it does not necessarily ensure that all citizens have equal opportunities and equal treatment.

Some proponents of egalitarianism believe that the capitalistic market economy should be replaced with a socialist economic system. Under socialism, a government, a committee, or another administrative body is responsible for making decision about the production and distribution of goods and services. Its roles are to promote equality and the common good (Reamer, 2018b). Whereas capitalism distributes resources according to each person's ability to pay, socialism distributes resources according to the Karl Marx (1875) maxim, "From each according to his ability, to each according to his needs." Under a Marxist definition of social justice, society should allocate resources based on meeting people's needs rather than their inherited status, wealth, or other personal attributes. At a minimum, society should ensure that basic needs (food, shelter, medical care) are provided to all people. If production in society is able to provide for more than just basic needs, then everyone should benefit equally from these additional resources. Ideally, society should not only provide for basic needs, but rather, provide what humans need to flourish (Dean, 2020).

Other proponents of egalitarianism support a mixed economy rather than a socialist one. A mixed economy is based on social democratic theory, which recognizes the limitations of a purely free market economy. According to this theory, free markets are dynamic and creative, encouraging people to invest and work hard. However, they may also create social dislocation and suffering, such as when there are boom and bust cycles of employment, large corporations taking advantage of their monopoly power, and unequal distribution of resources. In a mixed economy, much of the production of goods and resources remains in the hands of private companies and individuals; however, government plays a stronger role in controlling the market economy (Hacker & Pierson, 2016). Egalitarianism may be promoted through human rights laws, employee protection laws, publicly funded education, social security, government-regulated health care, and other types of social programs (Nuffield Council on Bioethics, 2007).

Some people conflate egalitarianism or socialism with authoritarianism or dictatorship. In authoritarian regimes or dictatorships, one party rules and people do not have political freedoms (e.g., the freedom to organize and support other parties, candidates, or policies). Egalitarianism and socialism are theories of justice and distribution of resources. Although some dictatorships and authoritarian regimes have claimed they are based on egalitarianism or socialism, these two theories of justice can be implemented in democratic manners (i.e., within political systems that embrace open elections with multiple political parties and political freedoms).

All governments use policies to influence human behavior. The ethics of a particular policy depends on the type of influence, as well as the policy goals (Sunstein, 2016). For instance, American society allows the state to incarcerate people for committing serious crimes. Incarceration is a significant infringement of personal **autonomy**; however, society authorizes governments to restrict people's autonomy when they commit serious crimes. For problems such as smoking, not wearing seatbelts, or engaging in risky sports, society would not approve of incarceration. However, society may approve of the government using public education, tax incentives, and regulations to encourage people to engage in healthy and prosocial manners. When we elect governments, we provide them with a mandate regarding what types of behaviors to encourage or discourage (Sunstein, 2016). Egalitarians may vote on the basis of which politicians will promote greater fairness and social justice. Libertarians may vote on the basis of which politicians will promote greater freedom and smaller government.

John Rawls, a *liberal egalitarian*, developed his theory of justice based on a *veil of ignorance*. He asks what types of policies or distribution of resources you would propose if you did not know your abilities, needs, or position in society (e.g., whether you had a disability, whether you were part of a particular minority, whether you worked in a high-status position, or whether you had unusual preferences). He suggests that, under the veil of ignorance, most people would oppose discrimination and support egalitarianism (Rawls, 1971). If you did not know whether you were blind, whether you were a refugee fleeing persecution, or whether you were gay, for instance, you would probably support the needs of the people in each of these situations (Pollock, 2017). Rawls's theory fits with social work perspectives, including protection of the most vulnerable in society. Rawls also believed in the notion of a social contract, an implicit agreement between government and members of society that we should cooperate for the benefit of the whole community, including those with greater needs. Liberal egalitarians believe that it is ethical to sacrifice some individual freedoms in order to empower the government to support community interests.

Although no society has been able to achieve absolute equality, egalitarianism (like libertarianism) does not have to be an all-or-nothing proposition. Social workers may promote policies that improve equality among different groups and individuals, even if 100 percent equality is elusive. Social workers may disagree with one another about the best way to promote equality. Still, social workers overwhelmingly agree that promoting social justice and combating inequality are key components of their professional mandate.

As suggested earlier, libertarians might argue that social work's value of "respecting the dignity and worth of all people" means that social work promotes social justice in terms of individual rights and responsibility. Egalitarians might argue, however, that respecting dignity and worth comes through policies that treat every-one equally. Egalitarianism rejects the libertarian principles of allocating resources on the basis of social merit or the ability to pay. The social work values of "service" and "respect" suggest that all people have a right to needed resources, not just people who can afford them or people who hold high standing. Despite the differences between libertarianism and egalitarianism, they are not polar opposites. Often, we can promote policies and practices that foster both freedom and equality. When these principles come into conflict, then we may use the Framework for Managing Ethical Issues (in Chapter 2) to work through the competing interests, obligations, and options.

Capabilities Approach

The *capabilities approach* to social justice suggests that we should empower people to maximize their potentials (den Braber, 2013; Banks, 2022). To empower people, we can help them enhance their abilities, for instance, their skills, knowledge, support systems, and resources. Amartya Sen, Martha Nussbaum, and other proponents of capabilities suggest that this approach promotes freedom, social functioning, and overall well-being (Nussbaum, 2011; Sen, 2010). Whereas egalitarianism and Rawls' theory of justice focus on distribution of resources, the capabilities approach focuses on building people's capabilities so they can make choices and maximize their potentials as they see fit (Reisch & Garvin, 2016). Some people may want to use their capabilities to obtain a good job, to have a safe and comfortable home, or to live a long, healthy life. Others may use their capabilities to be creative, spiritual, or generous to others.

The capabilities approach fits well with social work values such as respect, dignity, and autonomy because it empowers people to determine their own futures (Carlson et al, 2016). By fostering the capabilities of individuals, families, groups, or other systems, social workers generate conditions in which people have greater control over their lives and their futures. Further, a capabilities approach is not simply reactive to problems; it helps prevent problems and affords people with the strengths, resources, environments, and opportunities that they need to thrive. It also empowers them to participate more meaningfully in political, social, economic, and other decision-making processes affecting their lives.

Note how the capabilities approach applies in the online services situation. Rather than focusing on who gets access to technology or in-person services, social workers would focus on the capabilities of the older adults. Thus, workers could partner with each client, jointly assessing their needs and wishes, and determining what they can do to empower clients to fulfill those needs and wishes. For some clients, this may mean helping them learn to use technology more effectively. Still, the focus of help depends on the client's own goals. Assume a client feels isolated and wants more social interaction. Workers could help the client by fostering capabilities that would allow the client to have greater social interaction, for instance, developing community-based recreational activities for older adults, helping clients develop skills to engage with others through technology, or ensuring the community has free or affordable transportation to enable clients to see friends and family in person.

By empowering clients, we not only help them achieve their original goals, but we also foster capabilities that help clients enhance other areas of life (Finn, 2021). Whereas libertarianism focuses on liberties such as freedom of religion, conscience, and assembly, the capabilities approach fosters freedom by empowering people with the skills, knowledge, resources, and supports to help them fulfill their own dreams and wishes.

Restorative Justice

Restorative justice (RJ) focuses on how we should respond to crimes, transgressions, problematic behaviors, perceived injustices, and injuries (Vieille, 2013). The traditional criminal justice system is based on retributive justice. *Retribution* suggests that when people commit a crime, they should be held accountable through fines, incarceration, or other punishments determined by an impartial judge. RJ rejects the notion that we should punish people for their crimes. RJ emphasizes engaging people affected by the crime in a process designed to address their needs and repair the harm (Zehr, 2015). Whereas retributive justice centers on the person who committed the crime, restorative justice also involves people who were harmed and people who can help make the situation better. Restorative justice rejects an adversarial approach and individual responsibility in favor of collaboration and communal responsibility (Finn, 2021). RJ provides people opportunities to heal and to prevent similar problems from arising in the future (Office of Juvenile Justice and Delinquency Prevention, n.d.; Restorative Justice, n.d.).

To apply RJ to the online services situation, assume the program director was responsible for closing down in-person services and many older adults in the community experienced harm as a result (e.g., a client who could not access services online became despondent and died by suicide; another client fell in a bathtub and broke a hip because EFG Services was no longer performing home visits and safety assessments). Rather than having a trial to determine whether the director acted badly or violated any laws (e.g., the Americans with Disabilities Act), an RJ approach could be implemented through mediation. The mediator, an independent third party, would bring the program director and relevant stakeholders together (e.g., other agency professionals, older adults, family members, and community representatives). The mediator would facilitate communication between the participants, helping them explore what has happened, share their experiences, and validate one another's stories (Barsky, 2017a). The mediator would also facilitate a joint problem-solving process, helping everyone work toward solutions to address the harms already experienced and to prevent future harms. For instance, they might help the agency raise funding so that it could restore in-person services for those in need. Alternatively, they could identify other service providers in the community to provide in-person services. The program director might accept responsibility for developing better interagency collaboration for the benefit of older adults.

Mediation is just one example of a restorative approach to dealing with past harms, crimes, and misbehaviors. Family group conferences, healing circles, community impact panels, and other collaborative processes may also be used to foster RJ (Office of Juvenile Justice and Delinquency Prevention, n.d.). Although RJ was originally developed as an alternative within the criminal justice system, RJ has also been used to deal with misbehavior in schools, child protection issues, wars, and other types of conflict.

Whereas some forms of social justice focus on creating fair distributions of resources or equal rights (Cottone et al., 2022), RJ focuses on repairing harms. RJ fits with social work values such as human relationships, self-determination, and respect for the dignity and worth of all people. Rather than labeling someone as an offender and imposing punishments, RJ encourages people to work collaboratively to address needs and repair harms (Zehr, 2015). Although people who cause harm may be held accountable, they are held accountable in terms of redressing the harm and taking steps to restore themselves and others to full health and social functioning. RJ views justice in relation to the search for truth and accountability, as well as fairness in processes and outcomes (Bharara, 2019). RJ processes promote better relationships between people who caused harm and people affected by the harm. Given the focus on accountability, collaboration, and communication, RJ processes may also lead to apologies, forgiveness, and interpersonal healing (Barsky, 2017a). RJ shares some common features with the capabilities approach, as both forms of justice build people's capacities and allow them to determine their own goals.

For a comparison of egalitarianism, libertarianism, capabilities, and restorative justice, please see Table 3.1.

ECONOMIC, ENVIRONMENTAL, AND TECHNOLOGICAL JUSTICE

Although the NASW Code does not specifically mention economic, environmental, and technological justice, various social work policies and scholarly articles have recognized that we need to pay greater attention to these dimensions of social justice (Council on Social Work Education, 2022; Reyes Mason & Rigg, 2019). Social work has long embraced the person-in-environment perspective; however, the environments that social workers tended to emphasize were social systems such as family,

Table 3.1. Theories of Justice

	Egalitarianism	Libertarianism	Capabilities	Restorative Justice
Underlying values and ethical principles	Equity, equal opportunity, fairness, shared (community) responsibility	Freedom, autonomy, productivity, economic growth, individual responsibility	Enhance abilities, empowerment, social functioning, freedom to achieve well-being	Repairing and preventing harm, community and individual responsibility, empowerment, action, human relationships
Examples	Universal health care, free college education, nondiscrimination policies regarding employment or housing, protection of vulnerable populations	Free markets to purchase goods and services, democratic political system, limited government, client self-determination, no redistribution of wealth through taxes	Educational accommodations for people with special needs, sustainable economic development, political participation, supports for physical and mental health	Victim-offender mediation, healing circles, family group conferencing, truth and reconciliation processes, apology and forgiveness.

work, school, and peers. Proponents of economic, environmental, and technological justice suggest that social workers could benefit from deeper understanding of these dimensions so they can address them more deliberately and effectively.

To foster *economic justice*, social workers may help clients and communities address unemployment, poverty, income inequality, workplace discrimination, affordability of goods and services, and other economic concerns. Simply helping people find jobs is not sufficient, particularly when many jobs are part-time, low paying, or lack benefits such as health insurance, childcare, and paid maternity leave. Promoting economic justice may include promoting tax structures and social policies that encourage companies to pay fair wages and provide better work conditions. Social workers may also advocate to reform banks, insurance companies, and other financial institutions that have perpetuated economic injustice by imposing higher fees or restricting access to people based on poverty, race, immigration status, or other socioeconomic factors. When working with individuals and families, promoting social justice may include helping individuals and families develop financial capabilities, such as budgeting, investing, improving credit ratings, and building assets (Doran & Bagdasaryan, 2018). Economic issues are closely linked with other social justice issues, including access to good health and mental health services, housing, education, and recreation opportunities.

Environmental justice focuses on the relationship between people and their physical environments, including the quality of their air, water, land, and buildings. From a rights perspective, all people should have access to healthy physical environments in which to live, learn, and work (Environmental Justice, n.d.). From an equality perspective, all people should have the same degree of protection from environmental and health hazards, such as lead in drinking water, radiation from nuclear power plants, hurricanes, floods, and fires. Unfortunately, people living in poverty, older adults, indigenous peoples, and other vulnerable populations are often subjected to greater risks (Reyes Mason & Rigg, 2019), for instance, having garbage dumps, high voltage powerlines, factories, or highways that increase environmental risks in their neighborhoods. The impacts of social and economic disparities have been highlighted by global concerns such as the COVID-19 pandemic, floods and fires associated with climate change, and depletion of natural resources. When hurricanes, fires, droughts, or other environmental disasters arise, social workers may work with first responders and others to protect lives and to rebuild communities. However, economic justice also requires proactive steps, including policies and practices designed to prevent environmental disasters and to promote healthier living environments (Bright, 2021). Finally, environmental justice means providing community members with opportunities for full and meaningful participation in decision making about environmental issues, including how to ensure a fair distribution of the burdens and benefits in responding to these concerns.

Technological justice may be defined in relation to people's rights to equal access to technology, to decide whether and how to use technology in their personal and work lives, and to equity in how the benefits and costs of technology are shared among different individuals, groups, and communities (Hermann, 2019). Technology includes digital technologies such as computers, tablets, smart phones, and artificial intelligence. Technology also includes physical machinery and devices such as cars, artificial organs, manufacturing apparatus, and power-generation plants. Inequitable access to technology is often due to poverty; inequitable access can also exacerbate poverty. Access to technology is a critical social justice issue as so many aspects of our lives are affected by technology. Given society's growing dependence on technology, it is much harder for people without access to technology to acquire good educations, well-paying jobs, food, information, and other needs (Hermann, 2019). Lack of access to technology may also inhibit relationships with family, friends, and other social support systems (Alonso, 2016; Barsky & Sinha, 2022). Further, technological inequalities make it more difficult for certain groups to participate in political processes, community organizations, and social movements (Mathiyazhagan, 2021).

Access to technology does not mean that everyone should be required to use technology—or to use the same technology and in the same ways. The principle of autonomy suggests that people should be free to decide whether or not to use particular technologies. As the online services case suggests, some people may prefer in-person services to services mediated through technology for various reasons (e.g., privacy concerns, challenges in using technology, or personal preferences).

New technology may bring about many benefits including greater manufacturing productivity and profits, access to information and education, more efficient delivery of services, and more comfortable living environments. However, technology may also lead to pollution, unemployment, social dislocation, proliferation of hate propaganda, and other problems. Technology has also allowed for accumulation and analysis of massive databases that may be used to generate knowledge and foster advancements in medicine, mental health, and social services (Steiner, 2020). At the same time, we should ensure that the manner in which data is collected does not infringe on personal privacy and that vulnerable populations also have access to data so that they can participate fairly in policy formation processes (McNutt, 2019). Technological justice means ensuring that the most vulnerable people in society receive an equitable share of the benefits of technology and are protected from its negative effects (Mathiyazhagan, 2021; Ortega et al., 2018).

APPLYING SOCIAL JUSTICE IN PRACTICE

The forgoing discussion defines social justice and describes various dimensions of social justice that we should consider when working with clients and communities. Now, let us consider the ways in which the NASW Code suggests that we can put social justice into practice through our work with policy, communities, organizations, individuals, families, groups, and research.

Policy Practice and Community Organization

Standard 6.01 of the NASW Code describes social workers' duty to promote social welfare and social justice:

> Social workers should promote the general welfare of society, from local to global levels, and the development of people, their communities, and their environments. Social workers should advocate for living conditions conducive to the fulfillment of basic human needs and should promote social, economic, political, and cultural values and institutions that are compatible with the realization of social justice.

Note that this standard suggests all social workers should promote social justice, not just those who specialize in community and policy practice. Accordingly, even social workers who practice primarily with individuals, families, or groups should advocate for social justice. Promoting justice may include promoting justice on a case-by-case basis; however, it is also important to identify and root out institutional racism, xenophobia, and other forms of oppression.

Standard 6.01 is an aspirational standard, expressing the ideal that all social workers have a responsibility to address social injustices. Under this standard, we should continuously strive for the ideal of social justice. Unlike baseline standards, aspirational standards do not identify a floor beneath which social workers would be deemed in violation of their ethical duties. Standard 6.01 allows social workers to determine which social justice issues to pursue and through which means. So, how can we establish which social justice issues to prioritize and pursue? Some workers have their own pet causes due to familiarity with them from personal, family, or professional experience. Thus, social workers who have experienced racism, religious persecution, or transphobia might advocate to redress those issues. Workers serving clients with mental health or addiction issues might advocate for their rights. Alternatively, workers might prioritize current issues requiring immediate attention, for instance, ensuring that people without health insurance have access to health services during a pandemic (Berger & Miller, 2021). To reiterate, the NASW Code does not dictate which social justice issues to pursue as long as each of us accepts responsibility to promote some aspects of social justice.

Standard 6.02 builds on a capabilities approach to social justice, encouraging social workers to "facilitate informed participation by the public in shaping policies and institutions." Thus, social workers could participate in voter registration drives, ensure that vulnerable populations have access to accurate information about social issues, and create forums that facilitate meaningful involvement of diverse constituencies in public policy formation. Under this standard, social workers do not impose their values or views on the people they are engaging, but rather, empower people to express their own values and views during elections, legislative hearings, town council meetings, administrative debates, and other policy-making processes (Kirst-Ashman & Hull, 2018a).

Standard 6.03 guides workers to "provide appropriate professional services in public emergencies." In the aftermath of a terrorist bombing, for instance, social workers from outside the area directly affected might offer their services to help people who were dislocated or traumatized by the bombing. Workers might also fundraise or gather resources needed by people who lost their homes and possessions. Standard 6.03 fits with social justice as meeting people's needs, but also ensuring that the most vulnerable are provided with needed services and resources.

Standard 6.04 encourages social workers to engage in social and political action for various purposes:

- to ensure people have equal access to resources and opportunities;
- to expand opportunities for all people and with special regard for vulnerable and oppressed people;

- to promote conditions encouraging respect for cultural and social diversity; and
- to prevent and eliminate discrimination against any person, group, or class on the basis of race, ethnicity, national origin, color, sex, sexual orientation, gender identity or expression, age, marital status, political belief, religion, immigration status, or mental or physical ability.

Note that these duties promote respect for the dignity, inclusion, and equality of all people, specifically urging us to act against discrimination and oppression. These duties operationalize an egalitarian approach to social justice. Standard 6.04 also guides social workers to improve social conditions and expand opportunities, particularly for people who are vulnerable or exploited. These duties fit with a capabilities approach.

Organizational Development

Whereas Part 6 of the NASW Code focuses on social workers' ethical responsibilities to society, Part 3 focuses on workers' responsibilities to their practice settings (e.g., social agencies, hospitals, schools, or community-based organizations). Standard 3.07 suggests that workers should advocate within and outside their practice settings to ensure the agency has sufficient resources to serve clients. They should also ensure that resources are distributed fairly. Thus, in an assisted living facility for adults with developmental challenges, social workers could advocate for suitable food, beds, restrooms, and other client needs. Workers could also foster equitable distribution, for instance, ensuring that the facilities are equivalent for clients of different ethnic backgrounds and that clients with wheelchairs have appropriate access to the building through ramps or other accommodations. Workers could operationalize Standard 3.07 through both egalitarian and capabilities approaches, advocating for equitable distribution of resources as well as providing services that empower clients to participate in decision making and maximize their potentials.

Note that promoting social justice within organizations could put us at odds with our employers. Assume that our assisted living facility requires English fluency as a requirement of admission. To promote social justice, we might consider advocating for the agency to hire bilingual staff to accommodate the needs of people who speak other languages. If we fear that administration may resent our advocacy and retaliate for criticizing the agency, we may experience moral distress (Groessl, 2017). We know it is right to advocate for the changes but we do not want to lose our jobs or be subjected to other punishment. As the Framework for Managing Ethical Issues suggests, it is important to use effective conflict resolution skills when managing ethical conflicts. Consider, how can we raise issues in an assertive rather than an aggressive manner? How can we validate administration's concerns (e.g., the costs associated with the proposed changes)? How can we engage in joint problem solving to promote equitable access to services and accommodate administration's concerns about costs? We may benefit from assistance from others, for instance, colleagues who could provide support, philanthropists who could donate funding, or attorneys who could provide legal advice.

Standard 3.09 reminds us that we should generally abide by commitments made to our employers, while also promoting social work's values and ethics. If an agency engages in discrimination, we should first work within the organization to try to effect change in a collaborative manner. In situations where the agency's policies and practices put us in serious conflict with our ethical duties and collaboration is not adequately addressing the issues, we may need to take additional measures. If an agency is neglecting the needs of people with particular disabilities, for instance, we may need to report the situation to adult protective services. If the agency is violating human rights laws, we may need to engage the state agency responsible for enforcing those laws. If the agency continues to engage in unjust, unethical, or illegal practices, we may need to leave the organization so that we are not condoning or participating in these practices.

Practice with Individuals, Families, and Groups

Part 1 of the NASW Code focuses on ethical duties to clients, including individuals, families, and groups. In terms of social justice, many standards in this part focus on justice as respecting individual rights rather than collective rights and community interests. Standard 1.01 declares our primary responsibility is to our clients. Standard 1.02 says we should respect our client's right to self-determination, to make their own choices and have control over their own lives. Standard 1.03 says that we should offer services on the basis of informed consent, meaning that clients have a right to accept or reject services based on their assessments of relevant information. Standard 1.07 says we should respect our client's right to privacy. Each of these standards is based on the principles of autonomy and choice, principles that fit with libertarianism.

The NASW Code does not suggest that clients have *absolute* rights to autonomy, self-determination, and privacy. As we will see in Chapter 4, there are a number of limits on these ethical duties, including situations when vulnerable populations such as adults with disabilities or children may be at risk. To protect people from serious, imminent, and foreseeable harm, for instance, we may need to share information about a client with others or we may need to initiate processes to have a client involuntarily admitted to a psychiatric facility. Standard 1.01 suggests, "social workers' responsibility to the larger society or specific legal obligations may on limited occasions supersede the loyalty owed clients." Accordingly, we may need to weigh the interests of society with the wishes and interests of our clients. Consider working with a group whose members identify as "Alt-Right," a White nationalist group. The members disclose that they are involved in an Internet campaign designed to defame and harass people of color. As their social worker, would you respect the members' right to self-determination and confidentiality, or would you promote social justice and act to prevent their racist actions? In Chapter 4, we will explore the tensions between self-determination and other ethical duties in further depth.

Another social justice concern arises when social workers are employed in systems of social control, institutions or organizations designed to enforce particular morals, laws, or norms. Although self-determination is held out to be an ethical cornerstone of social work, many social workers serve clients mandated into services through the criminal justice, child welfare, and mental health systems. From a social justice perspective, we need to consider under what circumstances is it ethically justified to restrict clients' rights to autonomy and self-determination, for instance, when clients have committed crimes, when children or other vulnerable populations are at risk, or when clients pose serious risks to themselves or others. Consider, also, how each of these systems focuses blame or responsibility on the individual, rather than the family, community, or social context. Poverty, discrimination, unemployment, and other social stresses may contribute to issues such as crime and child neglect (Asakura & Maurer, 2018). Lack of sufficient mental health services may contribute to incidents of suicide or homicide. As restorative justice suggests, rather than having systems based on individual blame and punishment, we should promote justice through communal responsibility and interventions designed to deal with the underlying causes of crime, child neglect, and other types of harm (Zehr, 2015).

Standard 4.02 states that we "should not practice, condone, facilitate, or collaborate with any form of discrimination." When working with individuals, families, and groups, we should advocate for fair and equitable treatment. Social work has a dual focus on social action and individual change (NASW Code, 2021). It is not sufficient for social workers to merely help clients cope with discriminatory systems. If we are working within discriminatory systems, we should advocate for systemic changes rather than simply advocating separately for each client we serve. In the 2021 revisions to the NASW Code of Ethics, new provisions were added regarding our duty to address injustices when serving clients. Standard 1.05(b) says that we should take action against oppression, racism, discrimination, and inequities. It also says we should acknowledge our own privileges in society (e.g., White privilege, male privilege, heterosexual privilege, able-bodied privilege). Standard 1.05(c) says we should engage in critical self-reflection so that we are aware of our biases and can self-correct when interacting with clients. These provisions emphasize our responsibilities to address injustices when serving individuals, families, and groups, even when addressing social justice is not the primary focus of our work.

One method of promoting social justice through direct practice with individuals, families, and groups is through conscientization, raising people's awareness of social and political concerns (Asakura & Maurer, 2018). Conscientization fits with a capabilities approach. It empowers clients with information, awareness, critical analysis, and understanding. As Brazilian educator Paolo Freire (1994) suggests, when we empower people with the abilities to think critically, organize, and advocate for themselves, we are promoting freedom and social justice. Consider a family with a daughter who has autism. The family may believe that she is having problems at school because she has a deficit or disorder. A social worker can help the family understand that when we define children with autism primarily on the basis of having a disorder, we place limits on them. Further, we ignore the responsibility of schools, families, peers, and others to foster environments in which children with autism may thrive. By raising the family's consciousness, they may become engaged in social action processes, such as educating and organizing others to foster environments that are understanding and inclusive of children with autism, supporting their strengths and interests rather than fixating on their differences or challenges.

When working with individuals, families, and groups, we should be aware that the personal is political. How we help specific clients is related to broader social justice issues (Finn, 2021). When we see that our clients are experiencing discrimination, exploitation, or other social injustices, we should consider not only how to help the client deal with these injustices, but also how we can promote social justice through social policy reform, organizational development, or other interventions at a broader systemic level. When we see client after client experiencing issues such as poverty, discrimination, and violence, our commitment to social justice suggests that we should not only help each client deal with these issues; we should also participate in social action to alleviate or eliminate these problems at community, regional, national, or global levels.

Research

Research may be defined as a systematic search for truth or knowledge. According to many research models, researchers are supposed to strive for objectivity and guard against bias (Grinnell, 2021). Researcher objectivity is intended to promote the validity, reliability, and trustworthiness of research. Although the notion of objectivity suggests that researchers should not base their research decisions on political factors, many research decisions have inherent political and social justice implications. Even when researchers strive for objectivity, the research itself is not value free. The basic decision of which issues to study, for instance, can affect the welfare of particular individuals or groups. If a researcher decides to study the impact of gun control laws, for instance, the knowledge gained can be used to make future decisions about gun safety and social policies. If a researcher decides not to study the impact of gun control laws, that decision also has an impact on social policies. Without good research, how can policymakers make informed decisions?

Although some types of research are intended to be neutral and impartial, other forms are designed specifically to promote social change (Hammersley & Traianou, 2011). In action research, the researcher and participants collaborate in designing and implementing the study. From the start, they intend to use the research to stimulate change. Consider a school in an economically disadvantaged neighborhood. Parents are concerned that their children are denied proper school facilities that are common in wealthier neighborhoods. They ask you to help design a research project to help them advocate with the county government for better facilities. Although it is ethical to help the group promote its agenda through action research, you will need to take precautions to ensure that the research is conducted according to rigorous research standards, including accuracy, honesty, and transparency (NASW Code, 5.02[o]). You should not simply design the research to make a predetermined political point or feel pressured into making findings that are not supported by the data.

A researcher's decisions throughout the research process can have significant impacts on social policy and social justice (Reisch & Garvin, 2016); for example, which populations to study, how to draw a representative sample, what type of data collection methods to use, what types of quantitative or qualitative data analysis to apply, how to interpret the findings, and where to publish the findings. When social workers design research or collaborate with others to implement research, they should be aware of the social justice implications of each of their research decisions.

When determining which populations to study, some researchers might opt to study a homogenous group, for instance, White males or adults between the ages of 18 and 65. Focusing on a homogenous population may assist the researcher by reducing the number of variables that could affect the findings. From a social justice perspective, however, the research is excluding certain populations. Researchers should consider including vulnerable and disadvantaged groups in their studies to ensure that the research attends to their needs and the findings are applicable to their situations. Consider a study on the effectiveness of a particular crisis intervention for people with suicidal thoughts. If people of color or people over 65 were excluded from various studies, how would we know whether this intervention is effective with these groups? When research proposals go through ethics review with an organization's Institutional Review Board (IRB), the IRB will consider whether particular groups are excluded from the research (Common Rule, 1991/2018). The IRB may not approve the research unless there is good ethical justification for excluding particular groups. A study restricted to women or genderqueer people, for instance, could be justified because similar research has already been conducted with men.

Sampling procedures may also lead to biases in who is included in particular research. If I were conducting a survey by telephone, for instance, I would be excluding people without phones. If I conducted my study in urban areas, I would be excluding people in rural areas. I would need good reasons for limiting my research in these manners or I would need to supplement my sampling procedures to obtain a more representative sample.

When considering data collection methods, researchers should ensure that people from diverse backgrounds can participate fully and equitably. Many studies require participants to provide written responses. If some research participants speak different languages, then researchers should consider the use of different languages or translators to be inclusive of these participants. If some participants have low levels of literacy, then researchers could consider allowing participants to audio record their responses.

Approaches to data analysis may also have social justice implications. Consider a large quantitative study on the relationship between income, nutrition, and obesity. If people of different ethnicities are lumped into one category, then the research will not attend to potentially important factors related to ethnicity. If the researcher tries to analyze the effects of research, but the sample of certain groups is too small, then the researcher may not be able to find significant effects for those groups. Although quantitative research can be designed to attend to differences between groups, researchers could also consider qualitative research to attend to these issues. Qualitative research may be used to explore meanings, perspectives, and experience of diverse individuals and groups (Grinnell, 2021). Whereas quantitative research may disregard certain research participants as outliers, qualitative research may explore these so-called outliers in greater depth. Qualitative research may also promote social justice, giving people voice by gathering their views and publishing them for particular audiences.

When researchers are interpreting data, they should be aware of potential biases and strategies for overcoming them. Assume that your study of the relationship between income and nutrition finds that people with higher incomes tend to eat more nutritious food than people with lower incomes. You might conclude that people with lower incomes do not care as much about their nutrition or require better education about nutrition. Both interpretations could be invalid. Perhaps the issue is related to lack of nutritious food in their neighborhood stores or simply the lack of affordable nutritious foods. To attend to issues of interpretation and diversity, you could include people from diverse backgrounds on their research teams. You could also supplement your research by presenting the initial research findings to people from the diverse community and inviting their feedback to help interpret the findings. By empowering people from the community, you are promoting social justice through participation.

Finally, it is important to consider how you publish your research findings. Program evaluations are often kept within the agency that conducts the research. Scholarly research is often published in scholarly journals and presented at academic conferences. From a social justice perspective, these methods of disseminating research are missing many people, including those who may be most affected by the findings. In a study involving people of Haitian descent with HIV or AIDS, my research team first presented the findings back to the community in which we conducted the study. This information not only empowered them with access to the research findings, but also helped us with our subsequent publications and presentations. We were able to take their feedback and incorporate it in in our discussions and recommendations. When presenting research, in writing or orally, we may promote social justice by offering suggestions about the implications of the research, including how to bring about good in the world (Bloor, 2010).

CONCLUSION

Although there is broad agreement among the social worker profession that social justice is a core ethical value, different social workers may have different ideas about the meaning of social justice and the best means to promote it. This chapter has provided a range of theoretical perspectives on social justice, as well as different contexts of practice in which social justice issues can and should be considered. Regardless of whether you are acting as a community organizer, educator, case manager, counselor, advocate, or in another social work role, it is important to have your own understanding of social justice and to ensure that you are attending to social justice issues throughout your practice. As social workers, we have a dual focus on individual and social change. Regardless of our preferred areas of practice, we have an overarching ethical obligation to act against racism, poverty, homophobia, sexism, ableism, classism, and other forms of discrimination and oppression (Bragg, 2022). To promote social, economic, environmental, and technological justice, we often need to work in collaboration with our clients, communities, work colleagues, and people in positions of power and influence. When people express different views on social justice, we can listen to and validate their perspectives, as well as inviting them to consider different approaches to social justice and ways of finding common ground.

DISCUSSION QUESTIONS AND EXERCISES

1. *Contrast*: Identify the similarities and differences between each of the following pairs of concepts:
    a. Egalitarianism and libertarianism
    b. Capabilities approach and egalitarianism
    c. Retributive justice and restorative justice
    d. Liberal democracy and autocracy

2. *Equality and Inequality*: A study at HFI University finds that students who are the first ones in their families to pursue higher education are at greater risk of not completing their undergraduate degrees than students whose parents and other family members have completed some form of higher education. HFI is considering whether to provide additional services and resources (such as mentoring and scholarships) for first-generation university students. Some administrators oppose this affirmative action proposal as discriminatory. How would you assess this proposal according to egalitarianism, libertarianism, and the capabilities approach to social justice? Which approach do you think fits best with social work's mission? Provide your reasoning.

3. *Health Care Ethics*: What aspects of the United States health care system are based on egalitarianism and what aspects of this system are based on libertarianism and capitalism? Consider private and public health insurance systems, private and public hospitals, and how health and mental health providers receive payment for their services. From an ethics perspective, what recommendations do you have to enhance the current healthcare system by promoting ethical principles such as social justice, autonomy, beneficence, nonmaleficence, and respect for the dignity and worth of all people.

4. *International Perspectives*: Review the International Federation of Social Workers' (IFSW, 2018) Global Statement of Ethical Principles at https://www.ifsw.org/global-social-work-statement-of-ethical-principles. How does Principle 2 define social justice? Which theories of social justice does this statement incorporate? How are the IFSW's descriptions of social justice different from the ones in the NASW Code of Ethics?

5. *Retributive vs. Restorative Justice:* City officials are trying to figure out how to deal with violence that has erupted in recent months. Police shot and killed an unarmed Black youth. Police say that the youth was caught shoplifting and started running away. This incident sparked anger in the Black community and beyond, leading to many protests. Although most of the protesters have been peaceful, some people have used the protests to destroy property and attack police. If the city were to use retributive justice processes to respond to the situation, what specific processes could they consider? If the city were to use restorative justice processes, what processes could they consider? What are the advantages and disadvantages of using a restorative process versus a retributive justice process?

6. *Action Research*: Wendall plans to conduct action research in collaboration with survivors of shooting incidents. The survivors are hoping to use the research results to advocate for laws restricting the availability of semiautomatic shotguns. A colleague warns against conducting this research because it is too political. How do the ethical principles of objectivity, social justice, and honesty apply to question of

whether social workers should conduct this type of politically motivated research?

7. *Strategies*: Select one of the following situations. Identify the type of social justice issue raised by the situation: social, economic, environmental, or technological. Describe at least one possible strategy that the social worker could use to address the issue for each of the following types of practice: policy and community; organization; individual, family, or group, and research. Identify which standard from Part 6 of the NASW Code applies to each strategy that you identify.

   a. Latoya is concerned that many of her social work colleagues have been subjected to harassment by supervisors in their agency. The workers are afraid to raise concerns for fear of being fired or subject to some other retaliation. The organization has a procedure for workers to submit grievances, but they are all handled by a program director who does not take harassment allegations seriously.

   b. JKL Community Services has decided to use artificial intelligence to determine whether children are at risk of child abuse or neglect. Hector, a social worker, has concerns that the algorithms used to determine risk are based on stereotypes. He believes that people from certain ethnic groups will be overrepresented among those who are identified at risk. Hector believes that trained social workers are better at making accurate, unbiased risk assessments.

   c. A regional planning committee is deciding how to prevent flooding in light of climate change and expectations for more flooding. Alice, a social worker on the committee, is concerned that areas with higher property values are being prioritized. People who live in economically disadvantaged districts will not be protected by dykes or other safeguards against flooding. People from those districts have not participated in the committee's hearings because they cannot take time from work and there is no public transportation to the area where the hearings take place.

   d. While conducting a home visit with the Burgess family, Rona discovers that Grandma Burgess has been sedated with benzodiazepines. Grandma has dementia and her son, Jake, is her legal guardian for medical decisions. Jake says Grandma had been very anxious and irritable lately so her physician prescribed sedatives. Rona is concerned that doctors are overprescribing sedatives to older adults like Grandma. Although sedatives make taking care of them easier, Rona is concerned about respect for the dignity and quality of life of older adults who are heavily sedated.

8. *Revisiting the Framework*: Review the following situation and apply the first three steps of the Framework for Managing Ethical Issues from Chapter 2. When engaging in the third step, critical thinking,

apply various theories of social justice, including egalitarianism and libertarianism.

A social work program provides respite care for parents and caretakers of children with severe physical disabilities. The program had been providing respite services to any caretakers, regardless of their income level. The program lost its state funding in recent budget cuts. Agency staff are thinking of continuing to provide respite care on a fee for service basis. They also plan to use some of the fees from paying clients to offer scholarships to other clients who cannot afford to pay for the respite care.

9. *Digging Deeper*: Select one of the following ethics theories or social philosophies for further research: Aristotle's Eudemian Ethics, Kant's Categorical Imperative, Hegel's Dialectics, Nietzsche's Superman (Uebermensch), Horkheimer's Critical Theory, Stoicism, Rawl's Theory of Justice, Nozick's Libertarianism, Martin Buber's Personalistic Ethics, Gustavo Gutiérrez' Liberation Ethics, Philippa Ruth Foot's Trolley Problem, Jean-Jacques Rousseau's Social Contract Ethics, Simone de Beauvoir's Feminist Ethics, Joan Tronto's Ethics of Care, Bantu Stephen Biko's Black Consciousness, Buddhist Social Philosophy, Soleveitchik's Halakhic Man (Jewish), Confucian Ethics, Avicennian Philosophy (Islamic), Aquinas's Four Cardinal Virtues (Catholic), Bernard Gert's Common Morality Theory, and Lao Tzu's Taoism. Read a scholarly book or article on your chosen ethical theory or moral philosophy. Summarize the key points of this theory or philosophy. Describe how you could apply the key lessons of this theory or philosophy to social work practice, including promotion of social justice.

10. *Motivation and Commitment*: Identify an area of discrimination, oppression, or social injustice that you have addressed or plan to address in your professional capacity as a social worker (e.g., racism, poverty, heterosexism, transphobia, ableism, xenophobia, misogyny, religious bigotry, mass incarceration, police brutality, health disparities, or classism). What have you done or what do you plan to do to act against this form of discrimination or oppression? What motivates you to promote social justice in this manner? What organizations or groups could you partner with in order to pursue your cause?

4

Client Autonomy, Self-Determination, and Informed Consent

LEARNING OBJECTIVES

Upon successful completion of this introduction, you will be able to

- explain the importance of client autonomy, self-determination, and informed consent in social work practice;
- foster self-determination with individuals, families, groups, organizations, and communities;
- engage clients in effective informed-consent processes, including discussions of service options, potential benefits and risks of choices, and voluntariness; and
- critically analyze situations in which there may be ethically justifiable limits on self-determination and informed consent.

Autonomy derives from Greek roots meaning "self-rule." The ethical principle of **autonomy** is based on the value of respect for the dignity and worth of all people. All people, as sentient beings (having awareness and feelings), deserve to be treated with dignity and respect (Beauchamp & Childress, 2019; Grimwood, 2019). Respecting dignity and worth includes respecting each person's freedom to make their own choices. Within social work practice, client autonomy is a core ethical principle (NASW Code of Ethics, 2021). We put client autonomy into practice by respecting clients' right to self-determination, the right to make decisions about matters affecting their lives, including whether to accept or reject particular services that social workers or other helping professionals may offer (NASW Code, S.1.02). We may also put autonomy into practice by empowering clients to make their own decisions and ensuring that their voices are heard in contexts outside of the social worker-client relationship. As we will see in this chapter, while social workers believe strongly in the principles of client autonomy and self-determination, these principles are not ethical absolutes. We need to be aware of situations in which there are conflicting values and interests, circumstances in which we may need to place limits on client autonomy and self-determination; for instance, we may need to prioritize life and safety when clients express plans to cause serious or fatal harm to themselves or others. Even when we are ethically justified in placing limits on autonomy and self-determination, however, we should consider ways to empower clients as much as possible, affording them as much freedom and choice as we can, while still attending to concerns about safety or other conflicting ethical principles.

CONSTITUTIONALLY PROTECTED FREEDOMS

The principle of autonomy is built into the First Amendment of the U.S. Constitution (1791).

> Congress shall make no law respecting an establishment of religion, or prohibiting the free exercise thereof; or abridging the freedom of speech, or of the press; or the right of the people peaceably to assemble, and to petition the Government for a redress of grievances.

Freedom of religion, freedom of speech, freedom of peaceable assembly, and freedom to petition the government mean that people should be allowed to engage in these activities without constraints from the government. These freedoms are cornerstones of a free and democratic society.

The Constitution regulates the relationship between the government and the people. Although these constitutionally protected freedoms do not directly define our duties as social workers, they do have relevance to many aspects of our practice:

- When promoting social justice, we should promote the freedoms of the individuals and communities that we serve.
- When we engage in social advocacy and community organization, our activities are protected by our freedoms of speech and peaceable assembly.
- When advocating for particular clients or communities, we may invoke the Constitution to advance their rights and freedoms.

Note that the freedoms expressed in the Constitution are not absolute freedoms. There are limits, for instance, when exercising one's freedom hurts other people. Although we have freedom of speech, this freedom does not allow us to use hate speech to promote violence against a particular group of people (Orwell, 2019). We must balance our rights and freedoms with those of others. "Your right to swing your arms ends just where the other man's nose begins" (Chafee, 1919, p. 957). Although we have freedom of religion, this freedom does not permit us to impose our religious beliefs on our clients. Although we have freedom to petition government, we should not abuse this freedom by issuing grievances based on lies or threats of violence.

Constitutionally protected freedoms are intended to protect all people from coercion and control by the state. As social workers, our primary obligation is to our clients (NASW Code, S.1.01). In our professional roles, we may need to limit our own freedoms for the good of the people we serve. We have special obligations to protect our clients from undue pressure or control. The NASW Code of Ethics incorporates the principles of autonomy and consent by specifying our duties to respect our clients' rights to self-determination and informed consent, as described below.

FOSTERING SELF-DETERMINATION

Standard 1.02 of the NASW Code states, "Social workers respect and promote the right of clients to self-determination and assist clients in their efforts to identify and clarify their goals." This standard sounds simple: Just ask clients what they would like to achieve and then ask how they would like to start working toward these goals. In practice, this standard is far more complicated. What if a client does not have clear goals? What if a client has diminished mental capacity due to a mental illness, substance use disorder, age-related dementia, or social stress? What if a client's goals are unwise, illegal, or irresponsible? What if social workers think they know what's better for the client? What if the client has no idea about how to achieve certain goals? What if the client has been ordered into services through the child protection system, criminal justice system, or mental health system?

Self-determination requires mutual work in the planning process. We do not merely stand back and say, "You're the client, so you make all the decisions." We might propose:

Let's talk discuss the concerns you raised in the assessment process and try to set some priorities. I'll ask questions. For instance, what are your main concerns? How do you think you might address these concerns? What have you tried in the past? I may have some suggestions about how to proceed. I want to help you consider different options so that you can determine the best way forward. You are in the best position to know what is best for you. As the client, you will make the final decisions.

We let clients know that, although they make the ultimate decisions, we may provide information and suggestions. Rather than telling clients what goals to pursue, we ask questions. These questions facilitate insight about possible issues and goals to pursue. We start with our clients, meaning that we validate their concerns and permit them to explain their concerns further. A client might initially express one goal but—with guidance from your questions—eventually decide to pursue others. Listening is an essential part of facilitating self-determination. We should attend closely to what clients are saying, clarifying their thoughts and motivations, and acknowledging any challenges that they may be facing. When presenting options for clients to consider, we help them assess the pros and cons of each choice and allow them to make the final decision.

Consider a client who recently immigrated to the United States. She says her goal is to find a job as a tax accountant, a career she had in her country of origin. You acknowledge her desire and gently ask questions to help her determine whether this goal is reasonable, at least in the short term. Upon further questioning and research, the client discovers that U.S. tax laws are very different. It would take more than 2 years of study for her to qualify for the same type of licensure she had in her country of origin. The client revises her short-term goals, agreeing to search for a different job to help pay her bills in the immediate future and to enroll in a parttime course to begin work toward U.S. accreditation as a tax accountant.

In some situations, we may think that we know better than clients about what courses of action are in their self-interest. We need to resist the temptation to be paternalistic. Even if we think that we know what is best for our clients, imposing our values and beliefs on them conflicts with our clients' autonomy and the right to self-determination.

LIMITS ON SELF-DETERMINATION

Self-determination and informed consent are not absolute rights. The NASW Code and various laws provide many exceptions. Standard 1.02, for instance, states that we may limit a client's right to self-determination when we believe the client's actions or potential actions raise "a serious, foreseeable, and imminent risk to themselves or others." If a client in crisis says that she wants to end her life, we would not be obliged to help the client fulfill this desire.[1] Rather, we would be obliged to take necessary steps to protect the client (e.g., provide crisis intervention counseling, develop a safety plan, or refer the client to an in-patient psychiatric facility). Likewise, if clients want to commit fraud, steal, or otherwise break the law, we are not required to support such self-determined acts. If we did, we could be held criminally liable as accomplices to the crimes.

Many social workers work with involuntary clients, people mandated by the court to receive services. Requiring clients to see a social worker infringes their

---

1. We will discuss dying with dignity and assisted dying later in this chapter. The ethics considerations are different for clients with suicidal ideation due to an acute crisis versus clients who are making a reasoned choice to end their lives.

right to self-determination. This infringement is ethically or legally justified, however, by a higher value. In child protection cases, for instance, protection of children from maltreatment is deemed a higher priority than noninterference with the autonomy rights of the family and parents. In mental health cases involving involuntary commitment of a patient, preventing clients from seriously harming themselves or others is deemed a higher priority than client autonomy. In criminal cases, protection of society from serious harm is deemed a higher priority than client autonomy. In each of these situations, we face challenging questions in terms of where to draw the line between conflicting priorities. At what point, for instance, does a child protection concern become serious enough to limit client self-determination? Consider a father who refuses to stop the car to let his children urinate, telling them to "hold it" until the end of a car trip. Does this situation warrant state intervention and limiting the father's right to decide how to raise his children?

When working with involuntary clients, we still have an obligation to respect client self-determination as much as possible (Standard 1.03[d]; Cottone et al., 2022). For instance, we should be honest about the consequences of a client's not cooperating with us. The client may decide to accept these consequences (e.g., having children removed from the home; being incarcerated). Using a client-centered approach, we could offer to help clients work on their own goals:

> I understand that if it were up to you, you wouldn't be here today. Since you
> have been ordered by the court to see a social worker, perhaps we can make
> the best of it... If you would be open to sharing your concerns, we could
> develop goals that fit with your wishes and needs.

Although the client comes into services as an involuntary client, we offer the client as much self-determination as possible. Ideally, we connect with a client in a manner that transforms the worker-client relationship from involuntary to voluntary.

A final limitation on self-determination arises when the mental capacity of a client is in question. If a client does not have sufficient mental capacity to agree to services, including a particular form of intervention, we should obtain the consent of a substitute decision maker (e.g., a parent, guardian, or person legally authorized to represent the client).[2] Clients may not have sufficient mental capacity to provide informed consent for a variety of factors: age and mental maturity, mental illness, cognitive functioning, disorientation, communication impairment, memory impairment, or uncontrolled substance abuse. Mental

---

2. The names of substitute decision-makers varies from state to state and also depends on the types of decisions they are authorized to make (e.g., guardian ad litem for litigation-related decisions, power of attorney for property decisions, or healthcare agent for medical decisions).

capacity may be a complicated issue. In terms of age, for instance, there is no one age whereby a person automatically has full capacity to agree to services. Although 18 is the legal age of consent for many purposes, younger children may be able to provide consent for certain types of services (depending on agency policy, state regulations, and so on; Cottone et al., 2022). In terms of mental illness, clients are not automatically deemed mentally incapacitated just because they have a diagnosable condition. We should assess mental capacity in relation to the social context, the client's current mental state, and decisions to be made. A client who has schizophrenia, for instance, may have adequate mental capacity while taking medication to control hallucinations, delusions, and other symptoms. Clients with mild brain damage may not have capacity to consent to a complicated and risky intervention but may have capacity to consent to a simpler and safe intervention. We are obliged to enhance clients' ability to provide consent. If a client is incapacitated due to high levels of stress, for instance, we could help the client deal with the stress first; once the client's stress has been reduced, the client may be able to provide consent. The main criteria for assessing a client's capacity to consent to services are whether the client understands and appreciates the nature of the services being offered, including their potential benefits and risks. Clients should also be able to evaluate service options in relation to their own values and express their wishes about their preferred service options (Bryan et al., 2022).

Although we typically engage clients in planning and ask for agreement to services during the beginning phases of social work, client self-determination and informed consent are ongoing processes. We should continuously pay attention to client wishes. We should allow clients to change their minds, renegotiate their contracts for work, and make new decisions on how to proceed. By respecting client rights to self-determination and informed consent on an ongoing basis, we ensure that they are working *with* their clients rather than *against* them.

COMPONENTS OF INFORMED CONSENT

Self-determination and informed consent are linked concepts. Both involve providing clients with service options and empowering them to make the best decisions for themselves based on relevant information. Standard 1.03(a) states:

> Social workers should use clear and understandable language to inform clients of the purpose of the services, risks related to the services, limits to services because of the requirements of a third-party payer, relevant costs, reasonable alternatives, clients' right to refuse or withdraw consent, and the time frame covered by the consent.

When discussing service options with clients, we should provide accurate information about possible interventions, how they work, their potential benefits, and their potential risks (Cottone et al., 2022). The informed consent process may also include an honest and open discussion of the risks and benefits of doing no intervention. In some situations, we give information in the form of advice, "I recommend that you try . . . because . . ." To provide clients with greater control over their decisions, we may provide information without specifically advising the client what to do or how to do it. Consider a client with an alcohol use disorder who says he wants to "get my drinking under control." We could educate the client about the effectiveness of different interventions and then allow the client to determine which intervention to pursue. Perhaps the literature shows that controlled-use programs are not generally as effective as abstinence programs for people with chronic alcohol use disorders. If the client still wants to try a controlled-use program, we should accept this choice and help the client with his goal. If our agency only offers abstinence-based programs, we could refer the client to a controlled-use program. In addition to explaining the types of services offered, we should explain agency policies, including any fees, eligibility requirements, criteria for termination of services, and expectations of the client.

Many clients conduct their own research (on the Internet or with friends) to inform themselves about various psychosocial conditions and methods of intervention. When clients make appropriate use of reliable information, they may present us with reasonable requests and suggestions. Challenges arise when clients rely on dated, inaccurate, or irrelevant sources of information, or when they misunderstand the information. We may facilitate informed consent by guiding clients to more reliable and relevant sources of information and by clarifying any misunderstandings.

Clear violations of informed consent include

- imposing decisions on clients through threats, coercion, dishonesty, or trickery;
- failing to provide clients with sufficient facts and knowledge to allow them to make informed decisions;
- explaining services or interventions using language that clients cannot understand;
- preventing clients from choosing to withdraw from services; or
- obtaining consent from clients who do not have the necessary mental capacity to provide consent.

In addition to discussing possible service options, we should discuss options related to the use of technology, for instance, whether services will be provided in-person, through videoconferencing, through text-based communication, or through other forms of technology (NASW Code, S.1.03[f]). When discussing options involving technology, we may help clients determine which methods of communication work best and ensure that clients have access to the technology under consideration. Ordinarily, we should not conduct electronic searches (using Google or other digital programs) on clients unless they have provided prior consent. Exceptions may be justified when a search is required to protect "the client or other people from serious, foreseeable, and imminent harm, or for other compelling professional reasons." If you are merely curious about what a client has posted on social media, you would need prior consent before searching the client's social media. If a client fainted in the agency and you needed to identify next of kin for assistance, then you could be justified in conducting an online search without client consent.

Remember, informed consent includes the right to *informed refusal*. Informed refusal refers to a client's right to reject services (or particular methods of intervention) without fear of negative consequences and with sufficient information to make educated decisions. Informed consent is an ongoing process of communication. It does not end when clients sign a consent form or orally agree to services. Throughout the helping process, we should continue to discuss their experiences with services, being attentive to whether they want to continue or terminate services (NASW Code, S.1.03[a]).

When working with *involuntary clients*, we should acknowledge that clients may not be able to provide voluntary consent. We should explain "the nature and extent of services" and the "extent of the clients' right to refuse services" (NASW Code, S.1.03[d]). Consider clients with probation orders requiring them to receive counseling for intimate partner violence. We could let the clients know that the order requires some type of counseling, but they have choices about individual versus group counseling, as well as the model of intervention used in counseling. We could also explain the number of sessions that clients are required to attend and that clients may continue beyond the minimum.

The NASW Code does not dictate whether consent should be oral, written, or digital. We need to consult agency policies and relevant laws to determine what form of consent is preferred or required. If you receive oral consent, then you should document consent in the client's records. Often, prudent practice suggests that we document the client's signature (on paper or digitally) to provide evidence that a client has agreed to services. We should not simply tell clients to sign consent forms. When working with clients who do not speak English or have low levels of literacy, we should offer options such as using a qualified interpreter, going through the consent form orally, using a simplified consent form, or providing a consent form in the client's preferred language (NASW Code, S.103[b]). Informed consent means checking whether clients truly understand and agree to the services and other terms stated in the consent. See Box 4.1 for an example of an informed-consent process.

BOX 4.1

JOSIE

Josie (16 years old) was admitted to an inpatient functional rehabilitation program for adolescents with chronic pain. The program is not aimed at curing pain, but rather helping patients manage their pain more effectively so they can enjoy a better quality of life at home, at school, with friends, and in the community. The social worker, Liam, is part of an interprofessional team that is working with Josie. In the script below, Liam is engaging Josie in an informed consent process, helping her determine her goals and plans regarding school. As you read the script, identify specific ways in which Liam effectively covers the main elements of informed consent (self-determined goals, options, pros and cons of different options, and voluntariness). Also, identify ways in which Liam could have been more effective with the informed consent process.

> Liam: Josie, your psychologist, Dr. Kendrick, asked me to speak with you to help make plans for school after you leave our inpatient program.
> Josie: I thought I'd just go back to homeschooling.
> Liam: That's certainly one option to consider. What are some of the advantages of continuing with homeschooling?
> Josie: Well, when I started to develop chronic pain, I couldn't keep up with classes at my old school. I missed lots of classes because I was in too much pain or because I had to go to so many doctor appointments. I was able to do things at my own pace and if I just needed time to do nothing, that was ok.
> Liam: So, homeschooling offered a lot of flexibility and comfort. You could do your work at your own pace. Was there anything not-so-good about homeschooling?
> Josie: Not so good? I felt pretty isolated. I lost touch with most of my friends. I started to think that I would never have a normal life, with friends or a job or anything.
> Liam: Feeling alone can certainly be one downside of home-schooling. So, although home schooling is an option, we can talk about different options before you decide. One of the things that we've found is that graduates of our inpatient program tend to do better when they return to a traditional school. One of the risks of being home-schooled is that you can fall back into patterns where pain controls your life. Now that you're learning to take charge of your pain and your life, you can return to school, you can enjoy more time with friends, and you can get involved in other activities that you enjoy.
> Josie: It's kind of scary. What if I just can't keep up with school?
> Liam: Keeping up with school is certainly an important concern. You're learning a number of important coping strategies so that can help you keep your pain in check. We can also connect you with new support systems.

Josie: What do you mean by support systems?

Liam: We can work with the school to make sure the school provides you with appropriate support, for instance, a special education plan and a guidance counselor to help advocate for you. After you leave our program, you could also see a mental health professional for ongoing counseling and support. Each of these options is up to you and what you think might be best.

Josie: I do like the idea of having a counselor, especially to help during times when I'm feeling overwhelmed. If I do go to school, should I just go back to my old public school or should I go to one of the special private schools for kids with problems?

Liam: Again, the type of school is a choice that you can make. Some of the advantages of public schools are that they are free, they have lots of different courses, and there are a lot of different students and after school activities. Some of the small, specialized schools can provide smaller teacher-student ratios and support, but they may not offer the same range of classes, clubs, and activities. Also, we may not be looking for a school for "kids with problems" but rather, a school that helps all students thrive.

Josie: I'm not sure what's best. Shouldn't my parents be in charge of these decisions?

Liam: You don't need to decide right now, so it's ok not to be sure about what to do. You're also right that we should speak with your parents. It's best if everyone can agree, so we do want to involve your parents. You're 16 and you're my primary client, so I am speaking with you first. I want to hear what you want. If you'd like, I can help advocate for what you want. Would you like me to arrange a meeting with you and your parents so that we can speak together?

Josie: I think I'd just like to think about it myself for a bit, and talk to my parents alone first. Would that be ok?

Liam: Absolutely, Josie. You know what's best for you right now, so I'm going to take my directions from you. If you change your mind, just let me know. If you'd like me to do some research about school options in your area, I could gather some information and share it with you.

Josie: That would be great. Thanks.

MENTAL CAPACITY AND SUBSTITUTE DECISION MAKERS

We should ordinarily obtain informed consent directly from our clients. When clients lack mental capacity, however, we should seek permission from an appropriate third party (NASW Code, S.1.03[c]). So, how do we know whether clients "lack mental capacity," and how do we determine who is an "appropriate" third party?

Mental capacity *refers to the ability of a person to think, understand, reason, appreciate, and remember.* When we have concerns about a client's ability to provide informed consent, we should conduct a formal assessment of four decision-making components: (a) the ability to understand relevant considerations, (b) the ability to understand and appreciate the risks and benefits of various treatment choices, (c) the ability to compare decision choices and think rationally about them, and (d) the ability to communicate a stable treatment choice (Bryan et al., 2022; Johnson & Karlawish, 2015). To provide functional assessments for mental capacity for the purposes of informed consent, we should be trained in assessing the four areas of decision-making capacity.[3] If we do not have such training, we can refer the client for a second-level assessment from a mental health professional with specialized expertise. However, assessment of mental capacity by the client's primary practitioner is often preferable because the practitioner has an ongoing work relationship with the client and is able to track the client's decision-making abilities, goals, wishes, and reasoning over time (Ganzini et al., 2005).

Clients may lack decision-making ability due to various factors including age, level of cognitive development, mental illness, dementia, or substance use disorder. However, we need to determine the client's ability to make particular types of decisions rather than simply assuming that a client lacks decision-making capacity due to their age, mental illness, or other condition. A 14-year-old child, for instance, may have sufficient cognitive abilities and maturity to consent to school-based academic counseling, but may lack capacity to consent to medically risky surgery. A person with schizophrenia may lack mental capacity while experiencing hallucinations; however, if the client's schizophrenia is under control through the use of medications or other treatments, the client may have sufficient mental capacity.

Mental competence *is a legal term referring to whether individual have the legal status to make certain types of decisions on their own behalf.* Whereas social workers and other helping professionals may assess a client's mental capacity, only a judge may determine and declare whether a person is mentally incompetent (Neilson et al., 2015). Unfortunately, some people use the terms *mental competence* and *mental capacity* interchangeably, leading to possible confusion for professionals, clients, and family members. Professionals, clients, or their families may go to court for a ruling on mental competence when there is a dispute about whether the client has a permanent decision-making incapacity or when there is a dispute concerning which person should be appointed as a surrogate (or substitute) decision maker.

---

3. If there is a court case to determine mental capacity (e.g., in an adult guardianship case), then the court may require a formal assessment conducted by a specially trained mental health professional, as designated by state legislation. Elements of assessments in guardianship cases typically include an evaluation of the patient's alertness and attention, information processing, thought disorders, and ability to modulate mood and affect. Some states require the use of specific assessment tools (e.g., MacArthur Competence Assessment Tool for Treatment, cited in Zlodre et al., 2016).

Although judges determine whether a person is mentally incompetent, their decisions are typically informed by testimony or documentary evidence from social workers or other mental health professionals. A decision to declare a person mentally incompetent does not depend on whether the person is experiencing mental illness but whether the person has a serious impairment in mental capacity (thinking, understanding, reasoning, and memory). If a judge declares a person mentally incompetent, social workers cannot override this decision simply by reassessing the person's mental capacity (Stein, 2007). A judge must hear evidence of the person's mental capacity and rule on whether to declare the person mentally competent.

Competence to make certain types of decisions may also be determined by age. Although the legal age of majority for many decisions is 18, state laws may provide different age requirements for different types of decisions and services. For instance, age requirements may range from 12 to 18 years old for consent to receive counseling regarding birth control options, school issues, or help with an emotional crisis.

As mentioned earlier, when a client lacks mental capacity or is deemed legally incompetent, we should seek consent for services from an appropriate third person.[4] The NASW Code does not define what constitutes an "appropriate third party," in part because this is a complex issue and in part because the terminology and criteria vary from **jurisdiction** to jurisdiction. Although you should check with your state laws for specific criteria, the following general guidelines describe who may be an appropriate third party in various circumstances:

- For children who are too young or who lack capacity to provide consent on their own behalf, we should seek consent from their parents or legally appointed guardians. Although it is often legally sufficient to obtain consent from one parent, it may be prudent to obtain consent from both parents to ensure that both parents are supportive of their child being in services. When parents are separated or divorced, we should ask who has legal custody (or decision-making responsibility) for the children. We could also ask for a copy of a separation agreement, court order, or other documentation to ensure we are obtaining consent from the appropriate person(s).
- For adult clients who lack mental capacity or have been declared incompetent, we should determine whether they have a durable power-of-attorney, advanced directives, court orders, or other documentation naming their surrogate decision maker. When clients do not have a legally appointed surrogate, we can seek consent from their next-of-kin, for instance, their parents or adult children (Wendler et al., 2016). If there

---

4. When a patient has a mental incapacity and a proxy decision maker provides consent, we should still request the patient's assent, thus demonstrating respect and affirmation (Johnson & Karlawish, 2015).

is a dispute about who should have decision-making authority,[5] then it may be necessary to go to court for a ruling.

Surrogate, substitute, guardian, conservator, and proxy are terms used by different states to describe people who have authority to make decisions on behalf of a person who lacks mental capacity or who has been declared legally incompetent (Howard, 2017). In most states, surrogates have fiduciary obligations to make decisions according to what the patient would have wanted under the circumstances. Surrogates should not simply make decisions based on their personal preferences.[6] Consider a Muslim client who lacks mental capacity and his children are his surrogates. During his life, the client observed Muslim traditions including eating halal foods (as prescribed in the Qur'an) and praying five times per day. His children do not observe these traditions; however, as his surrogates, they should support his preferred religious observances.

When working with clients who lack mental capacity or legal competence to provide informed consent on their own, we can demonstrate respect for their dignity and worth by inviting them to provide assent. Whereas *consent* is legally recognized permission to provide services, *assent* refers to agreement to participate in services from a person who lacks mental capacity or legal competence to give formal consent (Cottone et al., 2022). Thus, when working with a young child, we could seek *consent* from the parents and also ask for *assent* from the child. Consider a parent who brings a child to you for help with shyness. If the child does not want this help, you could discuss various options and try to build agreement with the parent and child about how to proceed. Although the parent is legally responsible for determining whether the child should receive services, you could explain how services may not be helpful if the child does not want them. Unless there is a serious, imminent risk for the child, it may be best to respect the child's wishes.

CONSENT IN FAMILIES AND GROUPS

In the earlier discussion of informed consent, the examples focused on individual clients. In this section, we will explore informed consent in the context of work with families or groups. When our client is a family or group, the client is both a

---

5. E.g., a person with dementia who has two adult children contesting who has authority to make medical decisions.

6. Under some circumstances, surrogates may make decisions based on best interests rather than what the patient would have wanted. For instance, when making financial decisions for someone who has not managed finances effectively, the surrogate may make financial decisions based on how a prudent person would invest or manage the patient's assets (Dayton, 2014). Surrogates need to know the laws of their particular states, as well as the terms of any court order, letters of guardianship, or agreement granting them decision-making authority.

distinct system and a collection of individuals. When everyone in the family or group agrees on their goals and how to pursue them, obtaining consent is relatively simple. When individuals within the client system have different goals, needs, preferences, and levels of power, however, obtaining consent is more complex.

Ideally, when we establish goals and plans for work with families, we build consensus among all family members participating in the helping process. Family members often come into the helping process with different understandings of the presenting problem and what they want to accomplish. By helping family members communicate, identify common concerns, and focus on mutual interests, we may be able to reach consensus on goals for work and the types of services they would like to receive.

Although children (and perhaps other family members) may lack the mental capacity to provide informed consent, this does not mean that we should ignore their thoughts or wishes (Cottone et al., 2022). First, we should respect all family members, and second, children are more likely to cooperate if they are empowered to help set the goals for work. As noted earlier, when children or other family members do not have the mental capacity to give *consent* from a legal perspective, we may seek their *assent* for services. We need to be aware of power issues in families. Children or frail elders, for instance, may be hesitant about sharing conflicting views. Because they are dependent on parents or other family caretakers, they may be concerned about reprisals if they assert their needs or wishes. In families with domestic violence, some family members may fear speaking up because it could lead to further maltreatment. To assess for potential issues of power and violence, we could speak with family members individually to determine whether family work is even appropriate. If family work is inappropriate due to power or safety reasons, we could refer clients to services on an individual basis. As we will see in our discussion of confidentiality in Chapter 5, we also need to consider our legal and ethical obligations to report maltreatment of children and older adults or people with disabilities who are dependent on others for their care.

When discussing informed consent with groups, we also need to consider how to deal with different wishes and perspectives of different group members. For some groups, the purpose, goals, activities, and policies are established before the group even meets. We inform potential members about the group, including the nature of the group, expectations of group members, potential benefits, and potential risks. We could also share information about their professional credentials and theoretical orientation, policies for entering or leaving the group, policies related to substance abuse, policies related to involuntary clients, confidentiality, policies regarding out-of-group contact among group members, procedures for communication between group workers and members, time commitments, and fees (Thomas & Pender, 2008). In these groups, informed consent occurs when clients agree to participate in the group.

For other groups, we empower group members to develop the group's purpose, goals, activities, ground rules, and policies. We should help the group develop guidelines for how group decisions will be made, for instance, by majority vote or by consensus. As when working with families, we should be sensitive to issues of power and persuasion within the group. We should strive for full participation of members in group decisions, without fear of retribution, disrespect, or reprisal for expressing conflicting views or preferences (Barsky & Northen, 2017). When making group decisions, some members may feel pressured by others and may have difficulty asserting their views (Corey et al., 2019). To assess whether members genuinely agree to participate in the group, as well as whether they agree to decisions being made by the group, we could meet individually with group members. See Box 4.2 for a sample consent form for group members.

We should view informed consent as an ongoing process, periodically checking in with the family or group members. Their goals and preferred services or activities may evolve over time. We can use conflict resolution skills to help members renegotiate their agreements for participation in family counseling or group work. In addition to negotiating the family or group's overall goals, we may help members negotiate goals particular to each person. This negotiation could include discussion of referrals for individual social work services or other types of support.

BOX 4.2

GROUP FOR MANDATED CLIENTS

Please review and critique the following consent form for a psychoeducational group designed for men who have been court-ordered into services due to criminal charges related to intimate partner abuse. Identify ways in which the form could be improved to ensure that prospective clients clearly understand what they need to know about the nature of the group, its benefits and risks, expectations of the participation, and the extent of their self-determination within the group.

* * * * *

1) Acknowledgments: I, _____ (group member name), understand that I have been court-ordered to participate in a psychoeducational group for people who have been charged with offences related to intimate-partner abuse. My signature below indicates that I am agreeing to participate in this group to fulfill the court order. I understand that I may withdraw from the group at any time. I also understand that if I do not complete all the conditions of my court order, there could be further consequences in court.

2) Nature of the Group: The group is a closed group of approximately 6 to 20 members who will meet on Monday evenings from 7 to 9 p.m. from January 11 to February 23. Each week, the facilitators will share information about the nature and causes of intimate partner abuse, as well as strategies to eliminate intimate partner abuse. The facilitators

will encourage members to participate in group discussions and
role-plays; however, members will not be required to speak or
participate in these activities if they choose not to do so.

3) Ground Rules: During the first meeting, the facilitators will help
   members develop ground rules to ensure safe and productive discussions.

4) Information Shared: The group facilitators may provide my probation
   officer, _____, with a report of whether or not I participated
   in each group session. The facilitators will not report the nature of my
   participation or what I say during the sessions, except in the following
   situations:
   a. If I violate any terms of my court order.
   b. If I share information indicating a significant risk that I will engage in
      intimate partner abuse, child abuse, child neglect, or other violence.

5) Benefits: The group is designed to provide insights into the causes
   of intimate partner abuse and to provide strategies for emotional
   regulation, awareness, conflict resolution, and self-control to reduce
   risks of violence and threats of violence. Facilitators will also encourage
   members to develop their own personal goals to work on during the
   group experience.

6) Risks: Participating in this group may cause some anxiety and
   discomfort, as members will be remembering and discussing unpleasant
   feelings and experiences. Members may request individual meetings
   with the facilitators to assist them with strong feelings of sadness, anger,
   fear, or frustration.

7) Partner Contacts: Agency social workers will periodically contact
   the partners or former partners of group members to check on their
   safety and concerns. The social worker will report any significant safety
   concerns about to the member's probation officer and the member's
   participation in the group may be terminated.

8) Fees: Members will pay $30 for each session prior to the beginning of
   the session.

9) I have read and understand the above information. My signature below
   indicates my agreement to the terms of group participation.

_____   _____

Signature of Group Member   Date

CONSENT IN ORGANIZATIONS AND COMMUNITIES

When the client is an organization or community, we need to identify who is authorized to provide consent on behalf of the community or organization. Assume that
the Victorius Park Community Association (VPCA) asks you to help them develop
a neighborhood safety program. As part of the informed consent process, you would

need to know who speaks on behalf of the association and who is responsible for making decisions, such as the decision to hire you and the decisions about the goals, methods, and strategies for the community safety program. When working with a community or organization, you could check its charter, bylaws, constitution, or policies to determine who has authority to provide consent. VPCA could have a formal hierarchical structure with an executive director or an executive committee that is authorized to contract with you. When setting goals and determining strategies, however, you and the executive may also decide to engage other community members for their input. It is prudent to determine who has decision-making authority and how decisions will be made early in the process of engaging with the organization or community. See Box 4.3 for an example of issues that may arise when different people within an organization or community express different views.

When working with organizations and communities, we may be involved in helping them make policy decisions and perhaps even political decisions. When helping with policy decisions, we should avoid imposing our values and beliefs (NASW Code, Ss.1.02 and 1.03). We can empower our clients, for instance, by providing them with access to information and research to help make their decisions. We can help them think through the issues in using critical thinking, problem-solving, and conflict resolution processes. Ultimately, however, the organization or community has the right to make its own decisions about goals and methods for reaching those goals. Assume that the executive committee of VCPA says that its primary goal is to eliminate drug trafficking and that it wants to increase police presence to do so. You

---

BOX 4.3

Sexual Harassment

QRS Corp was recently sued by a group of women who complained that they were sexually harassed over the course of many years. In response, QRS hires you, a social worker, to help them build a program to prevent sexual harassment in their workplace. The first person you meet is Ava, the Chief Executive Officer. Ava says she wants you to develop a sexual harassment policy and a structure for dealing with complaints of sexual harassment. You then meet with the company's board of directors. They instruct you not to develop a complaints procedure because they want to eliminate sexual harassment, not just respond to it. They suggest that you develop a program to create a culture of respect within the organization. You then meet with a group of frontline employees. They tell you that the organization is rampant with sexism and that the only way to deal with it is to fire the sexist supervisors and administrators and replace them with people who truly respect all people, regardless of their gender. How do self-determination and informed consent apply in this situation? How should you approach obtaining consent about the goals and methods that you should use to address the issues of sexual harassment in this company?

---

believe that it may be more effective to focus on why certain people in the community are using drugs and address these underlying issues. You may validate the committee's concerns, offer them research on the effectiveness of various programs in
other communities, and help them make their own decision about how to proceed.
Honoring client self-determination and informed consent is easier when we agree
with our clients about how to proceed; note, however, that clients still have a right
to self-determination and informed consent when we disagree.

CONSENT IN RESEARCH

The basic principles of self-determination and consent apply not only when we
serve clients, but also when we are working with research participants. Standard
5.02(e) of the NASW Code of Ethics suggests that researchers should request written, voluntary, informed consent from potential participants before engaging them
in research. Informed consent means that a person's decision about whether to
participate in research should be made by individuals (or their legally authorized
representative) without being pressured to hurry the decision, without coercion
or undue influence from the researcher, and with relevant information provided
in easily understood language (Common Rule, 1991, §46.116; Shah et al, 2020).
Different states have different regulations regarding informed consent, so it is
important to check local laws for possible restrictions on consent processes. For
instance, some state regulations provide a one-year time limit on consent, meaning that a client's consent must be renewed if the research or intervention extends
beyond one year. As described earlier, the informed consent process operationalizes
a core value of social work—respecting the dignity and worth of all individuals—by
letting them choose whether or not to participate in a particular study.

Standards 5.02(e), (f), (i), and (j) of the NASW Code identify specific types of
information that should be shared with potential research participants as part of
the consent process:

- the nature, extent, and duration of the participation requested;
- the potential benefits and risks of participation in the research;
- choices regarding use technology in the research (e.g., submitting
  responses through apps or websites);
- the voluntary nature of participation, including participants' right to
  withdraw from the research at any time without negative consequences;
  and
- access to support services (e.g., if the client experiences stress or other
  negative consequences from participation in the research).

Although consent to research should generally be fully informed, voluntary, and
written, these conditions may be waived under certain circumstances.

Fully Informed Consent

When people are asked to participate in research, they generally have a right to full, accurate, and honest information about the nature of the research, the risks and benefits of the research, and what is expected of them. Deception arises when researchers share inaccurate information or do not share full information. Covert research is research conducted without the knowledge or consent of the participants. Deception and covert research may be ethically justified under very limited, specific circumstances. According to §46.116 of the Common Rule, 1991, the general requirement of fully informed consent may be waived by an Institutional Review Board (of an organization that receives federal funding) only if all the following conditions are met.

- The research involves no more than minimal risk to the participants.
- Waiving the right to full and accurate information must not adversely affect the participants' rights and welfare.
- The research could not practicably be carried out without the deception or withholding full information.
- Whenever appropriate, the subjects will be provided with relevant information about the research after their participation.

Consider, for instance, a study by a public health department to evaluate the effectiveness of different posters designed to encourage people to use masks during a viral pandemic. The research proposal states that research assistants will observe people in subway stations, gathering information about how many people are using or not using masks, as well as the reactions of people who observe the posters. The proposal asks for the consent requirement to be waived. The risks to the people being observed are minimal. To ensure anonymity, the researchers are not gathering identifying information. The public health department plans to use the posters regardless of whether the research is permitted, so there is no additional intervention or risk from conducting the research. The researchers will be instructed to be honest if anyone asks them what they are doing in the subway stations. The researchers will also make their research results available to the community and local government, so they can make better informed decisions about the effectiveness of the posters. The research could not be conducted effectively if the researchers were required to obtain informed consent from each research participant, because telling them about the research may affect their mask-wearing behavior. For these reasons, waiving consent for this research could be ethically justified.

The following real-life examples highlight the problems that may arise when researchers violate the principles of fully informed consent:

- In the 1960s, Stanley Milgram studied obedience to authority by instructing research participants to press a button that would give electric shocks to people posing as "learners," each time the learners made a mistake. The learners were in a separate room, so the participants did not know that they were not actually shocking the learners. Some research participants continued to follow instructions to provide shocks even though the learners were yelling, banging on the walls, and pleading for the participants to stop shocking them (Yanow & Schwartz-Shea, 2018). The deception in this study was unethical because participants were not provided with fully informed consent and they were subjected to significant risks. A number of participants suffered psychological distress, which continued even after their debriefing and learning that no people actually received shocks. Further, when some researchers use deception, potential research participants in future research may have difficulty trusting other researchers and may refuse to participate.

- In the 1990s, Arizona State University researchers collected blood samples from over 200 members of the Havasupai (indigenous) tribe for the stated purpose of examining links between genetics and diabetes. Without informing participants, the researchers shared blood samples with other researchers who studied schizophrenia, inbreeding, evolution, and migration (Marley, 2019). Using the blood samples for additional purposes violates informed consent. People have a right to know how their research samples will be used. This research could have been conducted by requesting fully informed consent, so there was no ethical justification for not obtaining proper consent. Further, there was harm to the research participants. The research findings that the Havasupai people migrated from Asia went against their traditional belief systems, causing emotional distress. The ethical violations resulted in a lawsuit (which was eventually settled), loss of funding, and a damaged reputation for the university. They may have also damaged the trust that Havasupai people and other vulnerable groups may have regarding participation in future research.

In Chapter 11, we will further explore the importance of honesty and integrity in social work practice and research.

Voluntary

Voluntary consent means that potential research participants should have the ability to freely choose whether or not to participate in research, as well as whether or not to terminate participation early. Voluntariness is violated when researchers coerce, threaten, or impose negative sanctions, or withhold help or benefits if someone refuses to participate. Although we should avoid coercing clients into consenting to research, there may be ethically **justifiable** limitations on voluntariness in relation to evaluation research. Many social work agencies require clients to participate in an evaluation of their programs as a condition for receiving services. At a minimum, we should explain what the evaluation entails, what information will be gathered, and how it will be used. Requiring clients to participate in evaluation may be ethically justified because the purposes of the evaluation are to determine whether services are effective, how services can be improved, and whether certain services should be modified or stopped because they are ineffective or risky. Evaluation is particularly important for novel interventions and for services that entail significant risks to client health or well-being. If clients want services but do not want to participate in the evaluation, we could offer to refer them to services at another organization. We should not abandon clients in need (NASW Code, S.117[b]).

Written

Obtaining consent in writing (digitally or on paper) is generally preferred to oral consent because it provides proof that research participants did consent. Written consent also offers participants an opportunity to review the terms of the consent in detail and on their own time. They may also ask questions if they do not understand particular terms. The requirement for consent in writing may be waived under certain conditions:

- when the risk of the participating in the research is minimal and the research involves no procedures that would normally require consent (e.g., telephone or online surveys about topics that do not entail significant risks);
- the signature on the informed consent document would be the only record linking the participant to the research and the main risk of harm to the participant would be a confidentiality breach (e.g., people involved in intimate partner abuse); or
- participants are members of a cultural group in which signing forms is not a usual or acceptable practice.

When we are not requiring written consent for a particular study, we may use our notes to document that we engaged participants in an oral consent process. To protect client privacy, we should not document participants' names or other identifying information.

For a sample consent to research form, see Box 4.4.

BOX 4.4

EFFECTIVENESS OF A GRIEF SUPPORT GROUP

LMN Agency has recently developed a support group for people grieving the recent loss of a spouse or partner. LMN is planning to study the group's effectiveness. The agency develops the following consent form for potential research participants. Critique this form in terms of how well it addresses key components of informed consent, including an explanation of the nature of the research, its benefits and risks, expectations of research participants, access to support services, and voluntariness of participation in the research.

* * * * *

1) **Title of Research Study:** Study of the Effectiveness of a Grief Support Group

2) **Purpose:** This research studies the effectiveness of a recently developed support group for people who are grieving the loss of a spouse or intimate partner.

3) **Procedures:** This study will draw participants from the Grief Support Group at LMN Agency. Among the people who express interest in participating in the support group, half will be randomly assigned to start the group right away and half will be asked to wait 8 weeks for a second round of the group. Participants of both groups will be asked to complete a 30-question survey at the beginning of the 8 weeks and a similar questionnaire at the end of the 8 weeks. Six questions will focus on demographic information (age, gender, culture, socioeconomic status, length of relationship, and education level). Twenty questions will focus on grieving processes, including feelings of isolation, loneliness, sadness, anger, moving on, and acceptance. The last two questions will allow participants to provide comments about their experiences in the group and suggestions for improvement. The questionnaire will take 15 to 30 minutes to complete. You will have the option of completing the two questionnaires on paper at the agency or online at a time and location convenient to you.

4) **Voluntariness:** Your participation in this research is purely voluntary. If you decide that you do not want to participate in this research, our staff can refer you to another support group or to other grief counseling services in the community.

5) **Risks:** The risks of participating in this study are minimal. Some people might feel anxiety because the survey includes questions about their reactions to the loss of a spouse or partner. If you do feel anxious and want a referral to a counselor, our researchers can provide information about available services.

6) **Benefits:** For participating in this study, you will receive a $75 gift certificate for a local grocery store. You will not receive other direct benefits other than the possibility of further insights into the grieving

process. The researchers hope this research will benefit our community by documenting the effectiveness of the support group and helping us improve it.

7) **Data Collection & Storage:** All information gathered from you is confidential and anonymous. The questionnaires will not contain your name or other identifying information. Only the researchers will have access to the questionnaires, which will be destroyed by shredding (for paper records) and deletion (for electronically stored data) within two years of completing this study. All findings from this study will be reported as group information, so that no individual can be identified. Nobody else will have access to the information collected about you, unless required by law. We may publish what we learn from this study. We will not include your name or identifying information in any publications.

8) **Contact Information:**
   - If you have questions about the study, please contact the primary investigator, Anyka Garber at [phone number] or [email address].
   - If you have questions or concerns about your rights as a research participant, please contact the Research Integrity Office of LMN Agency at [phone number] or [email address].

9) **Consent Statement:** I have read or had read to me the information describing this study. All my questions have been answered to my satisfaction. I am 18 years of age or older and freely consent to participate. I understand that I am free to withdraw from the study at any time without penalty. I have received a copy of this consent form.

Printed Name of Participant: _____

Signature of Participant: _____ Date: _____

CONCLUSION

To demonstrate respect for the dignity and worth of clients and research participants, we need to honor their rights to self-determination and informed consent. In addition, clients are more likely to follow through on services and achieve positive results when they are involved in setting goals and actively involved in determining how to make changes in their lives. As you ponder how to engage people in informed consent processes, think about what information they need to know and would like to know in order to make good decisions for themselves. Remember that informed consent is not a "one-and-done" event, but rather an ongoing process. Continue to share information and invite feedback. Screen for concerns regarding the person's decision-making capacity and consider whether parents, proxies, or others may be needed for substitute consent. As advocates and support persons, also assess for situations where your client's rights may be limited by other professionals or service providers. Be ready to lend support and empower them. Be aware of situations in which limits on self-determination may be ethically justified, such as when working with a client who poses serious, imminent, and foreseeable risks to others. Still, strive to empower all clients and research participants with information, options, understanding, and support (Hepworth et al., 2023).

DISCUSSION QUESTIONS AND EXERCISES

1. *Freedom of Religion and Speech*: Armand belongs to a religion that commands members to spread the word of the religion and encourage others to join. As a social worker in a state-funded shelter for people who are homeless, Armand is supposed to respect client self-determination. Armand believes that freedom of religion means that he should be able to educate and urge clients to join his religion. He also believes the Constitution's provisions on free speech give him the right to say what he wants to clients. How would you help Armand understand the limits on freedom of religion and free speech when acting as a social worker?

2. *Marital Advice*: Raven (24) has been seeing Wanda (her social worker) for help with self-esteem issues. During their third meeting, Raven tells Wanda that her wife, Penny, has been having an affair. Raven asks Wanda if she should leave Penny. Raven feels very angry and hurt. She is hesitant to leave Penny because "Penny has been so good to me." She also relies on Penny for financial support. Wanda thinks it would be best for Raven to leave Penny because Penny has been emotionally abusive. Should Wanda provide Raven with the advice that she is requesting? What should Wanda do to facilitate empowerment and self-determination?

3. *Group Rules*: Tina is facilitating a task group that is developing a child care program in an assisted living facility for older adults. Tina wants the group to run efficiently, so she plans to present the following ground rules to the group in their first meeting: (a) Everyone will use respectful language. (b) Everyone will listen carefully to one another to understand what they are saying. (c) To ensure the group is making decisions with valid information, the facilitator may fact-check what members are saying. (d) The purpose of the child care program is to provide older adults with an opportunity to spend time with and help young children. What issues does Tina's plan raise in relation to informed consent? What should she do to comply more effectively with Standard 1.03 of the NASW Code?

4. *Informed Consent Violations*: For each of the following situations, identify which paragraph of Standard 1.03 that the social worker is violating. Describe how the worker's actions are inconsistent with informed consent:
   a. Earl (22) has severe memory issues as a result of a traumatic brain injury. While meeting with Earl's older brother and father, the social worker asks his older brother to sign the consent to services form.

   b. A client tells her social worker that she is an heiress from a family that became wealthy from selling fine art. The worker thinks the client may be experiencing delusions, so he conducts an online search to verify the client's story.

   c. A social worker refers a client who is very lonely to a social support group. The worker wants the client to follow through, so she highlights the group's benefits and avoids discussing potential downsides.

   d. A social worker advises a client to use a meditation app to help him deal with stress. Unbeknown to the worker, the client does not have a phone or other device to make use of the app.

5. *Free Will*: A professor requires you to read a book on "free will" as part of your social work ethics course. By doing so, is the professor violating your rights to self-determination or informed consent? Provide your reasoning, referencing the NASW Code of Ethics.

6. *Age of Consent*: The age of consent varies from state to state. It also varies depending on the purpose of consent. Research the laws in your state to identify the age of consent for

   a. medical treatment or counseling services (and are there different age requirements for emergency medical services, substance abuse treatment, birth control, abortions, school counseling, and vaccinations); and

   b. sexual intercourse (and does it depend on the age of the sexual partner and whether that person is in a position of authority).

   To conduct your research, you may start by accessing information from online gateways such as https://schoolhouseconnection.org/state-laws-on-minor-consent-for-routine-medical-care, but also check the actual statutes to ensure the information is accurate and up-to-date.

7. *Parental Consent*: Frieda (13) asks her school social worker for counseling to help her with anxiety issues. Frieda says that she does not want her parents to know she is seeking counseling. Although state law and school policy allow the Frieda to consent to counseling, why might it be helpful for the social worker to discuss the possibility of asking her parents for their consent? What are some possible reasons that Frieda does not want her parents to know she is receiving counseling?

8. *Intoxicated Client*: Dexter walks into an addiction treatment center requesting admission so he can detox from opiates. As Belinda (the intake social worker) is asking questions, she realizes that Dexter is intoxicated. His speech is slurred. He has difficulty focusing and reasoning. He is nodding off. Belinda wonders whether Dexter has sufficient mental capacity to provide informed consent to treatment. What are Belinda's options for obtaining consent? What should she do, and why?

9. *School Research*: Everist would like to conduct research on the effectiveness of a social-emotional learning program at a high school

where he serves as a social worker. From whom should he seek consent and assent? Under what conditions could the obligation to obtain consent to this research be waived? Provide reasons for your answers.

10. *Post-Test Counseling*: Xavier goes to a health clinic to be tested for HIV. The social worker, Gwen, meets with Xavier to discuss the results of his test. Xavier says, "I changed my mind. I don't want to know." How should Gwen respond? Make use of the Framework for Managing Ethical Issues to assess this situation and consider various options, taking ethical principles such as self-determination, informed consent, protection of life, and quality of life into account. How might her decision differ depending on whether Xavier tested positive or negative?

11. *Involuntary Client*: Zhanna is a family support worker for a child protection agency. She is meeting for the first time with Dorothy (18) who has had her baby, Eli, taken into foster care due to concerns about her ability to parent. Dorothy wants Eli returned to her as soon as possible. A court order says that Dorothy needs to prove she is competent to take care of Eli before he can be returned to her care. How should Zhanna explain service options and informed consent to Dorothy, maximizing her choices and self-determination, and acknowledging that she is an involuntary client? Write a script or video a role-play demonstrating what Zhanna should say.

12. *Consent Monitor*: Rosario works as a consent monitor at a hospital. Her job is to ensure that the requirements of voluntary and fully informed consent are met when patients provide consent to risky or novel surgery. During a routine fetal ultrasound, physicians diagnose Fatima's baby with spina bifida. When Rosario asks Fatima what she understands about the surgery, she says, "My doctor told me that my baby has a hole in the spine and that they need to operate on the baby before birth. I'm not sure why they can't wait until after the baby is born. It's kind of scary, but I trust my doctor so I don't really have any choice other than to go ahead with the surgery." Based on this scenario, what additional questions should Rosario ask Fatima in order to ensure the criteria for informed consent are met? What additional information should Rosario ask the doctors to explain to Fatima?

13. *Family Planning Association*: The RST Family Planning Association hires Noor to act as an advocate on their behalf. Initially, Noor believes that RST wants her to help them advocate for better funding for programs to prevent unwanted pregnancies, to promote good sexual health, and to educate prospective parents about how to reduce certain risks during pregnancy. Noor discovers that one of RST's primary goals is to counsel women who are contemplating an abortion to consider other alternatives. Noor is concerned that RST would be violating client self-determination and informed consent. Who is Noor's client in this situation? What are her ethical obligations? How should she manage any conflicting obligations?

5

Privacy, Confidentiality, and Exceptions

LEARNING OBJECTIVES

Upon successful completion of this introduction, you will be able to

- demonstrate respect for client's right to privacy;
- engage individuals, families, groups, organizations, communities, and research participants in meaningful discussions of client confidentiality and its limits;
- critically analyze situations in which client confidentiality conflicts with other ethical obligations, including the safety of the client, children, vulnerable adults, or others; and
- limit disclosures of confidential information when the client is required by law or ethics to disclose certain information without the client's consent.

As we learned in Chapter 1, respect for the dignity and worth of all people is a core social work value. Social workers put this value into practice by respecting the rights of clients and research participants to privacy and confidentiality. *Privacy* refers to the right to keep personal information to oneself. In a free and democratic society, we respect one another's right to privacy as protection against unwarranted intrusion from the state or other actors. The ethical principle of **confidentiality** suggests that when we gather private information from others, we should maintain the privacy of that information by refraining from sharing it with others. In the first section of this chapter, we explore how social workers respect privacy by gathering information only if they have client permission and the information is relevant to the client's purposes in seeking services. In the middle sections of this chapter, we will learn how to discuss the nature, extent, and limits of confidentiality when working with individuals, families, groups, communities, organizations, and research participants. We will also study how the ethical, legal, and policy frameworks for confidentiality may vary depending on the particular context of practice.

Box 5.1 provides a situation raising a number of ethical issues related to the material in this chapter. As you read this chapter, consider how the social worker should have attended more effectively to client privacy and autonomy.

BOX 5.1

ONLINE SEARCHES

Noela is preparing to facilitate a group for people transitioning to retirement. To screen for possible safety issues, she conducts online searches of everyone who has applied to join the group. She discovers that one applicant, Lexy, has been posting conspiracy theories on several ultra-right social media sites. Although Lexy does not make specific threats, she suggests that Jews should be exterminated because they are responsible for spreading horrible diseases to innocent people. Noela thinks it would be best if she does not admit Lexy into the group. She is particularly concerned about potential risks to Jewish group members. Lexy wonders whether she should contact the police to investigate Lexy and remove her deplorable posts.

What ethical issues does this situation raise in relation to conducting online searches on potential clients? Once Noela has read Lexy's online posts, what are her ethical obligations according to the NASW (2021) Code of Ethics? How should she manage ethical concerns regarding client confidentiality, group safety, public safety, and discrimination?

GATHERING PRIVATE INFORMATION

In social work, we often need to gather personal and private information from clients. Sometimes, we ask for information about very sensitive topics, such as sexuality, HIV status, political affiliation, mental health history, criminal history, bowel movements, or income (Hammersley & Traianou, 2011). However, we should only gather private information from and about clients when two conditions are satisfied: (a) The information serves an important social work purpose, and (b) The client provides consent to gather such information. As Standard 1.07(a) of the NASW Code suggests, social workers should avoid "soliciting private information from clients unless it is essential to providing services or conducting social work evaluation or research." In other words, social workers should not ask questions or pry into personal issues with clients if the information is not relevant to the nature of the work they are doing. For instance, if I am helping a client apply for social assistance, it would be appropriate for me to ask about the client's income and economic situation. The client's political affiliation, however, is not relevant to our work, so I should not ask about it.

You may be surprised to learn that your own field agencies might be contravening this standard. Some agencies require workers to complete intake forms that include questions on topics irrelevant to the work being done. Consider asking for a client's religion. The question may seem simple and innocuous. For some clients, the question may feel very intrusive. Consider clients who have experienced religious bigotry. Some Wiccans (or Witches) keep their religion a secret, wanting to avoid discrimination or intolerance. If you ask such a client about her religion, she may feel pressured to lie or to disclose information against her will. Although a client's religion may be significant for some social work purposes, it may not be important for others. Accordingly, it is unethical to ask about a client's religion unless it serves a purpose for the work you are doing.

Remember to consider privacy from the client's perspective. A personal question that seems respectful and important to you may seem rude and intrusive to a client. When clients say they do not want to discuss particular issues, you could invite them to discuss why they do not want to share this information. Ultimately, respect the decision about whether to share particular information. As you build trust with the client, the client may eventually be more willing to share sensitive or potentially embarrassing information.

In addition to respecting client privacy when gathering information from them, we should also respect client privacy when considering whether to gather information from others. If we want to gather information from the client's family, physician, peers, teachers, or others, we should obtain client permission in advance (NASW Code, S.1.03[a]). If we want to conduct an online search to gather information about the client, we should let the client know why we want to conduct a search and request the client's permission. Requesting permission to gather information demonstrates that we respect the client's right to privacy. Social workers can justify conducting an online search without client consent if there are compelling professional reasons (NASW Code, S.1.07[q]). If a client was experiencing suicidal ideation because of something posted on social media, for instance, a social worker might be justified in searching for the post in order to help prevent serious, imminent harm to the client.

NATURE AND EXTENT OF CONFIDENTIALITY

Once a social worker has gathered private information from a client, the worker has a professional obligation, called *confidentiality*, to safeguard this information. Offering confidentiality is vital to engaging clients. It encourages confidence and trust in the worker (Bryan et al., 2022). Clients may be reluctant to share private information for a variety of reasons. Consider a client who has herpes or who has been sexually abused by a relative. The client may feel embarrassed, perhaps because of social stigma associated with herpes or incest. The client may fear negative repercussions, such as losing family support, health insurance, or employment. The fear may or may not be based on an objective assessment of reality; regardless, fear makes it difficult for the person to share the information. By reassuring clients that whatever they disclose will be kept confidential, social workers provide clients with a safe place to talk and work through their concerns. During an initial meeting with a client, you might explain,

> As a social worker, I respect your rights to privacy and confidentiality. I hope you will be able to share whatever information is necessary to help us assess your concerns and work on your goals. I want to assure you that, for the most part, whatever we discuss stays between us.[1] I will not share your personal information with your family, friends, employers, or others unless you provide me with clear instructions to do so. If you have any questions about privacy and confidentiality, this is a good time to discuss them.

Clients from diverse backgrounds may have different understandings and responses concerning confidentiality. Some clients may not believe a social worker will keep information confidential because they are used to having people in their communities share information. If one person knows the client has herpes, for instance, there is no way to control the rumors from spreading. Providing the client with a written confidentiality contract or policy may reassure the client. In some cases, it may take days or weeks to build clients' trust to the point that they will believe you will keep the information private.

Some of the more obvious breaches of confidentiality occur when a worker

- discusses a client's situation with friends or family, out of amusement or to solicit their support;
- discusses a client's situation with a supervisor or other agency coworkers in a venue where other clients or outsiders can hear the discussion;
- discloses client information to professional colleagues from another agency, without the client's permission;
- shares client information on social media; or
- gives a friend an old work computer without deleting all client files, backups, and information trails.

Some social workers believe they are free to discuss a client's situation with others, so long as they do not mention the client's name. This practice is risky because the worker may not know when others could identify a client from the information provided. Assume you tell your parents about a client who has a pierced upper lip. The next day, you and your parents are walking down the street and bump into the

---

1. Exceptions to confidentiality are described later.

client, who says hello. Your parents can now connect the confidential information with the client.

Social workers are permitted to share client information with supervisors and other agency staff provided the sharing is for professional purposes. In other words, workers should not engage in idle gossip about clients. Workers may share client information during case conferences to obtain feedback on past efforts or how to proceed with the client in the future. Social workers should let clients know, in advance, that certain information will be shared with others in the agency:

> I meet with my supervisor on a weekly basis to discuss my work with clients. I will also take notes about our work, including your goals, plans for work, and progress toward those goals. My supervisor and the program director review my client files each month to ensure that I am following agency policies.

The specifics of what you tell your client about confidential and shared information depend on the particular situation, agency policy, and client interests. When you start work at a new agency, check your agency's policies and procedures to determine which additional laws and policies, if any, will govern your practice. While you are a student, you should advise clients that you are a student and that you will be discussing your work in your practice classes, but on an anonymous basis. Anonymity means that you are describing some of your work but omitting identifying information. You might even change some identifying information (e.g., the client's name, age, ethnicity, or family structure) to disguise the client's identity further. If you plan to write a paper or conduct a class presentation based on your work with a particular client, you could show respect for your client's right to privacy by asking the client for specific permission.

> I am studying social work and taking a course on practice with individuals. With your permission, I'd like to make a brief presentation to my class of 12 students, based on my work with you. I will not share your name or any other information that identifies you. If you prefer that I don't discuss your situation, I will respect your decision and it will not affect our work here. Before I ask for your permission, what questions do you have about this presentation?

Some social work programs do not require students to ask for such consent, provided the student does not share identifying information. Still, asking for consent is prudent, respectful practice. Avoiding identifying information about a client during a class presentation may not be sufficient to protect the client's privacy. On occasion, I have noticed that some students will recognize another student's client because they are working with the same person but at a different agency. I now advise my classes, "If you think that you might recognize a client that another student is presenting, please excuse yourself from the class as soon as possible."

Social workers should structure their practice to support client privacy and maintain confidentiality. Steps to maintain confidentiality could include

- closing the office door and ensuring others cannot listen to private client conversations;
- using secure digital systems for videoconferencing, email, and other electronic communications (Mishna et al., 2021);
- maintaining paper copies of client records in a locked cabinet and digital records in a system secured with encryption and password protection (NASW et al., 2017); and
- not sharing client information with others unless the client provides explicit consent or when required by law to do so (Fisher, 2016).

Note that social workers believe, "Once a client, always a client." When a client dies, the client's right to confidentiality continues (S.1.07[w]). By honoring client confidentiality forever, we demonstrate respect for the client's privacy and wishes. We should not share client information with surviving friends and family—or with journalists and reporters—unless the client provided explicit consent to share such information upon the client's death.

Families

The forgoing examples relate to social work with individual clients. The basic principles of privacy and confidentiality apply equally to work with families: we should not gather information from or about families unless it serves a relevant social worker purpose, and once we gather information, we should not share that information with people outside the family without the family's consent. Confidentiality in family work may have additional complications, however, because we need to consider issues of privacy and confidentiality between family members, as well as the possibility that different family members may have different wishes about whether certain information should be shared with people outside the family.

First, consider privacy and confidentiality between family members. Assume you are working with Dan (12 years old) and his parents, Hank and Winnifred. Dan's parents divulge their intention to divorce but ask you not to share this information with Dan due to his current state of depression. This situation raises a potential ethical dilemma. On the one hand, the parents have asked you to keep information about their impending divorce confidential. On the other hand, you have an obligation to be open and honest with all family members as your client. Dan has an interest in knowing about his parents' plans. If he finds out that you have been keeping a family secret from him, he may feel that you have breached his trust.

Under Standard 1.07(f) of the NASW Code, you should seek agreement among family members regarding how you will manage issues of confidentiality between family members. Ideally, you have developed this agreement during the initial stages of work so your clients know the parameters of the confidentiality before they make key disclosures (Neilson et al., 2015). One approach entails maintaining confidentiality for information shared in individual meetings. You could explain:

> From time to time, I may need to speak with family members separately. One reason for individual meetings is to provide you with an opportunity to discuss matters that you might not be prepared to share with other family members. I will respect each family member's confidentiality, meaning that I will not share what anyone says in an individual meeting with other family members. At times, I may encourage the sharing of information. I may also need to share information if a serious risk of personal harm arises and I need to take steps to ensure someone's safety.

The advantage of this type of arrangement is that each family member will have a safe place to disclose concerns that they might not otherwise share. This allows us to process each individual's concerns, perhaps empowering the individual to share the concerns with other family members. In some instances, we will need to maintain confidentiality in order to protect certain family members from harm. Assume you are providing couples counseling and decide to begin by meeting individually with Hank and Winnifred. Both agree the individual meetings will be confidential. The individual meetings allow you to explore concerns about intimate partner abuse. In her individual meeting, Winnifred says she dreads couples counseling because Hank is abusive. After further assessment, you suggest terminating couples counseling before they have their first joint meeting. You help Winnifred develop a safety plan, including a referral to an agency that provides support to survivors of spousal abuse. You do not want to set up Winnifred for further abuse. When you meet with Hank, you discuss Hank's concerns and find a reason to suggest individual counseling rather than couples counseling. Because Winnifred and Hank have agreed that the individual meetings are confidential, you are not obliged to disclose Winnifred's concerns about abuse.

The primary downside of offering confidentiality for individual meetings is that we may be placed in the position of maintaining family secrets (Neilson et al., 2015). Consider a family receiving counseling for communication problems. The grandfather calls you to say that he has been having intimate relations with a new friend, but he does not want his family to know because he thinks they will disapprove of the relationship. To promote better communications, you encourage him to share this information in the next session. He refuses. You are obliged to respect the grandfather's confidentiality. Unwittingly, you have become triangulated into the family's problems, including keeping secrets rather than communicating directly.[2] If other family members discover the secret, they may think you have been colluding with the grandfather.

---

2. In some instances, you may need to terminate services unless the client agrees to share the secret with other family members. Consider, for instance, a parent who tells you her child is adopted. The parent tells you not to share this information with the child. The child thinks she is adopted and the parent wants you to pretend the child is not adopted.

An alternate approach to confidentiality among family members is to say that any information shared with you individually may be shared with other family members (Shaw, 2015). You could explain:

> My role is to be social worker for the whole family. To fulfill this role, I need to be able to share information from one person to another. If one of you wants to meet with me but says I cannot share what you say with anyone else, then I would have to tell you that I cannot make such a promise. If you need to talk privately with a social worker, then I could refer you to another worker for individual counseling.

This approach puts family members on notice that you may share information disclosed by one person with other family members. You may use discretion about what to share and what not to share. This type of contract ensures that you are not stuck maintaining family secrets. On the downside, individuals may not share information that could be useful to the counseling process. As you can see, there is no perfect solution to the issue of confidentiality among family members. Regardless of which approach you use, make sure you inform your clients of your agency's policy and your own guidelines regarding whether and how confidential information will be shared among family members (NASW Code, S.1.07[g]).

Note that sometimes you may be working with various family members, but your client is just one individual within the family. Your primary ethical obligations, including the duty of confidentiality, is to the individual family member. Assume Obadiah brings his 15-year-old, Sol, to you for counseling. Obadiah wants you to find out what is troubling Sol, who seems very sad and aloof. Although Obadiah is the referral source and payer for services, Sol is your client. You advise Obadiah and Sol that it would be best if they agree that most of what Sol shares with you will be kept confidential; you would make an exception to share information with Obadiah to prevent serious, imminent harm to Sol or another person. Obadiah says he wants Sol to share anything that is bothering him. He agrees that counseling should be a safe and confidential space for Sol to speak with you. During counseling, Sol identifies as nonbinary but does not want Obadiah to know. You explore Sol's reasons for not wanting to share this information and you respect Sol's decisions. You have provided Sol a safe place to discuss gender-related concerns. You can now empower Sol to decide whether and when to come out to Obadiah.

Note that you might have different agreements among family members depending on the child's age. For younger children, the parents and child may agree to share more information from counseling with the parents. For older children and teenagers, family members may agree to limit information sharing to concerns related to serious, imminent risks.

We have been discussing the social worker's obligation to maintain confidentiality of information gathered from the family. It is also prudent to discuss whether and how family members may share information from counseling with others. To build trust and allow family members to feel free to share potentially embarrassing information in counseling, it may be helpful for family members to agree that they will not share the information disclosed in counseling with others unless everyone in the family explicitly agrees that this information may be shared. For instance, family members may want to share certain information with the child's teacher but may not want that information shared with friends or other family members.

When using videoconferencing, online apps, or other technology to facilitate family interventions, social workers should address how confidentiality will be maintained and how family members can take precautions to maintain their own privacy (Doss et al., 2017). Consider a worker who invites children to use an online app to draw their family. Apps designed specifically for social work services should allow for encryption, password authentication, and other confidentiality protections. If the app does not have such protections then the children and their parents should be informed of such. Even if the app is relatively secure, the worker could provide confidentiality suggestions such as using private rather than public computers or tablets, logging off programs after use, and deleting any drawings, text messages, and back-ups once they are no longer needed (NASW et al., 2017).

Groups

Confidentiality in groups is vital to fostering a safe environment for members to share personal information in an open and honest manner (Toseland & Rivas, 2017). Section 1.07(f) of the NASW Code specifically advises group workers to seek agreement among clients regarding each individual's right to confidentiality and each individual's obligation to protect the confidentiality of others in the group. Whereas professional social workers automatically have an obligation to safeguard the confidentiality of clients, clients do not have such an obligation to one another unless they agree to it. By engaging group members in confidentiality discussions, you can educate them about the nature of confidentiality within a group and surface any concerns they may have: Is it safe for me to talk about things that I consider private; what happens if other group members start to gossip about me; and what can I do if information from this group gets leaked to my family, friends, or employer? You may inform group members that you cannot guarantee that all members will honor their agreements about confidentiality (Standard 1.07[f]).[3] For instance, some members may tell their friends about the group or share information on their

---

3. For an open group that allows new members to join at any time, you could meet individually with prospective members prior to joining the group to ensure they understand and agree to the group's confidential policies.

social media. By discussing these potential issues at the outset of the group, you may enhance members' commitment to keep each other's information confidential (Barsky & Northen, 2017). Consider the following exchange between a social worker, Stedman, and two group members:

CLAUDIA: How do I know whether I can trust people that I don't even know? If my boss finds out some of the things I've done, I could lose my job.

STEDMAN: That's a valid question. What do others think about Claudia's concern?

CHERYL: We're all in the same boat. Why would I gossip about Claudia outside the group? I wouldn't want anyone to do the same to me.

STEDMAN: Good point. We all have the same interest in respecting everyone's privacy, but we can only do this if we have trust in each other. Claudia, what else could we do to help you feel more comfortable sharing personal information in the group?

The process of discussing confidentiality issues within the group helps build commitment, group cohesion, and trust. Having a written pledge that formalizes the confidentiality agreement could further the commitment. A written pledge also provides clients with legal recourse if a fellow group member happens to breach confidentiality. In practice, group clients rarely sue one another for breach of confidentiality.[4] Still, written consent clarifies everyone's obligations and reinforces the seriousness of the commitments (Corey et al., 2019).

Groups often operate under a guideline that each group member is responsible for deciding what personal information to share with other members: Nobody (worker or client) should share another client's personal information with other group members without the client's consent. Thus, if you receive a telephone call from a group member explaining that she is too drunk to attend a session, you may not tell the group about this call unless the client specifically authorizes you to do so. Likewise, if two group members meet privately, neither one should share what the other says in this private meeting without the other's explicit consent.

Different groups may develop different agreements or ground rules around confidentiality. Support groups, counseling groups, and therapy groups tend to have relatively strict confidentiality guidelines. In these contexts, confidentiality ensures a safe venue for people to open up and share private information (Toseland & Rivas, 2017). In contrast, many task groups operate on the principles of openness and freedom of information rather than confidentiality. For instance, a social action group may want its information to be shared with the public in order to persuade others to

---

4. Low rates of lawsuits between group members may be due, in part, because it is difficult to prove that someone breached confidentiality and because it is difficult to show that such a breach caused specific damages to the client.

support their cause. Some task groups require confidentiality in terms of who says what during internal discussions, but issue a report or public document stating their conclusions or recommendations. Given the vast array of different approaches to confidentiality, group workers should clarify the extent of confidentiality for each group and ensure that group members agree from the outset of the group.

When conducting groups through teleconferencing or videoconferencing, social workers should address additional methods to ensure confidentiality. To avoid unauthorized access to group interactions, workers may advise members how to use strong passwords or other forms of authentication to log onto the teleconference or videoconference. Workers could also discuss precautions such as using computers or other devices in a private setting (e.g., a room at home without others present), logging off the computer, and ensuring that sessions will not be recorded or saved by group members (NASW et al., 2017). A potential advantage of teleconferences is the ability of members to maintain anonymity. Because members do not see one another, they are less likely to recognize each other in public. Members could also avoid sharing their full names or other identifying information.

Record keeping raises additional concerns about confidentiality. If you write one progress note for each group session, then confidential information about each individual is included in the same document. If you write individual progress notes for each individual, then you may not be able to document interactional issues that arose during the group session. Further, you will have to write some of the same information for each client, making documentation more time-consuming. One way to manage group work records is to write one group record that includes global group information (but excluding any information that identifies any particular group member), plus individual progress notes in each client's records that are pertinent to each particular client (Polowy & Morgan, 2004). When clients ask to see their records, they will be able to see information about the group and their own participation, without having access to personal information about others in the group. If one client's records are **subpoenaed** by the court, you can easily provide the client's records without breaching the confidentiality of others.

Organizations and Communities

Although Standard 1.07 includes confidentiality provisions regarding practice with families and groups, it does not specifically mention practice with organizations or communities. When working with organizations and communities, clarify which types of meetings and communications are confidential and which are not. There may be different confidentiality rules depending on the nature and purpose of the interaction.

Assume you are advocating on behalf of an organization that is promoting sustainable development. During planning meetings, the organization may want you to keep information confidential so as not to tip off potential adversaries or draw attention to their proposed strategies before they are finalized. Once the strategies have been finalized, the organization may ask you to share information broadly, helping them advocate for sustainable development.

Some organizations act under laws or agency policies that require free access to information. Government and publicly funded organizations, for instance, may operate under "open government," "freedom of information," or "sunshine" laws. Such laws require meetings to be open to the public. They are intended to promote transparency, ensuring that the public can scrutinize how government decisions are made and how public funds are used. The federal government and each state has its own rules, defining what types of meetings and information are open to the public and which types can be kept private (Reporters' Committee for Freedom of the Press, n.d.). Typical exceptions to public access to information include information related to national security, private information related to specific individuals, and deliberations of political committees. Each jurisdiction has its own rules concerning which types of information and meetings are open and which are protected by privacy or confidentiality rules. For private organizations, internal policies indicate which types of information may be shared and what types of information should be kept confidential. Social workers need to be familiar with the laws and policies governing openness and privacy within their organizations.

Prudent practice suggests having confidentiality conversations at the outset of work. By engaging members of the organization or community early in the process, you can construct agreements about what types of information may be shared, when, and with whom. Assume that you are helping a community group develop and implement a grassroots voter registration drive. The group may want you to share information to mobilize people to register to vote; however, they may ask you to keep certain information private, for instance, their donor list and personnel issues. You may use written agreements to ensure everyone understands and abides by the terms of confidentiality.

Research Participants

When social workers engage potential research participants in the informed consent process, they should explain what steps they will take to protect the participants' right to privacy. Standards 5.02(m) and (n) of the NASW Code direct social workers to safeguard the anonymity or confidentiality of participants and the data obtained from them (see also Common Rule, 2018, §46.116(a)[5]). Researchers ensure *anonymity* by collecting data from clients in a manner such that even the researcher cannot associate which participant provided which data (e.g., by asking participants to complete surveys without including their names or other identifying information on the forms). Maintaining *confidentiality* means that the researchers know which data belong to which participants, but they do not release any identifying information when they publish the findings of the research. In other words, they protect the identities of the research participants (Grinnell et al., 2018). Additional methods of maintaining confidentiality include:

- assigning each research participant a code number and using code numbers rather than names throughout the data collection, analysis, and publication processes;
- maintaining paper records or documents in locked file cabinets, with access limited to the research team;
- using secure, encrypted programs and passwords for digital data collection, storage, and transmission; and
- disposing or erasing records within a specified timeframe (e.g., within 12 months of completion of the research).

Maintaining confidentiality may be challenging when research is based on a sample drawn from a relatively small, interconnected community (e.g., a small town, a cultural minority group within a larger city, or people with a relatively rare psychological disorder). Consider a social worker conducting qualitative research in an agency serving people with multiple sclerosis, a condition that causes numbness, pain, and impaired physical functioning. If the researcher reports on individual experiences or specific events, people within the agency may be able to recognize the people being described. For instance, if the researcher reports on a client experiencing severe depression, agency staff could identify this person. Researchers can minimize the risk of others being able to identify which information is coming from which research participant by reporting cumulative data (e.g., rates of depression among all clients) rather than stories related to particular individuals. If the researcher is planning to publish information that could be attributed to particular individuals, the researcher should disclose this risk to research participants. The participants can then decide whether to continue with the research and if they continue, then what information they are willing to share. See Box 5.2 for an example of how confidentiality may be explained in a consent to research form.

Standard 5.02(m) advises social workers to inform participants of any limitations of confidentiality (see also Common Rule, §46.116(a)[5]). The following section describes limitations to confidentiality that may apply when working with clients or research participants.

EXCEPTIONS TO CONFIDENTIALITY

So far, we have focused on maintaining confidentiality for clients and research participants. *Confidentiality is not an absolute right, meaning there are several exceptions to confidentiality.* To engage clients and research participants, reassure them that you

BOX 5.2

CONFIDENTIALITY IN RESEARCH

Roni is designing a study about implicit bias, exploring unconscious attitudes, stereotypes, and associations about race. She plans to invite students in her social work program to respond to videos of social work interviews with racially diverse clients. Please review and critique the following excerpt from an informed consent form that Roni plans to ask her research participants to sign. Identify this statement's strengths and limitations regarding its explanation of confidentiality. Provide suggestions to correct for any limitations.

> Informed Consent: For this study, you will be provided with an app that you can upload to your cellphone or computer. The app will present a series of video clips showing social workers meeting with diverse clients. For each video clip, the app will offer four possible choices about how you would assess the client's situation. Select the option that you think is most appropriate. All of your responses will be collected through an encrypted program on an anonymous and confidential basis. We will not collect any identifying information other than your age, socioeconomic status, ethnic background, and IP address. Only the people working with or overseeing the study will see your individual data, unless otherwise required by law. Your responses will be stored for 2 years and then deleted. Any data that is published from this study will be presented on a cumulative basis. Your name and identifying information will not be included in any written or oral presentation of the research findings.

respect their right to confidentiality; also, be honest about the limitations of confidentiality. By letting clients know the limitations as soon as possible, you allow them to make informed decisions about what information to share or withhold from you. People are more likely to develop a trusting relationship with you when you explain that *confidentiality is limited* because this declaration shows that you are being honest (Rogers, 1957).

The exceptions to confidentiality are many. In fact, there may be so many that explaining all of them to a client may be confusing and take too much time. Some agencies and workers opt to use a brief global statement on the exceptions:

> Generally, what we talk about stays between you, me, and the agency. I will not share information with anyone outside the agency except as required by agency policy, the social work code of ethics, and relevant laws.

This brief statement covers all possible exceptions and allows clients to ask about specific exceptions. You may also explain the most likely exceptions to arise, given the nature of your work and the types concerns that may be raised by the client. The more common exceptions include client consent to release information, health information shared with insurance providers, information required by subpoena to be shared in court, suspicions of child abuse or neglect, suspicions of abuse or neglect of vulnerable adults, public health laws to prevent spread of infectious diseases, information required to prevent serious, foreseeable, and imminent harm to a client or others, and exceptions that are specific to certain practice contexts.

Client Consent to Release Information

Clients own the confidentiality of the information they share with you. Accordingly, they may waive all or some of their rights to confidentiality. When clients provide permission to release information to another agency or person, then you may share information with that agency or person (Ss.1.07[b] and [d]). From a legal perspective, it is safest to obtain express written consent stating precisely what information is to be released, to whom, and on what date(s). Some agencies have specific forms that must be used for any release of information. Other agencies allow release of information upon oral consent. You could document oral consent in your case notes, although this is not as strong evidence of consent as a form signed by the client (Barsky, 2012). When a client provides consent to share confidential information with another professional, that professional also has a duty to respect the client's confidentiality (NASW Code, S.2.02). When sharing client records, it is prudent practice to include a statement that the information is confidential and should not be shared with others unless the client provides express written consent.

Healthcare Information Shared with Insurance Providers

A federal law, the Health Insurance Portability and Accountability Act (HIPAA, 1996), permits healthcare providers to provide routine information to insurance providers for the purposes of requesting reimbursement (U.S. Department of Health and Human Services, n.d.).[5] Healthcare is defined broadly to include physical-medical care and mental health services, so it does apply to many services provided by social workers. HIPAA purports to balance the need of protecting client confidentiality with the needs of healthcare providers and insurance companies to share information. You have probably noticed that whenever you initiate services with a doctor, dentist, or other healthcare provider, you are asked to sign a document that tells you how information will be shared with your health insurance

---

5. Although HIPAA only requires service providers to provide clients with notice that they are releasing routine information to insurance providers, state laws or social work ethics may impose higher standards of practice (e.g., requiring that social workers request specific consent from clients to release such information).

company and others. Often, healthcare providers ask patients to sign such documents with little explanation or discussion. HIPAA legislates minimum standards for protection of client rights, as described in the following paragraph.

Under HIPAA, healthcare providers do not actually need client consent to share basic patient information with insurance companies. *Providers are **required to give patients notice of their rights** and the practices of the entity, but providers are **not required to obtain a signed consent form** for release of information for purposes of treatment, payment, and healthcare operations.* Providers must make good-faith efforts to obtain client's *written acknowledgment of receipt* of the notice of privacy rights and practices. Still, this written acknowledgment is not the same as consent. It only requires that providers *try to obtain it.* HIPAA does require providers to obtain specific written authorization for sharing of "nonroutine information." For instance, routine information such as the patients' name, diagnosis, and course of treatment could be transmitted to an insurer without having to ask the client to sign a specific authorization or consent. You may reassure clients that disclosures will be limited to information necessary for insurance reimbursement. If you need to share nonroutine information (such as detailed progress notes), request the client's written consent. If a third party wants access to a client's progress notes or details of interviews, the provider should ask the client for written authorization. If you have any questions about what is routine or nonroutine information and your agency is covered by HIPAA, your agency should have a privacy official to answer HIPAA questions. You may find additional HIPAA information on the NASW website (https://www.socialworkers.org/Practice/Clinical-Social-Work/HIPAA). HIPAA includes other specific provisions for ensuring client confidentiality, including guidelines for training employees, writing agency policies, and record keeping.

From an ethics perspective, you may go above and beyond these HIPAA requirements, for instance, explaining the client's right to confidentiality and what information will be shared, and asking the client for consent rather than just acknowledgment. Agency policies and practices may differ, with some agencies opting to do the minimum required, since obtaining an acknowledgment is simpler and faster than obtaining written consent.

Subpoena

A subpoena is a summons requiring a person to provide written or oral evidence in a court process. When you receive a subpoena, you may be required to submit your records and/or testify at court proceedings (Borkosky, 2020). To determine whether the document you have received is an enforceable subpoena, seek advice from your agency's privacy officer or attorney, or from an attorney that you hire to act on your behalf. An attorney can also provide advice about whether you or your client can challenge the subpoena by filing a motion (Ordway & Casasnovas,

2019). The court will then decide whether to order you to testify or submit your client records. Not all subpoenas are enforceable. Subpoenas may be challenged on the grounds that they are vague, they do not identify the proper person to submit evidence, they are requesting evidence that is not relevant to the court case, or the subpoena was not served properly. Clients may also claim *privilege,* that is, a legal protection for information learned in a confidential relationship (Cottone et al., 2022). When privilege is recognized, the information you have gathered from clients is protected from disclosure in court; that is, courts cannot compel you to testify about confidential client information (Caldwell, 2017; *Jaffee v. Redmond,* 1996).

Privilege may be established by case law or statutes for certain professional relationships (Borkosky, 2020). One of the oldest and most recognized forms of privilege is attorney–client privilege. This privilege allows people to consult lawyers without fear that they may be called as witnesses. Privilege for clinical social workers was first established in the case of *Jaffe v. Redmond* (1996). Since then, social work licensing laws have also granted privilege for licensed clinical social workers. Workers should consult their licensing legislation or speak with an attorney to determine whether their licensure is covered by privilege, and under what circumstances. Privilege laws vary from state to state; for instance, some state statutes provide privilege for individual, family, and group counseling; others cover only individual counseling. Some state statutes are silent on the issue of whether family and group counseling are covered by privilege, making it difficult to know with certainty whether these types of counseling are covered by privilege (Cottone et al., 2022).

There are no general privilege laws covering social workers who are not licensed. However, when a social worker is working under the auspices of licensed professionals who are covered by privilege, courts may extend privilege to the unlicensed social workers working with them (Barsky, 2012). There are also state and federal laws that limit compellability of professionals as witnesses if they work in certain settings, for instance, substance use disorder treatment programs (SAMHSA, n.d.-a; Confidentiality of Substance Use Disorder Records, 2017) and shelters for survivors of domestic violence (Family Violence and Prevention Services, 1994, 42 USCA §10401). For an example on how to respond to a third party who requests confidential client records, please see Box 5.3.

Suspicion of Child Abuse or Neglect

State laws require social workers (and many other helping professionals) to report *reasonable suspicions of child abuse or neglect* to proper authorities. These authorities may be the state's child protective services, police, or other agencies designated by state laws (see https://www.childwelfare.gov/topics/systemwide/laws-policies/statutes/manda). The purpose of this exception is to protect vulnerable children. The law requires workers to report child abuse and neglect even when they do

BOX 5.3

SARAI

Social workers need to be prepared for how to handle requests for client records from third parties. Review the following scenario and critique how the social worker handled the situation. What did she say to protect client confidentiality? To what extent was she able to be honest and open, and to what extent did she need to withhold client information? What suggestions would you have for Sarai on how to improve her responses and resolve the conflict with the attorney in a professional manner?

Sarai provides social work services in a rehabilitation facility for people recovering from physically injuries. She receives a call from an attorney, Kerry, and the following conversation ensues:

Kerry: One of your clients, Eveline Alcindor, is involved in a court case, claiming damages for the injuries she suffered in a workplace accident. Could you please send a copy of her records to me immediately? Our first court date is this Friday.

Sarai: I'm sorry. Due to confidentiality and privilege, I am unable to confirm whether or not this person is a client of mine. If your client Ms. Alcindor wants to obtain records then she needs to provide us with a consent to release confidential information or you need to provide us with a legally enforceable subpoena for her records.

Kerry: I already sent a subpoena for her records but you did not respond. Do I need to file a complaint against you?

Sarai: I understand your concerns. You have an upcoming court case and you would like to receive your client's records as soon as possible. If our office receives a subpoena, then it is usually handled by our legal department. Would you like to speak with them?

Kerry: I don't have time for a run-around. Could you please just speak with Ms. Alcindor and verify that she wants you to send us her records?

Sarai: If you would like your client to contact me, please have her do so.

Kerry: Are you daft? I just asked you to speak with your client. She is in your facility. Just go and talk with her.

Sarai: I'm sorry. I need to go now. Have a nice day.

not think the person will re-offend. States maintain a database of child abuse and neglect reports, helping them monitor and enforce child protection concerns. Note that the worker does not need firm evidence of child maltreatment, but rather, enough information to support a reasonable suspicion. It is the child protection system's responsibility to investigate and assess suspected child maltreatment.

Abuse, Neglect, or Exploitation of Vulnerable Adults

State laws require people to report various forms of maltreatment of frail elders, people with disabilities, or other vulnerable adults. Maltreatment may include physical, emotional, or sexual abuse, financial exploitation, abandonment, neglect by caretakers, and self-neglect. Adult protection laws differ from state to state, including who is covered by the laws and what types of concerns are reportable. See the National Center on Elder Abuse (n.d.) website at https://ncea.acl.gov or the American Bar Association at https://www.americanbar.org/content/dam/aba/administrative/law_aging/2020-abuse-definitions.pdf?eType=EmailBlast Content&eId=ed64ab8e-28fa-405b-930d-f4d812fb840d for state laws, contact information, and adult protective services in your area. For services and reporting requirements related to maltreatment of people with disabilities, search your state government's website, which can be found at http://www.usa.gov/Agencies/State_and_Territories.shtml.

Note that legal duties to report adult protection concerns are different from the duties regarding suspicions of child abuse or neglect. Child maltreatment reporting requirements apply for abuse or neglect of any child under 18 years. Adult protection reporting requirements do not apply to abuse of any adult. They apply only to those specifically defined under the state's laws. For instance, the laws typically cover adults who are vulnerable due to disabilities or age-related frailty, particularly if they are dependent on others for their care. The reporting requirements do not apply when the person being mistreated is an adult who is not dependent on others due to disability or other circumstances. Assume you are working with a client who says her spouse is physically abusive. The client has a right to confidentiality; if the client does not want you to report the abuse to police or other authorities, you should honor the client's right to confidentiality. You may continue to work with the client, jointly develop a safety plan, empower the client with information and access resources, explore options, and continue to monitor the situation. If, however, the client is dependent on the person causing the abuse or neglect (e.g., due to a disability), the situation is reportable. If you are uncertain about whether a situation is reportable, then consult your supervisor. You may also contact adult protective services and explain the situation without providing identifying information; adult protective services can help you determine whether the situation is reportable.

Public Health Laws

Although health information is generally protected by confidentiality laws, there may be specific laws requiring disclosure of information to public health officials. In response to a viral pandemic, for instance, states may pass laws requiring that information about people who test positive for the virus be provided to public health officials so they can conduct contact tracing. Contact tracing allows public health officials to inform people who may have been infected and to prevent further spread of the virus. Social workers who are legally required to share information with public health officials should try to do so with client consent. They should also limit sharing information to that which is legally required (Camper, 2020). Note that public health officials may be allowed to inform people exposed to viruses or other communicable diseases without disclosing the identity of the person who exposed them.

Information Required to Prevent Serious, Foreseeable, and Imminent Harm

An exception to confidentiality arises in situations where social workers need to share client information with others in order to protect the client or another person from serious, foreseeable, and imminent harm (S.1.07[c]).[6] If a client says he is thinking about suicide, for instance, assess the actual risk of suicide. Given this assessment, you may then decide what steps are appropriate given the current risk level: for instance, consult a supervisor, refer the client for a second-level assessment by an appropriate mental health specialist, engage family members so they can monitor suicide risk, or initiate proceedings for involuntary admission to a psychiatric facility. Ideally, you should take any of these steps with client permission. If the client refuses permission, you may need to disclose some confidential information to others to safeguard the client. Limit your disclosure of confidential information to that which is necessary to prevent the harm (e.g., provide police with the client's name, location, and nature of the risk, but do not share details of the client's life that are not pertinent to protecting the client).

Similar standards apply for a client who threatens to kill or seriously injure another person (Barsky, 2020c). The worker should assess the risk, try to engage the client voluntarily, and determine what steps are necessary in order to safeguard the other person from harm. Some social workers assume that they must report any threats to the potential victim, citing the Tarasoff v. Regents of the University of California case (1976). Tarasoff involved a university student (Poddar) who told his psychologist (Moore) that he intended to kill a woman (Tatiana Tarasoff). Moore assessed Poddar as dangerous and called the campus police. The police took

---

6. Until 2018, this standard stated that the others needed to be identifiable persons. By removing the term "identifiable," this section envisions situations where social workers may disclose confidential information to protect unidentifiable others (e.g., a client who threatens to bomb an unidentified school or to rape an unidentified sex trade worker).

Poddar into custody but released him after questioning, believing he would keep his promise to stay away from Tarasoff. Shortly after, Poddar killed Tarasoff. Tarasoff's parents sued the university and its employees for failing to notify her. On an appeal of a lower court decision, the California Supreme Court initially ruled that the psychologist had a "duty to warn" the intended victim. The case later returned to the Supreme Court and the court clarified that the psychologist had "duty to protect" the intended victim. The court ordered the defendants to pay damages to the family.[7] Accordingly, social workers and other mental health professionals should take whatever steps are necessary to prevent harm. Warning the victim may or may not be required, depending on the circumstances. In some cases, the victim is not known or cannot be found. In other instances, warning the victim could increase the risks. Because assessing risk and determining appropriate actions are complex and perilous processes, you should consult your supervisors about how to proceed when you sense a risk of serious harm to the client or others (Corey et al., 2019; Reamer, 2021c). Other steps to protect an intended victim from harm may include providing crisis intervention counseling and contracting, referring the client to services on a voluntary basis, escorting the client to another facility for a second-level assessment, initiating involuntary committal to a psychiatric facility, and calling the police or other authorities (e.g., child protective services or adult protective services). Social workers should clearly document their risk assessments, consultations, and steps taken to prevent harm in order to provide evidence of how they discharged their ethical and legal duties.

The question of whether you have a legal duty to warn or to protect potential victims varies from state to state (check National Conference of State Legislators, 2018 for your state laws). Some states impose a duty to warn when there is a general threat or a threat against the general public (e.g., Arizona, Delaware). Other states establish a duty to warn only when a threat is to a readily identifiable victim (e.g., North Dakota). Still other states have no legislation or case law clarifying whether social workers and other professionals have a legal duty to warn (e.g., unlicensed social workers in Florida; Polowy & Gorenberg, 2004). Note that social workers may have an *ethical duty to protect* the client or others from serious, imminent, and foreseeable harm even if there is no *legal duty to protect* clients.

---

7. Tarasoff is a California case and is not binding on other states. Although most states have followed Tarasoff, some states have case law or statutes saying that mental health professionals are not liable for damages as a result of failing to protect a person from harm (National Conference of State Legislatures, 2018). The NASW Code of Ethics makes it clear that social workers should protect clients from harm. Each state, however, may have different statutory or case law about what steps are required (e.g., warning the potential victim, contacting the police, or taking other steps to protect the potential victim) and the consequences of breaching this duty (e.g., whether the social worker is liable for damages or whether the worker's licensure could be suspended or revoked).

To begin a discussion about the exceptions to confidentiality, you might explain

Under my agency policy and professional code of ethics, there are some important exceptions to confidentiality. For instance, if I become aware of a situation that puts a person at serious risk of harm, I must take appropriate actions to prevent that harm. It is also possible, though quite rare in my experience, to be called to court to testify. If there are any occasions that might require me to share your information with other people, I will try to discuss this information with you first, so I can ask for your permission.

Context-Specific Exceptions

Some exceptions to confidentiality are related to specific types of agencies or contexts of practice (Caldwell, 2017). Probation officers, parole officers, and other professionals working within the criminal justice system, for instance, may be required to share information with the court if the client violates a law, including the terms of a probation or parole order. They may have some discretion about what information to share and under what circumstances, particularly if the violation is relatively minor. Still, they should inform clients that certain information may be shared with courts. Similarly, forensic social workers who gather information for child custody cases, mental health hearings, or other court purposes should inform clients that they will be reporting certain information to the court.

In school settings, social workers may need to share certain information with school administration or parents (Cottone et al., 2022), even when the situation is not specifically related to protecting someone from "serious, imminent, and foreseeable risks" (Polowy & Felton, 2008). Under various school regulations or policies, workers may be required to report when students bring weapons or drugs to school, when students are involved in gang activities, when students engage in underage sexual activities, or when students are pregnant. School social workers should advise students and their parents or guardians about these limitations on confidentiality so they can make informed decisions about what to share or not share with their school social workers. To explore additional ethical issues regarding confidentiality in a school context, please see Box 5.4.

Social workers in the child protection system are required to share certain information with the court. Assume you are working with a teenager who has been taken into foster care due to neglect. You should inform this client about what types of reports that you will be making and who will have access to this information (e.g., the court, the client's attorney, and the parents).

Social workers working in hospitals, assisted living facilities, and residential treatment facilities have legal duties to report certain types of problems to the agencies that regulate these institutions and facilities. For instance, if a client in an assisted living facility discloses an abuse incident committed by a staff member, the worker

BOX 5.4

CONFIDENTIALITY IN A SCHOOL SETTING

Avril is a social worker in a middle school. Ms. Eberts (a teacher) refers Romel Atkers (a 5th grade student) to work with Avril due to behavior concerns. During Avril's first meeting with Romel and his parents, she explains that everything they discuss will be completely confidential. She says she will respect their privacy by not sharing information with anyone else. She asks them to sign a release form so she can speak with Ms. Eberts and also so she can observe Romel in the classroom. Romel and his mother sign the form. Avril says Romel's father does not need to sign the form because one parent's signature is enough.

Romel tells Avril that he often got into fights because other students tease him about being Bengali. His parents say that they do not approve of Romel getting into fights, but that Ms. Eberts does nothing to protect him. Avril meets with Ms. Eberts who says that Romel initiates fights and has impulse control issues. She does not believe anyone is picking on Romel because of his ethnicity. Avril observes a class and notes that some students are teasing Romel. Ms. Eberts seems to ignore their behavior and chastises Romel when he becomes upset. Avril informs the principal about Ms. Eberts' discriminatory treatment of Romel.

During the next meeting with Romel and his parents, Mr. Atkins asks Avril why she spoke with the principal about Ms. Eberts. He says they did not give Avril permission to speak with the principal and now they are worried that Ms. Eberts will be even tougher on Romel.

What rules or guidelines should Avril have considered when determining her obligations regarding confidentiality with students and their families? In what ways did Avril explain privacy, confidentiality, and exceptions appropriately? What else should Avril have explained during her confidentiality discussion with the Atkers?

---

may be legally required to report that incident even if the client does not provide permission to do so. Social workers need to be apprised of their obligations under the laws and policies governing their practice so that they can properly inform clients about the limits of confidentiality—and take appropriate steps to report information or protect people from harm should the need arise.

Discussing Exceptions to Confidentiality

Although you should inform clients about the general exceptions to confidentiality, it would not be realistic to explain all the details of each and every possible exception to confidentiality. Begin with a clear overview of the nature and limits of confidentiality. Allow the client to ask for further details. Tailor your explanation to the client's situation. If you know that child protection concerns might arise, you could specifically mention these. If you know the client feels too stressed to follow a long explanation during initial engagement, provide a shorter statement initially and save the details for a later session. Avoid overwhelming clients with all the standards and ethics of practice, particularly since they are likely thinking of more pressing personal concerns during their first session with you. You may discuss additional ethical issues as they become relevant to the services being offered.[8]

Some agencies use written confidentiality contracts or digital forms that explain the nature of confidentiality and its limitations in greater detail. Before asking a client to sign such a form, be sure to review important points with the client. Ensure that the client is not overwhelmed with detail and technical language. Engage clients in a discussion of confidentiality rather than a lecture or one-way explanation. Encourage clients to ask questions and suggest changes to what is included in your standard confidentiality agreement.

One ethical distinction that often creates confusion is the difference between past harm and future harm. As described above, *social workers may have an ethical obligation to protect people from serious, foreseeable and* **imminent** *harm. Social workers do not generally have an ethical obligation to report* **past** *harm, regardless of how serious it was* (NASW Code, 2021, S.1.07(c); Polowy & Gorenberg, 2004).[9] For instance, a client may disclose that she killed her mother. A social worker does not necessarily have a duty to report this to the police, as heinous as this crime may seem. If the worker believes the client is going to kill her father, then the worker has a duty to protect the father. This obligation arises out of future risk, not past harm. Remember, your primary role is to help clients by providing counseling and other services, not to act as police or police informants to enforce criminal laws. Offering confidentiality to clients permits them to discuss past crimes in a safe place and relationship. By giving clients a safe space to discuss past crimes with you, clients may eventually decide to speak with an attorney and may decide to turn themselves into authorities.

Specific types of social workers have duties to report or act on past crimes. For instance, probation officers must document past crimes and report these to the court. Probation officers and other court-affiliated officials have a duty to the criminal justice system, not just the client. They should explain this duty to clients, allowing clients to make informed decisions about what to disclose and what not to

---

8. The challenge is knowing what is relevant, and when. If you delay explaining the child abuse reporting obligation, for instance, clients may feel duped if you later state that you have to report them to child protection authorities.

9. Some states, such as Kansas, permit disclosure of criminal acts or violations of law. Remember, a law *permitting* disclosure is not the same as a law that *requires* disclosure.

disclose to their probation officers. To determine whether you have an obligation to report murder or other past crimes, check your agency's policies, service contracts, and laws that regulate the agency.

Another important distinction is the difference between a "duty to report" and a "justification to report." *If a law, policy, or code of ethics says that you* **must** *report certain information, then this constitutes a duty to report. If a law, policy, or code of ethics says that you* **may** *report certain information, then you may report this information if you have a reasonable ethical justification.* Some agencies permit workers to report past crimes. In other words, they are not required to do so but they are allowed to do so. Note that the use of different terms such as *shall, must, should,* and *may* in laws, policies, and codes of ethics will have an impact on the nature of the worker's obligations. Further, if you have questions about whether to report a past crime admitted by a client, consult with your supervisor, agency attorney, or other ethics experts designated by your agency.

CONCLUSION

Respecting client privacy and confidentiality shows respect for their dignity and worth. It also helps build trusting work relationships with clients. By engaging clients in meaningful discussions of confidentiality and its exceptions, you can clarify expectations and ensure that clients understand your ethical, legal, and agency-based responsibilities. You can also tailor your confidentiality agreements to meet the needs of the client. Although some clients may not authorize you to share information with family, friends, or other professionals, other clients may want you to do so (Cottone et al., 2022). For instance, they may authorize you to speak with a particular friend as an emergency contact or they may want you to share certain information with a family member.

To ensure that you and your clients share a clear and mutual understanding of confidentiality and its limits, it is generally prudent practice to have clients sign confidentiality agreements or release forms that authorize sharing information with others. If you do need to disclose information to others, you can refer the client back to the agreement and explain why you need to share the information. Ideally, obtain client consent before sharing information with others. Limit the sharing to information that is required (e.g., to protect people from serious harm or to fulfill a legal obligation such as child abuse reporting laws). When in doubt about whether or not you need to disclose information without client consent, consider whether it would be helpful to consult with a supervisor, ethics expert, or attorney. They can help you interpret relevant agency policies, ethical standards, and laws. They can also help you explore various options and work through a framework for managing ethical issues, such as the one presented in Chapter 2. As social workers, we respect client's rights to confidentiality and privacy; at the same time, there may be situations in which we have to balance these rights with other interests, including preservation of life, honesty and transparency, accountability, and protection of vulnerable individuals and groups from various types of harm.

DISCUSSION QUESTIONS AND EXERCISES

1. *Discussing Confidentiality*: How would you explain confidentiality and its limits when engaging clients or research participants in the following situations?
   a. You are a high school social worker facilitating a group for students who have engaged in acts of cyberbullying.
   b. You have been hired by a foodbank to conduct interviews with people who make use of the foodbank's services to determine what additional types of services the agency could provide.
   c. You are providing case management services to Ms. Haggerty (77 years) and her adult children, Seth and Cora. Ms. Haggerty has been developing a severe hearing impairment and needs help coordinating services with an audiologist, otolaryngologist, and a support group.
   d. You are providing parenting skills training to Marikje (23). Child protective services referred Marikje to you due to abuse of her 5-year-old child, Miguel.
2. *Violations and Dilemmas*: Review each of the following situations. Identify whether the situation involves a violation of confidentiality or an ethical dilemma. Explain how you would respond to each situation, using the framework for managing ethical issues in Chapter 2.
   a. Svetlana provides confidential counseling to Esteban, who is very anxious about his recent engagement to Estrella. Svetlana accidentally sends a psychosocial assessment to Estrella, who has a similar email address. Estrella reads the report and finds out Esteban has been having intimate relations with other women. She calls off the engagement.
   b. Willard is conducting an intake assessment with Olivia (32) to determine whether she meets the eligibility requirements for a substance abuse treatment program. During the assessment, Olivia discloses that she has sold fentanyl (a very strong pain medication) to students at a local school. Willard wonders whether to keep this information confidential or whether he has a legal obligation to contact police or child protection authorities. Olivia is furious about the possibility of being reported because Willard said the interview was completely confidential.
   c. Ashley facilitates a group designed to help recent immigrants adapt to their new country. At the outset of the group, members agree that they will keep each other's information confidential. One group

member, Marty, lets the group know that he has been using his cousin's health insurance because he cannot afford to pay for a doctor. Another group member, Dara, says that the group needs to report Marty to authorities. Ashley says that the group should keep Marty's insurance fraud a secret as long as he agrees to stop using his cousin's health insurance.

d. Precious is conducting an evaluation of the services of a neonatal intensive care unit. One of her research participants, Giro, discloses that a nurse administered the wrong medication to his daughter. Precious says she is required to report this medical error to hospital administration so they can investigate the matter and take appropriate steps. Giro asks Precious not to report the nurse because he does not want to get her in trouble. His daughter experienced significant negative effects from the medication error (including sleep disturbances), but is feeling well now.

e. Renita was recently released from an inpatient treatment center where she received services for schizophrenia. Felice, as social worker, calls Renita to set up a follow-up appointment to monitor her progress and identify any further needs. Renita says she is too busy to come to the center for the follow-up. Felice offers to meet Renita using a free videoconferencing app that they can upload to their personal cellphones.

3. *Hepatitis*: You are working in a shelter for people experiencing homelessness. You notice that one client, Alex, has yellowish skin and eyes. Upon questioning, Alex says he has been suffering from fatigue, bruising, and itchy skin. You recommend that Alex see a physician because he may have Hepatitis C. Alex refuses because he does not trust physicians. You are also concerned that Alex is sexually active and in close quarters with other clients in the shelter. What ethical and legal responsibilities should you consider? What are your options and which options should you pursue with Alex?

4. *Social Robot*: Jenna, a social robot entrepreneur, approaches you to provide your social work expertise in developing the software for a social robot designed for older adults with moderate dementia. The robot will engage them in social conversations, play games, and assess their cognitive functioning. When consulting with Jenna, what suggestions would you have regarding issues related to client confidentiality, adult protection issues, and possible reporting obligations? (cf., Barsky, 2020b)

5. *Foster Parents*: You are starting a support group for foster parents to help them deal with emotional, behavioral, and social concerns that may arise in their relationships with their foster children. What types of policies should the group have in terms of maintaining privacy and confidentiality? Should group members be allowed to share private information about their foster children? Should group members be

allowed to discuss information about the biological parents? What obligations would you have if a member disclosed that their foster child was experimenting with marijuana? Provide your rationale, referencing the NASW Code of Ethics.

6. *Small Community*: Adina practices social work counseling in a small community[10] where almost everybody knows one another. When anyone comes to her office, others may suspect that they are her clients. When one client leaves and another is in the waiting room, it is likely that they know one another. When Adina goes shopping, banking, or walking in the community, clients often come up to her to say, "Hello." How should Adina explain client privacy and confidentiality in a manner that recognizes the challenges of practicing in a small community and still offers clients a sense that they can speak with her in confidence?

7. *Gossip*: You are part of an interprofessional team in the psychiatric department of a hospital. You notice that some professional colleagues chat informally about patients, joking and sharing rumors. When you suggest that they refrain from these conversations, they say that there is no harm joking around and that they are not violating patient confidentiality because they all work for the hospital. What are the possible harms? How would you explain the importance of refraining from gossiping about patients?

8. *Police Request*: You are conducting research to study the perspectives of people who have experienced identity theft and fraud. The police contact you to request records about a particular research participant. They say they need this information to prosecute an important case and to ensure others are protected from identity theft. How should you respond to the initial request to the police? What other actions should you take, and why? Under what circumstances should you share your information with the police? Under what circumstances should you refuse to share your records?

---

10. Examples small communities could include rural communities, small towns, an LGBTQ+ community, a school community, or close communities of people who share the same ethnic, religious, or linguistic background.

6

Professional Competence, Incompetence, and Impairment

LEARNING OBJECTIVES

Upon successful completion of this introduction, you will be able to

- determine when you have appropriate competence to provide particular services and when you should refer clients to other professionals who have more appropriate competence;
- raise awareness of situations in which your ability to practice may be impaired due to physical, psychological, or social concerns;
- implement strategies to enhance your ability to practice in a competent manner, including practice with technology; and
- assist colleagues with concerns about competence or impairment using restorative and corrective approaches.

Competence is a core social work value. Competence refers to the combination of knowledge, self-awareness, critical thinking, and practice skills that we as social workers need to provide particular services in an effective manner (Senger & Wiest, 2022). If we want to do good (beneficence) and avoid causing harm (nonmaleficence), we should strive for higher and higher levels of competence. Under Standard 1.04(a) of the NASW (2021) Code of Ethics, we should practice only within our areas of competence. Before providing services that are new to us, we should build our competence through "appropriate study, training, consultation, and supervision from people who are competent in those interventions or techniques" (NASW Code, S.1.04[b]). In this chapter, we will explore various types of competence that we need in order to practice ethically, including generalist, specialist, and technological.

Note that the term *competence* is used throughout this chapter to refer to professional competence and, specifically, the social workers' ability to provide services in a safe and effective manner. References to competence in this chapter do not refer to the mental competence or capacity of clients. However, this chapter does explore impairment issues that may be experienced by social workers; for instance, when a worker's ability to practice effectively may be impaired due to physical or mental illnesses, social stress, or other conditions affecting the worker's ability to function. To ensure competent practice, we need to be aware not only of our skills and knowledge, but also of any personal or social conditions that could hinder our ability to practice. The purpose section of the NASW Code highlights the importance of social workers engaging in self-care to ensure that they can continue to practice in a competent manner. Note also that professional competence includes cultural competence (Standard 1.05). Given the importance and breadth of issues related to race, ethnicity, sex, gender, disability, and other aspects of diversity, we will explore issues related to cultural competence in Chapter 7.

AREAS OF COMPETENCE

Generalist Competencies

The skills and knowledge that we need as social workers depends on the type of work we are doing, including the professional roles we are performing, the intervention models we are using, and the particular needs of the clients we are serving. All social workers with a Bachelor of Social Work degree or who have completed the generalist curriculum of a Master of Social Work program should be competent in the following generalist social work roles: case manager, group facilitator, advocate, policy analyst and developer, community organizer, service broker, counselor, mediator, integrated technology provider, and researcher (Hepworth et al., 2023; Zastrow & Hessenauer, 2021). Within each of these roles, we may use various models of intervention, for instance, a task-centered approach to case management, a social action approach to advocacy, an interest-based approach to mediation, a client-centered approach to counseling, or a quantitative approach to research. Within each approach, we need to learn how to put our knowledge and skills into practice. As advocates, for instance, we should be competent at assessing power dynamics, developing strategic plans, building credibility and trust, articulating our causes, implementing our advocacy plans, and evaluating their effectiveness. In terms of meeting client needs, we need to be able to adapt our roles and models of practice to the clients' unique situations (Barsky, 2019a). For instance, the communication skills needed to counsel children will be different from those needed to counsel adults. Likewise, a case manager assisting a person with cancer will require different knowledge and skills than a case manager assisting a survivor of childhood abuse. Generalists typically avoid giving clients advice; generalists help clients identify their own solutions and connect clients with specialists when they need specific legal, medical, mental health, financial, or other advice.

As you engage in your social work education, note that your classroom, online, and field experiences are designed to help you develop and demonstrate nine core social work competencies as defined in the Council in Social Work Education's (2022) Educational Policies and Educational Standards:

1. Demonstrate Ethical and Professional Behavior
2. Advance Human Rights and Social, Economic, and Environmental Justice
3. Engage in Antiracism, Diversity, Equity, and Inclusion in Practice
4. Engage in Practice-Informed Research and Research-Informed Practice
5. Engage in Policy Practice
6. Engage with Individuals, Families, Groups, Organizations, and Communities
7. Assess Individuals, Families, Groups, Organizations, and Communities
8. Intervene with Individuals, Families, Groups, Organizations, and Communities
9. Evaluate Practice with Individuals, Families, Groups, Organizations, and Communities

You will also have opportunities to develop additional competencies, going above and beyond the core.

As a student early in your social work education and career, you might wonder how you can assist anyone in a fully competent manner; after all, you are still learning. Remember, your competence to serve clients is connected with your ability to use supervision. During your field practicum, your supervisor should be assessing your competence on an ongoing basis, selecting clients and helping processes appropriate to your current skills and knowledge, and providing you with the support that you need to serve these clients. It is vital to build trust with your supervisor so that you feel comfortable discussing any concerns that you may have. "I've never worked with someone experiencing hallucinations. I'm not sure how I'm supposed to help." Your supervisor can help you build competence through coaching, role-plays, observing other workers, readings specific to serving your client population, online trainings, and other forms support (Hafford-Letchfield & Engelbrecht, 2020). You may also request support from your course instructors, for instance, consulting about the latest evidence-based practices (Gambrill, 2019) and how to develop the required skills.

Regardless of our primary areas of practice, we should all have knowledge and skills to handle urgent situations; for instance, a client with suicidal or homicidal ideation, a client experiencing abuse, or a community or organization under threat due to an active shooter, terrorism, hurricane, earthquake, pandemic, or other emergency situation (Alston, et al., 2019; NASW Code, S.6.03). We do not need to be proficient in providing all the needed services; however, as generalist social workers, we should at least be prepared to assess risks and needs, connect people with appropriate services and support systems, and address immediate risks.

The ethical principle of competence not only requires that we *possess* competence; we must actually *practice* in a competent manner, that is, in a manner consistent with the most current theory and research (NASW Code, 2021). The purpose of this principle is to promote effective practice, including the maximization of benefits and minimization of harm to clients, communities, research participants, and others we serve. Assume you are facilitating a support group for marines recently returning from active duty in a war zone. If you do not facilitate the group in a competent manner, the group is less likely to fulfill its goals. Further, you might cause harm, such as retraumatizing the marines and making it more difficult for them to fulfill their responsibilities with family, work, and others in their lives.

Social workers often work in teams, the advantage being that we can draw from the strengths of each person on the team, maximizing our combined knowledge and skills. When working in teams, we need to clarify one another's roles and stay within each of our areas of competence. Assume you are a social worker in a neonatal intensive care unit, working collaboratively with physicians, nurses, respiratory specialists, dieticians, and pharmacists. Your role includes helping family members adjust to having a baby with special health needs and risks. The baby has been experiencing bradycardia (slowing of the heartbeat). The parents ask whether this condition causes permanent brain damage. How would you respond? Do you have the requisite knowledge and skill to answer directly? If you determine that is more appropriate to refer the parents to another professional, which team member has the appropriate competence?

When we work in teams, we should ensure that our team as a whole has the appropriate competence to perform our required tasks. Consider a quantitative research project in which you are partnering with another social worker to study the effectiveness of a program for children who stutter. The required competencies include conducting a literature review, hypothesis development, research design, construction of research tools, engaging research participants, obtaining informed consent, data input, and statistical analysis. Which skills do you currently possess? What would you do if you or your collaborator did not have sufficient competence in statistical analysis? Is it ethical to simply hire a statistician to analyze the data, even if you do not understand how the data was analyzed? When you conduct and publish research, you are jointly responsible with your research partners for ensuring that the research is conducted in an ethically responsible manner (NASW Code, S.6.02[q]), taking safety, confidentiality, informed consent, honestly, accuracy, and research effectiveness into account.

Note that competence is not just a baseline standard, a minimum level of professional knowledge and skill that we need to perform our services. Competence is also an aspirational ethical principle. As the Principles section of the NASW Code suggests, we should continually strive to enhance our competence so we become the best social workers that we can be. One of the wonderful aspects of social work practice is that we are always learning and improving. Some ways that we can continue our process of professional development are

- engaging in professional conferences, in-person trainings, online educational opportunities, and role-plays and other experiential learning exercises;
- reading current research and scholarly literature;
- monitoring our practice through self-reflection, journaling, and critical thinking;
- making use of supervision and peer consultation for constructive feedback on our professional work, assistance with self-awareness, and guidance for how we can improve our services with current or future clients, research participants, coworkers, and others; and
- contributing to social work's professional knowledge bases by engaging in research and evaluation, and sharing our findings through agency-based reports, professional magazines and websites, scholarly research articles, and professional conferences.

Note that when we conduct research and share our findings, we are not only contributing to the knowledge base of the profession; we are also enhancing our own knowledge and expertise.

Specialist Competencies

Although social workers with generalist education and experience have the competence to provide many types of services, they may need additional knowledge, training, and skill development to provide specialized services. For instance, generalist education should provide you with the competence to perform psychosocial assessments, including assessments of client strengths, needs, and motivations; however, you would need additional training and credentialing in order to provide specialized assessments, such as psychological diagnoses, forensic analyses, or personality tests. Consider, for instance, a client who presents with feelings of sadness, hopelessness, and low levels of motivation. As a generalist social worker, you may document this information; however, you should not diagnose this client as having depression. If you believe it would be helpful for the client to receive a diagnosis, you should refer the client to a licensed social worker or other mental health professional who has the appropriate training and credentials for performing diagnoses. Licensing laws in most states permit licensed clinical social workers to diagnose. Some jurisdictions do not include diagnosis within the scope of allowed practice for social workers, so it is important to know your own state's laws (Shah et al., 2019).

Although some distinctions between generalist and specialist practice are relatively clear, some practice areas are more challenging to distinguish. Consider, for instance, the difference between counseling (as a generalist function) and psychotherapy (as a specialist function). In both functions, helping agents use a variety of communication skills to engage with clients and help them enhance their biological, psychological, social, and/or spiritual functioning and well-being. Generalist counseling helps clients with *here and now* concerns, such as the ability to perform the tasks of daily living and to function in one's usual roles (e.g., as a parent, partner, student, or employee). Specialist counseling may address here and now issues, as well as *historical and unconscious* issues. For instance, hypnotherapy uses guided relaxation and concentration to help clients reveal and process unconscious memories and conflicts. Some psychotherapies focus on specific concerns, for instance, sexuality therapy, trauma therapy, and grief therapy. Check your state laws to determine which types of training, accreditation, or licensure are required for specialized functions such as DSM diagnoses, sexuality therapy, and other forms of psychotherapy (see https://www.aswb.org/licensees/about-licensing-and-regulation/social-work-regulation). Specialized functions may entail higher levels of risk than generalist functions; accordingly, licensing laws are meant to promote higher levels of education, training, oversight, and accountability for professionals practicing in these areas.

Generalist social workers often develop specialized knowledge and skills in order to work in particular agencies or contexts of practice. As a school social worker, for example, you may require specialized competencies for fostering social-emotional development in children, advocating for educational system reforms, and engaging parents and families to support their children's educational needs. As an adult guardianship worker, you may require specialized competencies in assessing risks of abuse and neglect, working collaboratively with lawyers and others in the adult guardianship system, and developing resources for families in need of respite care for adult family members with special needs.

For additional examples of competencies required for particular contexts of practice, see the NASW's practice standards and guidelines at https://www.socialworkers.org/Practice/Practice-Standards-Guidelines. Also, see Box 6.1 for an example of a social worker who provides services outside her areas of competence. As you read the scenario, think of which other professionals would have been more competent to provide these services.

Technological Competence

With the growing use of technology to facilitate social work practice, we need to develop competence not only in various methods and models of practice, but also in how to use technology effectively when we engage, assess, plan, intervene,

BOX 6.1

WOMEN'S SHELTER

Brandy's BSW field placement is in a shelter for female survivors of intimate partner abuse. Her main roles are to assess client needs, provide supportive counseling, and connect clients with appropriate services. One of her clients, Charna, says that she left her children at home with her husband, Wendel, because she was scared that he might kill her if she tried to bring the children to the shelter. Brandy expresses empathy and informs Charna that she is there to listen and provide whatever kinds of support that Charna needs. Brandy suggests that they should not discuss the details of the abuse that Charna experienced so as not to retraumatize her. Brandy asks if she can examine her back for bruises or scars as evidence of abuse. Charna removes her shirt to allow Brandy to gather evidence. Brandy advises Charna that the bruises are "not so bad" and that Charna would be unlikely to obtain a restraining order if she went to court and accused Wendel of assault. Brandy counsels Charna to move to a new city, obtain a job, and earn enough money to be able to pursue custody of the children in family court. Charna asks whether she should close her joint bank accounts or withdraw all the money. Brandy responds that, for tax purposes, it would be better to withdraw all the money and open a new account in the name of a revokable trust in her benefit.

1. Identify each action that Brandy has taken or service that she offered that falls within her areas of competence.
2. Identify each action or service that falls outside Brandy's areas of competence.
3. For each service falling outside of Brandy's professional competence, what type of professional would have been more appropriate to provide services?

evaluate, and terminate our work with clients, communities, and research participants (Barsky, 2017b; NASW Code, S.1.04[d]; Reamer, 2021c). If you are facilitating group work through videoconferencing, for instance, you may need to know how to schedule meetings, invite group members, explain how to log into and participate in the video conference, and use videoconferencing functions such as recording, white boards, breakout rooms, and chat boxes. In addition to learning the instrumental tasks of using technology, you should also research best practices in how to conduct group processes through videoconferencing:

- How can you verify the identities of group participants and ensure that only those who are authorized to participate in the group have access to the videoconference?

- What specific skills and strategies should you use foster trust and meaningful relationships with clients who may initially feel reluctant to engage through videoconferencing?
- Should group members be required to turn on their cameras or should they be allowed to participate through audio only?
- What arrangements should you have in place to deal with sudden problems that may arise (e.g., glitches in the teleconferencing program, a group member who expresses suicidal plans, or a member who is intoxicated during the videoconference session)?

We need to be competent in assessing people's ability use to technology (NASW Code, S.1.03[g]). We should also ensure that we select technologies that fit best with each client's needs, interests, abilities, and goals. Consult research to determine what types of technology work best for which purposes and with which types of individuals, groups, or communities (Gambrill, 2019). When engaging community members in a mental health awareness project, for instance, would it be better to communicate through online videos, text messages, interactive games, or another technology? If certain community members have low levels of literacy, do we know how to enable tools that translate text into audio messages?

To learn how to use technology effectively, we can often benefit from collaboration with experts in computer science and information technology. Assume you are studying the spread of false information on social media. You are looking for a qualitative data analysis program that can help you code, interpret, and analyze online discourse. By consulting experts in qualitative research software, you can learn how to use the software more effectively. When using automated research tools, make sure you understand how these tools work. A program could provide you with a beautiful "heat map" to help people visualize your data; however, you need to know what a heat map is if you are going to include one in your research.

For additional examples of "what could go wrong" when we do not have sufficient competence in the technology we are using, see Box 6.2.

REFERRALS

If you are sensing that you have much to learn in order to be a competent social worker, take heart: All social workers, even the most experienced, have a lot to learn. As Socrates said, "The only true wisdom is in knowing you know nothing." In social work, having the wisdom to know what we do not know is imperative. It allows us to know when to ask for help to enhance our own knowledge and when to refer clients to others who can provide more effective help.

When facilitating referrals, ensure that the professional to whom you are referring the client is competent at providing the services needed by the client. Inappropriate referrals can cause significant harm to clients and lead to malpractice

BOX 6.2

ADVOCACY WITH TECHNOLOGY

Floran is a social work advocate with the Strom Coalition for Digital Privacy, an organization that advocates for better protection of personal information and privacy for information transmitted over the Internet. The coalition asks Floran to develop a website that invites people to join the coalition and donate money to the cause. Floran is a skilled web designer in terms of creativity, technical ability, and attention to detail. Unfortunately, he has not kept current in relation to website security and accessibility issues for people with disabilities.

Shortly after the website is launched, the coalition receives complaints from 12 people with concerns about unauthorized charges on their credit cards. Floran suspects that someone has hacked the website, gaining access to credit card information submitted by supporters. Floran is not sure how many other supporters may have been affected. He was aware of the risks of unauthorized access and identity theft, but he thought that proper security was built into the web designing program that he was using. In addition, the coalition has received a demand letter from a Blind person, suggesting that the website is not accessible to people with visual impairments. For example, the website contains many photos and other graphics. Floran should have provided alternate text or descriptions for nontext context. Also, the website requires a mouse to navigate to different pages and information. Floran should have enabled keyboard commands for people to allow people with visual impairments to navigate the website. Although Floran was vaguely familiar with the Americans with Disabilities Act, he had not thought about how to make the website accessible to people with disabilities.

- In what ways did Floran breach his duty of professional competence?
- With whom should he consult to determine how to clean up this mess?
- What options should he consider in responding to the security breach?
- What options should he consider in responding to the concerns about accessibility?

You do not need to know all the answers about how to respond to this situation; however, you should know the limits of your knowledge and competence. You should also know about possible sources of information, support, and advice so that you can properly address the types of issues that Floran is facing.

---

lawsuits (see Chapter 12). Assume you are working with a refugee from Ukraine who complains of sleep problems. You refer the client to a counselor who specializes in sleep issues; however, the counselor does not specialize in trauma and has not worked with clients from Ukraine. Because you did not check to ensure that the referral was a good fit for this client, you could be held responsible. When making referrals, avoid simply providing clients a list of random service providers, phone numbers, or websites. Take the same care as you would if you were connecting a beloved family member with a service provider. Assess the clients' needs, goals, preferences, and wishes. Identify potential service providers who are competent to address each of these factors. If you are not already familiar with a potential provider, contact the provider and ask questions to ensure the provider is competent and a good fit. Whenever feasible, provide clients with more than one potential provider so they can contact each potential provider and select the most appropriate one. Offering multiple possible providers supports the principles of self-determination, empowering clients to make the best choices for themselves. Follow up with clients to ensure that they connect with the provider and feel satisfied. As Standard 1.17(b) suggests, we should not abandon clients and we should ensure they have continuity of services. If you refer clients to a provider with a waiting list, for instance, you could offer to continue to work with the clients until they are able to see the provider. See Box 6.3 for an example of a situation in which a social work student, Sofia, says she cannot serve a particular group of people. Consider whether it is appropriate Sofie to refuse to provide services due to conflicting religious beliefs and lack of prior experience in working with such a group.

Given that we are competent to provide certain types of services but not competent to provide others, it is important to develop a strong network of professional support (Daley, 2021). We may have people within our agencies with whom we can consult or refer clients. We should also get to know other service providers and professionals, so we can access their support when the need arises. When I was working with clients affected by substance abuse, I visited several treatment centers so that I could get to know the staff, as well as the facilities and the programs that they offered. Visiting the centers also helped their staff get to know me. Developing good working relationships with colleagues at different agencies helps us serve our clients more effectively, including when we need to work collaboratively to ensure that our clients are benefiting from our combined knowledge, skills, and expertise.

Traditionally, we tend to think of referrals in terms of linking clients with agencies and other helping professionals. We could also think of referrals in terms of referring clients to use particular technologies that provide services. Consider the use of chatbots, devices programmed to respond automatically to questions, comments, and conversations with one or more people. Communication between the person and device may be through text, oral messages, images, or a combination. Chatbots may be programmed to assist people with various biopsychosocial issues, such as parenting, sleep, exercise, problem-solving, depression, and anxiety (Ahmed et al., 2021). Although it is relatively easy to suggest that clients use chatbots, referring them to chatbots is similar to referring them to other professionals. We should not make referrals unless we are familiar with the professional, agency, or chatbot to which we are referring the client. We need to know that the specific referral is appropriate for the client. Assume you are working with parents experiencing challenges communicating with their adolescent child. You believe they

BOX 6.3

COMPETENCE TO SERVE A GAY CLIENT

Review the following conversation between a social work student, Sofia, and her field instructor, Frankie. In her field placement, Sofia assesses clients for eligibility for social assistance due to disabilities. Use the Framework for Managing Ethical Issues in Chapter 2 to identify and analyze the primary ethical issues, weigh the relevant ethical obligations, brainstorm options, and determine the best option to implement.

Sofia: Thanks for seeing me, Frankie. I'm supposed to assess a new client, Gerard. I think you should assign him to another social worker.

Frankie: Why is that?

Sofia: Well, Gerard is gay and homosexuality goes against my religion.

Frankie: I'm not sure what a client's sexual orientation has to do with his application for social assistance. We're a federally funded program that is supposed to offer services to everyone—without discrimination.

Sofia: And that's why I think we should refer Gerard to another social worker—so I won't discriminate against him. Also, I'm not competent to serve gay people. I've never worked with them. The Code of Ethics says I should refer people if I'm not competent to serve them.

Frankie: The Code of Ethics also suggests all people have a right to access to services and to be treated with respect. How do you think Gerard would feel if you said you cannot serve him because he is gay?

Sofia: I don't have to tell him why I can't work with him. You could just assign another worker.

Frankie: You mean we should not be fully honest with Gerard?

Sofie: No. You can be honest. I think you could just find a social worker who is more competent to help this population.

(For an article exploring related concerns, see Jacobsen & Levy, 2018)

---

may benefit from a chatbot designed teach parents how to communicate more effectively. Before referring them this chatbot, however, you would need to know the specific types of information and supports that the chatbot provides. You could then determine the goodness of fit with your particular client family; for instance, if the adolescent has a learning disability or a substance abuse problem, is the chatbot properly programmed to help with these circumstances? Finally, when referring people to use chatbots, you should know how to complement the client's use of the chatbot with your direct services. For example, should you be monitoring their experience online so that you can provide feedback, identify any problems, and build on what they are learning in your counseling sessions? What does the research suggest about the best way to integrate chatbot experiences with in-person social work interventions? Given the rapid changes in technology and its applications to social work practice, we need to keep up-to-date on the current research and best practices with technology.

IMPAIRED PRACTICE

Impaired practice refers to situations in which we have physical, psychological, social, or spiritual conditions that hinder our ability to provide services in a competent manner. If you have a migraine, for instance, your ability to see, think, and process information may be severely diminished. If you are experiencing depression, you may feel tried, unfocused, helpless, or irritable. If you are going through an acrimonious breakup with an intimate partner, you may feel distracted, angry, or vulnerable. If the death of a loved one is causing you to question the meaning of life, you may lose motivation and energy to serve your clients. In each of these situations, if your ability to practice social work is significantly impaired, you should take a break from providing services and give yourself time to work on your well-being before returning to practice (Reamer, 2015). If you are working in an agency setting, your supervisor can help find coverage for your clients and responsibilities. If you are working in private practice, you may need to refer your clients to other professionals or agencies so they are able to receive continuity of services and support (NASW Code, S.1.15).

To guard against impaired practice, it is important to engage in personal and professional self-care (Miller et al., 2019). Personal self-care includes strategies that promote physical, psychological, social, and spiritual well-being (e.g., exercising, positive self-talk, recreational activities with friends, and meditation). Professional self-care refers to strategies designed to maintain healthy life-work balance and to build resilience against work-related stresses (e.g., taking time for lunch, engaging in supervision, not taking work home, taking pride in doing a meaningful work, using stress management, and engaging in continuing professional education). Self-care means being proactive, reducing risks such as burnout, compassion fatigue, vicarious trauma, and other impairments that may affect the quality of our work.

We all experience personal problems at various points in our lives. As professional social workers, we need to be aware of any instances in which personal problems interfere with our work. In many cases, we can persevere and continue to work even as we are experiencing these problems. It is incumbent on all of us, however, to be aware of situations when we need to take a break or step aside for the good of our clients. Examples of personal problems affecting work include not following through on commitments to clients, reacting to clients out of anger or defensiveness, crossing professional boundaries, and not respecting client rights such as confidentiality and informed consent (Dolgoff et al., 2012; Hepworth et al., 2023). The earlier that we are aware that personal issues are affecting work, the sooner that we can access help and take corrective actions.

CORRECTIVE AND RESTORATIVE APPROACHES

The preceding sections focus on ethical responsibilities to practice within our areas of competence and to refer clients to others when we lack competence to provide particular services or when we are experiencing conditions that impair our ability to practice in a competent manner. In this section, we focus on our ethical responsibilities when our professional colleagues have conditions impairing their ability to practice or when they lack professional competence.

Colleagues with Impairments

Standard 2.08(a) suggests that when we have direct knowledge of a social work colleague with an impairment, we should "consult with that colleague when feasible and assist the colleague in taking remedial action." Thus, if you saw me come to work inebriated, you could talk to me directly and work toward a corrective plan. For instance, you might encourage me to go home rather than serve clients while inebriated; you or my supervisor could contact my clients to reschedule their appointments. If I need assistance with an alcohol problem, you could encourage me to seek professional help. Note that Standard 1.08(a) suggests that you need "direct knowledge" of an impairment to trigger the obligation in this standard. What would you do if one of my clients told you that I seemed depressed and that I was not doing my job properly due to depression? When you have hearsay information (from a secondary source) rather than direct information, it may be best to gather additional information rather than simply rely on the secondary source. For instance, you could make your own observations about whether I exhibit signs of depression or incapacity. You could also check in with me to determine whether I am aware of any concerns affecting my ability to practice.

Standard 2.08(b) suggests that if you speak to a colleague about an impairment and the colleague does not take adequate steps to address it, you should pursue the concern "through appropriate channels established by employers, agencies, NASW, licensing and regulatory bodies, and other professional organizations." Thus, if you work in an agency, your next step could be to speak to my supervisor, who can then address the issue with me. Note that the purpose of sharing information about my impairment is not to be punitive, but to help me and to ensure clients are receiving safe and effective services. You may ask my supervisor whether the issue needs to be reported to any professional organization to which I am affiliated. If the matter can be resolved within the agency, then it may not be necessary to take the concern beyond the agency. If there is an ongoing concern about my impairment and risks to clients, then it may be prudent to also report me to any relevant professional bodies (e.g., if I am a licensed social worker, then to my licensing body; if I am an NASW member, then to NASW). Different agencies have different policies about where to report concerns about employees. In some agencies, you may be asked to report concerns about colleagues to human resources, the program director, your own supervisor, or a risk management officer. The purpose section of the NASW Code indicates that while we are responsible for our own self-care, our agencies are also responsible for supporting our self-care and ability to practice. Examples of agency support for self-care and responding to impairment issues may include ongoing supervision, paid sick leave, employee and family assistance programs, and adjusting work expectations to accommodate a worker's special needs. If your agency does not provide adequate support for self-care (including support for impairment concerns), then you may use the language in the NASW Code to advocate for better support. To consider additional issues that may arise when responding to impairment issues, see Box 6.4.

BOX 6.4

COLLEAGUE WITH DEMENTIA

Wren is a social worker in a community health clinic. Recently, she has noticed that one of the clinic's senior physicians, Dr. Donato, is having memory problems. Wren suspects that Dr. Donato is developing age-related dementia. He has forgotten appointments, names of patients, and their reasons for seeking services. Wren does not want to hurt Dr. Donato's feelings by suggesting that he may not be competent to continue practice, so she speaks with her supervisor, Salima, about her concerns. Salima tells Wren that Standard 2.08 does not apply to this situation because Dr. Donato is a physician, not a social work colleague. Salima also notes that they are not in a position to diagnose whether Dr. Donato actually has dementia. Salima is hesitant to report Dr. Donato to the board that licenses physicians because he is a well-respected physician and the clinic needs him. What are the ethical issues raised by this situation? Even if the NASW Code does not address impairments of non-social work colleagues, what ethical principles or duties should Salima and Wren consider? What options should they consider? What should they do, and why?

Colleagues Providing Services Beyond their Competence

Whereas Standard 2.08 refers to incapacity of colleagues, Standard 2.09 deals with incompetence of social work colleagues. Similar to 2.08, Standard 2.09 suggests that if we have direct information about the incompetence of colleagues, we should first talk with them "to assist the colleague in taking remedial action." If the colleague does not take adequate steps to address the incompetence, then we should determine how to take corrective actions through the colleague's employer or professional organization.

Assume that a client, Paul, tells me that he is very upset with his former social worker, Juanita, because "she did not know what she was doing." The information that Paul provides is second-hand information, so I do not assume that Juanita lacks professional competence. I listen to Paul and show empathy. I ask Paul to clarify what he meant when he said Juanita did not know what she is doing. Paul says Juanita was using hypnotherapy to help him with anxiety. She uncovered a memory that Paul was sexually abused as a child by his father. Initially, Paul believed this memory was true and confronted his family. After months of family turmoil, Paul now believes that Juanita induced a false memory. Paul asks what he can do to hold Juanita accountable. I am not a licensed attorney, so I do not provide legal advice. I help him discuss options that he may have considered, as well as options that he could consider: speak with an attorney, invite Juanita to participate in mediation, explore the grievance procedure at Juanita's agency, or consider whether to initiate a professional review process with NASW or another professional body to which Juanita belongs. Paul says that he does not want to pursue any of these options. He says the experience with Juanita and his family was very distressing and he does not want to relive the trauma any further. So, should I report Juanita to her agency or professional body? Generally speaking, I should respect the client's right to self-determination and confidentiality, meaning that I would not make reports without the client's permission. I could discuss any concerns with my own supervisor, for instance, do I have any other reporting responsibilities? Also, is there another way to ensure that future clients are not subjected to risky practices?

Our legal and ethical obligations depend on the type of work that we are doing. Assume that two children reported that a social worker had physically mistreated them. You may need to share this information with their parents so the parents could also be involved in the decision about how to respond.

Remedial and Corrective Responses

Speaking with colleagues about impairments or incompetence can be challenging. Ideally, our colleagues will acknowledge the concern and take remedial steps; however, our colleagues may respond with denial, anger, confusion, or rationalization. As a new social worker, if you do not feel comfortable discussing these concerns with a colleague, speak with your supervisor for guidance and support. There are various of models of practice that may be helpful for engaging colleagues in these types of conversations. The Transtheoretical Model of Change, for instance, may be useful for helping colleagues raise awareness and think about potential impairments (Prochaska & Norcross, 2018). Rather than labeling colleagues as "incompetent" or "ill," for instance, we can focus on particular behaviors that raised the concerns. Motivational Interviewing provides strategies such as developing a collaborative partnership, focusing on self-efficacy, offering choices, and building on the other person's internal motivation to help them make changes (Hepworth et al., 2017). Whenever engaging colleagues about concerns related to competence or impairment, the focus should not be on punishment or retribution. Focus on corrective actions such as how to restore competence and how to ensure that clients receive safe, effective services. Support the use of restorative processes, such as mediation and learning discussions (Barsky, 2017a). Avoid adversarial processes, such as debates or arguments. The purpose of engaging your colleague is not for you to provide therapy or counseling, but to encourage the colleague to seek appropriate help.

Unjustified Allegations

Standard 2.10(e) recognizes that not all allegations of unethical conduct are justified. It guides us to defend colleagues who are unjustly charged with unethical conduct, including incompetence or impairment. Advocating on behalf of an unjustly charged colleague can be daunting. Assume that you think your agency's administration is attacking a colleague's competence based on racial bias. You know you should speak up on your colleague's behalf, but you fear retribution from administration. This is not an ethical dilemma because you have a clear obligation to defend colleagues who are unjustly charged. However, it is an issue of ethical distress. As with other issues of ethical distress, it may be helpful to identify and work with others who share your concerns. They may be able to offer moral support and strategies. They may also be willing to help you and your colleague advocate with administration. For another scenario involving an unjust charge against a colleague, see Box 6.5.

BOX 6.5

IMPAIRMENT OR DISCRIMINATION

RBG Justice provides advocacy services for families that have been denied social assistance. Social work advocates frequently need to travel to conduct home visits and to attend appeals processes. RBG's program director recently told one of the advocates, Augusta, that she needs to retire because she has epilepsy and it is too risky for her to drive. Sherell, a social work field student, thinks the program director is discriminating against Augusta based on a disability. Sherell would like to advocate on Augusta's behalf but fears that she could fail her field placement if the agency thinks she is a troublemaker. What ethical obligations should Sherell consider? Who could she consult for help with decision making? How could she raise her concerns in a professional, assertive manner, while also minimizing the risks of retaliation from the agency?

CONCLUSION

Within the social work profession, we value competence because we want to ensure that our clients and communities receive safe and effective services. When offering services to clients, we need to explain the types of services that we are competent to provide. When clients need services that go beyond our competence, we should be honest about the limits of our competence and offer to connect them with professionals who have the requisite knowledge, skills, and credentials to serve them. As we will see in Chapter 13, staying within our areas of competence is a key risk management strategy: if we want to prevent harm to clients and avoid lawsuits or other grievances, we need to know the limits of our competence and practice only within those limits.

As social workers, all of us are expected to have certain generalist competencies, including the abilities to engage, assess, intervene, and evaluate our practice. Some competencies are specific to the types of work we do and the contexts where we practice. Some areas of practice and services require advanced training and credentials. One of the wonderful aspects of social work practice is that we are always learning and developing our knowledge and skills. At the same time, we need to be aware of any personal concerns that may hinder our ability to practice. By being aware and taking corrective actions as soon as possible, we can ensure that our clients and communities continue to receive safe and effective services. Social work is not an individual sport or practice. We must be open to accessing help from supervisors, colleagues, referral sources, and other helping professionals. Accessing help assists us, as well as our clients and the communities we serve.

DISCUSSION QUESTIONS AND EXERCISES

1. *Impairment or Incompetence*: For each of the following situations, identify whether the ethical issue is related to an impairment, a lack of competence, and, or a lack of credentialing:
   a. Garth provides family therapy even though he is not licensed and has no prior family therapy training.
   b. Lorinda conducts ethnographic interviews for a study on child sexual abuse. During the interviews she starts to cry because the stories trigger memories of her own abuse.
   c. During a job interview, Zofia tells a prospective employer that she has excellent community organization skills. In fact, she experiences panic attacks when she has to speak to large audiences and she is not familiar with evidence-based community organization strategies.
2. *Developing Competence*: Your supervisor says she would like you to facilitate a mutual aid group for caretakers of adolescents with schizophrenia. Identify 5 competencies that you currently possess that

you would need to facilitate this group. Identify 5 competencies that you would need to develop to facilitate this group. Describe 3 strategies you could use to develop the knowledge and skills that you will need to facilitate the group.

3. *Rural Community*: A regional hospital refers Nancy and her infant daughter, Amelia, to see you for support services. Ever since Amelia was diagnosed with Down syndrome, Nancy has been having difficulty coping. She is uncertain about how to raise a child with Down syndrome, she questions whether she is responsible for Amelia having Down syndrome, and she is worried about "who will take care of Amelia when I grow old and die." Although you have worked with children, you have not worked with children with Down syndrome. You do not feel as if you have the knowledge or skills to help Nancy and Amelia. At the same time, you live in a rural community and there are no other social workers within 150 miles who have the proper expertise to help them. You do not want to ignore clients in need or put them at risk. Analyze your options and explain how you would respond to this referral.

4. *Moral Strength*: Your field instructor asks you to work with a client who recently had both legs amputated due to necrotizing fasciitis (a flesh-eating bacteria). Assume that you do not think you have the knowledge or skills to serve this client. You also feel afraid to tell your supervisor that you do not feel competent to help this client because it could affect your grades and ability to pass the field placement. What are the relevant ethical obligations to consider? How can you meet these ethical obligations and manage the ethical distress that doing so may cause?

5. *Technologically Challenged*: You are working in an agency that uses electronic records. One of your colleagues, Alfie, is not very proficient with the technology. You have noticed that he miscodes certain information and leaves many fields blank. You offer to help Alfie enter client data more effectively. He responds angrily, "Mind your own business." Why might Alfie respond with anger when you have simply offered help? Explain what steps you would take next and provide your rationale.

6. *Referrals*: For each of the following client situations, identify whether you are competent to provide the services or whether you would refer the client(s) to another professional. If you would refer the client(s) to another professional, identify what type of credentials the other professional should have (according to your state's licensing or credentialing bodies).
    a. Alyssa requests individual counseling to help her with time management.
    b. Evgeni and Sasha want you to help them decide whether to pay off their credit card debts before paying rent or investing money in retirement savings.

    c. A community association asks you to lobby the state legislature to fund a new public school for the community.

    d. You have been helping Miguel deal with anxiety. He asks his physician for medical use marijuana. The physician wants you to provide a diagnosis documenting that he has an anxiety disorder.

    e. Uri identifies as "gender nonbinary." They ask if you can provide integrative therapy (a combination of counseling, meditation, massage, and other holistic mind-body approaches) to help them gain a greater sense of peace and psychological freedom.

7. *Punitive vs. Restorative*: Quinn is a research assistant for a social work professor. After publishing one of their studies on the effectiveness of school mentoring programs, the journal editor discovers that the data analysis is flawed and the conclusions are not supported. Although Quinn had good intentions, he did not have appropriate statistics knowledge and skills to conduct the required analysis. Provide two examples of punitive responses that Quinn could receive for his lack of competence. Identify two examples of restorative justice approaches that could be used to respond to this situation.

8. *Student Competence*: Stella is a social work student. Stella's field instructor, Brianna, has assigned Stella to facilitate psychoeducational groups for teens who have engaged in bullying behaviors. To evaluate Stella's competence for her midterm evaluation, Brianna observes Stella facilitating a group. Brianna notes that Stella demonstrates low levels of empathy and has difficulty engaging group members. In addition, Stella is not assessing group dynamics, managing group conflict, or conveying information in an effective manner. Brianna informs the field coordinator that she wants to terminate Stella's field placement because her lack of skills and knowledge is putting clients at risk. What type of corrective action plan could Brianna, Stella, and the field coordinator put in place so that Stella can build her competence without putting clients at risk?

9. *Scope of Practice*: Arvid is a medical social worker. Many nurses are unavailable for work due to a communicable infection that has spread across the hospital. Arvid's supervisor, Darleen, has asked him to assist with nursing functions, including preparing patients for surgery, monitoring and changing patients' intravenous bags, and checking patients' pulse and blood pressure. Arvid advises Darleen that these functions fall outside his scope of practice. Darleen responds that she would not ask him to assume these duties, but their primary duty is to their patients and this is an emergency situation. What ethical standards should Arvid consider? Based on these ethical considerations, how should Arvid respond to Darleen's request?

10. *Information versus Professional Advice*: Providing information to clients means giving them facts. Providing professional advice means giving

people opinions or making recommendations based on professional knowledge and judgment. As social workers, we may provide basic information about legal, financial, or medical issues if we are knowledgeable about these topics and can provide accurate information; however, we should not provide legal, financial, or medical advice because these types of advice fall outside our areas of competence and scope of practice. For each of the following situations, describe whether the social worker is offering information or advice.

a. Jung tells a client with a sore abdomen that he has appendicitis.

b. Uli tells a client that a felony is a more serious crime than a misdemeanor.

c. Amir explains that the stock market has been volatile in the past year.

d. Harriet encourages a client to plead guilty for shoplifting so she will receive a less serious sentence.

e. Bella suggests that a client pay down her mortgage before paying off her credit card debts.

f. Anya informs a pregnant client with concerns about Tay-Sachs disease that she can talk with her obstetrician about the possibility of genetic testing.

11. *Self-Care*: Identify 3 examples of personal self-care and 3 examples of professional self-care that you currently practice on a regular basis. Identify 2 additional examples of personal and professional self-care that you think would be helpful. How do you think these examples would be particularly helpful for you? What challenges, if any, would you need to overcome in order to put these examples into practice?

12. *Dealing with Defensiveness*: You have a field placement with a court diversion program where clients charged with criminal offences are referred to your agency for psychosocial assessments, victim-offender mediation, and other problem-solving services. You have recently been mugged by someone with a knife. Your supervisor suggests that you take time off for self-care. She is concerned that working with people charged with similar acts of violence could be traumatizing. Returning to work without taking time off for self-care could also affect your ability to serve clients. Why might you feel defensive about your supervisor's suggestion? In other words, what fears or concerns might you be experiencing in response to being asked to take a leave of absence? How could you manage these fears or concerns? What positive messages could you tell yourself in terms of your values, what you want to gain from your field experience, your supervisor's intentions, your abilities, and your choices? When deciding about whether to take a leave of absence, which standards of the NASW Code should you consider?

7

Cultural Competence, Humility, Awareness, and Responsiveness

LEARNING OBJECTIVES

Upon successful completion of this introduction, you will be able to

- approach practice with diverse clients and communities through the lenses of cultural humility, awareness, and responsiveness.
- identify and avoid microaggressions, disrespect, and other potential violations of the NASW Code of Ethics in relation to culture and diversity.
- manage ethical issues that arise when social workers, coworkers, clients, or research participants have conflicting values.

When social workers consider the ethics of working with people from different cultures, they often use concepts such as **cultural competence**, **cultural humility**, cultural awareness, and cultural responsiveness. For the purposes of this chapter, *culture* refers to a group of people with shared values, beliefs, norms, rituals, traditions, language, history, social structures, foods, and/or art forms (NASW, 2015). For ease of reference, I will refer to this list of values, beliefs, and so on as *cultural attributes. Cultural groups* may be identified by their age, sex, gender, race, ethnicity, nationality, religion, immigration or refugee status, disability, marital status, socioeconomic status, or other social identity grouping. Standard 1.05(a) of the NASW Code of Ethics (2021) states, "Social workers should demonstrate understanding of culture and its function in human behavior and society, recognizing the strengths that exist in all cultures." This strengths-based standard operationalizes the core social work values of *competence* and *respect for the dignity and worth of all people.* In terms of competence, Standard 1.05(b) suggests that we should "demonstrate knowledge that guides practice with various cultures" and "demonstrate skills in the provision of culturally informed services that empower marginalized individuals and groups." The second part of Standard 1.05(b) states, "Social workers must take action against oppression, racism, discrimination, and inequities, and acknowledge personal privilege." This statement operationalizes the ethical principle of promoting **social justice**, including antiracism, diversity, **equity**, and inclusion. It is not sufficient that we avoid engaging in racist, oppressive, or discriminatory acts; we have a positive duty to help our clients by addressing various forms of racism, oppression or discrimination that they may be experiencing.

The concept of *cultural competence* indicates that social workers should possess specific knowledge, practice skills, and attitudes that are required to work effectively with people from particular cultural groups. Thus, if you were working with a Latin American family that was dealing with divorce, you should know about that culture's beliefs, rituals, and expectations regarding marriage, divorce, and child rearing. Further, you should be able to select models of practice and intervention skills that are culturally appropriate in light of the family's Latin American background. In terms of attitude, you should embrace learning about Latin American culture and respect cultural differences rather than judge this culture as better or worse than your own culture (Sue et al., 2016). You should also understand that there is no single Latin American culture: there are many differences depending on the clients' country of national origin, socioeconomic status, level of acculturation, and other within-group differences. Culture affects how people seek and make use of help. When working with clients from diverse cultural backgrounds, it is helpful to explore how cultural attributes may be affecting their ability and preferences for making use of our help. Ultimately, cultural competence leads to better outcomes for the people and communities we serve (NASW, 2015).

To develop cultural competence, we may cultivate relevant knowledge, skills, and attitudes through various means: attending classes, conferences, or online training; reading cultural research and scholarly literature; engaging in supervision or consultation with people who are knowledgeable about the culture; and learning while working with clients from the particular background (NASW, 2015). Cultural competence is not simply about tolerating differences, but rather accepting, embracing, and celebrating them. Cultural competence requires the ability to put cultural knowledge and awareness into practice through the use of culturally informed skills and helping processes. In addition to helping clients on an individual basis, cultural competence also requires us to engage in activism and advocacy to redress discrimination and promote social justice (NASW, 2015).

If you are relatively new to social work practice with diverse populations, you might wonder, "How can I possibly be expected to know about every culture or every diversity group?" True, there are so many groups that this seems like an impossible expectation. You might also contemplate whether you can simply refer clients to social workers from their own background. While this may be a solution on a case-by-case basis, it does not resolve the basic ethical imperative that social workers should be prepared to serve people of diverse backgrounds. Refusing to serve clients who are culturally different from ourselves may constitute discrimination. Even if you have good intentions in referring diverse clients, they may perceive these referrals as prejudice or rejection. Rather than simply referring diverse clients to other social workers, consider whether you can effectively serve them with the help of ongoing supervision, consultation, and training. In addition to general diversity education, we can learn from culture-specific training and from consultation with experts in particular cultures. As discussed later, we can also use ethnographic interviewing to learn from our clients.

The notion that we may become competent in another person's culture may sound arrogant or presumptuous. Can we truly appreciate another person's culture by simply reading a book or attending a training? How do we know whether the cultural competencies that we are learning are valid or whether they are based on biases or inappropriate assumptions (Berger & Miller, 2021)? Rather than viewing cultural competence as an outcome, it may be better to view it as an ongoing process. We need to use a combination of approaches to work toward higher levels of cultural competence. The process is fluid, as we continue to learn throughout our careers and interactions with various clients. Cultural competence not a binary choice (i.e., that one is either culturally competent or incompetent); rather, we should think of cultural competence as a continuum. Although we have some level of cultural competence now, it is important to continue to strive for greater and greater competence.

In 2021, the NASW introduced the term *cultural humility* into the NASW Code of Ethics. Standard 1.05(c) defines cultural humility in terms of "engaging in critical self-evaluation (understanding their own bias and engaging in self-correction), recognizing clients as experts in their own culture, committing to lifelong learning, and holding institutions accountable for advancing cultural humility." Cultural humility starts with the premise that we do not know everything about another person's culture and we need to hone our knowledge, skills, and attitudes to work with them in a culturally appropriate manner. Cultural humility fits with virtue ethics, inviting us to be humble about what we know (Caron et al., 2020). Being humble means that I do not see myself as better than anyone else. It also means that I am ready to question what I think I know and I am open to learning from others (Higgins, 2021). If I am not Bangladeshi, I may learn about Bangladeshi culture but I can never fully appreciate the experiences of living as a Bangladeshi individual in the same way as a person who is Bangladeshi. I have an outsider's view rather than an insider's view. Rather than presenting myself as an expert in my client's religion, traditions, worldviews, experiences, and so on, I present myself as a learner. I reflect on my biases and I strive to maintain an open heart and open mind. Even if I have prior experience working with people from Bangladesh, I do not assume that my prior knowledge applies uniformly to each new client. I treat my clients as experts in their own lives. To demonstrate humility and respect, I acknowledge that I do not understand Bangladeshi culture in the same sense as my clients; I value the opportunity to learn from them (NASW, 2015; NASW Code, S.1.05[c]). Cultural humility requires an ongoing commitment to reflection, self-awareness, and learning (Thurber, 2020).

To avoid making assumptions about another person's culture, I need to be aware of ways that culture affects my own values, beliefs, and other cultural attributes. What may seem "normal" or "healthy" within my life experience may or may not be normal or healthy for people from different backgrounds. For example, given my life experiences and social identities, I believe that parenting responsibilities should be shared equally, regardless of the parents' genders. When I work with clients who value gender-specific roles in parenting, I need to be aware of our cultural differences and avoid imposing my values on them (Maschi & Leibowitz, 2018). I also need to explore any biases, prejudices, fears, and areas of ignorance that may affect my ability to work effectively and ethically with people from diverse backgrounds (NASW, 2015). Rather than assuming that I have no biases, I acknowledge that I may have learned biases such as racism, sexism, homophobia, xenophobia, or ableism. By acknowledging these biases, I can work to ensure that they do not inhibit my ability to engage, assess, and respond to the people I serve in a culturally appropriate manner (Rogerson et al., 2021). As I work with clients from different backgrounds, I consider how various systems affect their belief systems, their sense of self, their family and social relationships, and the situation that brought them into services (Gottlieb, 2020).

Despite our best efforts to incorporate cultural humility in our work, we may make mistakes. For instance, we may make assumptions based on stereotype or we may use culturally insensitive language. Making mistakes is part of the learning process. We need to have the humility and moral courage to acknowledge our mistakes, apologize, learn from them, and do better in the future (Gottlieb, 2020).

Cultural awareness refers to being mindful of similarities and differences between people from diverse backgrounds. To employ cultural awareness, we need heightened consciousness of our own cultural characteristics as well as those of the people we are serving. The focus of our awareness depends on the type of work we are doing. For instance, if we are providing services through technology, we need to be aware of how the clients' culture may affect their ability to access and use the technology (NASW Code, S.1.05(d)). I may be comfortable communicating through virtual reality; however, my client may not be so comfortable due to factors related to age or socioeconomic status. Cultural awareness includes being aware of issues related to social location, power, privilege, and oppression (NASW, 2015).

As a white male (my social location), I have many privileges: when I apply for a job, I do not have to wonder whether my prospective employer might discriminate against me by assuming that I will need time off to have a baby; when my car is pulled over by police, I do not have to fear that police are going to assume that I am dangerous because of my race and therefore be more likely to shoot me; and when I read mainstream history books, I do not have to be concerned that people of my gender and race will be excluded. Even as I strive to understand the experiences of discrimination and oppression of those who come from different backgrounds, I know that I cannot fully appreciate their experience. As a gay man, I understand the impact of homophobia on my life; however, I do not assume that my experiences of homophobia are the same as a client's experiences of racism or xenophobia. When clients share their experiences of discrimination or oppression, I gain insight into their lives. I show gratitude to my clients for helping me understand them. I constantly strive for better and better understanding. To heighten my self-awareness, I can make use of supervision or peer consultation.

Cultural responsiveness refers to using our awareness of cultural dynamics and engaging with clients in a manner appropriate to their values, beliefs, traditions, and other cultural attributes. Assume we are helping an Indigenous community develop strategies to enhance their rates of high school and college graduation. Some community members question the value of "White man's education" given their experiences in school: being treated with disrespect by non-Indigenous teachers and students; exclusion of Indigenous worldviews and history in the school curriculum; and lack of connection between what they were learning and the careers that they expected to have. By striving to appreciate these concerns from the community's perspective, we can partner with them in a culturally responsive manner. For example, we can work together to promote greater use of Indigenous educators, school climates that are more respectful and supportive, and curricula that attend to the needs and expectations of Indigenous students. My actions with and on behalf of the community are informed by their values, beliefs, and other cultural attributes.

Now that we have explored the meanings of cultural competence, humility, awareness, and responsiveness, the following section provides an opportunity to explore how to implement them in an aspirational manner; that is, how can we promote the best practices and ideals of working with clients from diverse backgrounds? In contrast, the section on violations provides examples of social work behaviors that fall below the baseline of acceptable practice in terms of cultural awareness and responsiveness. This section highlights actions that we should avoid because they are disrespectful, dismissive, or harmful. In the next section, we will consider how to manage value conflicts based on cultural differences. The final section provides guidance on how to foster a culture of antiracism, diversity, equity, and inclusion in our work environments. Throughout this chapter, reflect on the scenarios through a cultural lens: How are my thoughts, feelings, and reactions related to my social location and the cultural groups to which I belong?

CULTURAL HUMILITY AS AN ETHICAL ASPIRATION

Cultural humility is a lifelong commitment and process rather than an outcome to be attained in a fixed period of time (Abe, 2020). Because we are continuously striving to better understand our client's culture, cultural humility is an aspiration.

When we begin work with clients, we may not know everything that we need in order to provide services in a culturally responsive manner. Perhaps the most fundamental element of culture humility is caring. When we truly care for our clients, we want to understand them from their perspectives. We want to honor their values, beliefs, and other cultural attributes. As we learn about our clients, we also engage in self-reflection, learning how we and our clients are similar in some ways and different in others (Abe, 2020).

Assume you have read scholarly articles suggesting that Chinese people traditionally value harmony and, therefore, may avoid dealing with conflict in a direct manner. You have read research suggesting that responding to Chinese people with a firm "no" is culturally disrespectful. While there may be some truth to this information, it may or may not apply for a particular client with whom you are working. Also, if you do not understand the entire cultural context of these tidbits of information, you may misapply them. Cultural norms for managing conflict may be different, for instance, if the people involved are elders, siblings, children, or professionals from outside the family. Accordingly, even if you know something about the ways that Chinese people traditionally deal with conflict, you should maintain an open mind and learn from directly from your clients about how they deal with conflict. Avoid *stereotyping*, assuming all people from the culture are the same. Also, avoid *essentializing*, taking one piece of information about a diversity group and treating that piece of information as if it is the definitive aspect of their culture. People have a variety of different qualities. Avoid reducing any individual or group to just one trait to describe them. Strive to understand various aspects of their cultural values, norms, and other cultural attributes. To explore how cultural humility applies in an intercultural situation, see Box 7.1.

Ethnographic interviewing is a method of using cultural humility to engage with clients or research participants. In ethnographic interviewing, we adopt a

---

BOX 7.1

THE PATELS

The Patel family recently emigrated from India. Raj Patel (21) has recently been diagnosed with cancer. The physicians believe that Raj will die within a year and that no medical treatments would be effective in extending his life. Raj's parents say that they do not want Raj informed about his diagnosis. According to their belief system, it is better to protect Raj from the stigma and stress associated with the diagnosis. Sheila, a hospital social worker, believes that withholding crucial medical information from Raj would be a breach of his right to informed consent and self-determination. How do Sheila's professional values conflict with those of the family? How can Sheila and the medical team approach this situation using cultural humility, awareness, and responsiveness?

---

person-centered approach, allowing the speakers to tell their stories, share their views, and describe themselves as they wish. Rather than generalizing that everyone from a particular cultural group has similar characteristics, we learn about each person's unique experience and interpretation of their culture. We begin by explaining our purpose. "I want to make sure I am offering you appropriate services. If it is okay with you, I'd like to ask some questions to help me better understand your cultural background." If the client offers permission, we can then ask them to discuss their social identity. "How would you describe your cultural background?" or "How do you identify in terms of your sexual orientation?" We do not make assumptions. We ask for clarification to ensure that we are understanding accurately. "You said your parents taught you the value of 'respeto.' Could you please give me some examples of what you mean by respeto?" Rather than asking for an abstract definition, we ask for concrete examples or stories. After asking general questions about the client's culture, we may then ask questions about their values, norms, and other cultural attributes as they relate to the work we are doing with them. "I understand that your boss referred you to our program for help with alcohol use. As someone who identifies as Puerto Rican, I'm wondering how you feel about this referral." The client may choose to answer this invitation in a variety of ways, for instance, focusing on cultural beliefs about alcohol or discussing thoughts about a boss who refers a client for alcohol treatment services. When the client responds, we may demonstrate active listening by restating what the client says using the client's words. We avoid using different words because they may have different connotations than the client intended. We might start with broad questions such as, "What are some of the most important cultural values that you learned as a child?" We avoid asking yes/no questions, such as, "In the Puerto Rican community, are there lots of stigma around seeking help from social workers?" Closed questions tend to lead the discussion in a particular direction rather than empowering clients to choose how to respond and describe what they feel is most important. Closed questions may also be based on assumptions that do not apply to our clients' situation and experience.

When considering our clients' values, beliefs, traditions, and other cultural attributes, it is important to consider the intersectionality of their social identities; that is, the ways in which race, gender, religion, disability, and other aspects of diversity have complex and overlapping effects (Cottone et al., 2022). Assume that you are working with a client who identifies as a stutterer. The client's experiences of being a stutterer may be very different if the client is female versus male or nonbinary, lower versus higher economic status, Sikh or Muslim, and so on. Within some groups, for instance, stutterers may experience less support and more alienation than within others. Thus, it is vital to ask clients about various aspects of their social identity and how each has an influence on their values, beliefs, and other cultural attributes. When assessing intersectionality, we should also consider how racism, sexism, homophobia, religious bigotry, and other forms of discrimination are affecting the clients and communities we serve (NASW, 2015).

When meeting with clients from diverse backgrounds, remember to take time for self-reflection (Rogerson et al., 2021). Reflect on what you learned about yourself, including your reactions to the ways in which the client's values, beliefs, traditions, and so on are different from your own. Consulting with your supervisor may also assist with the reflection process. Supervisors can help you identify assumptions or biases that you may have held. They can also support you in your ongoing process of learning from your clients.

VIOLATIONS OF CULTURAL AWARENESS AND RESPONSIVENESS

The previous section describes cultural humility as an aspirational goal. In this section, we will consider specific violations of cultural awareness and responsiveness. By being aware of these violations, we are in a better position to avoid them; also, if we do engage in violations, we can apologize and correct for them in a timely and respectful manner. Key violations include showing disrespect, ignoring culture, imposing values or beliefs, and using culturally inappropriate assessments or interventions.

Showing Disrespect

Showing disrespect means treating others in an insulting or hurtful manner. To determine whether a particular act is disrespectful, we need to consider the perceived impact on the people affected by the act. Microaggressions are unintentional acts of disrespect (Sissoko & Nadal, 2021). In other words, people may feel disrespected whether or not we intended to act in a disrespectful manner. Microaggressions may be based on implicit bias (unconscious stereotypes, attitudes, or beliefs about certain groups). Examples of disrespect include

- misgendering (e.g., referring to a transgender woman as "he");
- labeling people rather than allowing them to self-identify (e.g., calling someone African American when they identify themselves as Black);
- speaking about culturally taboo topics in an insensitive manner or expecting clients to discuss them without first requesting permission (e.g., speaking the name of an ancestor with a client whose cultural beliefs suggest that using the name of a dead person disturbs their spirit);
- asking questions or making statements based on cultural assumptions or stereotypes (e.g., asking Asian Americans if they are good drivers; asking Jews if they would like to live in Israel);
- denying experiences of racism or oppression (e.g., telling Mexican Americans that their career success shows that racism is not a problem in this country);

- mimicking a client (e.g., imitating a person's accent or cultural mannerisms); and
- praising a person with a disability or mental health issue in a patronizing manner (e.g., "It's so inspiring that you, as a Blind person, were able to finish high school.").

Through *self-awareness*, we strive to communicate respectfully with clients, research participants, and others. Through *other-awareness*, we can alert ourselves to situations where others perceive our talk or actions to be disrespectful. We can then apologize, accepting responsibility, expressing remorse, and taking steps to avoid disrespect in future interactions. "I understand that my question about death was insensitive. I am committed to learning more about your culture and showing greater respect. Moving forward, I will ask for permission before we talk about potentially sensitive issues to ensure that I am respectful of your values and beliefs. Please let me know if there is anything else that I can do to make amends."

Ignoring Culture

Whereas showing disrespect is a form of *malfeasance* (violating an ethical duty by acting in a way that hurts another person), ignoring culture may be characterized as *nonfeasance* (violating an ethical duty by not acting in accordance with an ethical duty). As social workers, we have an ethical duty to consider the culture of the people we serve (Standard 1.05[a]). Taking culture into account not only shows respect for our clients; it also fosters more effective services.

According to the Golden Rule, we should "do unto others as we would have them do unto us." In Leviticus 19:18, this maxim is framed as "Love thy neighbor as thyself." Variations of the Golden Rule may be found in other religious scriptures and cultural teachings. Some people view the Golden Rule as a universal ethical principle, applying across all cultures and belief systems. After all, shouldn't we treat others in a positive manner, just as we would want others to treat us in a similar manner? Perhaps. Unfortunately, the Golden Rule has an element of color blindness. If we are to treat others as we would like to be treated, then we are ignoring our differences, including differences related to race, ethnicity, disability, religion, socioeconomic status, and so on. In contrast to the Golden Rule, the Platinum Rule suggests that we should "treat others as they would like to be treated." When I meet people in a professional capacity, I like to shake hands. When I meet a client who—for religious or cultural reasons—does not believe that shaking my hand is appropriate, I should respect my client by not shaking hands.

Examples of ignoring culture include

- assuming that the client's values, beliefs, and other cultural attributes are the same as those of the majority in your location (e.g., in the

United States, valuing individuality, believing that America is a land of opportunity, or celebrating Christmas);

- not including images of people from diverse backgrounds on your agency's website, brochures, office pictures, or artwork;
- conducting assessments without asking questions about culture or demographics;
- refusing to discuss the effects of racism, sexism, religious bigotry, or other forms of oppression (e.g., telling clients to accept personal responsibility for unemployment or other problems when at least part of the problem may be related to discrimination);
- advising clients that you treat everyone the same (e.g., informing clients that when you look at them you do not see color); and
- telling clients from different cultural backgrounds that you know exactly how they feel (e.g., assuming that your life experiences, opportunities, and stresses are the same as theirs).

The antidote to the problem of ignoring culture is not to assume that all of a client's concerns—or strengths—are associated with culture. We should be open to considering culture and provide clients with opportunities to discuss culture. Although cultural factors may be very important, we should also consider clients' individual strengths, needs, concerns, and differences.

Just as we need to consider ethical limits on the Golden Rule, we also need to consider limits on the Platinum Rule. Although we should consider how clients from diverse backgrounds would like to be treated, we may face ethical dilemmas when their wishes conflict with our other ethical and legal obligations. Consider some clients who ask you to develop a Whites-only support group because they feel that people of color are inferior. Although you have an ethical obligation to support client self-determination, following their request would violate your obligations to support social justice and counter racism.

Imposing Values or Beliefs

In social work, we often say that we should meet clients where they are. As Standard 1.01 of the NASW Code suggests, our primary professional obligation is to our clients, not to ourselves. When we impose our cultural values or beliefs on clients, we may be violating this standard, as well as the principles of cultural awareness and responsiveness.

As underscored throughout this volume, self-awareness and other-awareness are vital to managing ethical issues in a deliberate manner. You may value personal freedom, the ability to do what you want to do without interference from others. You may be working with a client who values the authority of their imam, priest, minister, or other spiritual leader. If you instruct this client to make up her own mind rather than follow the instructions of her spiritual leader, then you are imposing your values. Similarly, you may believe that corporal punishment hurts children and should never be used, whereas a client believes that corporal punishment needs to be used to promote respect and prosocial behavior. Although you may believe that you are right and the client is wrong, simply imposing your beliefs runs counter to the principles of cultural humility, respect, and self-determination.

Whereas cultural **absolutism** refers to the conviction that our own values and beliefs are superior to those of others, cultural **relativism** suggests that we need to understand other people's values and beliefs from their cultural frameworks. We should not be chauvinistic and we should not make value judgments based on our own worldviews. When a client observes the instructions of their spiritual leader, we should strive to understand this choice from the client's standpoint. Although some people may see heeding the instructions of a spiritual leader as a sign of weakness or disempowerment, the client may view her behavior as a sign of restraint, respect, and commitment.

By applying cultural relativism, we can validate our clients' values and beliefs. Validating their values, and beliefs, however, does not necessarily mean that we agree with them. Saying, "I understand that you grew up in a family where spanking was seen as an effective way to correct a child's behavior," does not mean that you believe spanking is effective. You are showing that you understand. You are with-holding judgment. You are not imposing your values and beliefs.

As we will see in the section on conflicting values and beliefs, there are situations in which we cannot simply validate and support clients' values and beliefs. We may need to discuss other ethical and legal obligations, including duties to protect people from serious harm. Although we should generally support a client's right to follow spiritual authority, for instance, we may be justified in intervening to protect a client who is in serious danger due to manipulation (e.g., by a cult leader). In the corporal punishment situation, we may generally respect a parent's right to use culturally sanctioned methods of child discipline; however, when the form of discipline amounts to child abuse (as determined by local laws), then we have a legal duty to report the situation to child protection authorities. We do not judge the parent's culture as bad or immoral; however, we do have a duty to help protect vulnerable children from abuse.

Examples of imposing values and beliefs include

- telling clients who value taking care of elders to start prioritizing their individual needs (e.g., by putting an elder in assisted living rather than taking care of the elder at home);
- requiring clients to recite prayers from our own religion;
- advising lesbian clients that same-sex relationships are sinful (Mason et al., 2022); and
- educating immigrants to assimilate into the mainstream local culture (e.g., by giving up rituals and traditions to fit in).

To avoid imposing values and beliefs, we can use a person-centered approach, showing interest in our clients' culture, learning from them, and taking the lead from them in terms of what they would like to change or achieve and what types of help they would appreciate.

Using Culturally Inappropriate Assessments or Interventions

When selecting assessment tools and models of intervention, we need to ensure that they are culturally appropriate for the people we are serving. Ideally, each assessment tool and model of intervention has been designed for people who have the same ethnicity, religion, age, gender, sexual orientation, and other cultural attributes as our clients. When certain tools and models have not been designed for our particular clients, we should consider whether they can be adapted for culturally appropriate use with our clients or whether we need to select more appropriate tools and models. We should also ensure that our models of intervention not only address cultural stresses and concerns, but also build on the strengths and resiliencies within the cultural group.

Consider the use of genograms for assessment purposes. Although genograms have been designed for many different family structures, traditional genograms are not inclusive of people who do not fit into binary definitions of gender and sexuality. In traditional genograms, males are represented by squares and females are represented by circles. Although transgender people could be represented by a circle in a square or a square in a circle, these symbols do not accurately represent the experiences and identities of transgender people. A transgender woman, for instance, does not identify as a man on the outside and a woman on the inside (a circle in a square). A transgender woman identifies as a woman. Other concerns with traditional genograms include absence of symbols for people who identify as gender fluid, queer, pansexual, asexual, two-spirit, and other nonbinary genders and sexualities. Rather than using traditional genograms, we need to develop genograms that are inclusive and respectful of the full range of genders and sexualities. Using a person-centered approach, we can allow clients to select which symbols that they want to use to identify their genders and sexualities (Barsky, 2020d).

Traditional family systems models contain cultural biases. For instance, they often assume that a nuclear family is the primary family unit (i.e., a two-parent family with children). In some cultures, the primary family unit includes grandparents, aunts, uncles, and other relatives. Family units may also include fictive kin, people who are considered family by love and social bonds even if they are not related by blood or marriage. Traditional family systems theories suggest that certain types of family structures are more functional than others; for instance, boundaries between parents and children should be flexible (not too weak and not too firm). This framework could lead us to assessing some families as dysfunctional just because the family has different boundaries. What may look like an enmeshed and troubled family to an outsider, may be a well-functioning family from a perspective within the culture. Accordingly, we should use family systems models that are inclusive of various cultures and do not assume that just one form of family structure is functional or preferred. In addition, family systems models should take environmental factors into account, including the experiences of racism or other forms of oppression (James et al., 2018).

When engaging in community organization, we need to ensure that we select culturally appropriate ways of engaging members of the community. Within cultures that value hierarchical structures, we may first approach leaders as defined by the community (e.g., elected officials, elders, or spiritual leaders). Within cultures that are more egalitarian, we may first approach people based on interest or need rather than status. Using a partnership model, we take our lead from the community as to what is a culturally appropriate approach, consulting with community members rather than making assumptions about what is best for them. Rather than acting as leaders or experts in the community's needs, we act as facilitators (Thurber, 2020). We do not assume that everyone in the community has the same beliefs, values, and needs. In addition to exploring the perspectives of the overall community, we explore the beliefs, values, and needs of various groups and individuals within the community.

In terms of research, we should consider which methods of research may fit best with various diversity groups. Regarding socioeconomic status, for instance, if we conduct research through websites or other technology, we may be excluding people who cannot afford or may not trust the technology. If we conduct quantitative research using survey questions with multiple-choice answers, we may need to ensure that the choices are inclusive of people from diverse backgrounds and identities. To be inclusive, we could pilot test the surveys with different groups and we could also include a choice for "other," allowing individuals to add their own desired response if the predetermined choices to not fit (Grinnell, 2021). Using a participatory action approach, we could include people from diverse backgrounds as partners in developing and implementing our research. Rather than a top-down approach in which we act as experts, we partner with our research participants and allow them to help with designing the research, including determinations about what research questions to study, what research methods to employ, how to gather data, and how to write, publish, and make use of the findings.

We want to avoid situations in which we base our research on stereotypes or assumptions. Further, we should be careful about potentially negative impacts from our research. Consider, for instance, the genetic research that was conducted based on blood samples from the Havasupai tribe in northern Arizona. Without informing research participants, researchers used the blood samples to study schizophrenia and migration patterns. In addition to not obtaining informed consent, the researchers did not respect cultural concerns about studying these topics (Marley,

2019). By empowering our research populations and participants as partners in our research, we can ensure that research is performed in a culturally informed and responsive manner. We can jointly choose research that supports cultural groups (including our understanding of their strengths and concerns) and avoid research that is culturally offensive. For another example of a culturally inappropriate intervention, please see Box 7.2.

BOX 7.2

IMMIGRATION SERVICES

Velma facilitates a psychoeducational group for immigrants from China, Vietnam, and Laos who identify as Hmong. As part of the program, Velma teaches group members American customs for dressing, grooming, and social etiquette so that they will fit into American society. She advises the group that adapting to American culture is important if they want to get jobs and avoid discrimination. She suggests that if anyone asks about their backgrounds, they should simply describe their country of origin and not try to explain what it means to be Hmong. Velma also introduces members to common American foods, suggesting that it is easier to give up their traditional cuisine and adopt local customs. In what ways are Velma's methods of helping this group culturally inappropriate? Using cultural humility, awareness, and responsiveness, how should Velma have approached working with this group?

VALUE CONFLICTS

Value conflicts are situations in which we and our clients, coworkers, or others are operating on differing values. Often, value conflicts stem from differences between our cultures, ethnicities, and other aspects of diversity. Because values define what we hold to be dear or deeply important to us, value conflicts can be very challenging. Assume that due to my spiritual background, I value the sanctity of life. My client, Warren, comes from a different spiritual background that values personal dignity and choice—even over life. Warren is suffering severe pain from a malignant tumor. His condition is incurable. Physicians suggest he will die within 6 months. He asks me to assist in ending his life. On the one hand, I value life. On the other hand, I value respect for the dignity and worth of all people, including the right of clients to make self-determined choices. I do not want to impose my values on my client and I have a professional duty to provide services to my client. Still, if I assist with his dying process, I am contravening my values.

As social workers, we should respect our client's values. At the very least, we should show compassion and understanding. "I understand your desire to die with dignity. You're not only suffering physically, but you've also lost a lot of independence and the ability to engage in meaningful activities." In some instances, having a values conflict does not mean that we need to act in a way that contravenes our values. If Warren had not asked me for assistance in dying, for instance, I could respect his choice without having to take active steps to facilitate his dying. I could be there for him and, as a social worker, I could continue to assist him in other ways. Because Warren did ask me for assistance with dying, I have an ethical duty to provide some type of help. If I live in a jurisdiction where there is a legal process to facilitate dying with dignity, then I could provide him with referrals to health professionals who work within that system (Wiebe et al., 2018). By connecting Warren with appropriate services, I am prioritizing my values for service and respect for my clients. I do not impose my value for the sanctity of life on my client. Even referring Warren to other professionals may feel as if I am going against my values. I may need to work through these personal-professional value conflicts by speaking with my supervisor.

So, how do I respond if I live in a jurisdiction where medical aid in dying is not legal? I can educate Warren about local laws. I can also help Warren consider other options, for instance, if he is in pain, what are the options for pain management and palliative care? If Warren lacks meaningful activities, I may be able to work with Warren to identify meaningful activities (e.g., spending time with friends or family). Although I do not assist Warren with terminating his life, my justification is not because of my values, but because of the laws.

The concept of *cultural relativism* suggests that we need to understand people's values and ethical choices in the context of their own culture (Churchill, 2020). Rather than judging a client's choices as if I was making a decision, I need to consider the client's values, beliefs, situation, and experiences. Assume you are working with Alma, a client who tells you that she has been going to work every day even though she has a highly contagious disease. You are concerned that she is putting other people at risk. Your values tell you that caring for the health and welfare of one's work colleagues is important. It may seem as if Alma values going to work more than caring for her colleagues. Note, however, that the two of you may be coming from different sociocultural backgrounds. If you have a job that provides paid sick leave, then it may be relatively easy for you to miss work when you are sick. If Alma is paid only for the time that she works and does not have sick leave benefits, then she may need to work even when she is sick. If she does not have savings, then missing work may mean that she has no money for food or other necessities for herself and her family. By understanding her situation more fully, you can appreciate why she is making particular choices. You can then problem solve with her to develop a better solution: for instance, advocating for her to receive sick benefits, identifying other sources of financial support, or determining whether there is a way for her to continue to work without putting herself or her colleagues at risk (e.g., working remotely).

Sometimes, we need to help families, organizations, or community groups manage value conflicts between individuals or subsystems. Consider, for instance, a culturally based community group that invites you to help fundraise for scholarships for people who could not otherwise afford college. Some community members want the scholarship money to be available for anyone in the community, regardless of gender. Other members suggest that the funding should only be open to men because they are the ones who will need well-paying jobs to take care of their families. Both groups value education; however, the first group values egalitarianism and the second group values gender-specific family roles with men as breadwinners and women as nurturers. So, how would you help the community deal with this conflict? You will need to consider your role. Have you been hired to act as a neutral facilitator to help the group determine how to proceed? Alternatively, is your role to advocate for particular values, such as social justice, equality, or empowerment? If your role requires you to be neutral, then you can facilitate discussion around the issues and encourage the group to develop a solution that works for everyone; however, neutrality means that you should not advocate for particular values or solutions (Barsky, 2017a).

CONCLUSION

As with other ethical obligations, the duties of cultural competence, humility, awareness, and responsiveness are best achieved within a supportive organizational environment. To foster a culture of antiracism, diversity, equity, and inclusion, we need to work jointly with our colleagues and agencies to develop policies and practices that truly value people of various backgrounds and social identities (NASW, 2015). Through agency-based research, training, consultation, and conversation, we can expand our cultural knowledge and skills, building on the cultural strengths of our clients and helping them deal with challenges related to discrimination and oppression. We should commit ourselves and our organizations to develop culturally responsive services (NASW Code, S.1.05[c]), including services designed to meet the needs of populations that have been historically oppressed, underrepresented, and underserved. We need to ensure that our services are accessible to people of various backgrounds, reaching out to different groups to explore how our services can be made more accessible (Piggott & Cariaga-Lo, 2019). We need to nurture our moral courage to do what is right for the people we serve, even when faced by challenges within or outside our organizations. Antiracism, diversity, equity, and inclusion should be infused in all aspects of our organizations— not only in service delivery, but also in the organization's hiring, development, and retention of staff, community relationships, and strategic planning. When we have greater diversity within our organizations, we can learn from one another and make sure that we are responsive to the diverse groups that we serve (Elässer et al., 2020). When planning programs and determining policies, we should promote meaningful participation from clients and other representatives of diverse communities so that our decisions reflect their specific needs, concerns, wishes, cultures, and experiences (NASW, 2015). Finally, we need to develop heightened consciousness of the ways that cultures interact, including the cultures of our clients, communities, practice settings, and ourselves.

Promoting a culture of antiracism, diversity, equity, and inclusion is not just a belief or an act. It requires an ongoing commitment that we build into our character. As philosopher Ralph Waldo Emerson suggested, "Sow a thought and you reap an action; sow an act and you reap a habit; sow a habit and you reap a character; sow a character and you reap a destiny." When we sow antiracism, diversity, equity, and inclusion into our destiny, everyone flourishes.

DISCUSSION QUESTIONS AND EXERCISES

1. *Conceptual Comparison*: What are the similarities and differences between the following four concepts: cultural competence, cultural humility, cultural awareness, and cultural responsiveness. Assume that you are working with Wasuda, a client who identifies as Blind and Kenyan. Wasuda has asked you to help her with parenting skills. She has a 5-year-old daughter that she describes as rambunctious. How would you apply the four cultural concepts to your work with Wasuda?

2. *Self-Awareness*: For each of the following situations, rate the level of difficulty that you may have working with the client, organization, or community due to conflicting values or beliefs. Use a scale of 1 to 5, with 1 being very easy and 5 being very difficult. After rating each item, explain how you determined your numerical rating, including what aspects of your ethnicity, race, spirituality, gender, socioeconomic class, or other aspects of social identity and location are informing your values and beliefs.

   a. A client family comes from a culture in which adult children follow their parents' choices about whom to marry, what careers to pursue, and where to live.

   b. A community asks you to help them overturn a city bylaw that requires criminal background checks for people who want to purchase guns.

   c. An 85-year-old client asks you to assist with ending her life when the pain from her fatal health condition worsens.

   d. A foodbank wants to change its policies so that only people who can prove they are actively looking for work will be eligible to receive food.

   e. A social work supervisor expresses misogynistic attitudes, suggesting that men are better organizational leaders than women.

   f. A group member who identifies as genderfluid asks the group to refer to the member with the pronouns "they, them, and their."

3. *Cultural Assimilation and Integration*: When people from another country assimilate, they adopt the host country's values, worldviews, food, language, norms, and other cultural attributes, rejecting or losing cultural attributes from their country of origin. When people from another country integrate, they retain many aspects of their original culture and blend them with aspects of the new host culture. How long have you and your ancestors lived in this country? If your family came from another country, in what ways have you and your family experienced cultural assimilation or cultural integration? If your family identifies as Indigenous, what are some ways that your family continues to embrace Indigenous culture and what are some ways that your family has adopted different cultural qualities?

4. *Privilege and Oppression*: Identify a famous politician, artist, entertainer, educator, social worker, or athlete that you admire. What are this person's social identities in relation to race, ethnicity, nationality, spirituality, socioeconomic status, disability, sex, gender, sexual orientation, and other aspects of culture? Based on what you know about the person's social identities, what types of privilege and oppression do you think this person has likely experienced throughout life? How do the intersections of this person's social identities relate to the advantages and disadvantages that this person has experienced in life?

5. *Traditional Medicine*: Susi is working with Claudette, a client of Haitian descent who recently tested positive for HIV. Claudette refuses to take medications prescribed from mainstream doctors. She says she will use traditional Haitian root medicine because it is safer and much more effective. Susi consults with HIV experts. They tell her that the root medicine which Claudette is considering is ineffective. Susi believes that Claudette will develop full-blown AIDS if she does not begin antiretroviral therapy. She wonders whether Claudette should be declared mentally incapacitated because she is rejecting life-saving treatment. Identify two possible responses from Susi that violate the principles of cultural awareness and responsiveness. Describe how Susi could approach working with Claudette in a culturally appropriate manner.

6. *Exclusive Forms*: You are meeting with a new client and completing your agency's online intake forms. The form has dropdown menus for demographic information such as ethnicity, religion, and gender. Your client identifies as Catalonian, humanistic, and genderqueer. None of these categories exist in the dropdown menus. The closest categories in the menus are Latino/a, no religion, and transgender. There is no option for "other." How should you complete the intake forms and what is your ethical reasoning?

7. *Access*: Hari works for a mental health agency. He notices that the agency has very few clients of Filipino descent even though the surrounding

community has a large number of Filipinos. When he asks his supervisor about doing outreach to the Filipino community, the supervisor suggests that their primary obligation is to their clients and that they cannot divert resources to serve people who are unwilling to come into the agency. What are Hari's ethical obligations? How might Hari persuade his supervisor to address concerns about potential cultural barriers to service?

8. *Groups*: You are designing a support group for people with gambling addictions. How would you ensure that your group is designed in a culturally appropriate manner for helping clients from a particular diversity group (e.g., people who identify as Jamaican Americans, Baptists, older adults, or Deaf individuals)? Does the group need to be facilitated by a social worker who comes from the same diversity group as the clients? Why or why not?

9. *Violations*: Explain how the social worker in each of the following situations violates the principles of cultural awareness and responsiveness. Identify whether the violation is an example of demonstrating disrespect, ignoring culture, imposing values or beliefs, or using culturally inappropriate assessments or interventions.

   a. Violet comes from an individualistic culture. She tells a client from a **communitarian** culture that it is abnormal for parents to expect their children to live at home until they are married.

   b. Dietrich uses a lot of paraphrasing and reflection of feeling to show empathy and build trust with an Indigenous (Native American) client. Within the client's cultural frame, it is more appropriate to demonstrate listening through silence rather than through restating what the person has just said.

   c. When speaking with staff at a day program for people with autism, Gayla suggests that they should teach these clients social skills so they can interact better with neurotypical people.

   d. Raoul is facilitating a group for people who have experienced hate crimes. The group includes people who identify as either Japanese American, LGBTQ+, or Hindu. He informs the group of its rules for communication as follows: We will speak in respectful language; we will focus on what we have in common rather than what separates us; and we will focus on the future rather than the past.

   e. Edwina is working with a client who identifies as Thai. She refers the client to a Chinese community center so the client can connect with people from her own culture.

10. *Ethnographic Interviewing*: Identify a person from a culture or diversity group that is different from your own. Ask whether the person is willing to talk to you about cultural differences and similarities as part of a class project. If the person agrees, engage in a discussion about values, beliefs, traditions, and norms regarding parenting, how to raise children, and

what it means to have a good life. Share your values, beliefs, traditions, and norms so the two of you can identify commonalities and variances. If you and the person that you interview feel it is appropriate, you may share photographs or visit one another's neighborhoods to gain a sense of the similarities and differences in where you live. Take notes so you can share your findings with your class.

11. *Conflicting Values*: You are working with the Torres family. The parents affiliate with a church that accepts a strict interpretation of scriptures related to marriage. They believe marriage is a religious sacrament between a man and a woman. They also believe that sexual relations are appropriate only within the context of marriage. They have recently discovered that their 16-year-old daughter, Paulina, is experimenting sexually with friends from school. During a family counseling session, they threaten to punish Paulina for violating their religious scripture and disrespecting the family. Paulina says that she does not care about religion and that she is free to make her own choices about sex and religion. As a social worker, what is your role in helping family members manage their conflicting values? How do the concepts of cultural relativity and cultural absolutism apply?

12. *Beliefs versus Behaviors*: Ignacio works in a program that provides hot meals to older adults who are living independently but have limited financial means and social support. One of Ignacio's clients, Mr. Abdul, identifies as Muslim. Ignacio tells his supervisor that he does not like Islam because it goes against his religious beliefs, including a belief that only Jesus can save people from their sins and the Pope is an infallible leader, guided by the Holy Spirit. Ignacio says he will not impose his beliefs on Mr. Abdul, but he feels sorry for Mr. Abdul as being misguided by his religion. Analyze whether Ignacio has violated Standard 1.05 regarding cultural competence and humility. What should Ignacio's supervisor say to him in response to his disclosures about his religious beliefs?

13. *Assisted Living*: Mary and Terry reside in an assisted living facility for older adults. Mary has dementia and is no longer able to care for herself. During a case conference, the physician (Dr. Wright) decides to move Mary to a higher level of care, meaning that Mary and Terry would have to live in separate areas of the facility. Terry is adamant that they continue to live together. They have been married for over 40 years. You are a patient advocate for Terry and Mary. You understand that Mary needs a higher level of care and that hospital policy requires each person to live in the section of the facility that matches their level of need. What are the conflicting values in this situation? What is your role in helping the facility and deal with these conflicts? Apply the Framework for Managing Ethical Issues to analyze the nature of the conflict, the ethical

and legal obligations to consider, and possible options to manage the issues.

14. *Organizational Culture*: Reflect on your experiences with your current college, university, or social work program. In what ways does the organization foster a culture of antiracism, diversity, equity, and inclusion (ADEI)? In what ways could the organization do a better job of fostering a culture of ADEI? What are two specific actions that you could take in order the help the organization enhance its culture of ADEI?

8

Professional Boundaries, Dual Relationships, and Conflicts of Interest

---

LEARNING OBJECTIVES

Upon successful completion of this introduction, you will be able to

- explain your ethical duties in relation to maintaining appropriate boundaries, avoiding dual relationships, and avoiding conflicts of interests;
- maintain appropriate boundaries with clients, supervisors, supervisees, coprofessionals, and research participants (including physical, emotional, social, and spiritual boundaries);
- critically analyze professional situations to determine whether dual relationships should be avoided and when it may be ethically justified to enter dual relationships with appropriate safeguards; and
- identify potential conflicts of interests and implement strategies to avoid or manage them in an ethical manner.

As Standard 1.01 of the NASW Code of Ethics (2021) suggests, our primary commitment as social workers is to our clients. We have a *fiduciary relationship* with our clients, meaning that we are in a position of confidence, trust, and reliance. We are obliged to put client interests above our own. These **fiduciary** obligations stem from the nature of social worker-client relationships in which clients rely on workers to act in their best interests. We need to take precautions to ensure that our relationships with clients are structured in a manner that benefits clients and safeguards them from harm. To advance clients' interests and protect them from harm, we need to maintain professional boundaries, avoid dual relationships, and prevent conflicts of interests. In this chapter, we will explore ways to fulfill these ethical obligations, as well as ways to manage risks when it is difficult or impossible to avoid dual relationships and conflicts of interest.

MAINTAINING APPROPRIATE PROFESSIONAL
BOUNDARIES

Professional boundaries define what types of roles and behaviors are appropriate and inappropriate within the context of a particular professional relationship. In its simplest terms, maintaining appropriate boundaries means staying within our prescribed roles. As an ethics professor, it is appropriate for me to provide students with information about ethical social work practice, to engage them in discussions of challenging ethical dilemmas, and to grade their papers or presentations in relation to their ability to apply critical thinking and analysis. It is not appropriate for me to sell drugs, impose my personal beliefs, or berate students.

When we interact with clients in a manner that is uncharacteristic of our usual social work roles and behaviors, we are *crossing boundaries*. Boundary crossings are not necessarily ethical violations. Some boundary crossings may be helpful to our clients; however, boundary crossings may also entail significant risks to you and the client. **Boundary crossings** become **boundary violations** if there are problems with our intent or the effect of the crossing on the client (Gutheil & Brodsky, 2011; Madura, 2018). In terms of intent, the behaviors of social workers should be guided by what is in the best interests of the client's wellbeing. If I am acting in a manner to gratify myself—emotionally, financially, or otherwise—then I am not serving the client in a professional manner. Proper intent is important, but even with proper intent, a boundary crossing can turn into a violation. Suppose you offer to drive a client home, thinking that driving client would be better than having the client walk home in a snowstorm. If nothing bad happens, the client benefits from this boundary crossing. Although you mean well, if something inopportune happens to the client during the car ride, you may be held responsible for a boundary violation. Typically, social workers do not drive clients home. Unless the agency specifically authorizes you to drive clients, you are taking a chance and may be held liable for any resulting harm. Different ethicists, practitioners, and agencies have different views on whether practitioners should engage in boundary crossings with clients (Corey et al., 2019). Some believe that being too strict with professional boundaries causes more harm than good for clients. Others believe that strict boundaries are required to preserve effective helping relationships and to reduce risks to the worker, the agency, and the client (Zur, n.d.). When in doubt about whether a particular type of interaction with a client is appropriate or inappropriate, consult with your supervisor. For additional examples of boundary issues, please see Box 8.1.

Given that the nature of appropriate boundaries differs from context to context, different parts of the NASW Code of Ethics apply to social workers' relationships with clients versus their relationships with supervisees, coprofessionals, and research participants. The following sections explore the nature of boundaries in each of these contexts, as well as boundary issues that are not explicitly covered in the Code: boundaries between group members and boundaries in practice with communities and organizations.

BOX 8.1

PHYLLIS

Review the following situation and identify examples of boundary crossings and boundary violations. For each example, identify potential risks to the clients, Phyllis, and her agency. As you read through this chapter, consider what Phyllis could do to minimize the risks.

> Phyllis is a social worker of Navajo descent who works in social services for the Navajo nation. Because Phyllis lives in the community where she works, she often interacts with clients outside her work environment. When she meets clients in grocery stores or at the park, she will say hello and chat with them. She avoids discussing information shared by clients during her counseling sessions. In her personal time, Phyllis helps facilitate Blessingways, which are Navajo healing ceremonies. Sometimes, she encourages clients to participate in Blessingways. Phyllis does not require clients to participate in them. She lets clients know that the services she provides will not be affected depending on whether they attend the Blessingways. Sometimes, when clients are not eligible for aid from Social Services, Phyllis buys food or clothing for them. Occasionally, clients repay Phyllis when they have enough money. Sometimes, they help her around the office, tidying up, answering phone calls, and cooking lunch.

Social Worker–Client Boundaries

When working with individuals, families, and groups, we should explain our roles, so clients will have reasonable expectations about the nature of our relationship and how we will interact (NASW Code, Standard 1.03). In a counseling role, for instance, you might explain that you will help your clients assess their strengths and concerns and develop a plan of action to address those concerns. If a client requests legal or medical advice, you may explain that those types of help fall outside your scope of practice. You could also provide examples of the types of help that you do provide (e.g., stress management, communication skills training, or referrals to other professionals). If a client asks personal questions as if you were a friend, you could explain how your professional relationship differs from a social relationship. Maintaining appropriate boundaries promotes effective practice and protects clients from exploitation, biased treatment, misunderstandings, and other potential harms (Reamer, 2021c). In terms of maintaining appropriate boundaries, we should respect our clients' right to appropriate physical, sexual, psychological, social, and spiritual boundaries, as described below.

1. PHYSICAL BOUNDARIES

When determining "what is an appropriate physical boundary," we should consider questions such as how close we sit to a client; whether it is appropriate to touch, kiss, or hug a client; and whether physical interventions such as massaging, bathing, or physically restraining a client are appropriate social work roles. In most social work roles, our physical contact with clients is limited. Whereas physicians conduct physical examinations that involve touch and massage therapists touch clients as part of their treatment, social workers typically do not use touch for assessment or intervention. We rely primarily on communication through voice, body language, and writing. Standard 1.10 of the Code advises workers not to have physical contact with clients "when there is a possibility of psychological harm to the client" (S.1.10). The challenge is knowing when there is a possibility of psychological harm. Arguably, there is always a possibility. Consider touching a client's arm to offer condolence and support. The client reacts with fear due to a history of sexual abuse that was not previously disclosed. You meant well, but there was a risk.

Professors, field instructors, and agency supervisors may warn students and supervisees not to touch clients, and especially not to hug them. They may be trying to provide clear, black and white guidelines for what types of behavior are inappropriate. But is it okay to comfort a distraught client by holding hands or some other form of touch? Once again, it depends on the context. What does your agency policy say? What does the client's culture say? How might the client interpret your touch? What does your model of practice say? Suppose, for instance, that your agency subscribes to integrative mind–body therapy and this therapy requires you to touch a client in a particular manner. If the client has consented to the therapy, with full knowledge of its risks and benefits, you would be permitted to touch the client in accordance with your agreement with the client.[1] Still, you should be sensitive to the client's needs and refrain from touch that may be harmful. For beginning social workers, it may be safest to avoid types of physical contact that could be interpreted as sexual or unwanted. Even when deciding whether to shake hands, check the client's body language to see if handshaking is welcomed. Within some cultures, for instance, unrelated women and men are prohibited from having physical contact.

When determining the appropriateness of touch, we should consider what is generally accepted by our context of practice, as well as the possible interpretations of clients. A hospice for people with cancer may permit some forms of hugging between staff and clients. Although hugging is generally permitted, we should still assess how a particular client may interpret the hugging at a particular moment in time. If we think the client may perceive the hug as a sexual advance, then we should avoid hugging. If we think the client will interpret the hug as merely an expression of professional caring, then a hug may be appropriate. Before hugging

---

1. Given the potential risks of an intervention that involves touching, use risk management techniques such as documentation (e.g., ask the client to sign a consent form that includes the risks and benefits of the intervention, and document your reasons for using this particular intervention in the client's case records; Caudill, n.d.). Another risk management strategy is to have a second staff member present to observe the intervention.

clients, we could ask for permission. Requesting permission shows respect for client self-determination. Asking for permission, however, does not necessarily prevent a boundary violation. The client may feel pressured into consenting. Further, the client may interpret the hug as an invitation to develop a nonprofessional relationship, such sexual relationship or friendship (as described later). When I worked in a group home for children with emotional and behavioral challenges, we were permitted to hug a child under specific circumstances: if the child initiated the hug and if other staff were present. The group home informed all children and staff about these conditions, so everyone knew what was appropriate or inappropriate. To maintain clear boundaries and reduce risks, many social work organizations advise social workers not to hug clients.

2. Sexual boundaries

To establish trust and build good working relationships with clients, we may demonstrate empathy and concern. Being professional does not mean being dispassionate or indifferent. We may even express loving care to our clients. There is a difference, however, between love demonstrated through professional care and love that crosses into the realms of romantic intimacy, infatuation, or physical love. Standard 1.09 of the NASW Code specifically prohibits social workers from engaging in sexual relationships with clients and former clients. The prohibition against sexual relationships not only includes physical sexual relationships, but also interactions of a sexual nature that occur through verbal or written communication, including sexting or other forms of sexual communication through technology (Cottone et al., 2022; Reamer, 2021d).

The prohibition against sexual relationships with clients and former clients does not have exceptions when clients agree to the relationships. It is also no excuse to say that the relationship was based on "true love" or that the client benefited from the relationship. When clients make use of our services, they may be placed in vulnerable situations. They may become emotionally distraught or confused. They may confuse our professional help and caring with romantic love (Koocher & Keith-Spiegel, 2016).[2] They may view us as authority figures who can tell them what to do. They may feel they have to comply with our suggestions, perhaps viewing us as experts or guardians of their interests. By prohibiting sexual relationships with clients, the NASW Code makes it clear that protecting clients from harm is one of the worker's highest priorities.[3] Standard 1.09(c) says social workers "should not engage in sexual activities or sexual contact with former clients," indicating this

---

2. Clients may be particularly vulnerable if they are recently separated, lonely, or in an abusive relationship.

3. The NASW Code also advises social workers not to have sexual relations with people related to their clients, particularly if that might have a negative impact on a client. For instance, dating a client's former spouse may infuriate your client.

restriction lasts forever. We may not terminate work with clients to pursue romantic relationships with them. Further, we may not engage in sexual relationships with former clients, even many years after termination.

In addition to the prohibition against sexual relationships in the Code of Ethics, social work licensing laws and agency policies may also prohibit sexual relationships with clients. Despite knowing about these clear prohibitions, some social workers still have sex with clients. Although some workers knowingly exploit vulnerable clients to have sex, many slip into having romantic relations with clients without intending to get into such situations and certainly without intending to hurt their clients (Reamer, 2021a). To help prevent yourself from violating sexual boundaries with clients, make sure you are aware of any romantic feelings that you have toward your clients—or that your clients have toward you. Sexual attraction may lead you to feelings of anxiety, confusion, or guilt (Koocher & Keith-Spiegel, 2016). Romantic feelings toward clients may cloud your thinking and lead to inappropriate choices in the professional helping process. Make sure you deal with these feelings as soon as possible, through supervision, therapy, or other forms of support (Reamer, 2021a). When boundaries start to become unclear, take steps to restore appropriate boundaries. If a client emails you sexually explicit jokes or memes, let the client know that sharing these types of humor fall outside the boundaries of your professional relationship. If a client invites you to supper or a community event, discuss your professional role and why meeting socially would be inappropriate. If effective work becomes impossible due to a client's attraction to you, or vice versa, consider terminating your professional relationship and referring the client to another professional. If a client claims she became depressed or traumatized after having sex with you, it is no excuse to say that the client consented to or initiated the intimacy. As a professional, you are responsible for maintaining appropriate boundaries:

> Thank you for your invitation. I know we have established a good working relationship. I genuinely care about your wellbeing. Although the social worker-client relationship is meant to be a caring and safe relationship, it is a professional helping relationship, not a social or romantic one. If we were to meet socially, how might this affect our working relationship?

Although it should simply be common sense, the Code of Ethics also explicitly prohibits social workers from sexually harassing clients. Prohibited forms of sexual harassment include making sexual advances, requesting sexual favors, sharing sexualized images, and making jokes of a sexual nature, whether the harassment is communicated in-person or through technology (S.1.11). What constitutes sexual harassment should be judged, in part, from the client's perspective. You might plan to show a movie with sexual content to a group of clients, thinking that watching the movie will be therapeutic. If some clients could be offended by the movie, you should let them know the nature of the movie in advance, allowing them to decide whether or not to watch it. Likewise, you might write that a client is "promiscuous" in the client's records, thinking it is just an accurate description of the client's pattern of having sex with multiple partners. The client might view this term as judgmental and derogatory. When considering what to say to a client or what to write in a client's file, consider how the client might interpret and view your message. If the client might take offense, find a different way to convey your message.

3. PSYCHOLOGICAL BOUNDARIES

Boundaries help us create safe psychological spaces for clients to discuss their concerns (Cottone et al., 2022). By making boundaries explicit, we let clients know the parameters around what types of interactions are appropriate or inappropriate. When we inform clients that we are offering them a safe place to discuss their personal feelings and concerns, part of making the place truly safe is respecting client's psychological boundaries. During the beginning stages of work, for instance, we may start with relatively easier questions. When we do ask about topics that may cause the client to feel anxiety, embarrassment, or stress, we give clients control over whether and when they want to answer these questions. "If it's okay with you, I'd like to ask some questions about what led to the breakup with your partner." If a client expresses reluctance about discussing a particular topic, we can explore the client's reasons, but ultimately, respect the client's decisions. "It sounds like you still feel embarrassed about the breakup. You're the client and you're in charge of whether or not we discuss this issue." Topics that some clients may find particularly challenging to discuss include drug use, crime, personal or familial mental illnesses, death, and experiences of abuse or other forms of trauma. As social workers, we may have good reasons to open discussions about these issues; however, we should not ask questions about these topics if they are not related to the purposes of our work with our clients (Standard 1.07[a]). When we do engage clients in such conversations, we can continue to give them control over how much information they want to disclose. "We've set aside some time to talk about your end-of-life care. I understand that this can be a sensitive topic. Feel free to let me know when it's okay to continue the discussion, as well as when you might like to take a break." As the client shares information, we can validate their feelings and experiences, while also paying attention to any verbal or nonverbal cues indicating the client does not want to discuss these matters further.

Another way to maintain appropriate psychological boundaries with clients is to ensure that we use respectful language. Standard 1.12 prohibits the use of derogatory language with clients. We should not label clients as crazy, dysfunctional, or stupid—directly with clients, through technology, or in their records. Derogatory language may have negative effects on a clients' emotional wellbeing, as well as on our professional relationships with them. As with other boundary issues, we should consider the appropriateness of language from our clients' perspective. If a client self-identifies as Queer, for instance, then it is appropriate to refer to the client as Queer. For other clients, Queer may be interpreted as pejorative or demeaning. If we sense that a client is troubled by the language that we are using, we should apologize and ensure that we use more appropriate language moving forward.

4. SOCIAL BOUNDARIES

When establishing appropriate social boundaries with clients, we need to consider how social worker–client relationships are different from other types of relationships, such as parent–child relationships, friendships, or commercial business relationships. As social workers, our time with clients should be spent in a purposeful manner, working on our clients' goals and fulfilling the mandates of our agencies. Ordinarily, as social workers, we do not meet clients for lunch or social gatherings, we do not attend their weddings, we do not exchange birthday gifts, and we do not go on vacations together. Engaging in these types of activities could distract us from serving our clients and focusing on their needs. They could also confuse clients about the nature of our professional relationship, with the possibility of leading to dual relationships (as described later).

One of the most frequent questions among students in my introductory social work practice courses is whether it is appropriate to disclose personal information to clients. My not-so-simple answer is, "It depends." Some agencies and supervisors discourage social workers from self-disclosing in order to maintain clear boundaries with clients. Others provide more nuanced guidance about whether and when it is appropriate to self-disclose, allowing social workers to use their professional judgment based on the particular circumstances of the relationship with a client. Sometimes, when clients ask us personal questions, they are concerned about whether we are a good match to work with them (Reamer, 2021a). A couple who asks about questions about your age or marital status, for instance, might be interested in whether you have sufficient knowledge and life experience to help them. A potential advantage of self-disclosing is that it fosters trust (Gutheil & Brodsky, 2011). When working with client with substance abuse problems, disclosing that you are in recovery may help the client feel connected with you. One of the risks of self-disclosure is that the client may start to see the relationship as more of a friendship rather than a professional helping relationship. In addition to taking time away from focusing on the client's concerns, self-disclosure could also lead to a breakdown in trust. Assume that you self-disclose having mental health issues. The client might view this information as a weakness rather than a strength. Alternatively, your self-disclosure could signal that it is safe for the client to share personal mental health concerns with you. When you are unsure about whether to disclose personal information with your clients, consult your supervisor. Your supervisor can help you assess the potential benefits and risks of self-disclosure. If self-disclosure is motivated by your need for validation or support from the client, then self-disclosure would be inappropriate.

As noted earlier, whereas boundary violations are exploitative and harmful to clients, boundary crossings may be helpful to them. Although many social workers would not ordinarily take clients for lunch, when I conducted outreach with youth living on the streets, my agency authorized me to take them for lunch. Taking clients for lunch gave me an opportunity to provide clients with a basic need (food); it also provided an opportunity to engage them and assess whether they could use any psychosocial services or supports. To reduce the risks associated with boundary crossings, I let clients know that I was acting in my work capacity and that it was my agency (not me) paying for the meal. I informed clients that I could not guarantee the confidentiality of our discussions while meeting in a public venue and that we could meet in my office if they wanted a more private setting. Our agency worked with the restaurant staff so that they knew to give us space and avoid listening to our conversations. I also informed friends that if they saw me having lunch with someone that they did not know to avoid asking me who they were. I wanted to preserve my clients' right to privacy as much as possible.

When considering engaging in a boundary crossing with clients, it is prudent practice to

- ensure that you have prior approval of your agency (on a case-by-case basis with your supervisor or by agency policy);
- document your interaction with the client and explain why you engaged in a boundary crossing (e.g., "I escorted my client to his mother's funeral because he was highly anxious about going alone and requested my support. My supervisor authorized this request."); and
- discuss possible risks of the boundary crossing with your client and seek agreement on how to minimize these risks (e.g., "I want to respect your right to confidentiality. If anyone at the funeral asks how I know you or your mother, how would you like me to respond?").

Whether a particular type of social interaction with clients is appropriate depends on the particular context and circumstances (Madura, 2018; Zur, n.d.). The idiosyncratic nature of boundaries makes it difficult for professional associations, agencies, and legislatures to dictate specifically what is appropriate and what is inappropriate. For instance, some agency policies suggest that workers should not accept gifts from clients. Accepting gifts might be viewed as accepting bribes or placing expectations on clients to remunerate workers beyond their usual salaries. Clearly, if a client offers you $10,000 to provide them with preferential treatment, it would be inappropriate to accept this gift. What if a 5-year-old client offers you a picture she has drawn? Would it be inappropriate for you to accept it? Arguably, accepting the gift is in the client's best interests because accepting the gift validates the client's gesture of thanks. Arguably, accepting the gift does not violate professional boundaries because the gift was not costly to the client and there are no concerns that the gift is a bribe. If we change the circumstances slightly and you asked the client to give you a picture, this may violate professional boundaries. The client may feel pressured into giving the gift, perhaps seeing you as a person in authority and not wanting to displease you. Within some cultural communities, refusing gifts may be perceived as rude or uncaring (Daley, 2021). Accordingly, social workers should take the client's culture into account when considering whether or not to accept a particular gift. As you can see, the standards demarcating appropriate and inappropriate boundaries are not as clear as black and white. There are many gray areas.

When we communicate with clients through smart phones, email, texting, avatars, videoconferencing, or other technology, we need to consider how to maintain appropriate boundaries in relation to the timing, content, and professionalism of the communication (NASW et al., 2017; Mishna et al., 2021). In terms of timing, speak with clients about appropriate times for communicating with you. For instance, you may say that you are available by phone during regular business hours, but that it is okay to leave certain types of phone messages or secure text messages at any time. It is also important to let clients know when they can expect you to respond.

> "If you leave a voice or text message, I can usually respond within 24 hours or by the next regular business day. If you have an emergency situation, please do not leave a message. For emergencies, please contact a mental health crisis hotline or web service, go to the emergency room at a hospital or urgent care facility, or call 911."

You could also provide specific phone numbers or websites for emergency services that may be particularly suited to your clients' cultural background or psychosocial needs (e.g., for a client applying for refugee status, you could provide a number for legal services).

In terms of content, inform clients about the types of information that they may convey through various forms of technology. For instance, you may advise clients that it is okay to use email or voice messages for setting up or rescheduling appointments, but that they should save discussion of personal or confidential concerns for discussion during videoconferences or in-person meetings. When you respond through email, secure text messaging, or other forms of technology, model effective social-worker client communication. Avoid casual conversation, poor grammar, and language that may seem unprofessional. Casual (nonpurposeful) conversation may lead clients to treat the relationship as if you are a friend rather than a social worker. Friendly chitchat, funny emojis, vulgar jokes, and using acronyms could result in miscommunications. They could also reflect poorly on your professionalism. Avoid using technology to discuss non-work-related concerns (NASW Code, S.1.06[e]). Before sending messages, proofread them and ensure that you are maintaining appropriate boundaries.

Although social workers (and all people) are entitled to freedom of expression and association, we need to be aware of the possibility of boundary crossings or violations when we communicate through social media or other communication technology (Reamer, 2021c; Smith et al., 2021). Standard 1.06(f) notes that we need to be aware that *posting personal information on professional websites* or other social media could cause boundary confusion. If your agency has a Facebook site, for instance, it would be inappropriate to post messages on this site asking if anyone can recommend a good restaurant or electrician for you. Standard 1.06(g) informs us to be aware that personal affiliations may increase the likelihood that clients may discover them on social media or other forms of technology. Assume that you plan to join an online dating service. Before doing so, know that the information you submit online could be accessed by current or future clients.

The NASW Code does not prohibit us from posting personal information online; still, it does encourage us to use professional judgment about whether and how to post personal information online. Some social workers reduce risks by avoiding posting information online. Others try to restrict access to personal information by setting privacy settings on their social media (National Association of Social Workers et al., 2017). Know that even when you limit access to private information on social media, friends or acquaintances might repost or share the information (Smith et al., 2021). When others share your information, the information may become accessible to the public, including to your clients. Note that there have been many instances in which social workers and other helping professionals have posted information online that later resulted in serious professional concerns. If you have posted racist or prejudicial jokes or images, for instance, future clients or employers may have concerns about your commitments to equality, integrity, and social justice. Before posting information on social media, take a moment to consider the possible impacts on your professional career, including the impacts on your relationship with clients. To maintain an ethical presence online, ensure that the language you use in your posts is respectful, honest, and grammatically correct—whether you are posting information for personal or professional purposes. A good test of whether a certain posting might lead to trouble is, "How would I feel if my employer or my parents saw this posting?" Standard 1.06(h) says social workers should avoid accepting requests from or engaging in personal relationships with clients on social networking sites or other media. Once again, it is important to maintain appropriate boundaries whether communicating with clients in person or through social media and other technology.

To foster appropriate boundaries with clients, it may be useful to share your agency's policy on social media and other technology as part of the informed consent process. The policy may indicate, for instance, that you are not permitted to accept "friend" requests or otherwise connect with clients on social media (Cottone et al., 2022). By informing clients about appropriate boundaries during the initial stages of work, you may pre-empt awkward situations in which you may have to decline friend requests from clients (Reamer, 2021a). Although we may try to limit the personal information that we post on the Internet, clients may still have access to personal information on the Internet over which we have no control

(Daley, 2021). If clients initiate discussions about personal information that they have gleaned from the Internet, we may need to discuss ways to keep the focus on the client's needs and concerns.

When feasible, we should avoid using personal phones, computers, email accounts, and other personal technology for work purposes (NASW et al., 2017). Providing clients with our personal phone numbers or email addresses, for instance, can blur professional boundaries. Clients might interpret your providing access to personal devices as an invitation to communicate with you outside of the usual parameters of your work relationship. Some workplaces may expect you to use personal devices for work purposes. You may let them know that using personal devices for work purposes can lead to boundary crossings or violations. If you and the agency do agree that you will use personal devices for work purposes, then identify possible risks and methods of reducing those risks. If you are using a personal phone for work purposes, you could add a second phone number to your phone that you would give to clients and work colleagues. You could then respond to calls to your work number only during work hours, fostering appropriate boundaries for you and your clients.

5. SPIRITUAL BOUNDARIES

In terms of spiritual boundaries, it is generally appropriate to explore clients' spirituality, including whether they are affiliated with any religions or other spiritual groups, what types of prayer, meditation, or other spiritual practices that they engage in, and what gives them a sense of meaning or purpose in life. Spiritual wellbeing is closely connected with physical, psychological, and social wellbeing, so we may help clients make better use of various forms of spirituality (Canda et al., 2020). The ethical obligation of cultural competence includes attending to religion and spirituality (Cole, 2021). It would be inappropriate, however, to impose religious or spiritual beliefs, rituals, or associations on our clients. We should not assume that clients have a particular spiritual affiliation or that their spiritual beliefs mirror ours. Likewise, we should not judge clients if they do not have spiritual connections or if their spirituality is different from our own.

Standard 1.06(b) states that social workers should not exploit clients for religious purposes. This means that we should not evangelize clients or try to impose our religions on them (Canda et al., 2020). Some agencies operate under the auspices of a particular religion. They may incorporate prayer, religious beliefs, and faith-based interventions in their practice. To maintain appropriate boundaries, social workers practicing within faith-based agencies should inform potential clients up front about any religious content or requirements of their programs. This allows clients to provide informed consent if they agree to the religious components of the program. When clients do not want to participate in a programs due to its religious components, then the worker should refer the client to a program that provides a better fit with the client's needs and wishes (S.1.16[a]).

So how should you respond if a client asks you to pray or participate in a religious ritual that does not fit with your belief system? Because the client initiates the request, acceding to the client's wishes does not mean that you are imposing religion on the client. Still, you may consider praying with the client to be a boundary crossing because it does not fit within the usual roles of a social worker. If you choose to participate in prayer with the client, you should do so because doing so supports the client's interests and wishes. Alternatively, you could maintain your usual professional boundaries and offer the client alternatives. "I understand that prayer is very helpful for you. As a social worker, it is not my customary role to pray with clients. If you would like, we could arrange time for you to pray before or after our sessions together."

Similarly, if a client asks you about your religion, you should decide whether to disclose your religious beliefs and affiliations based on what is best for your client, including how to maintain an effective work relationship. Before answering the client's question, you might begin with an empathy statement. If you believe that the client wants to know if you are a good match for them in terms of religion, you might respond, "When you asked about my faith, I wonder whether you want to know whether I can understand and respect your faith." This statement provides the client with an opportunity to explain why they asked about your faith. You could then respond with a brief disclosure about your faith and redirect the conversation to the client's needs and concerns. Alternatively, you could provide reasons for not disclosing your faith. "In our agency, we work with people of various religions and forms of spirituality. Our client's interests come first. Rather than spending time talking about my religious affiliations and beliefs, let's focus on the reasons you came for services."

Maintaining appropriate religious and spiritual boundaries can be particularly challenging when a social worker believes that a client is acting in a manner that conflicts with the worker's core religious beliefs and values. We may use "ethical bracketing" to stay within our professional roles, setting aside our personal beliefs and values in order to provide services in accordance with our professional values and ethics (Cottone et al., 2022). We should not judge our clients or impose our values and beliefs (Canda et al., 2020). In our personal lives, we may encourage family, friends, or acquaintances to follow our religion or spirituality. When serving as professional social workers, however, we should not do so with our clients.

Supervisor–Supervisee Boundaries

Within social work, supervisor–supervisee relationships include agency-based supervisors and their social work employees or interns, educators and students, and researchers and research assistants. In each of these situations, the supervisee relies on the supervisor for coaching, education, guidance, and support. Depending on the situation, supervisors may also be responsible for monitoring and evaluating the supervisees' performance and making decisions about hiring, firing, promotions, grading, and completion of courses. Although both supervisors and supervisees are responsible for maintaining appropriate boundaries, supervisors should take primary responsibility for ensuring appropriate boundaries given their positions of power, expertise, and influence. Standard 3.01(b) states that supervisors are responsible for setting clear, appropriate, and culturally sensitive boundaries. Assume that, as a social work student, you invite your field instructor to attend a party to celebrate your graduation. Attending a graduation party falls outside the usual roles of a field instructor, so attending could be viewed as a boundary crossing. However, if there is little risk of exploitation or confused boundaries, attending your graduation party is not a boundary violation. Your field instructor may determine that it is culturally and professional appropriate to attend, particularly if your grades have been submitted and perceptions of biased treatment are unlikely. Alternatlively, your field instructor might decide not to attend your graduation in order to maintain professional boundaries (NASW, 2013).

The appropriateness of boundaries varies with the context of work and the theoretical framework for practice. Larger institutions and agencies may have more hierarchical structures, with more rigid boundaries between supervisors and supervisees. Smaller institutions and agencies may have less hierarchy and more flexible boundaries. Supervisors operating from feminist perspectives also strive for more egalitarian relationships and more flexible boundaries with supervisees (Arczynski & Morrow, 2017). The boundaries that supervisors establish with supervisees may be used as models by the supervisees for their relationships with clients. To help supervisees understand how supervisor–supervisee relationships are parallel to social worker–client relationships, supervisors should discuss how their boundaries are similar to and different from the boundaries that the supervisor believes the supervisee should establish with clients. Some supervisors establish collegial, almost friend-like, relationships with supervisees. Although supervisors retain some professional distance due to their status and functions within the organization, supervisor–supervisee relationships often involve less power difference than social worker–client relationships.[4]

Although supervisees are not vulnerable in the same ways as clients, it is important for both supervisors and supervisees to ensure that supervisees can operate in a safe working environment, free from harassment, coercion, unwarranted criticism, exploitation, or other risks of harm. Standard 2.06 explicitly prohibits supervisors from engaging in sexual relationships with supervisees. Similarly, Standard

---

4. Of course, there are many occasions when the power differential between supervisor and supervisees is very large (e.g., when supervisees are working on a probationary basis so the supervisor may determine whether or not they should be hired on a permanent basis).

2.07 prohibits them from sexually harassing supervisees, whether in person or through technology.

As coprofessionals, supervisors and supervisees may work as partners to help the supervisees learn and develop as professionals and to ensure that they are performing their jobs effectively. During the course of your work together, you and your supervisor may agree to share certain personal information with each other. Supervisor–supervisee relationships may be friendly, but they are different from nonworkplace friendships. Supervisors and supervisees should acknowledge the differences in their roles and the power within their relationships. Supervisors and supervisees may negotiate the types of roles and boundaries that they feel are appropriate, as well as any safeguards that they may need to take. Standard 3.01(c) says supervisors should not engage in dual relationships with supervisees if there is "a risk of exploitation for or potential harm to the supervisee." Standard 3.01(d) has a similar prohibition of dual relationships between educators or field instructors and students. Accordingly, it would be inappropriate for your professors or field instructors to ask you to babysit or paint their house. Even if you think it would be helpful to earn money for these services, think of how your relationship as a student could be affected if something went wrong while babysitting or painting. As the section on dual relationships below notes, if you can avoid dual relationships, you can avoid the risks that these relationships entail. One challenge in terms of defining appropriate boundaries is identifying when a boundary crossing may lead into a dual relationship. Having a working lunch with your supervisor is appropriate; having a romantic lunch with your supervisor is not.

Clinical supervision is a relation-based process in which a supervisor may ask you to reflect on your work with clients (Hafford-Letchfield & Engelbrecht, 2020). Your supervisor may invite you to discuss personal thoughts, feelings, or biases that may be affecting your work (NASW, 2013). To maintain appropriate boundaries, it is important to distinguish appropriate clinical supervision from psychotherapy. Remember, if you are seeking therapy, the focus is helping you with your personal psychosocial concerns. If you are seeking clinical supervision, you and your supervisor should focus on your professional roles and your work with clients. Thus, it would be inappropriate to ask your supervisor to treat you for trauma issues; however, if past traumas were affecting your work with clients, your supervisor may demonstrate empathy, assist you in setting appropriate boundaries with clients, and provide you with professional self-care strategies (Miller et al., 2019). If you need therapeutic help, your supervisor could assist with a referral for therapy. If you think that your field instructor is overstepping the bounds of an appropriate supervisory relationship, share your concerns in an assertive and respectful manner. "I'm not comfortable speaking about my personal mental health history. Could we please focus on how I can help this client . . . " If you do not feel comfortable discussing these concerns with your field instructor, then you may ask your field faculty liaison for assistance.

Boundaries between Coprofessionals

In social work practice, we often work with other social workers and professional colleagues. We may consult with one another, building on one another's expertise and offering each other support. We may develop goals together with our clients and collaborate on the best ways to serve them. Also, we may refer our clients to other professionals, within or outside our agencies (Interprofessional Education Collaborative, 2016). As with supervisors, we can certainly be friendly with coprofessionals, while still maintaining appropriate boundaries. For instance, we may joke around and share personal information with colleagues as long as such socializing does not interfere with our work. Standard 2.01 suggests that we should collaborate for the good of our clients and that we should also treat one another with respect, avoiding unwarranted criticism. Assume that a client says he is having difficulties with a psychologist at your agency; you have also had misgivings about this psychologist. Despite your concerns, it is important to remain professional and avoid "bashing" your colleague. You may offer the client support, as well as guidance on how to address their concerns (e.g., the client may speak with the psychologist's supervisor). Standard 2.04 suggests you should not exploit clients in your dispute with a colleague. For instance, you should not set up a client to complain with your program director on your behalf when the complaint has more to do with your agenda rather than with the client's concerns.

Be careful about posting messages about colleagues online, even anonymously. If you have a concern about a colleague, address that concern directly with the colleague. It you are unable to address the concern in this manner, then make use of the agency's process for handling complaints and, if warranted, consider filing your concern with the professional's licensing board or professional association (as discussed further in Chapter 12).

The NASW Code does not prohibit social workers from having friendships, romantic relationships, or other nonwork relationships with professional colleagues. Some employers may have restrictions on romantic relationships between employees. Although professional colleagues may be permitted to have romantic relationships, before entering such a relationship, consider the possible effects on your work relationship if the romantic relationship runs into trouble. If you have a friendship or romantic relationship with a colleague, make sure that you do not allow this relationship to interfere with your professional judgement or ability to serve your clients effectively. When referring clients to colleagues, for instance, your decision should be based on the client's best interests. Rather than simply referring clients to friends, determine who is the most appropriate match for each client. For referrals, it is often prudent practice to provide clients with more than one name, encouraging them to check each potential service provider to decide the best fit for themselves.

Boundaries between Group Members

Standards 1.06, 1.09, 1.10, and 1.11 of the NASW Code define how social workers should maintain appropriate boundaries with clients: They should not engage in dual relationships with clients, they should not have sex with clients, they should avoid physical contact when there is a possibility of psychological harm, they should avoid engaging with clients online for nonwork-related purposes, and they should not sexually harass clients. Although these standards apply to group workers, they only apply between the worker and each client; they do not establish boundaries among clients within a group. While the NASW Code does not provide guidance on how workers should manage boundaries among group members, social workers should attend to these boundaries (Barsky & Northen, 2017).[5] Facilitators may help groups determine what types of boundaries and relationships are appropriate by building agreement among members. In particular, facilitators could consider developing group guidelines for the following issues:

- What types of touch, if any, are permitted between members during group sessions?
- What types of interactions, if any, are group members permitted outside of group sessions—group-related support, social relationships (including online social networking), sexual relationships, or work relationships?
- To what extent are group members permitted to confront one another within the group?
- To what extent are group members allowed to ask each other about potentially sensitive topics, including politics, sexuality, religion, and criminal activity?

As with confidentiality, group workers cannot guarantee that members will respect whatever boundary guidelines are established. Accordingly, workers should discuss proposed guidelines and use consensus-building techniques to establish commitment from group members. Assume you are facilitating a group for clients in a substance use disorder treatment program. You might propose the following guidelines:

- To ensure that everyone feels safe in group, group members will not hug, kiss, or touch other members, other than to shake hands (which is permitted).
- Group members may socialize and support one another outside of the group, provided they have permission from one another.
- Group members may not engage in sexual relationships with one another.

---

5. From an ethics perspective, the obligation to attend to boundaries between clients could arise out of Standard 4.01(c) on competence and the need to practice based on recognized social work knowledge.

When you discuss the proposed rules, members might ask why they can socialize but cannot engage in sex. You could then engage them in a discussion of the benefits and risks of various group guidelines so the group can gain insight into the purpose of the guidelines and build consensus. During early stages of recovery, people may be vulnerable emotionally and socially. Engaging in romantic relationships could lead to relapse. Intimate relationships could also affect the rest of the group, particularly when romantic relationships experience conflict. An advantage of allowing nonromantic relationships within the group is that group members can provide one another with social support.

Different groups may require different guidelines about group boundaries and relationships between members. When I facilitated a group for men with a history of abusing their intimate partners, my agency discouraged group members from socializing with one another outside of group. The agency did not want members sharing information or support outside of our meetings because the agency believed this could lead to further intimate partner abuse (e.g., sharing tips on how to control a partner without leaving physical evidence of abuse). In contrast, when I facilitate task groups or mutual aid groups, I often encourage members to get to know one another outside of scheduled group meetings in order to build comradery and support. Regardless of the type of group that you facilitate, consider what types of relationships to promote between group members and how you can help the group establish appropriate boundaries.

Boundaries in Practice with Communities and Organizations

Although social workers practicing with communities and organizations need to be aware of boundary issues, the types of boundaries expected of these types of practice are different from those in practice with individuals, families, and groups. In family work, for instance, you should not practice with your own family. In community or organizational work, you may be a part of the community or organization that you are helping. Accordingly, it may be ethical to interact with members of the community for nonwork purposes, for instance, meeting for social events or engaging together in social action (online or in-person). Assume that you organize recreational activities for a community center. During work hours, the center expects you to focus on organizing these activities. Unless it is part of your job, it would not be appropriate to use your job to encourage the center's members to join you in social action. During nonwork hours, however, you and the center's members could engage together in social action.

Social work pioneer, Jane Addams, encouraged social workers to live and interact in the same communities as the people with whom they were working (Bertram, 2017). Rather than maintaining rigid boundaries, encountering people within the community on a daily basis allows us to gain a better understanding and compassion for the people we are serving. If we know how a particular immi-grant community is being affected by current social policies, for example, we will be better positioned to advocate for reforms based on the true needs of this community.

Each community and organization has its own norms and expectations about personal boundaries, including boundaries with the social workers serving them. In some communities and organizations, boundaries with social workers may be relatively informal or relaxed (Daley, 2021). People may refer to social workers by their first names, engage them in personal conversations, and meet for various social, religious, and educational activities. Other communities and organizations may have stricter boundaries. People may address social workers with formal salu-tations, avoid personal conversations, and frown upon interacting outside their work responsibilities. When we work with specific communities and organiza-tions, we need to clarify what types of boundaries and relationships are appropri-ate. Some boundaries may be defined in an organization's official policies; however, other norms may not be defined explicitly.

Researcher–Research Participant Boundaries

In many forms of research, we are supposed to maintain objectivity in the pursuit of knowledge and truth (Grinnell, 2021). One strategy for maintaining objectivity is to preserve relatively firm boundaries with research participants. For instance, we avoid sharing personal information including personal phone numbers, personal opinions, or personal mental health concerns with research participants. We let people know the purpose of our research and we keep our conversations focused on this purpose. In double-blind quantitative studies, research participants do not know who we are and we do not know who they are. These precautions protect our research against biases and perceived biases. Even in studies that are not double blind, we limit self-disclosure to keep the focus on the thoughts, feelings, or experi-ences of our research participants.

We construct different types of boundaries with research participants depending on the type of research. In qualitative and ethnographic research, for instance, we may immerse ourselves in the settings we are studying so there is a more personal relationship with research participants (Denzin & Lincoln, 2017). We continue to focus our relationship on the purpose of the research; however, we may build rapport through sustained interaction and demonstration of care and concern for the participants. We may also observe participants in their homes, communities, or other natural environments. In action research, we act as partners with our research participants. We work together in various stages of the research process, sharing responsibility for developing research questions, methods, instruments, data gath-ering, and analysis. As with other social work functions, researchers engage people in informed consent processes to ensure that they understand and agree to the expected relationships, boundaries, and ways of interacting with the social worker.

Before asking research participants about past traumas, losses, or other concerns that are potentially embarrassing or anxiety-inducing, we ensure that they are aware of and agree to being asked these questions. We should guard against exploiting research participants or being too intrusive (Sobočan et al., 2020). For instance, if I know that research participants are emotionally vulnerable because they recently lost their parents, I need to respect their boundaries and avoid pressuring them into answering questions just to suit my research agenda. I need to stay within my role as a researcher and avoid providing counseling or other social work interventions.

DUAL RELATIONSHIPS AND CONFLICTS OF INTEREST

Boundary violations, dual relationships, and conflicts of interest are different but related concepts. As noted earlier, *boundary violations* arise when we interact with clients in a way that is inconsistent with the traditional roles of a social worker, resulting in harm or exploitation to the client. **Dual (or multiple) relationships** arise when we engage in more than one type of relationship with a client, for instance, a social worker who provides services to a friend, a family member, or a business associate. **Conflicts of interest** arise when we have two or more types of relationships with a client that may give rise to conflicting ethical or moral obligations. Often, dual relationships involve boundary violations, for instance, a social worker having sexual relations with or a borrowing money from a client.

Standard 1.06(a) of the Code of Ethics says, "Social Workers should be alert to and avoid conflicts of interest that interfere with the exercise of professional discretion and impartial judgment." We should generally avoid conflicts of interest because they present us with competing motivations, obligations, or concerns that may hamper our ability to act in our client's best interests. Assume your client is looking for an attorney to assist with her divorce. Coincidentally, your spouse is an attorney. It would be inappropriate to refer your client to your spouse because your marital relationship does not allow you to make an unbiased decision about whether your spouse is the best referral for your client. Further, your client may think you are exploiting her for personal gain, regardless of your intentions.

For an example of dual relationships in an organizational context, please see Box 8.2.

Risks of Exploitation and Harm

Under Standard 1.06(c), social workers should avoid dual relationships when there is a risk of exploitation or harm to the client. If a close friend comes to you for services, you would be wise to refer this friend to someone who does not have a prior

BOX 8.2

AUNTIE BOSS

You have recently graduated with your social work degree. Congratulations. Your Auntie Em offers you a job as a social policy analyst in a private nonprofit agency that advocates for survivors of tornadoes and other natural disasters. Assume that you are competent and motivated to perform this work. Given your personal relationship with Auntie Em, should you accept this position? What benefits and risks should you consider? How might other agency employees perceive you? Which standards in the NASW Code of Ethics should you consider? If you decide to accept the job, what kinds of guidelines or boundaries should you and Auntie Em set to minimize risks related to the dual relationship? How is a dual relationship with an employer different from a dual relationship with an individual client?

---

personal relationship. Otherwise, your friendship could interfere with your ability to serve the client in a professional manner. Perhaps the client will expect you to act as a friend rather than a professional. Perhaps other clients will believe that you are favoring a particular client, given your friendship.

One of the core values of social work is human relationships. As noted earlier, our work with clients is predicated on building trusting relationships with the people we serve. We have special fiduciary obligations to clients because they often come to us in vulnerable situations. They may be mentally distraught, depressed, financially impoverished, or otherwise experiencing stress. They may feel embarrassed or exposed because they are revealing personal or family secrets. They may be relying on us for advice, support, guidance, or access to resources (e.g., if we are deciding whether a client is eligible for social assistance). Because we are in positions of trust with our clients, we need to act in ways that foster and preserve trust. We should not taint our relationships with anything that can be perceived as taking advantage of clients. Legally and ethically, if we betray a client's trust, we may be held accountable.[6] Whenever feasible, we should avoid conflicts of interest. Avoiding conflicts of interest fits with the principles of honesty and integrity. By being honest and ensuring the integrity of our relationships with clients, clients are more likely to have confidence and work with us in a collaborative manner. We are also more likely to serve clients by using prudent, professional judgment, unfettered by conflicting relationships and obligations (Dolgoff et al., 2012).

To demonstrate the risks and realities of conflicts of interest, assume you are a child protection worker in a rural community. You are the only child protection worker within 100 miles. You receive a call alleging child abuse by Ned, your

---

6. Malpractice lawsuits, licensing grievances, and other forms of accountability for breach of trust and other forms of malpractice are explored further in Chapter 12.

neighbor. If you accept the case and start an investigation, you risk a conflict of interest. You and Ned have an ongoing personal relationship. You might feel inclined to "go soft" on him, wanting to retain good relations as neighbors. If anything goes wrong—for instance, you leave the child in Ned's care and Ned abuses the child further—people may assume you did not do your job properly due to this conflict of interest. On the other hand, if you refuse the case, who would conduct the investigation? For pragmatic reasons, you might need to accept the case. However, you should take the following steps to minimize risks:

- Check agency policy to see how conflicts of interest should be handled.
- Discuss the conflict of interest with your supervisor for guidance on whether to accept the case, whether there are other options, and how to ensure the child abuse investigation is conducted with as much objectivity as possible.
- If you accept the case, discuss the possible conflicts of interest with the client and the steps necessary to minimize the risks (e.g., explaining how your role as social worker is different from your role as neighbor).

If another child protection worker is available, you could simply refer the case to that social worker. If a dual relationship is unavoidable, you should set clear boundaries for your work with Ned. Whether or not a dual relationship is unavoidable or potentially beneficial, we should discuss possible conflicts of interest with clients and develop strategies to manage the risks. If any harm befalls clients or others due to conflicts of interest, we may be held liable for damages.

Unavoidable or Justifiable Dual Relationships

Although Standard 1.06 cautions social workers against entering dual relationships or situations where conflicts of interest might arise, it does not completely prohibit them. As the previous example suggests, some dual relationships are unavoidable or inevitable (Reamer, 2021a). In some situations, you might have appropriate justification for the dual relationship—for instance, you may be the only practitioner available to provide services. Alternatively, it might cost less time and money if the client received services from one professional with dual roles rather than having to see two separate workers for related issues. In residential addiction treatment programs, for instance, group facilitators sometimes provide individual counseling to group members. By allowing group facilitators to do individual work, social workers can build on what the client is doing in group work. The situation is not without risks. For instance, the worker needs to ensure that information shared individually is kept confidential from other group members unless the client provides specific permission to share information with the group.

Another challenging setting is school-based practice. School social workers constantly need to manage dual relationships because they work with clients who have relationships with one another. Thus, they may need to establish certain boundaries, such as not talking with one student about another student. If one student has concerns about the worker serving their friend, the worker could consider referring one student to a social worker outside the school. Referring out should be the exception rather than the rule. In most situations, the worker should be able to establish appropriate boundaries with students who know one another so that each student can trust the social worker to address their individual rights, needs, and wishes.

Dual relationships may be unavoidable for social workers working in prisons, residential treatment programs, military units, tightly knit cultural communities, small towns, and other situations where the worker has many clients who know one another (Koocher & Keith-Spiegel, 2016; Reamer, 2021a). In small and tightly knit communities, clients are more likely to know personal information about you, including where you live, where you shop, who you have dated, and what types of social activities you enjoy (Daley, 2021). It may be difficult or impossible to avoid dual relationships when we live in close proximity with our clients or when we have common interests such as religious worship, political activism, recreational clubs, or online gaming. In these situations, we can inform clients that we may be serving others in the community who know them, but we will protect privacy by ensuring their confidential information is not shared with other clients from the community. We may also need to discuss the differences in boundaries when interacting socially in the community and when engaging in social work services. You might explain, for instance, how greeting one another with a kiss may be appropriate within a personal relationship, but not within a professional social worker–client relationship. Similarly, idle chitchat may be appropriate socially, but conversation is more purposeful when meeting in a professional context. Even within communities where everyone seems to know "everyone else's business," we can take steps to distinguish professional relationships from personal ones and maintain the integrity of our professional relationships with clients.

Some social workers use an empowerment model that strives to reduce the professional distance between clients and social workers; according to this model, living in the same community and having nonsexual, nonexploitive dual relationships with clients may be acceptable and even valuable (Bryan et al., 2022). Note that Standard 1.06 speaks about maintaining culturally appropriate boundaries. Within some cultures, the fact that a social worker knows clients outside of their social worker-client relationship may be seen as an advantage. Within some Indigenous communities, for instance, clients may be more trusting of people that they know from their community (Halverson & Brownlee, 2010). Within the Deaf community, clients can benefit from having social workers affiliated with the Deaf community.

Dual Roles

Another form of conflict arises when a social worker plays two different roles with the same client system. Assume that I am helping a client cope with trauma following a sexual assault. If the client subpoenas me to testify in a subsequent criminal case against the person who assaulted her, I will face a conflict of interest (NASW Code, 1.06[d]). My role as a counselor is much different from my role as a potential witness (Barsky, 2012). Accordingly, I should explain the nature of these two roles so my client can make informed decisions (along with her attorneys) about whether to call me as a witness. To pre-empt this type of conflict of interest, we could ask new clients to agree (in writing) that they will not subpoena us to testify in any court proceedings. Courts may overrule these types of agreements, so we could still be required to testify (Ordway & Casasnovas, 2019); still, we are putting clients on notice that our main purpose in meeting them is to provide counseling or other social work services, not to testify in court.

When working with involuntary clients in the criminal justice or child protection systems, we play dual roles. In the criminal justice system, we act as helping agents for our clients and we also promote public safety and personal accountability in our role with the criminal justice system. In the child protection system, we act as helping agents for our clients and we also promote the safety and welfare of vulnerable children. Although we retain our usual ethical obligations to respect client confidentiality, self-determination, and informed consent, we also have duties to the system that employs us, placing limits on our ethical obligations to clients (Rooney, 2018). If I were working within a parole department and a client disclosed violating a law or court order, I may need to report this information to the court despite my usual duty of client confidentiality. If you were working with a family whose child was in foster care and the biological parents asked you to return the children to their custody, you would have to weigh the children's safety and wellbeing with the parents' right to self-determination. When we work in systems with dual obligations, we need to explain our dual obligations so our clients are aware of the limitations on self-determination, informed consent, and confidentiality. Notifying clients about our dual obligations demonstrates our honesty and allows them to make informed decisions about the information that they choose to share or not share with us.

Pre-Empting Conflicts of Interest

In terms of practice, we should assess for possible conflicts of interest from the first stages of engagement. When we foresee potential problems, we should address them as soon as possible, pre-empting further issues. Assume you are facilitating a stress management group and discover that a potential member will be your daughter's teacher next year. You could open a discussion of this issue as follows:

> I understand that you teach at Aristotle Elementary. That's where my daughter goes to school. Since you will be her teacher next year, perhaps we could discuss the possibility of referring you to another social worker. I want to make sure that you receive the best help possible and avoid problems that could arise if you were to become both my client and my daughter's teacher.

By engaging the client in this discussion, you empower the client to make her own decision. If the client does not want to be referred to another worker, you could discuss the risks of dual relationships and the benefits of a referral:

> I agree that we could work very well together. My code of ethics, however, says I should avoid conflicting roles, ensuring all clients have a social worker who can focus on their best interests. How do you think our stress management work could be affected if my daughter was disruptive in class and you did not think I was handling it well as a parent?

By identifying and handling potential conflicts of interest early, you can reduce risks and promote higher levels of client trust.

When working with families, we need to clarify which family members are the clients, as well as the nature of our ethical duties to the other individuals (S. 1.03[d]). If you are working in an assisted living facility for older adults, for instance, your clients might be the older adults rather than the whole family. You could inform your clients and their families that your primary obligations are to the clients. You might also explain that you will respect the rights to confidentiality and self-determination of the whole family; however, if there are conflicting interests within the family, you will need to prioritize your individual client's wishes and best interests.

Conflicts of interest may also arise when social workers and clients have conflicting values and convictions (Chechak, 2015).[7] Consider social workers who—because of strong personal values or religious beliefs—do not want to work with LGBTQ+ clients. We should not reinterpret the code of ethics through the lens of our personal beliefs; we should abide by the code and determine how to manage our value conflicts. As social workers, we believe clients should have access to needed services, so simply denying clients service could be an ethical violation. Similarly, we should not

---

7. Cognitive dissonance theory suggests that people with conflicting demands or beliefs experience stress (Chechak, 2015). When social workers experience cognitive dissonance due to value conflicts, they should consider supervision to help them explore ethical ways to manage the conflicts.

impose our religious beliefs, for instance, by trying to convert LGBTQ+ clients to be heterosexual or cisgender.[8] Some workers might decide to refer LGBTQ+ clients (Standard 1.06[a]), thus avoiding the conflict of interest and allowing the client to obtain services elsewhere. "I feel that you might benefit from a counselor with greater experience working with LGBTQ+ clients" (Scales & Kelly, 2016, p. 245). However, simply referring LGBTQ+ clients to others due to value conflicts could be considered a microaggression, an insult or rejection of a client. We should consider the impact of refusing to provide services to clients because of their sexual orientation, beliefs about abortion or gun control, political or religious affiliation, or other factors that may conflict with their personal values or beliefs (Corey et al., 2019). In small communities or in specialized agencies, for instance, refusing services may mean the client has no reasonable alternative to receive appropriate services. We should resolve value differences by not allowing our personal values or beliefs to interfere with our professional obligations. If we are not able to do so, we should consider whether social work is an appropriate profession. For instance, proselytizing or trying to convert clients goes against social work ethics. If we want to proselytize, perhaps we should choose a profession that permits proselytizing.[9]

Additional Conflicts of Interest

In addition to a general statement that we should avoid conflicts of interest, the NASW Code suggests avoiding conflicts of interest in the following circumstances:

- Standard 1.06(h)—Engaging with clients on social networking sites or other electronic media for non-work purposes (e.g., posting Tiktok videos of yourself singing karaoke on a client's Facebook page).
- Standard 1.13(b)—Bartering with clients (e.g., asking clients to pay for services by doing chores or giving you something of value that they have created).
- Standard 4.07(a)—Soliciting potential clients who are vulnerable to undue influence, manipulation, or coercion (e.g., going to a funeral and handing out business cards to mourners).

---

8. American Civil Liberties Union (n.d.) suggests, "Religious freedom in America means that we all have a right to our religious beliefs, but this does not give us the right to use our religion to discriminate against and impose those beliefs on others who do not share them."

9. Consider Kim Davis, a court clerk in Kentucky who defied a court order to issue marriage licenses to same-sex couples, or Julea Ward, a counseling student in Michigan, who was dismissed from her professional program because she refused to counsel LGBTQ clients, despite being given opportunities for remediation (Neilson et al., 2015). Although these situations did not involve social workers, they demonstrate how one's legal and ethical obligations to employers and clients may supersede personal values and beliefs.

- Standard 4.07(b)—Soliciting testimonial endorsements from clients or others who may be vulnerable to undue influence (e.g., asking clients with mental health issues to post a positive review on your work website).
- Standard 5.02(p)—Dual relationships with research participants (e.g., asking your family members to participate in your research).

The Code does not prohibit these dual relationships absolutely, but it does discourage them when there are risks of harm to our clients or research participants. Assume that you are conducting research on a program in which you are also a social work service provider. If you invite your clients to participate in the research, you are engaging in dual relationships (Sobočan et al., 2020). Although your intentions may be good, you need to be aware of potential risks: your clients may feel pressured into participating in the research and you may be encouraging them to participate even if it is not in their best interests (Morain, & Joffe, 2019). To ensure that clients do not feel pressured by you during the informed consent process, you could have a third party inform them about the research and ask for consent. To ensure that client interests are paramount, the third party should explain the risks and benefits of participating in the research, allowing the clients to make fully informed decisions. If you are asking your own clients to participate in research, it is important to reassure them that they have a right to refuse to participate in research. To ensure that clients do not feel coerced, avoid any suggestion that they will be denied services unless they participate in the research.

CONCLUSION

As social workers, our relationships with clients and research participants are based on trust. To preserve trust and ensure the highest levels of integrity in our work, we need to maintain appropriate boundaries. We should also avoid dual relationships that could raise conflicts of interest or other risks of harm to the people we serve. To determine what types of behaviors are appropriate or inappropriate within a particular professional relationship, we need to consider our roles and mandate, as well as the culture, needs, and vulnerabilities of those we serve. We should be particularly careful not to exploit people who are in vulnerable situations, but rather, focus on their interests and ensure that we do not impose our values, beliefs, or opinions.

Some dual relationships are unavoidable or ethically justified (e.g., when working with small, closely-knit communities or with organizations where clients know one another). When we do enter dual relationships, we need to consider ways to minimize the risks associated with conflicting roles and obligations: consulting with our supervisors; ensuring clients and research participants are informed about potentially conflicting obligations; and problem-solving potential concerns around confidentiality, self-determination, client safety, or other ethical obligations. When we are uncertain about how to handle potential or actual conflicts of interest, we should review the NASW Code for guidance. We may also need to consult our supervisors, attorneys, or professional associations to help us determine the best way to proceed. Often, when social workers get into trouble related to boundaries and dual relationships, it is not because they lack empathy or concern for their clients; instead, it is because they are acting out of care but extended help to clients in a manner that is risky and outside the usual boundaries of professional social work practice.

DISCUSSION QUESTIONS AND EXERCISES

1. *Distinctions*: Why is it important for social workers to maintain appropriate boundaries, avoid dual relationships, and prevent conflicts of interest? What are the differences between these three concepts?
2. *Conversations*: Assume that you are counseling a teenaged girl via videoconferencing. The teenager's father, Mr. Kawai, has been listening to some of your conversations with her. He calls you one day and says he would like to hire you to be the human resources officer in a large business that he owns. You are tempted to accept the job offer as it pays very well and you find human resources work very interesting. What sections of the NASW Code should you consider as you decide how to respond? What specifically would you say to Mr. Kawai?
3. *Self-Disclosure*: Identify the potential benefits and risks of self-disclosure in the following situations.
   a. A social worker who facilitates grief and loss groups lets members know that he believes in reincarnation, suggesting this belief system can help them with the mourning process.
   b. A research participant asks a social worker who is interviewing him (for a study on discrimination) whether she has experienced discrimination. The worker describes how teachers belittled her because of her race.
   c. A social work intern tells her field instructor that she has panic attacks when speaking in front of large groups. The field instructor discloses she overcame anxiety about presenting in front of large groups by using positive self-talk.
   d. A child protection worker tells a parent that she will be away from work for a few weeks because she needs to take care of a sister who is ill (she does not disclose that her sister has cancer and is undergoing chemotherapy because the client also has cancer).
   e. A social worker interacts with clients through videoconferencing from home. In the background of the workers' video frame, clients can see photos of her same-gender partner, a large dog sleeping on a couch, and dirty dishes stacked on the kitchen counter.

4. *Context*: Which of the following types of behaviors or interactions do you think is appropriate and which do you think might be boundary crossings or boundary violations? Provide your reasoning, including how the context of the situation affects your analysis. Identify any additional information you would need to know to determine the appropriateness of the worker's boundaries and behaviors.

   a. Upon seeing a 6-year-old client in the hallway, a school social worker gives the client a high five.

   b. As part of her psychosocial assessments in a program serving recent immigrants, a social worker asks clients whether they own guns, whether they have been vaccinated for communicable diseases, and whether they have committed any crimes.

   c. A social worker in a town of 30,000 people attends that same house of worship as many of her clients.

   d. While conducting a home visit, a social worker brings cookies for the children.

   e. After the final session of a support group for genderfluid clients, the group facilitator joins members for coffee and dessert at a restaurant.

   f. A social worker who provides discharge services for patients being released from hospital invites patients to join her social media so that she can maintain contact with them and ensure they are okay.

   g. Your professor invites your class to their house for the final class of the term so everyone can celebrate their progress and successes.

5. *Current vs. Former*: Under the NASW Code, social workers are prohibited from having sex with current or former clients. Although the Code prohibits social work supervisors and educators from having sex with *current* supervisees and students, it does not prohibit them from having sex with *former* supervisees and students. Why does the Code have different guidance for former clients versus former supervisees and students? Explain whether you agree or disagree with this distinction.

6. *Promoting Awareness*: Kyra works as a vocational counselor. Ever since a relative died from problems related to sickle cell disease (SCD), she has placed a poster in her office that promotes public awareness about SCD and the need for regular medical screenings. Although promoting SCD awareness is not an assigned part of her job, she also asks Black clients whether they are aware of SCD.

7. *Personal Trauma*: Assume you are working with clients who have experienced trauma. Your supervisor is concerned about how you are personalizing issues with a particular young client. Your supervisor asks whether you have experienced any childhood traumas. How would you respond? Explain your reasons, including how you and your supervisor should determine how to maintain appropriate boundaries in these circumstances.

8. *Personal Freedoms and Professional Obligations*: You discover that a coworker, Lana, is posting videos on the Internet describing the challenges of being a social worker. Although Lana is not disclosing

identifying information about any particular clients, you find her posts demeaning to clients (e.g., Lana refers to clients as needy and unstable). When you suggest that Lana take down the video in the interest of maintaining good relationships with clients, Lana says that freedom of expression is protected by the U.S. Constitution. What might you say to Lana in terms of how to balance her constitutional freedoms with her ethical obligations as a social worker?

9. *Research Thyself*: Ernest is studying the lived experiences of systemic discrimination on transgender people. Ernest identifies as a transgender man and an activist. Does this situation present Ernest with a conflict of interest? Why or why not? What are the potential advantages or disadvantages of a researcher coming from the same group that is being studied (Caron et al., 2020)? How is this situation different, if at all, from a cisgender social worker who is conducting research on the lived experiences of marriage for different-gender couples? Consider how deontologists and virtue ethicists might analyze the issues raised by this situation.

10. *Conflicts of Interest*: For each of the following situations, analyze the potential benefits and risks of engaging in a dual relationship. Based on your analysis, explain whether you would engage in the dual relationship, including what steps you could take to minimize the conflicts of interest or any other risks.

   a. You provide discharge planning services in a maternity ward of a hospital. One new mother says she is unable to take care of her baby because she has no job and cannot afford a decent home. She asks if you would like to adopt him. You have been wanting to adopt a baby. You think that adopting the baby could also help your client.

   b. You are conducting qualitative research on the impact of work stress. One of your research participants asks if you could coach her about work stress because she believes you are very knowledgeable and empathic.

   c. You work as a fundraiser for a camp for children with disabilities. A camp counselor asks you to go to a family wedding as their date.

   d. You facilitate a group for people with codependency. A client offers to post a positive review about your group on social media.

   e. You have a neighbor, Bob, who seems very depressed. His father asks if you can screen Bob for suicidal ideation to see if he needs to be hospitalized.

9

Responsibilities in Practice Settings

LEARNING OBJECTIVES

Upon successful completion of this introduction, you will be able to

- identify your ethical commitments to your practice setting in relation to record keeping, billing, client transfer, resource allocation, and following agency policies and contracts;
- manage conflicts that may arise between your ethical obligations to your clients, your practice setting, and society;
- advocate for your agency to ensure that its policies and practices support social work ethics (including client self-determination, informed consent, confidentiality, and social justice); and
- analyze the ethicality of whistleblowing and civil disobedience to address laws, policies, or practices that are illegal, unethical, or harmful.

Earlier chapters focused on our ethical obligations as social workers to promote social justice and to advance the needs and interests of our clients (including their rights to self-determination, informed consent, confidentiality, and fidelity). In this chapter, we turn our attention to obligations in the context our practice settings. Practice settings include social agencies, not-for-profit and for-profit treatment programs, private practices, humanitarian organizations, voluntary associations, research institutes, hospitals, schools, the criminal justice system, the child protection system, mental health facilities, military programs, assisted living communities, or any other organizations that employ social workers. For ease of reference throughout this chapter, I will refer to all these practice settings as *agencies*.

The first part of this chapter focuses on legal and ethical obligations within our agencies: maintaining client records, billing, transferring clients, and other duties determined by agency policy and employment contracts. The second part of this chapter delves into conflicts that may arise when our agency obligations conflict with other ethical obligations, such as our duties to clients and research participants. The third part explores civil disobedience, including when it may be ethically justifiable to violate a law or agency policy in order to change that law or policy. As you read through this chapter, consider the ethical duties and conflicts raised by the scenario in Box 9.1.

BOX 9.1

ESTRELLA'S CONFLICTING OBLIGATIONS

Estrella recently completed a field placement at the Aqua Family Center. Aqua serves families who have children with developmental challenges. Estrella just obtained a job with another agency, Burgundy Family Services. Burgundy's services are like those of Aqua, but in a different part of the city. One of Estrella's client families from her fieldwork at Aqua, the Bentleys, asks if she can continue to work with them at Burgundy. Estrella wants to honor the Bentleys' right to self-determination; however, she is not sure whether working with the Bentleys at Burgundy would violate any ethical or contractual obligations that she might have. She is also not sure with whom she should consult in order to decide what she should do. Consider the first four steps of the Framework for Managing Ethical Issues in Chapter 2. How would you advise Estrella about managing the issues raised in this situation?

OBLIGATIONS WITHIN AGENCIES

Ethical obligations within our agencies are defined in Part 3 of the NASW Code of Ethics (2021).[1] We also have agency-related obligations defined by our agencies' policies and employment contracts. As we go through each of these obligations, consider how they fit with our ethical commitments to professional competence, integrity, human relationships, access to service, and respect for the dignity and worth of all people.

Client Records

Standard 3.04 says we should maintain timely client records, accurately reflecting the services we provide. If we provide false, incomplete, or inaccurate records, we may be held liable within our agencies or through our professional regulatory bodies. Each client record should contain sufficient information to allow us to monitor progress from session to session, and to allow our agencies to monitor the

---

1. Given the focus of this textbook, this section highlights the obligations of frontline, generalist social workers within their agencies. Note that Part 3 of the NASW Code also includes ethical obligations of supervisors and administrators.

appropriateness and effectiveness of our services (Wilkins, 2017). Good record keeping demonstrates that we are providing competent and ethical services (Reamer, 2021c). If clients claim we have engaged in malpractice or unethical behavior, case records provide valuable information as to what issues arose, how we handled them, and the reasons for our decisions. Accordingly, case records may be vital to defend against lawsuits or professional ethics complaints. Good record keeping also ensures continuity of services. If we become ill, go on vacation, or cannot serve our clients for other reasons, our supervisors or another worker in the agency may review our records in order to follow up with our clients.

Each agency should have policies specifying what information should be kept in client records and for how long.[2] We should include only information relevant to work with the specific client—for instance, the client's presenting problem, the client's goals, and the information required for us to work with clients to fulfill these goals. To respect client confidentiality, we should exclude information that is not directly relevant to the services being provided (Polowy & Morgan, 2004). For instance, a client may disclose she is having an affair. If your role is to help find this client a job and the fact of her affair is irrelevant, then do not include this information in her record, even if you think this information is interesting. For another scenario involving client records, please see Box 9.2.

Federal laws such as Health Information Technology for Economic and Clinical Health Act (HITECH, 2009) and Health Insurance Portability and Accountability Act (HIPAA, 1996) provide special provisions regarding confidentiality of electronic health care records (U.S. Department of Health and Human Services, n.d.). If you are working within a health care system (including mental health), ensure that your records are gathered, managed, and stored in a manner consistent with these laws. When using technology, use encryption, passwords or other user authentication methods, and additional strategies to protect the confidentiality of client records and communications (NASW et al., 2017, Part 3). Under HITECH (2009), health care providers must report confidentiality breaches to patients, including the type of information involved and methods used to mitigate harm and prevent future breaches. If you are working in child protection, schools, or other non-health systems, then you and your agency should follow the record-keeping laws related to those systems (see also Chapter 11 regarding social work accountability and regulation).

Standard 1.08 of the NASW Code specifies that we should provide clients with reasonable access to their records. Reasonable access typically includes letting clients view their psychosocial assessments, progress notes, and any other information we include in their paper or electronic files. Beginning social workers

---

2. Typically, state laws and agency policies specify that records be kept for a minimum of 2 to 6 years. This ensures that the agency has records should a client return for services or should a client sue the agency for malpractice.

BOX 9.2

SHAKIRA

Shakira is providing case management services to Felix, a client transitioning from prison to the community after he completed his 6-year sentence for armed robbery. Shakira's agency is separate from the criminal justice system; however, it receives funding from this system to help clients make successful transitions to the community. Shakira has been helping Felix with issues related to housing, job retraining, and life skills. During one session, Felix and Shakira are discussing safety issues. Felix says that there have been several muggings in his neighborhood. He adds that he has been thinking of buying a gun to protect himself. Shakira reminds Felix that, as a person convicted of a felony, he may not be permitted to buy a gun. Felix responds that he will not buy a gun and that he wants to stay away from any further legal troubles. Shakira validates his decision. Felix asks Shakira not to write anything about guns in his case records because he does not want his records to state anything bad about himself. Shakira feels conflicted. On the one hand, Shakira believes that Felix is not planning to buy a gun and wants to support his wishes. On the other hand, she is concerned that she may need to document this discussion about guns because it is relevant to their work. What should Shakira do? What is your rationale for suggesting this course of action?

sometimes assume that they or the agency own the records and can decide whether to share them with clients; however, agency policies and laws provide clients with specific rights to access to their own records (HIPAA, 1996; Polowy & Morgan, 2004; U.S. Department of Health and Human Services, n.d.). We should withhold records only for exceptional reasons (e.g., when a client is currently homicidal and the case records identify where the potential victim may be found, or when protecting the confidentiality of a third person).[3] If you have questions about whether or when to share records with clients, consult your supervisor and/or the person in your agency designated to deal with records and confidentiality issues. Some agencies provide clients with instant access to electronic records through password-protected portals (sometimes called, "open records"). In these settings, we should be particularly careful about how we document client information, knowing that clients may see their records without the benefit of being with us to explain the content and respond to any concerns (e.g., imagine a client who reads that she tested negative for hepatitis and assumes that "negative" means she has hepatitis).

---

3. Legislation that mandates reporting of child maltreatment, for instance, typically allows non-professional reporters to remain anonymous. In other words, the person who is the subject of an abuse allegation would not have a right to find out who submitted the allegation. Social workers and other professionals typically need to identify themselves when they provide reports of child maltreatment.

Billing

In some agencies, services are free or they are covered primarily by health care insurance. In others, clients pay fees covering all or most of their services. For many beginning social workers, engaging clients in discussions about fees and billing may be uncomfortable. We want to ensure that services are accessible to all people in need. We may feel awkward asking people for money, particularly if we are concerned that they are unable or unwilling to pay. Still, as part of the informed consent process, we should let clients know the expectations around fees and payment in an assertive and kindly manner. Standard 1.13 states that we should ensure that fees are "fair, reasonable, and commensurate with the services performed." As a matter of honesty, we should not overcharge for our services or charge for services that are not needed or not performed. Consider a client experiencing high levels of distress. He may be willing to pay extra to see you right away; still, we should not exploit the client's predicament by charging extra.

Standard 1.13 also suggests that, when setting fees, we should consider the client's ability to pay. Within some agencies, we may be able to use a sliding scale by lowering fees for people with lower incomes. Within some agencies, sliding scales may be prohibited. Some health insurance and managed-care programs prohibit sliding scales or waiving fees and deductibles. Some agencies offer scholarships to clients in financial need. Others may advocate with insurance companies for reduced fees. Sometimes, we need to be creative in order to serve clients in an equitable manner, for instance, allowing certain clients to pay their bills over time or finding other agencies that can provide services for free or at reduced fees.

In terms of invoicing clients, our billing should reflect "the nature and extent of services" and "identify who provided the service" (S.3.05). Clients have a right to know the specific services for which they are being charged. For programs that provide one type of service (e.g., counseling), billing may be relatively simple. For hospitals, residential programs, and other practice settings that provide multiple services to each client, billing can be more complicated. Consider an in-patient addictions treatment program that charges $10,000 per week. Standard 3.05 suggests that clients have a right to know what portion of this fee is related to group counseling versus meals, individual counseling, recreational therapy, acupuncture, or other services offered by the program.

Client Transfers

When clients initiate moves from one agency to another, social workers at the receiving agency should consider the clients' needs and best interests (S.3.06). Assume that a client calls and tells you that he does not like a psychosocial assessment that he received at a prior agency; he asks you to conduct a new one. Before you accept the client for services, prudent practice suggests that you explore his relationship with the other agency, including potential benefits and risks of switching agencies. It may be beneficial for him to remain with the original agency, for instance, if there were issues that could be worked out through advocacy or conflict resolution. The client may be able to save time and money by staying with the same service provider. You could also avoid confusion and conflict with the other agency. Consider, for instance, a client who terminates services every time a worker asks difficult, but important questions. Standard 3.05(b) suggests that you should speak with the client about whether it would be useful to consult with the prior service provider. Consultation could help you serve him more effectively. Consultation also shows respect for the other service provider, allowing her to share input about what was helpful or unhelpful in prior services. Ultimately, clients have a right to self-determination, including the right to switch service providers and to decide whether or not we may speak with prior service providers as part of the transfer process.

Resource Allocation

As noted in Chapter 2, we have a duty to promote social justice. Within our agencies, Standard 3.07(b) suggests that we should advocate for "resource allocation procedures that are open and fair." Assume that your workplace has insufficient bathroom facilities for employees with special needs. Even if you are not directly affected, you should advocate for accessible facilities. Other examples of resources for employees include office space, technology, funding and time for continuing education, supervision, and means of supporting self-care (e.g., mental health days, employee assistance programs, and access to fresh air).

As a matter of integrity, we should be good stewards of our agencies' resources, including prudent use of our time, office space, and technology (S.3.09[g]). Given that agencies have limited budgets, we may need to make difficult choices about how to meet our clients' needs. We should make resource allocation issues in a nondiscriminatory manner, based on "appropriate and consistently applied principles" (S.3.07[b])). Assume that you are conducting a needs assessment but do not have sufficient time or resources to interview everyone in the community that you are studying. It would be inappropriate to gather information from only those people who are easiest to access (e.g., people with landline telephones or people who are home during the daytime). To ensure the needs assessment is fair and inclusive, you could identify a random sampling of people from the community. Alternatively, you could use purposeful sampling to ensure that research participants include people from various ethnic, socioeconomic, and religious groups.

As a frontline worker, you may need help from administrators to ensure that resource allocation within your agency is fair and sufficient to meet client needs. Standard 3.07(a) states that social work administrators should advocate for adequate resources to meet clients' needs. Often, we need to engage with funding bodies, government officials, or others outside our agencies to ensure that our agencies and clients have sufficient resources.

Commitments to Employers

Our ethical commitments to employers are based on the ethical principle of integrity, acting in an honest and trustworthy manner. Standard 3.09(a) of the NASW Code suggests that we should "generally adhere to commitments made to employers and employing organizations." We incur commitments to employers through agency contracts and policies. During the hiring process, employers may require us to sign employment contracts specifying our rights and obligations as employees (e.g., the pay we will receive, our hours of work, and the services we will provide). Some employers also ask us to sign additional forms, specifying our commitments to maintain client confidentiality, follow agency policy, adhere to state laws, abide by the NASW Code of Ethics, comply with work safety standards, or avoid conflicts of interest with the employer (e.g., setting up a competing private practice). If we do not comply with agency contracts or policies, then we may be subject to agency discipline, such as restrictions on practice, demotion, denial of promotion, or dismissal. As we will see in the following section, when our agency obligations conflict with our other ethical obligations, we may be faced with ethical dilemmas or situations of ethical distress.

CONFLICTING ETHICAL AND AGENCY OBLIGATIONS

Ideally, our *ethical obligations as social workers* are consistent with our *obligations to our agencies as employees*. For instance, Standard 1.03 of the NASW Code says we should provide clients with informed consent and our agency supports this ethical standard by ensuring that we make use of appropriate informed consent forms. In some situations, however, our agency obligations and ethical obligations conflict. The NASW Code envisions such situations and provides general guidance about how to manage such conflicts. Standard 3.09(b) encourages us to improve our agencies' policies and procedures, including the efficiency and effectiveness of our services. Consider a situation in which you facilitate groups for the Marines. Agency policy directs you to use a program designed to enhance the resilience of Marines who may experience trauma during active duty. You become aware of research that suggests this resiliency training program (RTP) is ineffective. According to Standard 3.09(b), you should advocate for the use of evidence-based interventions. What would you do, however, if your supervisor continues to direct you to use RTP? Standard 3.09(c) suggests that we should "take reasonable steps to ensure that employers are aware of social workers' ethical obligations as set forth in the NASW Code of Ethics." Accordingly, you could inform your supervisor that, under Standard 1.04(c), you have an obligation to serve clients in a competent manner and protect them from harm. Further, under Standard 3.09(d), you have an obligation to ensure that your agency's practices are consistent with the NASW Code. Ideally, you and your supervisor can develop a solution so that your agency practices are consistent with your ethical obligations. If you receive a complaint or malpractice lawsuit suggesting that you have violated your ethical obligations, it is no excuse to say that you were simply following agency policies.

The following sections explore how to respond to conflicting obligations, including seeking redress through channels inside or outside your agency. As you learn about different methods of managing conflicting obligations, consider how you might apply these strategies in the example presented in Box 9.3.

BOX 9.3

Needmore Eating Disorder Services

Zena has been working as a social worker with Needmore Eating Disorder Services (NEDS) for two years. She recently learned about a number of questionable marketing strategies that NEDS uses to attract clients to their residential programs. NEDS informs clients that, for each additional person that they refer to NEDS, they will be entered into a lottery for a free computer. NEDS also offers to waive copays and deductibles for clients who post positive testimonials about the program on social media. Zena is concerned that these marketing strategies reflect negatively on the integrity of the program and the professionals that work there. She is also concerned that these marketing schemes may violate state and federal laws, including the federal Anti-Kickback Statute (42 U.S.C. §1320a-7b[b]; see https://oig.hhs.gov/compliance/physician-education/01laws.asp). Zena is reluctant to discuss this issue with her supervisor, Solel, because she suspects that Solel supports this program and would simply dismiss Zena's concerns. Zena considers speaking with the executive director, Noam, who she thinks will provide a more sympathetic response to her concerns. What are the first steps that Zena should take to address her concerns about the agency's marketing practices? What communication and conflict resolution strategies should she use when speaking with others inside or outside her agency?

Managing Conflicting Obligations

In situations where following agency policy goes against the needs, interests, or wishes of clients, we might feel inclined to follow agency policy and inform clients that we have to do so (van der Tier et al., 2021). By following agency policy, we can stay out of trouble with our agency and perhaps win favor with our supervisors. We may also avoid or minimize anger from clients, given that we are laying responsibility with our agencies rather than assuming responsibility ourselves. Standard 1.01 of the NASW

Code states that our primary ethical commitment is to our clients. Accordingly, when agency policy conflicts with client needs, interests, and wishes, we should consider advocating for our clients. For instance, if a 24-year-old client is being denied services because agency policy restricts services to foster children under 24 years old, we could advocate for an exception for this particular client. Alternatively, we could advocate for new resources and services for clients aging out of the foster care system.

Saying that we have an obligation to ensure that our agency's practices are consistent with the NASW Code is relatively easy. Making this happen, however, can be challenging. We want to maintain good relationships with supervisors and others in our agencies. Further, we do not want to risk our jobs. If we challenge authority or act in a manner that seems disloyal to our employer, we may be ostracized or disciplined (Bibus, 2015). To manage discrepancies between our ethical and agency-based obligations, we can employ collaborative conflict resolution skills, including assertiveness, empathic listening, and joint problem solving (Barsky, 2017a). To raise your concerns about RTP, you might use an assertive I-statement. "I've been researching the effectiveness of RTP. I'm very concerned that RTP is not effective for increasing the resiliency of active military." You could also share copies of the research to support your concerns. If your supervisor says, "The Marines have invested a lot of time and money into RTP," you could show empathy by reflecting your supervisor's concerns. "I understand that the Marines have made a huge investment in this program. Switching to a different program could be costly." By validating your supervisor's concerns, you are showing respect and building trust. You could then invite your supervisor to engage in collaborative problem solving. "Perhaps we could review the research together to determine the most effective options for resiliency programs. We could also consider whether there are ways to reduce costs for training so that administration is more likely to support a change to a more effective program."

In addition to speaking with our supervisors about needed changes, we may need to engage with agency administrators, coworkers, or people outside the agency. Ordinarily, we should follow the chain of decision making and responsibility within our agencies, starting with our immediate supervisors and focusing on collaborative problem solving. Trying to resolve issues within our agencies demonstrates respect to our supervisors and work colleagues. It also avoids the risk of escalating conflict by going outside the agency. If we have exhausted in-house approaches to resolving ethical issues without coming to a reasonable solution, then we may need to consider whistleblowing.

Whistleblowing

Whistleblowing refers to any actions taken by employees or former employees that bring attention to illegal activities, unethical behaviors, or other serious problems within the agency (e.g., mistreating clients, financial corruption, exploitation of staff, or mismanagement of resources) (Ash, 2016). Whistleblowing is a form of advocacy (Raymond et al, 2017). It may include disclosures within an agency, such as when social workers take concerns about a clinical supervisor to a higher level (e.g., to the board of directors). Whistleblowing may also include disclosures outside the organization (e.g., to the media, funders, the public, or a governmental oversight body). Genuine whistleblowers are motivated by the hope that notifying people with power will result in holding wrongdoers accountable and prevent harm to others (Ash, 2016). Accordingly, whistleblowing fits with utilitarian ethics by promoting good in the world.

Within some organizational cultures, whistleblowers are shunned as traitors or tattletales. Some supervisors and coworkers may view whistleblowing as betraying friends, colleagues, and the agency, rather than promoting a just cause (Bibus, 2015; Raymond et al, 2017). Ethical standards for social workers suggest whistleblowing is not only permissible, but desirable when an agency's practices are unethical or unlawful (Ss.2.10 and 3.09[d] and [e]). Too often, social workers and other professionals have turned a blind eye to serious concerns (e.g., the abuse of children and older adults). They may rationalize that doing nothing is better than taking actions that may hurt the agency, their friendships, or their jobs. In some cases, social workers have been complicit in unethical and unlawful practices (Hayes, 2016).

When faced with decisions about whether to blow the whistle, we may experience moral distress. We know that the most ethical course of action is to take action to correct unethical or illegal behavior; however, the threat of retaliation or negative consequences can make it hard to do the right thing (Kölbel & Herold, 2019). Still, we should act for the greater good, not just what is good for ourselves. Whistleblowing takes moral courage, an essential virtue for confronting injustices, hypocrisy, and corruption (Papouli, 2019; Pope, 2015).

Green and Latting (2004) suggest that social workers use the following steps when deciding how to approach a situation that may require whistleblowing:

1. *Assess the situation, including your readiness to go forward.* Not every possible ethical violation requires whistleblowing. Before acting on a potential violation, assess the severity of the possible violation, the degree of harm it poses, and the reliability of evidence that you are depending on. If the violation or damages are not severe, try to resolve the issues through inside channels and avoid the riskier act of whistleblowing. As the cliché goes, "Choose your battles wisely." Ensure that you have sufficient evidence before making accusations that could harm others (Bibus, 2015). If you think that wrongdoing is taking place, but you lack good evidence, it will be difficult or impossible to make your case. Also, examine your own motivations to ensure you are acting out of genuine concern rather than anger, revenge, mistrust, or bias. Weigh the benefits of pursuing the cause versus the risks to yourself (e.g., alienation, harassment, or job loss), your clients (e.g.,

embarrassment, loss of services), and your agency (e.g., loss of face, funding, clients, or accreditation).

2. *Begin first with the alleged offenders.* If you decide to pursue the concerns, discuss them first with the alleged offenders (S.2.10[c]). This puts them on notice and allows you to assess whether the problems can be worked out amicably, without resorting to more formal, costly, or adversarial actions (Barsky, 2017a). Express your concerns in a calm, confident, and collegial manner. Allow your colleagues to explain their actions and vent their feelings by demonstrating empathy, patience, and sincere concern (Koocher & Keith-Spiegel, 2016).

3. *Establish a track record of credibility.* Develop credibility over time by practicing in an honest and professional manner. New workers and workers with spotty professional records may have a harder time convincing others that they are honest and properly motivated when they make allegations of impropriety against others. Make sure you have a positive track record before raising claims against others (e.g., wait until after you receive a positive performance evaluation before taking steps that may upset your supervisors). Build social capital within your agency by acting in a competent, honest, respectful, and reliable manner.

4. *Develop allies within the organization.* If you treat everyone else as if they are unaware or uncaring, they are more likely to act as adversaries. Explore who might support your cause and try to work together. Gather allies discreetly. Validate concerns of potential but wary allies. Empathize with their discomfort about becoming a whistleblower or advocating for a cause when there is a possibility of retribution.

5. *Gather corroborating evidence.* If you make an allegation and the only evidence is "the alligator's word" versus the "alleged perpetrator's word," you will have difficulty proving the alleged perpetrator did something wrong. Determine the accuracy and strength of your case (Koocher & Keith-Spiegel, 2016). Bolster your case by gathering corroborating evidence, such as eyewitnesses, documents, photographs, and other recordings of events (Barsky, 2012). Keep careful records (including a chronology of events) in case a grievance or court hearing is initiated against you as retribution for whistleblowing.

6. *Follow the agency's policies and procedures for expressing complaints.* Unless the situation is dire and urgent, follow the agency's usual protocols for raising concerns. Generally, this means proceeding up the chain of command or organizational hierarchy (e.g., speak to the worker, then the supervisor, then the program director, then the board of directors, then the governmental body responsible for the agency, if any). Following agency procedures demonstrates integrity and respect.

7. *Consult for support and expertise.* Given the emotional, social, legal, and financial risks involved with whistleblowing, consider consulting with others who can help with each of these risks—for instance, the NASW state or national ethics committees, state regulatory bodies,

knowledgeable colleagues, or legal counsel. Different consultants may offer you different types of information and advice.[4] Some may also offer you a place to vent anger, grief, despair, and other emotions. Do not consult with family members, friends, or your own therapist if doing so would require a breach of client confidentiality. In some cases, the agency violations do not involve confidential client information, so accessing help from family, friends, and therapists may be appropriate. You are permitted to consult with attorneys, professional ethics committees, and state regulatory bodies even if the issues involve confidential client information. Limit disclosures of client information to what is necessary, respecting client confidentiality as much as possible. The Government Accountability Project (n.d.) is a nonprofit group that offers information and support for whistleblowers (see http://www.whistleblower.org). IF YOU ARE CONCERNED ABOUT THE SERIOUS ETHICAL OR LEGAL VIOLATIONS WITHIN YOUR AGENCY BUT YOU ARE AFRAID TO ACT, CONSULT WITH OTHERS. Some of the most important social changes have occurred because someone took a risk. Still, you want to determine what risks to take based on the best information and advice available.

8. *Consider going outside your agency only as a last resort.* Before deciding to voice your concern with the media, the government, the court, or some other forum outside your agency, make sure you have considered every other alternative. Once you speak outside the agency, be prepared for the consequences. You may have to leave the agency and find another job. Make use of your supporters and consultants to minimize risks and maximize your chances of successful resolution of the conflict. Use what you are learning about advocacy in your social work courses, including those on policy development, community organization, and social change.

Ideally, social workers practice in work environments that support the same values and ethical principles as the social work profession. In practice, social agencies may experience many of the same social problems that exist in general society (e.g., corruption, discrimination, and abuse of power). Thus, social workers should foster agency cultures that facilitate disclosure of problems so they can be handled effectively within the agency (Bibus, 2015). When problems cannot be managed effectively within the agency, they should also be prepared to pursue change by going outside their organizational contexts.

Please review the case in Box 9.4. Given what you now know about whistleblowing, identify concerns about the way that the social worker engaged in whistle blowing.

---

4. E.g., attorneys can advise you on whether state or federal legislation provides whistleblower protection, permitting greater freedom to report wrongdoing without fear of firing, harassment, or other forms of retaliation by the employer (e.g., the Whistleblower Protection Act, 1989; see https://www.whistleblowers.gov/statutes for other statutes). Some legislation also provides rewards for people who blow the whistle on abuses within government agencies.

BOX 9.4

IKBIR

Ikbir is a community service worker at the Sikh Society of Banksville (SSB). One day, Ikbir overhears a work colleague, Katiya, talking with friends about SSB's executive director, Qudrat. As Ikbir listens from behind a screen, Katiya is sharing stories about how Qudrat made sexual advances which she felt she could not refuse. He hugged and kissed her. She felt embarrassed, disgusted, and disempowered. When Katiya's friends depart, Ikbir invites Katiya into his office to discuss what he overheard. Ikbir expresses empathy and concern. He then says that he can help her file a formal complaint against Qudrat. Initially, Katiya minimizes the concerns, suggesting that it was just a kiss and no big deal. Ikbir suggests that it is a big deal and that Qudrat needs to be investigated and fired. He expresses concern about other women that Qudrat may be mistreating. Katiya asks Ikbir to "just forget about it." She likes her job and does not want to lose it. Ikbir says she can hire an attorney and sue Qudrat. Once again, Katiya asks Ikbir to leave well enough alone. Ikbir reports Qudrat to SSB's board of directors. When the board asks for evidence of sexual harassment, Ikbir says that Katiya can verify what happened. The board invites Katiya to a meeting to hear her concerns. During the meeting, Katiya reports that nothing happened and that Qudrat is a wonderful executive director. Ikbir becomes incensed when he hears that the board is not investigating Qudrat any further. Ikbir confronts Qudrat in a staff meeting, saying, "I know that you've been harassing the female staff at this agency. You are a disgrace to this agency and to the values that we represent." Shortly after the meeting, Ikbir receives written notice that he is being fired for making defamatory comments that are harmful to the agency and the people it serves.

Analyze the steps that Ikbir took in this situation. Identify which steps that he took that were appropriate and which ones were not. What steps would have been more appropriate, both when Ikbir first spoke with Katiya and then after Katiya said that she did not want Ikbir to pursue the matter any further?

CIVIL DISOBEDIENCE

Civil disobedience refers to using "a public, nonviolent, conscientious yet political act contrary to law usually done with the aim of bringing about a change in the law or policies of the government" (Rawls, 1971, p. 354). Although some definitions of civil disobedience are limited to nonviolent actions directed toward government, civil disobedience could also include nonviolent actions designed to bring about changes in the policies and practices of an agency. Historical examples of civil disobedience include

- the Boston Tea Party (dumping tea into the harbor) to protest the British policy of taxation without representation;
- black-rights activist Rosa Parks refusing to sit on the back of the bus in a protest against racial segregation;
- antiwar activists staging sit-ins and blocking access to public buildings (Delmas & Brownlee, 2021);
- ACT UP's shutting down the Food and Drug Administration to raise consciousness about AIDS and to advocate for experimental drugs to be made available more quickly and more equitably (Schulman, 2021); and
- Colin Kaepernick of the San Francisco 49ers kneeling during national anthem, in violation of National Football League policies, to protest wrongful treatment of people of color (particularly by law enforcement officials).

Civil disobedience may be used by individuals, groups, and social movements in combination with other strategies to foster broader legal and social changes (Pineda, 2021).

Ordinarily, we should promote legal and agency policy reforms through legal means, such as lobbying government, advocating within the agency, mobilizing communities, and educating the public (Lens, 2004). However, the NASW Code envisions situations when we might be ethically justified[5] in violating laws or agency policies in order to pursue higher ethical objectives. The Purpose statement in the Code suggests that when ethical standards conflict with legal obligations, social workers "must make a responsible effort to resolve the conflict in a manner that is consistent with the values, principles, and standards expressed in this Code. If a reasonable resolution of the conflict does not appear possible, social workers should seek proper consultation before making a decision." Other than suggesting that we should seek proper consultation, the Code does not provide much guidance on when, if ever, we are justified in disobeying laws or agency policies in order to promote higher values. Perhaps the Code remains vague on this issue due to lack of consensus in the profession. The issue of civil disobedience is controversial, so it is challenging for organizations such as the NASW to provide members with specific instructions on when violating laws or agency policies may be ethical. The following discussion offers analysis of the ethical issues to be considered when determining whether and when we engage in civil disobedience. As with other ethical dilemmas, reasonable people may disagree about which responses are most ethical.

---

5. *Ethically justified* does not mean the same as *ethically required*. Although some workers might believe an act of civil disobedience is ethically justified, others may disagree, as they are not ethically required to participate in civil disobedience.

When considering whether a proposed act of civil disobedience is ethically **justifiable**, we should analyze three factors: the importance of the cause in relation to the seriousness of the legal or policy violation, the willingness of the parties to openly admit they are breaking the law or agency policy, and the willingness of the parties to accept the consequences of breaking the law or policy.

Importance of the Cause

Although the NASW Code instructs social workers to promote social justice and act against discrimination and oppression, each of us needs to make individualized decisions about which causes to pursue and how to go about pursuing them. Given limited time, energy, and resources, we need to prioritize where to place our efforts. The more important the cause, the more important it is for us to give the cause priority. As per **utilitarianism**, we might ask, "If I have to choose between various causes, which cause will promote the greatest good, for the greatest number?" Thus, based on Maslow's hierarchy of needs (Maslow et al., 1987), we could justify a decision to advocate for food for 100 starving clients rather than advocating for movie tickets for 100 mildly bored individuals. When considering the use of civil disobedience to pursue a cause, we should not only consider whether the cause is important in relation to other causes, but also whether it is so important that civil disobedience is justified.

Although civil disobedience may be useful in promoting **social justice**, it also entails various risks and costs. Ordinarily, we should follow the **rule of law**. Following the law promotes order, decency, security, liberty, and respect for the rights of others. If we could justify breaking laws or policies simply because we personally disagreed with them, society could fall into chaos and anarchy. Crime may be contagious. If one person is allowed to break the laws with impunity, then everyone else may feel they also have a right to break the law (*Olmstead v. United States,* 1928). Thus, social workers should ensure they have strong justification before engaging in civil disobedience.

For some social workers, breaking laws or agency policies is never justified. They may view following the law and policies as absolute duties. This duty does not necessarily prevent them from challenging laws or policies. They may believe it is ethical to advocate for changes, but only through legal means. For other workers, breaking laws or agency policies may be justified, depending on the consequences. To determine the ethicality of civil disobedience, such workers would ask, "Does the end justify the means?" Consider a group of African Americans who believe the state government has an unofficial policy restricting African American–owned businesses from obtaining an equal share of government contracts. They ask you (a community organizer) to help plan a protest and blockade that would involve circling the state capitol with vehicles to prevent legislators from entering or leaving the building. On its face, the cause appears ethical: challenging discrimination (S.6.04). But does this cause warrant the proposed form of civil disobedience? As a social worker, you should first help the group verify that discrimination is actually taking place. You could then help the group consider other means of promoting its cause: What forms of advocacy have they already tried, what alternative forms of advocacy are available, and which of these, if any, should be tried before resorting to the blockade? Civil disobedience should be viewed as a last resort, to be used only after the group has made good-faith attempts to change the laws or social policies through legal means (Delmas & Brownlee, 2021). You should also help the group explore the risks involved in a blockade—for instance, will it help or hurt their public image, what is the likelihood that protesters or others may be injured, how will the protest affect the running of the government, and what other unintended harm may arise? How willing is the group to accept these risks? How willing is the group to impose risks on innocent bystanders? For an example of civil disobedience involving agency policies, see Box 9.5.

In addition to having a good cause (or an end that justifies the means), some ethicists argue that there must be a reasonable chance of success in order to justify civil

---

BOX 9.5

FOODBANK FOR ALL

Enid is a social worker at a food bank that has a policy restricting services to American citizens and people with visas or other documentation to reside in the United States. After turning away many people without documentation, Enid decides that it is time for change. She approaches her supervisor and program director about the need to provide services to all, highlighting their ethical obligations as social workers to promote social justice and to ensure access to needed services, particularly to people in vulnerable situations. They respond by saying that they have limited resources and that they need to prioritize citizens and residents with documentation. They claim that they may lose government funding and donations if they start serving people without documentation. Enid thinks it is time to stand up for what is right. She considers providing food to whomever comes to the foodbank without asking questions about their residency or documentation. Under this option, she could provide food surreptitiously, so nobody else will know what she is doing. For a second option, she considers inviting a large number of people without documentation to come to the foodbank on a particular morning. She could use this event to make a public statement about the need for the foodbank to provide food to all people, regardless of their immigration status. Under option two, she could invite journalists and other media to raise awareness of her acts of civil disobedience.

What are the potential benefits and risks of Enid's two options? What steps should she take before deciding whether and how to engage in civil disobedience?

disobedience (Rawls, 1971). If the cause is futile, then why incur the risks? Others, from a **deontological** perspective, suggest that civil disobedience may be justified because challenging social injustice is the right thing to do, regardless of the consequences (Kant, 1979/Orig.1779). When analyzing the ethics of civil disobedience, it is useful for us to not only consider whether the cause is good, but also whether and how to take the consequences of the actions into account.

Openly Admit Breaking the Law or Policy

The primary purpose of civil disobedience is not to *violate* the law or policy, but to *change* it. Given this purpose, if we plan to participate in civil disobedience then we should be willing to admit that we are going to break existing laws or policies (Delmas & Brownlee, 2021). Our intent is not to hurt others, seek vengeance, or surreptitiously violate laws for personal gain. Rather, our intent is to promote social justice (Pineda, 2021). In San Francisco, for instance, public officials of the City and County of San Francisco acted unlawfully by issuing marriage licenses to same-sex couples, even though the existing law restricted marriage as between a man and a woman (*In re Marriage Cases,* 2008). Organizers of this act of civil disobedience ensured that the act was open to the public, inviting media to cover the event. The purpose of the event was not to flout the law, but to provide a test case for the fairness and constitutionality of the existing law. In contrast, consider a social worker who refuses to report child abuse because she believes mandatory reporting laws are ineffective at protecting children and harmful to social worker–client relationships. If the worker does not go public with her refusal to report abuse, then her actions are unlawful, but they are not acts of civil disobedience (Kalichman, 1999).

In the blockade example, impeding access to the state capitol is a public event. Proponents of the blockade are not simply acting out of anger or aggression toward authority. They are advocating for social justice (Delmas & Brownlee, 2021). Thus, as their community organizer, you could help them present the blockade to the public in a positive manner. For instance, you could work with the media in advance of the blockade to provide them with background information on the blockade, you could prepare protesters for how to respond to law enforcement officials in a nonviolent manner,[6] and you could help the protesters present themselves as courageous advocates of social justice, rather than "criminals" or "misfits." These strategies help reduce risks and increase the likelihood of successful social advocacy (National Lawyers Guild, n.d.).[7]

---

6. E.g., protesters could politely inform an arresting police officer that they would like to speak with an attorney before answering any questions.

7. See Chapter 13 for additional examples of risk management (e.g., documenting the rationale for civil disobedience, building supportive coalitions, and obtaining legal advice).

Accept the Consequences of Breaking the Law or Policy

The third standard for civil disobedience is that when we participate in the civil disobedience, we should be willing to accept the consequences of breaking the law or policy (Delmas & Brownlee, 2021; Rawls, 1971). Our willingness to accept the consequences of engaging in illegal acts gives us moral authority to commit those acts. We are not just paying lip service to support a cause; we are willing to make significant sacrifices for the cause.[8]

When we encourage others to participate in civil disobedience, we should ensure that they know they may be charged with and convicted of particular crimes. Many of the more common crimes associated with civil disobedience are misdemeanors: causing public nuisance, violating traffic control laws, trespass, unlawful assembly, failure to disperse, resisting arrest, and violating specific municipal codes (National Lawyers Guild, n.d.). The penalties for misdemeanors typically range from warnings to suspended sentences, probation, fines, and jail time of up to 1 year. More serious offenses, called felonies, may result from assaulting police officers, seriously damaging property, or using weapons to cause injury (National Lawyers Guild, n.d.). Felony convictions may lead to harsher sentences, including incarceration in federal penitentiaries. In addition, people with felony convictions must cope with a criminal record for the rest of their lives (barring a pardon from the state governor or U.S. president). For social workers, the impact of felony convictions may be severe, as some social agencies have policies against hiring workers with felony convictions. Further, social work licensing laws may prohibit licensure of social workers with certain types of felony convictions.

We may be held criminally responsible for helping with civil disobedience, whether or not we actually participate in the primary activities that violated the law. Assume, for instance, that you help organize a blockade of the Capitol, but you are not present for the blockade and the ensuing violence. As someone who planned the event, you could be charged with conspiracy or incitement.[9] If you assisted in the commission of the particular crimes (e.g., providing resources that the protesters used to commit the offense), you could be charged with aiding and abetting. If you helped protesters hide from the police after they committed the crime, you could be charged with obstructing justice or being an accessory to the

---

8. Consider, for instance, an activist who is arrested, but law enforcement officials agree to let the activist free if she promises not to re-offend. The activist might refuse this deal in order to maintain her moral authority and maintain pressure on the government. She might even engage in a hunger strike to demonstrate her moral commitment and put greater pressure on the government to change the unjust laws.

9. Note, for instance, how the U.S. House of Representatives impeached former President Donald Trump in 2021 for inciting an insurrection at the Capitol even though he did not participate directly in the violence at the Capitol.

offense (Legal Information Institute, n.d.). Some states, including Florida, have created new felony offenses and harsher penalties for rioting, damaging historic memorials, intimidation designed to change viewpoints, and cyberintimidation (Weiss, 2021).[10]

When we are advancing important causes, we may encourage others to join us in acts of civil disobedience. The principles of informed consent suggest that we should not lead clients or others into civil disobedience unless they are fully aware of the potential risks and benefits. Thus, all planners, organizers, supporters, and participants in civil disobedience should be apprised of the potential consequences of their roles. We must be particularly careful when working with vulnerable populations to ensure that we are not exploiting them or putting them at undue risk by encouraging them to participate in civil disobedience (S.6.04). When working with people with mental illness, for instance, we should ensure that they have mental capacity to decide whether to participate in civil disobedience. We should consider whether participation in civil disobedience could inflame issues related to their mental illness.

Although social workers and others considering civil disobedience should be willing to accept the possibility of criminal charges and convictions, they should also note that criminal prosecution and conviction are not certainties. Police have discretion in whether to press charges. In some instances, the legal violations or harm done are not serious enough to warrant charges. In other cases, the police may be sensitive to public support for the protestors or the possibility of public backlash from pressing charges against a group that is standing up for a good moral cause. Similarly, the prosecuting attorneys may decide to drop charges or plea bargain to reduce charges in return for a guilty plea. In court, alleged offenders could raise the defense that they were challenging unjust and unconstitutional laws. However, good conscience or intent (breaking the law to change it) is not necessarily a legal justification for crimes committed during acts of civil disobedience—particularly if the court finds the laws challenged to be valid (Delmas & Brownlee, 2021; Lambek, 1987). Individuals or groups considering civil disobedience should consult attorneys who specialize in this area. Attorneys can provide legal information as well as advice on how to manage the legal risks of civil disobedience (National Lawyers Guild, n.d.).

Note that the use of nonviolent strategies (including noncooperation with laws, passive resistance, work stoppages, and going limp at arrests) provides participants with moral justification for the means of their actions, not just their ends (Beer, 2021). When assessing the ethics of civil disobedience, we need to consider both the means (the specific strategies and tactics) and the ends (the desired outcomes).

---

10. These anti-intimidation and anti-rioting laws may be challenged in court as unconstitutional because they restrict free speech. There are also concerns that these laws could be used to target Black communities and other people of color.

We should remember that even when we have a good cause and when we use ethical means of civil disobedience, we may risk prosecution. Dr. Martin Luther King Jr., Claudette Colvin, Mahatma Gandhi, Nelson Mandela, and many other great civil rights advocates have spent time in jail, even though they were pursuing social justice through nonviolence.

Within agencies, violating policies—even with good intentions—can result in dismissal, demotion, or other forms of discipline by the agency. Still, there may be occasions where we accept these risks to correct injustices and stimulate change. Protecting our jobs and source of income is understandable. Still, if we remain silent and do nothing, then we become part of the problem rather than part of the solution. In the 1980s, activists used the moniker "Silence = Death" to symbolize the importance of everyone speaking up to address the AIDS epidemic. Many people did not speak up for fear of ostracization. As the concept of moral courage suggests, sometimes we need to do what is right even when we know that we may experience negative consequences from pursuing what is right (Papouli, 2019). Congressman and civil rights activist John Lewis referred to the use of nonviolence to stimulate social change as "good trouble" (Hayden, 2020).

Some social workers and agency administrators may be astonished to see an ethics textbook that provides guidance on how to break laws and agency policies. Likewise, if you were to suggest civil disobedience to your professional colleagues, you might be met with shock, dismay, or derision. Decisions to promote social justice by violating laws or agency policies should not be taken lightly. When colleagues raised doubts about the ethics or viability of civil disobedience, we can recall historical examples, such as those presented earlier. Some of our most important changes in laws and social policies have transpired due to civil disobedience.

Because many social agencies are funded and regulated by the state, social workers who wish to participate in civil disobedience may not be able to count on support from their agencies. We may need to participate in civil disobedience as private citizens rather than in our professional capacities. Even then, we may be subjected to discipline or dismissal from our agencies if they disapprove of our behavior—particularly if it leads to criminal prosecution.

CONCLUSION

As social workers, we have ethical obligations to promote social justice and to promote the wishes and wellbeing of our clients. We also have obligations within our practice settings, including those spelled out in agency policies and employment contracts. In many instances, our agencies' policies and practices support our ethical responsibilities. When our ethical obligations and agencies policies or practices conflict, however, we need to determine the best way to manage these conflicts. In some situations, we can advocate for changes in agency policies and practices so that they align with our ethical obligations. Ideally, we can use informal and collaborative approaches to bring about these changes. To address significant problems related to unethical, illegal, or harmful practices, we may also need to consider additional measures, such as whistleblowing and civil disobedience. Before using these measures, it is important to consult with others to ensure that these measures are warranted. In addition, it is important to work with others to improve the chances that these measures will be successful in addressing the problematic laws, policies, or practices. We can then ensure that not only is our cause good, but also the means of addressing our cause are good.

DISCUSSION QUESTIONS AND EXERCISES

1. *Violations*: Identify whether each of the following situations involves the violation of an ethical standard, and if so, which ethical standard it violates.

   a. A social worker waits 2 days before writing progress notes for a meeting with a particular client.

   b. A social worker accepts a client's health insurance for services and waives the client's copay because the client is financially stretched.

   c. A social worker conducts research with clients who are mourning the loss of a loved one. To identify a research sample, she includes clients who are coping relatively well and excludes clients who are having greater difficulty coping.

   d. A social worker facilitating a life skills training group is tired of working with a client who is constantly "rude and obnoxious." The worker transfers the client to another agency without telling the client or agency the true reason for the transfer. Instead, the worker says the client has "special needs" that cannot be accommodated at her agency.

   e. Agency policies allow employees up to 12 days per year for paid sick leave. Each year, a particular social worker takes off 6 days to go to a spa and have a massage. He views these days as mental health days, but he just tells his agency that he is sick and needs to take a day off.

   f. A client couple says they missed an appointment because their car was not working. Agency policy requires clients to cancel appointments at least 24 hours in advance, so the social worker charges the couple the regular fee for the missed appointment.

   g. The union at a community service association calls a strike to protest poor working conditions and low salaries. A social worker decides to cross the strike line and go to work because she believes that her duty to serve clients rises above any duties to the union or her agency.

   h. A social worker accepts job at an adoption agency that refuses to serve clients who identify as atheist.

2. *Manhattan Transfer*: Mitch has been providing counseling to Janet for 4 years. Janet lives in New Jersey but is planning to move to New York City. Mitch refers her to Vera, a social worker in New York. Although Vera is very competent, the main reason that Mitch referred Janet to her is because Vera is a close friend. Vera also refers clients to Mitch in return for his referrals. Vera and Mitch have a good personal relationship, making it easy for them to discuss the needs and concerns of the clients that they are referring to one another. What ethical concerns does this situation raise? How could Mitch make referrals in a more ethical manner?

3. *Request for Referral*: As part of your field education, you are providing intake assessments for people seeking inpatient treatment for gambling addictions. A prospective client, Borje, asks to have "a real social worker" conduct the intake assessment "not some student who doesn't know what they're doing yet." Your agency has a policy that the worker initially assigned to conduct the intake assessment is the one who conducts the assessment. How should you handle Borje's request? Use the first four steps of the Framework for Managing Ethical Issues in Chapter 2 to guide your thinking and to provide your rationale.

4. *Eligibility Dilemma*: You have been working with a client, Mikayla, who is aging out of the foster care system. She would like to continue to work with you; you would also like to continue to work with her, despite the agency's age restrictions. Mikayla has a history of abuse and abandonment. She finds it difficult to end relationships or start new ones. You think it would be in Mikayla's best interests to continue to work with her. What options should you and Mikayla consider? What are your ethical obligations to your client and your ethical obligations to your agency? How should you balance these obligations if they conflict? Under what circumstances, if any, might you consider working with Mikayla even if it goes against agency policy?

5. *Self-Care*: Quincy works in an agency serving clients who have experienced severe emotional trauma. Quincy is concerned about stress, vicarious trauma, and burnout. His agency does not provide social workers with opportunities for continuing education or self-care. Although his employment contract allows Quincy to have two weeks of paid vacation each year, Quincy is usually so busy serving clients that he rarely uses his vacation time. If he were to take a week off, his clients would be without help for a whole week. Which standards and language from the NASW Code could Quincy use to advocate for better support and resources from the agency? What types of personal and professional self-care could be useful for Quincy?

6. *Value Conflict*: Risha conducts psychosocial assessments for people seeking services at a reproductive assistance clinic. The clinic recently decided to offer ectogenesis, growing babies in artificial wombs

(Leonhard, 2016). Risha believes that ectogenesis is unethical because it is an unproven method of reproductive assistance. She thinks it is too risky and that it may offend some people's spiritual beliefs. She believes the agency is more concerned about building its reputation and making money than serving clients in a safe and ethical manner. What steps should Risha take to analyze the ethical issues and options for addressing her concerns? What guidance should she consider from the NASW Code?

7. *Research Pressure*: You are a research assistant helping to evaluate the effectiveness of biofeedback to assist people with anxiety-related problems. When analyzing the data, you find that biofeedback is not as effective as other methods of intervention. Your supervisor, Annette, plays with the data and writes the findings in a manner that strongly supports the biofeedback intervention. When you question Annette's analysis, she says that she needs to demonstrate the effectiveness of biofeedback so the agency continues to receive key funding. "It's for the greater good." You note that biofeedback is not dangerous, but it is not the best use of the agency's resources. You are experiencing ethical distress. You know that the analysis is flawed, but you are afraid to confront your supervisor. You do not want to lose your job and you are the main financial provider for your family. How can you foster and make use of moral courage in this situation? What steps should you take? Under what circumstances, if any, would you consider whistleblowing?

8. *Friend of Client*: You are a medical social worker who assists clients on dialysis and waiting for kidney transplants. One of your clients, Xiao, is related to a prominent malpractice attorney in your community. Your supervisor asks you to prioritize Xiao for transplant surgery even though there are other clients that should be prioritized according to the hospital's standard criteria. Your supervisor is afraid that if anything goes poorly with Xiao's situation, her lawyer-relative will sue the hospital. When analyzing the ethical issues raised by this situation, how do the principles of beneficence (doing good), nonmaleficence (do no harm), social justice, integrity, and fidelity to one's client and employer apply? What options should you consider if you cannot persuade your supervisor to use the hospital's usual criteria for prioritizing clients?

9. *Anonymous Report*: Gian is a case manager at an assisted living facility for older adults. He notices that some nurses use the same pair of gloves throughout their shifts. Agency policy suggests that nurses should change gloves between attending to each resident. Gian wants to address the issue but feels shy about speaking with the nurses. He does not want to cause any friction in his relationship with them. He considers making a phone call, on an anonymous basis, to a government agency that receives complaints about assisted living facilities. Which ethical standards should Gian consider when deciding what to do? What are the

possible benefits and risks of reporting this situation without providing Gian's name or contact information?

10. *Scope of Practice*: You work as a discharge planner in a hospital. The hospital is currently overwhelmed by a viral pandemic. The hospital is treating many more patients than it is equipped to handle. Also, the hospital is experiencing a shortage of nursing staff because many nurses have contracted the virus. Your supervisor asks you to assist with some nursing functions that are ordinarily beyond your scope of practice (e.g., physically moving patients from one area to another, monitoring intravenous bags, and administering medications). What ethical concerns should you and your supervisor discuss? Given the urgent nature of the need for someone to help the nursing staff, is it ethical for you to perform their functions? Why or why not? What other options could you and the hospital consider?

11. *Deportation Risk*: You are a school social worker. One of your clients, Teresa Alvarez (7), discloses that her parents sometimes hit her with a belt. Legally, you are required to report suspicions of child abuse to protective services. School policy also requires reporting suspicions of abuse. In this situation, you are reluctant to report Teresa's parents because they are in this country without documentation. You do not want to risk having them deported. You think that you could deal with the abuse issues yourself by meeting with the parents and educating them about the laws prohibiting them from hitting Teresa with a belt. You believe they want to obey the law and that all they need is some education. With whom should you speak before deciding how to proceed? How should you balance your ethical obligations to your client, her family, the law, and your agency?

12. *Information Leak*: Siri works for a community organization that investigates incidents of police brutality and advocates to reform law enforcement agencies. Siri hacks into the electronic records of the local police. She finds internal communications demonstrating how the police have covered up situations in which certain officers used lethal force based on racist assumptions rather than actual threats of harm. Siri leaks this information to the media and the Federal Bureau of Investigation. She ensures that they cannot trace the source of the information back to her. Has Siri participated in whistleblowing or civil disobedience? From a social work perspective, what ethical and legal standards should Siri have considered before leaking the information? What are the potential benefits and risks of her actions? Under what circumstances, if any, would Siri's hacking and leaking information be considered ethically justifiable?

10

Access to Services

LEARNING OBJECTIVES

Upon successful completion of this introduction, you will be able to

- explain the value of access to services from a social work perspective;
- identify potential barriers and facilitators of access to services;
- critically assess ways to overcome challenges and ensure access to services; and
- manage ethical dilemmas in which the principle of access to services conflicts with other ethical principles.

ocial work is renowned as a helping profession; accordingly, it should be no surprise that our profession values service. The principles section of the NASW Code of Ethics (2021) explains:

Social workers' primary goal is to help people in need and to address social problems

Social workers elevate service to others above self-interest. Social workers draw on their knowledge, values, and skills to help people in need and to address social problems. Social workers are encouraged to volunteer some portion of their professional skills with no expectation of significant financial return (pro bono service).

Given social work's core value of respect for the dignity and worth of all people, we believe that all people have a right to access to needed services. Access to services refers not only to access to social work services, but also access to healthcare services, education, housing, clean water, food, employment, legal services, immigration services, and other needs that may be experienced by individuals, families, groups, and communities. As the capabilities approach to **social justice** (introduced in Chapter 3) suggests, we can help people maximize their potentials by ensuring that they have access to services that support their freedom, social functioning, and overall wellbeing (Nussbaum, 2011; Sen, 2010). Given that many determinants of health and wellbeing are related to socioeconomic status and poverty (Fairchild et al., 2019), one of the primary ways that we can challenge social injustice and health disparities is promoting access to services (Berger & Miller, 2021).

In the first part of this chapter, we will explore various facilitators and barriers to access services. To ensure proper access to services, we need to take client diversity and social circumstances into account, including financial factors, age, gender, sexual orientation, disability, race, ethnicity, culture, and distance. We should also be prepared for emergency situations and service interruptions. When we initiate experimental interventions, we often provide them on a limited basis to determine their risks and benefits. When determining who should have access to experimental interventions, we should consider the principles of fairness, **beneficence** (doing good), and **nonmaleficence** (avoiding harm). The suggestions throughout this chapter for improving access to services are meant to illustrate various possibilities; they are not meant to provide an exhaustive list. You may discover other creative ways to facilitate access and overcome potential barriers. In the second half of the chapter, we will explore ethical dilemmas that may arise in relation to access to services, including the possible conflicts between teleological and deontological approaches to managing these issues. Finally, we will consider how to help people gain access to research to help them make well-informed decisions about services. As you read through this chapter, consider ways in which you can enhance access to resources through advocacy, resource allocation, and making changes in the ways that services are offered and delivered. Be aware of how your role within a particular agency or work environment may affect how you can enhance access to services (Banks, 2016). In some instances, we may be called upon to pursue changes for particular clients. In other instances, we may need to change policies, procedures, or laws to enhance access for particular groups, communities, or populations.

Box 10.1 provides a situation raising a number of ethical issues related to access to services. As you read the situation, consider each of the possible impediments to access and consider how the social worker might address them.

FACILITATORS AND BARRIERS TO ACCESS

Facilitators of access refer to factors that make it easier for people to use services which they may need to address any physical, psychological, social, or spiritual concerns. People are more likely to use services that have convenient hours and locations, high rate of effectiveness (Whittle et al., 2019), affordable fees, approachable staff, and equitable and clear agency policies. *Barriers to access* refer to factors that make it more challenging for people to use needed services. Examples of barriers include inconvenient hours and locations, exorbitant fees, unfriendly staff, and discriminatory or confusing agency policies. Barriers to service may also be related to the specific

BOX 10.1

The Guevara Family

Rocco, a 14-year-old student, was referred to the school social worker, Ziva, due to school attendance concerns. Rocco says he has been missing school to take care of his 72-year-old paternal grandmother, Sra. Guevara. The family came to the United States from Guatemala fifteen years ago. Although Rocco was born in the United States, he is uncertain about the immigration status of his family. Sra. Guevara has Parkinson's disease, a degenerative central nervous system disorder affecting her motor skills and ability to take care of herself. When Ziva asks Rocco about his parents, he provides vague responses concerning their whereabouts. He does not seem to want to discuss their situation. Ziva offers to help Rocco and his family by linking them with resources such as a long-term care facility or in-home care services for Sra. Guevara so that Rocco does not have to miss school. Ziva wants to help Rocco on a voluntary basis. Because Rocco seems reluctant to accept any type of help, Ziva thinks she may need to report the family to child protective services. She has tried to contact Sra. Guevara, but nobody answers the phone or responds to voicemail messages. Ziva discusses the situation with her supervisor, Mai, who suggests that they should consider potential barriers to services:

1. Rocco may feel defensive because he has been required to see a social worker due to truancy issues. His reluctance to talk about his parents may indicate a family secret or taboo topic that makes it difficult for Rocco to discuss these issues (e.g., immigration status). He may also feel caught between loyalty to his family and his desire to be successful at school (and wanting to avoid problems with both).
2. Rocco may question whether he can trust Ziva given their different cultural identities, values, norms, and beliefs. If Ziva is not aware of and responsive to cultural issues when offering help to Rocco and his family, then Rocco is less likely to accept her assistance.
3. Although Ziva has offered to link Rocco and his family with services, there may be financial barriers to accessing them. First, they may not be able to afford the services offered. They may not have health insurance and they may not be eligible for financial assistance. Even if the family is eligible for financial assistance, they may have a strong sense of pride, including the sense that accepting help is a sign of weakness or failure.

How could Ziva address each of these potential barriers? What strategies could she use to facilitate access to support for the Guevaras? What additional challenges to access may arise as Ziva tries to help the family?

type of service need; for example, people with dementia or mental health issues may be reluctant to use services due to social stigma related to dementia (Stephan et al, 2018). In terms of aspirational ethics, we should be proactive in promoting equitable access to services rather than simply responding to barriers on a client-by-client basis. In the following sections we will explore ways to facilitate access and help clients, organizations, and communities remove or minimize barriers to service.

Financial Factors

People with lower levels of income and wealth tend to have greater challenges with access to physical and mental healthcare services (Fairchild et al., 2019). These barriers to access lead to higher rates of illness and other problems related to health and wellbeing (Sabatello et al., 2020). On a macro level, we can promote better access to services by advocating for social policies that

- reduce levels of unemployment,
- ensure living wages,
- provide affordable and comprehensive insurance coverage for physical and mental health services,
- encourage free or affordable fees for services based on need, and
- educate people about how to identify and access services as needed.

On a micro level, we can help clients overcome financial challenges and access services by

- helping them identify services that are free or affordable,
- advocating for free or sliding scale fees based on the clients' ability to pay,
- identifying scholarships, insurance, or other sources of funding for clients in need,
- helping clients apply for or navigate through the complexities of health insurance, managed care, or other systems that fund services (e.g., submitting tax documents to prove financial need), and
- helping clients find jobs that provide good pay, health insurance, employee assistance programs (e.g., counseling), childcare, paid sick leave, and other employment benefits.

Consider the Guevaras' situation. Sra. Guevara is not receiving the types of care that she needs to help her with Parkinson's disease, creating hardships for her, Rocco, and the rest of the family. Ziva could reason that if the family does not want help, she should not force help on them. The principle of access to services, however, suggests that she should offer to help the family address potential barriers to access, including access to insurance or other funding sources to pay for needed services. As a social worker, Ziva has skills to help them navigate relevant healthcare and social assistance systems (Sabatello et al., 2020). She can also help the family determine what types of housing and support are most appropriate for the family.

When social workers charge for their services, they are supposed to ensure that their fees are "fair, reasonable, and commensurate with services performed" (S.1.13[a]). When clients cannot afford fees ordinarily charged by their agencies, they may advocate for exceptions to agency policy or they may work with the agency to ensure the client has access to needed services at another agency.

Age

Many health and social services are geared toward particular age groups, for example, services specifically for children, adolescents, adults, or older adults. Funding for afterschool programs might be limited to children under 13. An addictions treatment program might be limited to people over 18. Access to an assisted living facility might be limited to people over 65. Age restrictions may be based on ethical considerations, for instance, ensuring safe and age-appropriate services for children of different ages. In other instances, age restrictions may be unwarranted. When foster children turn 18, they may lose certain entitlements, despite their need for continued support into early adulthood. To facilitate access to services, we may need to advocate for changes in age-eligibility requirements in existing services. Alternatively, we may need to advocate for new services for particular age groups.

Assume you are working at a youth corrections facility designed for 12- to 17-year-olds convicted of criminal offences. At a case conference, the program director suggests transferring a 16-year-old girl to an adult facility because she has mental health and behavioral issues that the youth facility cannot manage. As a social worker who believes in access to services, how would you respond? What are the ethical arguments in favor of transferring the girl to an adult facility? What other options should be considered?

Age-related barriers to services may arise in relation to how services are delivered. Consider the increased use of technology with older adults, including social robots, sensors, GPS alarms and digital reminders, and telehealth services offered by videoconferencing (Frennert, 2020). Although many older adults may benefit from technology-assisted services, some may find it difficult to access these services due to challenges such as impaired memory, lack of familiarity with technology, or distrust with particular forms of technology. For a client with memory challenges, we could offer in-person services that do not require the use of technology or we could identify technology that is easier to use for people with compromised memory. We could also empower the client with support systems, such as a family member to assist with the technology. For older clients who lack familiarity or distrust technology, what strategies could you use to facilitate access to telehealth or other technology-assisted services?

Gender and Sexual Orientation

Trust is an important factor in relation to access to health, mental health, and social services. According to the Minority Stress Model, many LGBTQ+ individuals have concerns about having to disclose their sexual orientation or gender identity due to trepidation about discrimination and stigma. These concerns may lead LGBTQ+ individuals to delay or avoid seeking help, leading to adverse outcomes (Tabaac et al., 2020). To facilitate access to services, we can build trust by ensuring that we

- use **cultural competence** and humility (NASW Code, S.1.05) to develop the knowledge, skills, awareness, and responsiveness to provide services in a respectful and effective manner (including knowledge about heterosexism, biphobia, transprejudice, and other forms of discrimination that may be affecting LGBTQ+ individuals and communities),
- reach out to LGBTQ+ communities to let them know that they are genuinely valued and welcomed to make use of our services,
- ensure that clients are aware that services are offered in a confidential manner (particularly for clients who may be concerned about being outed to family, friends, employers, or others), and
- advocate for the needs, rights, and interests of LGBTQ+ individuals and communities (Youth Engaged 4 Change, n.d.).

Assume you are working in a community health clinic. Clinic staff want to ensure that the LGBTQ+ community feels comfortable accessing its health services; however, they are not sure what changes, if any, they need to make. Using a **cultural humility** approach (rather than assuming you know what the LGBTQ+ community needs), you could conduct a needs assessment. Working with LGBTQ+ community organizations, for instance, you could conduct focus groups to research potential facilitators and barriers to service. Alternatively, you could conduct research through an anonymous survey to gather recommendations for improving access. By starting with the clients, we are not only learning how to facilitate access more effectively, we are also showing respect for the dignity and worth of the community.

To ensure access to services for people from diverse sexual orientations, gender identities and expressions, and sexual orientations (SOGIEs), we should ensure that our agency policies, forms, and practices are inclusive of people from various SOGIEs. When we use binary language and categories such as male/female or heterosexual/gay, we are excluding people who may identify as genderqueer, gender nonbinary, transgender, genderfluid, bisexual, asexual, pansexual, and so on. We should allow people to self-identify, respecting their dignity and worth. To make our agencies safe places for people of all SOGIEs, we also need to ensure that all helping professionals and staff are properly trained, attentive to, and affirming of their identities, needs, and wishes (Johnson, 2019).

Disability

When we consider how to improve access for people with disabilities, we should take physical, sensory, psychological, and cognitive disabilities into account. For people with physical disabilities such as cerebral palsy, spinal cord injuries, or amputations, we can facilitate access through various forms of building design and assistive technology, including

- ramps or walkways that make it easier to walk or use wheelchairs,
- videoconferencing or other communication technology to allow clients to access services from their homes, hospital beds, assisted-living facilities, workplaces, or other locations, and
- locating services in areas that have accessible buses or other modes of public transportation.

Sensory disabilities include blindness, deafness, and other conditions that affect sight, hearing, touch, smell, or taste. Some methods of facilitating access to people with disabilities should be universally available (e.g., accessible transportation, professionals trained in serving people with disabilities, accessible office design, and assistive technology). Other methods may be offered on a client-by-client basis depending on individual needs. When offering services to deaf clients, for instance, we might offer services through sign language, texting, or other forms of communication. Rather than assuming what may facilitate access to services for particular individuals, we can invite them to let us know what works best. We can also use online information gateways to identify community resources to facilitate access to services (American Association for People with Disabilities, n.d.; Enabling Guide, n.d.).

Psychological disabilities include various forms of mental health issues (e.g., depression, schizophrenia, bipolar disorder, social anxiety disorder, phobia, and post-traumatic stress disorder). Symptoms of mental health issues such as stress, anxiety, hallucinations, or paranoia often make it more difficult for people to access services (National Alliance on Mental Health, n.d.). Once again, if we can start with our clients and meet their needs and wishes, we are more likely to ensure services are accessible. We can empower clients with paranoia, for instance, by asking what types of service environments may be more or less comfortable (e.g., avoiding crowded offices, one-way mirrors, voice-activated technology, or other devices that may exacerbate the client's paranoia). For clients with agoraphobia, we might offer home visits or teleconferencing rather than requiring them to come to our office. What types of accommodations might you offer to facilitate access to services for a client with obsessions about cleanliness and avoiding germs?

Some clients with mental health issues may be turned away from services due to concerns about violence or aggression (Whittle et al., 2019). Some concerns may be based on past behaviors, although some may be based on myths or biases. As social workers, we can educate service providers about the true nature of mental illnesses, including how to properly assess for and manage concerns about the safety of clients, staff, and others. People have a right to services regardless of their mental health status. The Americans with Disabilities Act (1990) is a useful tool for advocating for access for services, including situations in which agencies have denied services to people with mental health and behavioral issues. When people with disabilities need a legal advocate to ensure proper access to services, we can link them with attorneys and advocacy organizations that specialize in advocating for the rights of people with disabilities.

Cognitive disabilities refer to impairments in intellectual functioning such as dyslexia, dementia, and attention deficit disorder. To facilitate access for people with cognitive disabilities, we should offer accommodations in how services are utilized. Consider a substance abuse treatment program that ordinarily requires clients to be literate so they can complete written journals and assignments. To ensure access to people with limited literacy due to cognitive disabilities or other factors, the program could offer alternative methods of completing journals or assignments (e.g., through technology that reads questions and records answers for clients).

Another important way to enhance access to care is to offer integrated care (National Alliance on Mental Health, n.d.). Some services are very specialized, for instance, focusing only on physical care, mental health, or addictions, and not providing integrated services for clients with concerns in more than one realm of practice. We can play a vital case management role by ensuring that professionals from different agencies or professional backgrounds work together to meet all the clients' needs, including those related to disabilities.

People with profound disabilities tend to have particular challenges with access to services (Gao et al., 2019). Although the mission of social work includes attending to the needs of the most vulnerable populations in society, many agencies to not commit sufficient resources to ensure access for people with profound disabilities (Sabatello et al., 2020). Providing services for people with severe communication disorders, for instance, may entail higher costs because they require high staff-to-client ratios. People with disabilities tend to have lower levels of lower education and higher rates of unemployment and poverty, adding to the challenges of accessing services (Gao et al., 2019). Accordingly, we may need to allocate more resources to help people with disabilities rather than fewer.

Additional methods of facilitating access to services for people with disabilities include:

- fostering mutual aid and self-help groups in which people with similar disabilities support one another,
- designing services in a manner that offers clients greater freedom, choice, respect, and understanding,
- helping clients navigate complex insurance, health, and social care systems,

- reducing stigma around disabilities as pathologies or illnesses and building on client strengths,
- coordinating services between social workers, physicians, occupational therapists, physiotherapists, speech-language pathologists, and other service providers (Stephan et al., 2018; Hepworth et al., 2023), and
- reaching out to clients with mental health issues or other disabilities to help them understand how they may benefit from various services (Whittle et al., 2019).

Race, Ethnicity, and Culture

People who come from different races, ethnicities, or cultures may experience different facilitators and barriers to service. For instance, within some cultures, seeking mental health services is customary and valued. Within other cultures, mental health issues carry stigma and seeking mental health services may be viewed as a sign of weakness. When people are reluctant to receive certain types of services, we may need to reach out to them and help them deal with the challenges that make it difficult for them to access services (Whittle et al., 2019). Strategies for helping people overcome cultural stigma include

- starting with the person by demonstrating respect for the person's culture beliefs and values,
- helping the person explore their cultural beliefs and values and the possibility that accessing culturally responsive services may be helpful (NASW Code, S.1.05),
- engaging family, friends, or cultural leaders (with the person's permission) to explore how services could be provided in a manner that does not conflict with cultural beliefs and values,
- helping people explore service alternatives, and
- allowing people to make their own decisions (including the possibility of declining services at the present time) (NASW Code, Ss.1.02 and 1.03).

Consider a client experiencing hallucinations. You discuss referring her to a counselor at a mental health agency. The client says that, given her cultural and religious beliefs, there is no possibility that she could use their services. She says she would be too embarrassed. She fears how friends or family might treat her if they found out she was seeing a psychiatrist or other mental health professional. Starting with the client, it is important to validate her fears and concerns. You could also help her explore other options, for instance, accessing mental health services online or seeing a therapist who does not work in mental health agency. She could then access services privately, minimizing the chance that family or friends will find out she is using mental health services. If she has concerns about whether the therapist will respect her religion, you might help her identify a mental health professional or agency that operates from her cultural and religious perspectives. If she is not ready to access services now, you could leave the door open for a future referral.

For some prospective clients, immigration status may affect decisions about accessing services. Consider the Guevarra family from the case at the beginning of this chapter. Some family members may be in this country without legal documentation. Sra. Guevarra may be hesitant to access health because she does not want herself or other family members to be deported. She fears that healthcare providers may report her to the police. To respond to these concerns, you could help the Sra. Guevarra and her family identify programs that serve people regardless of immigration status and that have clear policies protecting client confidentiality. The family may also benefit from a referral to an immigration lawyer who can assess their situation and determine whether it is possible to secure a visa or other documentation allowing them to stay in the country without fear of deportation. The lawyer can educate them about their legal rights, possibly allaying fears about being deported.

When helping people from diverse backgrounds secure services, it is important to understand that one size does not necessarily fit all (Whittle et al., 2019). People may have different needs and preferences for services. Clients from a background that holds a strong sense of personal privacy, for instance, may prefer individual counseling. Clients from communitarian cultures may prefer support groups. Clients whose first language is not English may prefer services offered in their first language. We should also consider cultural norms and expectations related to dress, food, and religious observances. Clients who dress modestly may prefer agencies in which modest dress is the norm. Clients who observe particular religions may require agencies that can accommodate their dietary laws and religious holidays. When culture-related challenges arise, we may also need to advocate for changes within the agencies to ensure that services are accessible and culturally appropriate (Kirst-Ashman & Hull, 2018b).

An antioppression approach to social work highlights the need to address systemic racism and oppression to ensure equitable access to services and to redress disparities in health and social wellbeing (Berger & Miller, 2021). We can empower clients from diverse backgrounds to play active roles in the change process rather than act as passive recipients of help from well-intended social workers. Instead of advocating for access to services for particular individuals and groups, we can act as supporters, partners, or allies (Caron et al., 2020). For example, if I provide a group with information on how to advocate for services on their own behalf, they will be empowered not only for this particular situation, but also for future situations. I am also showing respect for the strengths and abilities of the people I am serving. Who can better know what needs to be changed than those people who are directly affected by systemic discrimination and barriers to access?

Distance

The distance between service providers and users can create significant challenges for many people (Rhoads & Rakes, 2020). Some people may not be able to travel long distances to access services because they cannot take time away from work, child-care, or other personal responsibilities. Others may not have access to private vehicles or public transportation. Problems related to accessing services may arise in rural or sparsely populated communities where people may need to travel long distances to more urban centers that have such services (Rural Health Information Hub, n.d.). Problems may also arise in urban areas, for instance, due to traffic congestion, insufficient transportation, or lack of paid time off work to seek assistance. Access to services may be particularly challenging for people who need highly specialized services (Whittle et al., 2019), for instance, people with dual diagnoses (e.g., substance use disorder and schizophrenia). Social workers can help people redress distance-related access issues by

- advocating for services to be located in accessible locations (e.g., near public transportation),
- connecting clients with services that can be provided through communication technology, such as videoconferencing (Fairchild et al., 2019; Rhoads & Rakes, 2020),
- ensuring that people from smaller communities have access to professional education so that they may provide their communities with services that require professional educations, and
- making use of informal support systems to supplement or fill gaps in formal support systems (e.g., developing self-help groups for people with common concerns).

Assume that you are a generalist social work practitioner assisting Zack, a client with a history of hallucinations, paranoia, and violent behavior. You work in a small community that does not have any facilities or professionals who specialize in these concerns. You are worried that you may not be able to manage these concerns on your own, particularly if risks of violence escalate. You ask Zack to consider telemental health services; he rejects this idea, fearing that others will listen in and send messages to control his thoughts and behaviors. You describe the security protections used to ensure that services can be provided in a safe and confidential manner. Zack continues to reject services. What additional options could you and Zack consider? In the short-term, you could work with Zack's family and friends (with his consent), helping them develop a plan to monitor Zack's wellbeing and know how to respond if new safety concerns arise. You could also explore whether Zack might be willing to go to an inpatient program in a larger center. You could explain that it would be better for Zack to admit himself now, rather than wait for a crisis situation in which he might need to be admitted on an involuntary basis (e.g., if he presents a serious, imminent risk to himself or others). If you are lacking the knowledge and skill to work with Zack, you and your agency might also secure specialized professional consultation to help you work with him. If there are no other suitable professionals in your community to work with Zack, you may be his only local source of professional support. To overcome various barriers to services, we often need to be creative. At the same time, we need to stay within our areas of competence (NASW Code, S.1.04).

Videoconferencing, telehealth, electronic records, and other types of technology can help reduce barriers to access related to distance and convenience. Unfortunately, many vulnerable populations lack access to technology-mediated services because they do not have access to computers, tablets, or smart phones. Older adults, people living in poverty, and less educated groups are disproportionately affected by lack of access to technology-mediated services (Chang et al., 2021). As social workers, we can advocate for in-person and low-tech options for services. We can also help make technology available to clients in need through fundraising and other creative options. For instance, we could work with public libraries and schools to help them develop private rooms where people in need can use computers to connect with health and social service providers.

Emergency Situations

Standard 6.03 of the NASW Code states, "Social workers should provide appropriate professional services in emergencies to the greatest extent possible." Emergency situations include terrorist attacks, pandemics, mass shootings, hurricanes, tornadoes, flooding, earthquakes, fires, or other natural or human-initiated disasters. When these types of disasters arise, service providers may become overwhelmed because of the extent and depth of the need that ensues. To ensure access to services in emergency situations, we should

- develop plans for how we will respond in specific emergency situations, including plans for how to manage work, family, and other social responsibilities (e.g., having a family member take care of our children to allow us to serve clients);
- engage in training on responding to emergency situations (including training on critical incident debriefing and helping people respond to traumatic situations) (Substance Abuse and Mental Health Services Administration, 2022); and
- offer services to existing clients and others in need, including work with existing services that respond to emergency situations (such as crisis intervention programs, emergency response teams, and humanitarian organizations that provide services locally or abroad).

During emergency situations, we need to respond quickly and effectively. We should be aware of potential risks and how to manage them. During a pandemic, for instance, what precautions can we take to protect ourselves and the clients we serve from a deadly virus (Camper & Felton, 2021). In the aftermath of an act of terrorism, we should be aware of fears or other feelings that could negatively impact our ability to help. If we need supervision or counseling, then we should access it and take care of ourselves (NASW Code, Purpose Section). If we are ready and able to help people in the aftermath of a disaster, then we should not only serve our existing clients, but consider whether we can provide services to other people in need, perhaps through collaboration with other organizations that specialize in emergency response.

Service Interruption

Prior examples of access to service focus on how we can ensure that clients originally have access to services. The NASW Code of Ethics reminds us that access to service also means that we should guard against interruptions in services (S.1.15) and we should not abandon clients in need (S.1.17). Interruptions in services may arise in a number of circumstances. For instance, we might not be available due to illness, mental or physical incapacity, travel, or family emergency. To ensure continuity of services, we need to be proactive rather than simply waiting for problems to arise. To pre-empt disruptions, we should work with our organizations to ensure that someone can see our clients when we are not available (e.g., a supervisor or coworker). We should also inform clients about whom to contact if we are not available. If we plan to move, switch jobs, or complete a field internship, we should develop plans with clients to ensure a smooth transfer to another worker. Referring clients does not mean simply providing the client with a name and phone number of another worker. When considering referrals with clients, we should have a full discussion of the client's needs and wishes, an explanation of service options, and perhaps a transfer meeting in which we meet with the client and new worker to ensure a smooth transfer (Hepworth et al., 2023).

When using technology to engage clients, we should inform clients about backup plans for situations in which technology is not working. If videoconferencing is disrupted, for instance, should the client contact you by telephone, email, or other means? When clients are having problems with their technology, who may they contact for assistance? When clients are having problems affording their technology, what types of assistance can your agency provide?

We should not abandon clients in need of services (S.1.17[b]). Consider a client who loses a job and can no longer afford services. The client may be at risk of suicide or other harms. To ensure continuity of services, we may consider

- providing services on a pro bono (free) or reduced-fee basis,
- connecting the client with other services that are free or that the client can afford, or
- securing payment from alternate sources (e.g., advocating for scholarships or insurance coverage for the client).

Standard 1.01 suggests that our primary obligation is to our client, meaning that there may be situations in which we prioritize our client's needs over our own. Consider a client that you find difficult or repugnant. Perhaps you feel repulsed by the way that the client speaks, smells, or behaves. You know that you should not be judgmental, but you are also aware that you should not abandon your client. You might consider referring the client to another service provider. Before doing so, you could speak with your supervisor to review the situation and to help you explore your countertransference (or thoughts and feelings) toward the client. Although a transfer to a new provider may be in the client's best interests, know that there are potential downsides to referring a client: the client may feel rejected or embarrassed, it may take the client time to connect with the new provider, the client may decide not to pursue further services, or the new provider may encounter similar concerns about the client. It might be better to work through the concerns in collaboration with the client rather than simply "unloading" them through a referral.

Experimental Interventions

When new interventions are being pilot tested, we often offer services to a relatively small group of clients. Because the risks and effectiveness of new interventions are not known, trying them with small groups allows us to assess the risks and benefits without exposing a larger group of people to the potential risks. Ethical issues may arise, however, when people want access to particular interventions but they are denied because the intervention is still under study (Moore, 2019).

Consider research into the effectiveness of a new model of psychotherapy for people with post-traumatic stress disorder. You have a client who could benefit from this model, but it is still under study and the client does not qualify for participating in the research. How can you fulfill your ethical duty to provide access to services for this client? You could consider the following options:

- Advocate for your client to be permitted to engage in the psychotherapy either as part of the research study or separate from it,
- Advocate for the client to be given priority on a waiting list for when the psychotherapy is offered to additional people,
- Explore other support or treatment options that may be useful to the client, either instead of the new psychotherapy or as a temporary measure until the new psychotherapy is available.

If the experimental intervention is being offered to a restricted segment of society (e.g., only males or only White people), then you may advocate that it should be offered to people in a more equitable manner. All interventions, whether experimental or not, should be equally accessible to all people unless there are compelling professional reasons to limit accessibility (Moore, 2019). In clinical trials of new medications, for instance, access may be limited initially to adults. Children may be more vulnerable to the risks of the medication. In these circumstance, testing the medication first with adults may be ethically justified. If you are working with a child who has not responded to other medications and there is a high risk of death without further assistance, however, you could advocate for an exception for this client due to the gravity of the need.

TELEOLOGICAL AND DEONTOLOGICAL APPROACHES TO ACCESS

As Chapter 2 describes, **deontology** suggests that we should abide by certain ethical principles regardless of the situation. The principle of *access to services* supports ethical principles such as protection of life, promotion of physical and psychosocial wellbeing, and advancing social justice (including elimination of health disparities between people of different racial, cultural, or socioeconomic backgrounds). Ethical challenges may arise, however, when we have limited resources and competing needs and interests. Assume, for instance, that you are helping one client and you receive a message that you have another client in crisis requesting your assistance. Do you attend first to the client you are currently seeing or the one with serious, immediate needs? In this situation, you might simply ask the current client if it is okay to attend to an emergency situation and offer to meet again as soon as feasible. In other situations, however, you could have two clients with immediate needs, making it more challenging to determine which client to help first.

Utilitarianism (a teleological approach to ethics) can be used to help prioritize clients and their needs based on their current circumstances and options (Bentham, 1823; Johns, 2016). Utilitarianism suggests allocating resources according to the greatest good; that is, how an individual, organization, community, or society can allocate a limited pool of resources in a way that maximizes benefits (or utility) for the greatest good (McAuliffe, 2014). The term *utility* refers to ability of any resource to produce the experiences of benefit, advantage, pleasure, good, or happiness, or to prevent the experiences of mischief, pain, evil, or unhappiness (Bentham, 1823). I can do greater good (or avoid greater harm) by serving a client experiencing suicidal ideation rather than assisting a client requesting help to apply for a bus pass. Although both clients need and deserve assistance, the second client's request is not as urgent. Thus, when we have competing interests, one method to prioritize use of our time and resources is to evaluate which options support the greatest good.

Allocating resources to situations where they will promote the greatest good fits with Standard 3.09(b) of the NASW Code. This standards suggests social workers should promote the efficiency and effectiveness of their services. Given that health and social service organizations have limited resources, considering the cost-effectiveness of service is part of being good stewards of our organization's resources. Still, decisions about how to allocate an agency's resources should also be based on fair (nondiscriminatory) factors (NASW Code, S. 3.07[b]).

As social workers, we have a historic alliance with people who are the most vulnerable in society, for instance, people living in poverty and people subjected to discrimination or oppression (Hepworth et al., 2023). If we focus only on serving the greatest good for the greatest number, then we may be ignoring the needs of the most vulnerable, particularly if their numbers are relatively small. If we apply the greatest good for the greatest number standard, we may also decline services to people with disabilities and other vulnerable populations because it is more costly to serve them (Sabatello et al., 2020). As social workers, we may advocate to reallocate resources to protect and serve the most vulnerable, even when this course of action does not benefit the greatest number in society. Consider clients who use wheelchairs. We could advocate for our agency to install wheelchair ramps and wheelchair accessible doors to ensure access to services for these clients, even when using the same financial resources could be used in another way to serve more clients (e.g., reducing fees for all clients or extending service times in the evening by one hour). Thus, when making decisions about the best way to allocate resources, we need to consider not only which course of action will lead to the greatest benefits, but also whose needs are the most important and urgent, and how to ensure both equitable access and cost-effectiveness in the services we offer.

Rationing services may require us to make value judgments in relation to people's lives, including the quality of their lives and their prognosis for survival (Sabatello et al., 2020). Assume you are working with Amari, a man recently admitted to hospital due to a work-related accident that caused severe internal injuries. Amari is unconscious. His parents (as next-of-kin) are authorized to make decisions on his behalf. Physicians suggest that the costs of surgery are high and he has no prospects for survival, with or without surgery. Amari's parents ask you to advocate for physicians to attempt surgery even though the physicians believe that surgery is futile. In your role as social worker, your primary commitment is to your client, Amari (S.1.01). Amari's parents honestly believe that he would have wanted the surgery, so it would be ethical to advocate for surgery on his behalf. The hospital, including is ethics committee, also has a responsibility to be good stewards of its resources. It may not allow surgery to be performed if there is no reasonable chance that it will be effective. The hospital does not want to waste resources. In addition to advocating for the parents' wishes, you may need to help them understand why the hospital opposes surgery. You may also demonstrate empathy, acknowledging their desire to take all steps possible to save their child's life, including heroic and costly measures.

If surgery is not a viable option, you could discuss options for compassionate end-of-life care, including pain management and family support (Richardson & Chowns, 2020). Often, social workers use a strengths-based approach to practice, building people's hope rather than tearing it down (Churchill, 2020). In Amari's situation, however, it would be dishonest to promote hope when there are no viable treatment options to save his life. To maintain **honesty**, you could validate the parents' thoughts and feelings. "I understand that you believe that surgery can help Amari and you are prepared to do whatever is possible to save him. Your love for Amari is deep and strong." At the same time, you should not provide false reassurance or information that their son's life can be saved.

Given that health and social service organizations have limited resources, they often need to make decisions about ways to ration resources and services. They may make decisions based on a cost-benefit analysis, weighing the costs and benefits of using resources for various purposes (Muscrove & Fox-Rushby, 2006). As noted earlier, decision making should be based on a broad range of ethical considerations, including equity, prognosis for survival, quality of life, promoting good, and minimizing or eliminating harm. Allocating resources should not be based on unethical considerations such as nepotism (favoring family or friends), discrimination (disfavoring people because they are members of particular groups), bribery, or coercion.

From an **egalitarian** perspective, we could argue that certain types of services and resources should be universally available (e.g., education, housing, healthcare). Universality supports the principles of *equity* and *respect for the dignity and worth of all people*. The main arguments against universality are related to the costs and efficiency of services (Zieff et al., 2020). People who oppose universal healthcare, for instance, may argue that it is very expensive and that governments are less efficient at utilizing resources than private individuals and businesses operating in an open market. From an ethics perspective, the question may not simply be a choice between universal medical coverage or privatization of the healthcare system, but rather, what combination of private and government-funded services produces the greatest good and also meets the needs of those who are most vulnerable in society? Following an evidence-based approach (Gambrill, 2019), we can evaluate research within and outside the United States to determine the best systems for pursuing our ethics objectives regarding access to healthcare or other services.

Some social policies, historically and currently, have based access to help on whether the potential recipient of aid is "deserving." Consider *universally accessible social assistance* versus *workfare*. Under workfare policies, access to social assistance is limited to people who participate in some type of work or job training. The purpose of limiting eligibility is to create incentives for people to work and be productive members of society. Critics of workfare suggest that it assumes people are lazy or dishonest, so they should not be trusted (Carey & Bell, 2021). Some people may have very valid reasons for not working, for instance, single parents who stay home to care for their young children or people find it difficult to maintain a job due to the effects of particular mental health disorders. Workfare proponents tend to justify their preference based on the ethical principle of personal responsibility. Workfare critics tend to prefer universality based on the ethical principles of equity and respect for the dignity and worth of all people. They believe that everyone deserves sufficient resources to have their basic needs met and that most people are motivated to work if they are able to do so. What are your thoughts about social assistance policies based on the notions of who is deserving or undeserving? What belief systems and ethical principles underlie your policy preferences?

ACCESS TO RESEARCH AND KNOWLEDGE

Until this point in the chapter, we have focused on access to services. Although *access to research and knowledge* is different from *access to services*, the two notions are related. If we want people to be able to make well-informed decisions about their health and social welfare, they should have access to accurate and reliable information. Consider Shyanne, a young woman who is trying to determine the best protection against sexually transmitted infections (STIs). If Shyanne speaks with someone who believes in abstinence until marriage, she may hear that she should stay abstinent until marriage. If she asks someone who believes strongly in the protective abilities of condoms, she may hear about the benefits of condoms. If she does an electronic search online, she is likely to find many different suggestions, some with and many without reliable research to support them. If Shyanne speaks with you (as a professional social worker), then you should not simply recommend one form of birth control or provide a recommendation based on personal opinion; rather, you should go through a list of options with Shyanne, helping her identify the benefits and risks of each (NASW Code, S.1.03). Because Shyanne does not have training in how to evaluate research, one of your roles could be to help make research findings and knowledge accessible to her. You could do so through various alternatives:

- If you are proficient in the research on preventing STIs, you could help summarize the research for her in relation to the options she is considering.
- You could refer Shyanne to a medical professional who is more knowledgeable about preventing STIs to explain her options and help her make an informed decision.
- You could help Shyanne identify and access valid, reliable, and plain-language information on STI prevention (e.g., on a government-sponsored website).

As Chapter 4 on informed consent explains, we can empower people to make the best decisions for themselves by helping them sort through their options for treatment or services based on sound research and knowledge.

On a macro level, we can also ensure that particular communities have access to information in a manner that is understandable and culturally appropriate. Assume that you are tasked with helping a community respond to a recent increase in STIs. To ensure people have access to valid and reliable information, you could

- work with teachers and healthcare providers to develop and implement educational programs;
- work with cultural group leaders to determine the best ways to share information in a culturally appropriate manner (e.g., attending to different religious or spiritual belief systems); or
- offer in-person or online forums for sharing valid and reliable information about STIs in a clear and compassionate manner.

If you discover potential barriers to accessing the information, you could work with community members to reduce or remove those barriers. Assume, for instance, that certain cultural groups believe it is inappropriate for people to engage in public discussions about sex in mixed-gender settings; however, they might be open to similar discussions involving one gender at a time. As indicated throughout this chapter, we need to work with the people we serve and invite their input to devise appropriate ways to make research, services, and other resources accessible.

CONCLUSION

As social workers, we play many different roles to facilitate access to services. As case managers, we assess people's needs and help them identify services and professionals that can address these needs. As advocates, we can help clients access services that are being denied by advancing their rights, helping service providers understand their needs, and working toward collaborative solutions (Hepworth et al., 2023; Whittle et al., 2019). We can also encourage interprofessional collaboration to ensure that services are integrated in an appropriate manner. Within our own agencies, we may need to advocate for clients within our agencies, for instance, to accept a client who does not meet technical eligibility requirements or who does not have insurance to pay for services. Sometimes, we may accept certain policies without questioning them (van der Tier et al., 2021). We may have more discretion than we initially think and our agencies may have more flexibility than written policies might suggest. We may need to be creative, searching for different sources of funding or creative ways of managing challenges such as distance, poverty, or discomfort with the way that services are being offered.

Lack of access to services is a key factor in relation to disparities in health and well-being. Given our belief in social justice and respect for the dignity and worth of all people, we need to play proactive roles in facilitating access to services. Finally, when facilitating access to services, we should ensure that the services are not merely accessible, but also timely, effective and culturally appropriate (Fairchild et al., 2019).

DISCUSSION QUESTIONS AND EXERCISES

1. *Pro Bono*: Janine is a social worker who practices as an end-of-life doula. She assists clients and their families with end-of-life caregiving, coordinating family caregiving, life review, palliative care, and bereavement support. Janine has been approached by Garnet, who has coronary heart disease. He would like to hire Janine but cannot afford her services. Does Janine have an ethical obligation to provide pro bono services? What other options should Janine consider? How should she respond?

2. *Family Secret*: You work in a family counseling program. You are meeting with Petra (21 years old) and her parents. Petra recently discovered that she was adopted. Petra asks you to help her access a professional genealogist and genetic testing service so she can locate her biological parents. Her parents say they do not want Petra to dredge up the past. They ask you to discourage Petra from searching for her biological parents. Also, they refuse to help Petra pay for a genealogist and genetic testing. What ethical issues does this situation raise and how would you resolve them (cf., Landers & Parrish, 2021)?

3. *Bartering*: You are providing support services to a client, Belle, who recently lost a job. Belle cannot afford paying for services out of pocket. Instead, she offers to help your agency develop a better online system for managing electronic client records. Belle has lots of expertise in this area and your agency could use her help. Under Standard 1.13, what ethical issues does this situation raise in relation to bartering for services? How should you respond to Belle's offer?

4. *Gender Affirming*: Horatio facilitates a psychoeducational group for parents of 8- to 16- year olds who have gender dysphoria, a condition in which people experience a high degree of distress because their biological sex does not match their gender identity. Ordinarily, Horatio provides information about various forms of gender affirming medical care, including pubertal blockers. These medications pause puberty, allowing the child, parents, and medical team to determine whether a child's gender identity is long lasting. The physical effects of gender blockers are reversible. Medical research suggests that pubertal blockers can be very helpful for the psychological wellbeing of some children who identify as transgender or gender nonconforming. Recently, the state government has passed a law deeming use of pubertal blockers to be a form of child abuse. The law imposes fines or imprisonment for anyone facilitating these procedures. Horatio wonders whether he should stop talking about pubertal blockers in his groups. He believes children and families should have access to such services, but fears criminal consequences for his clients, himself, and any other colleagues to offer gender-affirming medical services. Use the Framework for Managing

Ethical Issues to analyze how Horatio should address the issues described in this situation.

5. *Difficult Client*: You work in a hostel for adults experiencing homelessness. One client, Wendy, has been berating staff with racist comments. During a staff meeting, several people demand that Wendy be discharged immediately. You are concerned that if Wendy is discharged, she will be living in a dangerous situation on the streets. In the past, Wendy has engaged in risky sexual relations just to have a place to stay. Although you could refer Wendy to another hostel, you believe that she will face the same problems. You do not want to "dump" a client on another agency. You would rather resolve the issues within your own agency. As you discuss this matter with your work colleagues, how would you assess your professional obligation to ensure access to services with your obligations to promote social justice and to protect others from racist attacks? Which sections of the NASW Code of Ethics are most relevant to this situation? How would you feel if Wendy were directing her racist attacks against you? How might your feelings affect your thoughts about whether to discharge Wendy from the hostel?

6. *Machismo*: You are working with Raphael, a client who identifies as Mexican American. He has a low-paying job. He is struggling to pay for housing, food, and other basic needs. You offer to help him apply for social assistance to supplement his earned income. He explains his sense of machismo (masculine pride) and how he does not feel comfortable accepting handouts, even if he and his family are suffering. How should you respond, taking ethical considerations such as access to service, self-determination, beneficence (promoting good), and cultural humility into account?

7. *Vaccine Allocation*: A new vaccine has been developed to prevent spread of a virus during a global pandemic. Initially, there is limited supply of the vaccine. How would you apply the ethical principles of beneficence (doing good), nonmaleficence (avoiding harm), justice (equity), and autonomy (free choice) to allocate the vaccinations (c.f., Beauchamp & Childress, 2019)? According to these principles, how would you prioritize the following groups: older adults, children, healthcare providers, police, politicians, smokers, prisoners, citizens, noncitizen residents, and people with pre-existing health conditions that put them at greater risk?

8. *Vaccine Hesitancy*: Assume you are engaged in community work with a particular ethnic community that is experiencing relatively high number of deaths related to a global pandemic. Although vaccines can reduce the incidence of death and serious illness, many members of the community are reluctant to take the vaccine. Some view the vaccine as too risky, even though the national center responsible for approving vaccines says there is strong research suggesting the vaccine is highly effective and

entails low risks. Others note a history of racism, including mistreatment of their community by researchers and health professionals. How do the principles of access to services, autonomy and informed consent, community safety, and social justice apply to this situation? What processes and options should you and your colleagues consider in working with the community? What are the ethical arguments against simply saying that many members of the community do not want the vaccine, so we should simply leave them alone and let them make their own decisions?

9. *Access and Resource Responsibility*: You are working in a prison. An inmate named Marco (52 years old) wants to complete his high school education via a correspondence program for "a regular high school diploma." The prison says that they will provide him with free access to a GED program (general equivalence diploma), but they will not pay for a correspondence program. Marco does not have financial resources to pay for a correspondence program. He asks you to help him get into the correspondence program. You have doubts about whether a correspondence program is any better than an online GED. You do not want to waste time or resources for something that is not necessary. You also believe in advocating for client self-determination and access to needed resources. Use the Framework for Managing Ethical Issues to explore the options and determine how to proceed.

10. *Intake Priorities*: You are conducting intake interviews for clients seeking services at an inpatient program for people with substance use disorders. Your program has one bed available and three recent applicants for services. Your program will not have another bed available for several weeks and there are no other inpatient programs in your area. Which of the following people would you prioritize for inpatient treatment, and why?

    a. Serge (32 years) is the first of the three to apply for services. He was recently charged with drinking under the influence of alcohol. He reports drinking 3 to 6 beer virtually every day. He does not think he has a problem with alcohol. He is seeking services because he has an upcoming child visitation hearing as part of a divorce process. He wants to be able to show the court that he does not have a problem with alcohol.

    b. Arcadia (77 years) is in hospital, ready to be discharged after accidentally overdosing on pain killers (opiates). She has a history of depression. She has cycled in and out of treatment programs for many years. Her needs are the highest and most urgent. Given her past experiences in treatment programs, however, her chances of successfully completing the program are relatively low.

    c. Estelle (21), a genderfluid person, reports an addiction to marijuana. Although marijuana is not creating any immediate risks of harm,

Estelle says they cannot stop using marijuana without the assistance of an inpatient service. Estelle has lots of social support and their prognosis for success in the treatment program is very good.

What ethical principles or criteria are you applying? How, if at all, should you take each potential client's age, gender, and prognosis into account?

11. *Online Information*: Benny, a fourth-grade student, was referred to you (a school social worker) for help with peer relationships. You invite Benny's parents to meet with you to discuss Benny's situation. They tell you that they do not have time to meet you because they work full-time and have 5 other children to care for. They say they have already found information on a mental health website. They believe that Benny is on the autism spectrum. They say that this website provides them with all the information that they need to know. You explain the benefits of seeing a specialist who can assess and provide services for Benny. They decline services. You are conflicted because you believe that Benny has a right to receive needed services, but you also want to respect the parents' right to make decisions for the child. You wonder whether refusal to accept services amounts to medical neglect (which would need to be reported to child protective services). What are your ethical and legal obligations toward Benny and his family? How would you manage the conflicts between Benny's needs and his parents' wishes? How could you address potential barriers to services?

12. *Deserving or Not*: You work in an agency serving clients with pedophilia (people with intense sexual attractions to young children). A friend asks you how you can devote your life to working with "those people," suggesting that they are not worthy of help because of the harm they cause to children. Further, your friend suggests that people cannot be cured of pedophilia. What is the ethical rationale for devoting time and other resources to help people with pedophilia? How would you respond to your friend's question?

13. *Omelas*: Read the Ursula K. Le Guin's short story "The Ones Who Walked Away from Omelas" available at https://learning.hccs.edu/faculty/emily.klotz/engl1302-6/readings/the-ones-who-walk-away-from-omelas-ursula-le-guin/view. This story describes a serene utopian community, with one exception. What are the ethical lessons from this story in relation access to resources, social justice, respect of the dignity and worth of all people, and the greatest good for the greatest number?

14. *Access to Liver*: Kara has cirrhosis of the liver and in desperate need of a transplant. Although she is on a waiting list for a live organ donor, the wait could be over a year. She asks you to help her access a program in another country that offers donors without the long waiting time. You have ethical concerns about this foreign program because it pays donors for their organs, most of the donors come from meagre economic

circumstances, and the foreign government may be putting pressure on its citizens to provide donations. How would you and Kara assess the ethical and pragmatic issues in this situation? Ultimately, what would be the main reasons that you would either help or refuse to help Kara gain access to help from the foreign donor program?

15. *False Information*: You work for an organization mandated to help people with diabetes. You notice a number of popular medical websites have inaccurate information about diabetes, including methods of managing diabetes and medications that may be helpful. What strategies could you use to ensure that people with diabetes in your community have access to valid, reliable, and plain-language research and information about diabetes?

16. *Prevention and Intervention*: As a mental health advocate, you are preparing to speak at a state government hearing about whether to allocate additional funding to suicide prevention or suicide intervention programs. Some people suggest that the focus should be on prevention and wellness, including programs that promote good mental health and well-being (Chang et al., 2021). Others highlight the need to ensure that services are in place to serve those who are already in crisis. How would you apply a deontological approach to this issue? What ethical principles would you apply? How would you apply a teleological (utilitarian approach)? How would you define the "greater good" and the needs of the most vulnerable in this situation?

17. *Flawed Ethics*: For each of the following scenarios, identify the types of flaws in the decision-making process. Explain how these flaws conflict with ethical principles such as acting with integrity, promoting social justice, being fair, being good stewards of our agency's resources, and respecting the dignity and worth of all people.

    a. Ms. Sharp discourages a client, Gil, from applying for social assistance so that she can save taxpayer money and encourage the client to take individual responsibility for his life. Gil has excellent job skills, but he has been feeling depressed after the loss of his life partner (who was also the family's primary income earner). He says he's not ready to go back to work.

    b. Mr. Velo is advocating for better funding for afterschool programs in economically stressed neighborhoods. He discovers that a key state legislator had sexual relations with a student intern. Mr. Velo threatens to disclose the affair to the public unless the Velo supports a bill that would fund more afterschool programs. The legislator fears what disclosure will do to his family and career, so he decides to support the bill.

    c. A nonprofit community agency recently accepted a large donation from Epsi-Vapes, a company that sells vape products. The donation will allow the agency to expand services for children with learning disabilities. In return, the agency will rename itself Epsi-Vapes Community Services. Social workers at the agency are not comfortable with the decision because Epsi-Vapes markets vape products to children.

d. Bernice gets a job as an intake worker for Topnotch Assisted Living, a residential facility for older adults. Her aunt, Veronica, asks Bernice if she can get her into Topnotch. Veronica has challenges taking care of herself and Topnotch is a great fit for her needs. Bernice places her aunt at the top of a long waiting list.

e. Topher (a college student) wants his social worker, Naya, to refer him to individual counseling for help with test anxiety. Agency policy suggests that Naya should refer clients to group counseling rather than individual counseling because it is generally more cost effective. Topher says he values his privacy and does not want to participate in a group. Naya validates Topher's wishes, but refers him to group counseling, saying, "My hands are tied by agency policy. I am required to refer you to group counseling."

11

Honesty and Integrity

LEARNING OBJECTIVES

Upon successful completion of this introduction, you will be able to

- describe the importance of honesty and integrity in social work practice with individuals, families, groups, organizations, communities, coworkers, and research participants;
- compare and contrast integrity and honesty as values, virtues, and ethical principles;
- assess social worker behaviors to determine whether they are consistent or in conflict with the principle of integrity;
- develop strategies for responding to situations of moral distress;
- critically evaluate ethical dilemmas involving honesty and integrity; and
- apply the principles of integrity and honesty when conducting social work research.

Honesty and integrity are vital to ethical and effective social work practice. Building trust is the essence of engagement, the first stage of the generalist intervention model (Hepworth et al., 2023). Research suggests that genuineness is a core condition for building trust and maintaining positive helping relationships (Rogers, 1957). Whether we are working with clients, coworkers, employers, research participants, organizations, or communities, we are working in relationships based on cooperation and interdependence. To collaborate effectively, we need to demonstrate (on a consistent basis) that we are honest, genuine, and trustworthy (Appleton, 2010).

As helping agents, we serve in *fiduciary* relationships with our clients (Cottone et al., 2022). We ask them to speak freely and rely upon us. We invite them to share personal and potentially embarrassing information, promising that we will not exploit their vulnerabilities or confidences. As fiduciaries, we are very careful to do what is good for clients, focusing on their needs, interests, and wishes (Morrison, 2016). The moment that clients sense that we are being dishonest, inconsistent, self-serving, or irresponsible, we may lose their trust. Without trust, it is challenging, if not impossible, to work together in an effective manner. It is morally good for all people to act with integrity. Still, as professional social workers, we hold ourselves to higher standards than the general public because we are working with vulnerable populations such as young children, frail older adults, people with mental illness, and clients experiencing high levels of social stress.

In the first part of this chapter, we will explore the meanings of integrity and honesty in greater depth, including how they may be defined as values, virtues, or ethical principles and standards. The next section, "Violations of Integrity," provides examples of professional conduct that breach the ethic of integrity. Being aware of behaviors that violate integrity can help us steer clear of violations. If violations do arise, we can then take corrective actions as soon as possible. In the section entitled "Moral Distress and Moral Courage," we will explore situations in which we are aware of how to fulfill our obligation to act with integrity but we feel pressure to act in a way that violates integrity. We will then explore situations in which honesty and integrity conflict with other key ethical principles. To manage these conflicts, we will explore possible exceptions to honesty, as well as how to manage ethical dilemmas involving honesty. In the final section we will delve into the notion of integrity as it applies to research ethics.

Please see Box 11.1 for a situation raising ethical issues related to integrity and honesty. As you read this scenario, consider the perspectives of both the social worker and the group members. In analyzing this scenario, note that having good intentions as a social worker may not be sufficient. We should also consider the full impacts of our actions on the people we are serving.

DEFINITIONS OF INTEGRITY AND HONESTY

Integrity and honesty may be defined as values, virtues, or ethical principles. As **values**, integrity and honesty are ideals to which we aspire. We conduct ourselves in a manner inspired by honesty and integrity, not because we are required to do so by codes of conduct, agency policies, or regulatory laws (Schroeder et al., 2019). Rather, we practice these values because they are inherently good or desirable (Berling et al., 2019).

When we say that integrity and honesty are **virtues**, we mean that they are enduring qualities, integrated into our being (Aristotle, 2013). Integrity and honesty speak to the relationship that we have with ourselves, being true to our own values, morals, and ethics. They are related to emotional intelligence, our ability to recognize and manage our fears, values, emotions, and ethical principles (Appleton,

BOX 11.1

VIVVI'S GROUP

For each statement in the following situation, consider the extent to which the social worker, Vivvi, has breached her ethical duties to act honestly and with integrity. Consider also whether there are any ethical justifications that make it appropriate for Vivvi to withhold information or provide inaccurate information.

a) As part of her social work field placement, Vivvi facilitates a psychoeducational group for teenagers who have lost a family member due to suicide. In the first meeting, she explains that the purposes of the group are to assist members with feelings about the loss of their family member and to offer strategies for coping with their feelings.

b) One group member asks Vivvi about her qualifications to facilitate this group. Vivvi responds that she has a certificate in grief and loss. She wants members to know that she is competent to lead this group. Although she has completed a training course on grief and loss, she does not have any state-recognized certificates.

c) Another member asks whether Vivvi has personally experienced loss of a loved one due to suicide. She says she is not allowed to talk about her personal life because the focus is on the group members. Agency policy gives Vivvi discretion about whether to self-disclose. She does not have any personal experiences with losses due to suicide, so she did not want to answer the question directly. She wants members to trust and respect her.

d) A third member asks whether Vivvi will share anything they say with authorities. Vivvi acknowledges that she has a duty to report reasonable suspicions of child abuse or neglect, but that she would try to protect their confidentiality as much as is legally permissible.

e) Although the group is primarily a psychoeducational group, Vivvi plans to use hypnotherapy to help group members deal more effectively with their feelings of grief and loss.

f) One group member, Otis, is a distant relative of Vivvi (fourth cousin, once removed). She does not plan to treat Otis any differently from any other group member. She does not think it is important to disclose her relationship with Otis with the group. Further, she thinks that disclosing this relationship will do more harm than good (e.g., embarrassing Otis).

2010). For example, even if we feel tired, angry, or attacked, we still focus on the situation and needs of the people we serve. We do not want our personal feelings or situations to inhibit our ability to practice for the benefit of our clients. We can nurture virtues so they provide us with good moral dispositions, encouraging us to behave in a prosocial manner, even when it is challenging to do so (Fowers et al., 2021). Methods of nurturing integrity include

- making integrity a good habit by practicing it in our everyday life (not only in our roles as social workers);
- surrounding ourselves with people who embrace integrity as a virtue (including supervisors and other models of virtuous social work); and
- fostering self-awareness so that we can be deliberate about how we respond to situations that challenge our integrity.

As ethical principles, integrity and honesty refer to conducting ourselves in a trustworthy manner. The NASW Code of Ethics (2021) defines integrity in terms of three dimensions:

1) acting honestly;
2) using professional and personal self-care; and
3) acting in a manner consistent with social work's mission, values, and ethics.

Acting honestly goes beyond telling the truth and avoiding lies. Honesty includes being open and transparent. When clients ask for feedback, for instance, we should provide them with accurate information (Cottone et al., 2022). To act honestly, we should not withhold information or sugarcoat our feedback. In other words, honesty includes full disclosure of relevant information (Schroeder et al., 2019). Consider a client who has been diagnosed with pancreatic cancer. She has been advised by physicians that she has a very low chance of survival. A social worker might try to help the client feel better by suggesting, "With your positive attitude, I think you're going to beat the odds." Despite the worker's good intentions, this response lacks full honesty. It is not based on science or research evidence. In addition, the worker does not have the medical expertise required to provide this type of prognosis. See Box 11.2 for another situation raising issues related to honesty and bending the truth.

BOX 11.2

SUPPORT ANIMAL

You are helping a client, Ronald, apply for public housing. Ronald says that he cannot bring his emotional support animal into his apartment unless he has a letter from his social worker stating that he needs his Labrador Retriever for mental health purposes. You are not sure whether you are qualified to provide such a letter. Ronald assures you that any social worker can provide such a letter. You know that Ronald has experienced trauma. Still, you are not sure whether he needs a dog for emotional support. You want to help Ronald, so you are thinking of providing a very general letter explaining Ronald's situation and advocating for the housing authority to allow him to keep his dog in the apartment for emotional support. What issues does this situation raise in relation to integrity, honesty, and full disclosure? How should you balance these principles with your obligations regarding client self-determination and serving your client's best interests?

In addition to being truthful, acting honestly suggests we should honor our promises. We should not make promises that we know we cannot keep and we should keep the promises that we make. When we are unable to fulfill our promises, we should let those affected know why we are unable to do so and we should accept accountability. Assume that you promise to submit a client's application for Medicare, but you forget to do so. Given the broken promise, the client may have difficulty trusting you. To rebuild trust, be honest and take ownership of the problem. "I apologize for not submitting your application on time. I forgot and I want to make amends. I know you were counting on me to ensure you have access to Medicare as soon as possible [pause for response]. I will submit the application today and follow-up to ensure the application is processed as soon as possible." Owning up to mistakes can be embarrassing and challenging. As the section on "Moral Courage" below suggests, we may need to access support from supervisors or others to muster the courage that we need to address problems and do the right thing.

The second dimension of honesty, self-care, was added to the NASW Code's definition of integrity in 2021. This addition recognizes the ongoing need to take care of our physical health, psychosocial well-being, and spirituality in order to serve clients with integrity. If I work without taking breaks or holidays, for instance, I may become overstressed and burned out. If I do not access support from supervisors or colleagues, I may not recognize when personal problems are negatively affecting my work and the people I serve. If I am not centered by what is important in my practice as a social worker, I may stray from the core values and ethics of the profession. Accordingly, it is vital that we take care of ourselves through good nutrition, sleep, exercise, mindfulness, boundary setting, professional development, supervision, self-compassion, social support, and balance in our work and personal lives (Grise-Owens et al., 2022; Miller et al., 2019). We may also need to advocate with our agencies to ensure that they provide us with proper work conditions and support.

The third dimension of integrity requires acting consistently with our professional values and ethical responsibilities (Hultman et al., 2018). Accordingly, acting with integrity means being open and honest, fostering client self-determination, promoting social justice, practicing within our areas of competence, avoiding conflicts of interest, and adhering to our other ethical duties (Schroeder et al., 2019). Integrity also requires a willingness to be held accountable for our actions. When people raise concerns about our professional behaviors, we are open to listening. We are willing to admit when we are wrong or have caused harm. We apologize and we take corrective actions, as needed. Assume that a client raises concerns about the quality of a psychosocial assessment that you have prepared. As an accountable professional, you could share the client's concerns with your supervisor and jointly decide how to address these concerns. You could then discuss the revised assessment with the client to ensure that the concerns are properly addressed. By accepting accountability, you are showing that you are honest, reliable, and responsible. We will revisit the notion of accountability in Chapter 12, including when to consult attorneys about the legal implications of admitting mistakes.

When considering our ethical obligations, it is helpful to distinguish between situations involving *moral goods* and situations involving *absolute duties*. In situations involving a moral good, it is virtuous to act in a particular way even if we are not ethically required to do so. Assume you are facilitating a support group that asks if you can move its meeting time from Wednesdays to Sundays. You are not ethically required to move the meeting from your usual working hours to the weekend. Arguably, however, it is a good thing to do. Moving the group is accommodating the group members' needs and wishes. Alternatively, consider a parent who asks you not to report a situation of child abuse. Legally and ethically, you are supposed to report child abuse. It is not just a good thing to do. You have a positive obligation to protect children from harm (Reamer, 2021e). When acting with integrity, we fulfill our moral obligations. We also seek to do good, sometimes going beyond our baseline ethical obligations. When we go beyond our baseline obligations, we are employing aspirational ethics.

When clients, supervisors, or others question the integrity of our conduct, we should respond with empathy, compassion, and integrity. We may need to explain the reasoning for our decisions, demonstrating how we analyzed the situation and took relevant considerations into account. Assume that you are working with an interprofessional team and your colleagues question why you terminated work with a particular client. You could explain that you terminated work with the client because the client was violating agency policies: smoking in nonsmoking areas, missing scheduled appointments, and verbally abusing staff. To demonstrate integrity in your decision making, you could also discuss the full context of the decision. For instance, did you provide the client with feedback and give the client an opportunity to correct their behavior, did you assess underlying psychosocial issues that may have contributed to the problematic behaviors, and did you discuss possible referrals so the client does not feel abandoned? By helping others understand what factors you considered and how you took them into account, you are demonstrating **transparency**, reliability, and responsibility.

VIOLATIONS OF INTEGRITY

In this section, we explore various examples of violations of the principle of integrity. It is vital that we are able to recognize particular violations so that we can avoid them whenever possible. Further, if we or our colleagues engage in any violations, awareness helps us recognize problems and respond to them as early and effectively as possible.

One might think that anyone going into professional social work must be doing so for the right reasons and must possess a relatively high value for integrity. One might be surprised at how often social workers act in a manner that conflicts with integrity—for instance, taking advantage of clients by having sex with them, breaching agency policy or ethical standards, intentionally misguiding clients, or searching online for client information without client consent (Reamer, 2015; 2021c). Sometimes these acts are based on poor judgment in a particular situation rather than faulty values. Sometimes these acts are committed while the worker is under extreme stress—for instance, putting inaccurate information in client records due to fatigue from working overtime, or exaggerating one's efforts in order to look good to a supervisor who has unreasonably high expectations. Acting under stress does not excuse workers from acting dishonestly, but the context does help us understand the causes of the behavior. Social workers must not only want to act with integrity; they must commit themselves to developing working environments that promote integrity. Acting with integrity requires the willingness and ability to apply moral reasoning, as well as the capacity to empathize with the experiences and views of others (Morrison, 2016).

I can think of many examples when I did not identify an ethical issue until I debriefed with my supervisor. In my first field placement, I discovered that a client's infant daughter was playing with the client's bottle of methadone (a synthetic opiate used to treat heroin addiction). The child did not actually open the bottle and we discussed how the client would ensure that her methadone would be safely stored in the future. I thought this ended the issue until I met with my supervisor. My supervisor noted that agency policy required me to report this incident to child protective services. Initially, I resisted making the report as it could diminish the trust that I was trying to build with my client. By working through the issues with my supervisor, I realized that the resistance was coming from me rather than from my client. Essentially, I wanted to avoid conflict. When I actually discussed my duty to report with the client, she understood my obligation to protect the welfare of her child and thanked me for being honest with her. With the help of my supervisor, I was able to identify and manage an ethical issue that reduced risks to the client, her daughter, the agency, and myself. Sometimes, we engage in unethical behavior because we are not focusing our attention on the right issues. One of the values of supervision is that our supervisors can ensure that we do pay attention to relevant ethical considerations.

The following examples demonstrate a range of social work behaviors that conflict with integrity:

- Saying something that is untrue with the intent to deceive a client, research participant, colleague, or other person;
- Being negligent or reckless in stating information that is inaccurate;
- Making exaggerated statements;

- Basing statements on questionable research or evidence (e.g., cherry-picking research to prove a point that is not truly supported by the full body of evidence);
- Not sharing information that should be disclosed (e.g., a client's right submit a grievance about the worker's conduct);
- Sharing the benefits of a proposed intervention without also noting the risks; or
- Using personal (ad hominin) attacks to try to win a debate or argument.

Some of the most egregious violations of integrity involve intentionally providing false information in order to advance our own interests, without concern for how others may be hurt: for instance, lying to a client about the need for services so that we can make more money, even though the client no longer needs services. Violations of integrity, however, do not require that we hurt others or that we personally benefited from the violation. Consider parents who ask for feedback on their parenting style. You respond that they tend to expect perfect behavior and these expectations can hurt their child's self-esteem. Assume you did not conduct a proper assessment of these dynamics and the conclusions that you provided are inaccurate. The parents ignore your assessment. Although you did not lie or intentionally mislead your clients, your assessment may have been reckless or negligent. Although the parents dismissed your assessment and did not suffer significantly from your inaccurate statements, you have not lived up to the principle of integrity. The parents may lose trust. You may have hurt not only your own reputation, but also the reputation of other social workers. When people lose faith in a particular professional or a profession as a whole, it is challenging to rebuild that trust (Churchill, 2020).

The spread of misinformation throughout society has grown with the proliferation of social media (Pennycook et al., 2021). False information about vaccinations for COVID-19, for instance, caused many people to refuse vaccinations despite strong research evidence to support their effectiveness in reducing the incidence of death and serious illness. Conspiracy theories about "rigging" the 2020 presidential election led some people to question the legitimacy of the election of Joe Biden and incited them to attack the Capitol on January 6, 2021. Research into the spread of misinformation on social media suggests that when people choose whether to share certain content on social media, they often focus on whether the information fits with their political ideology rather than whether the information is accurate. People who might be tempted to share misinformation based on political ideologies are less likely to do so if they are asked to focus on the accuracy of the information before they decide whether to share it (Pennycook et al., 2021). These findings fit with the research on confirmation bias, our tendency to search for, rely upon, and favor information that supports our pre-existing values and beliefs. As we evaluate information, we need to be aware of possible biases and self-deception about the validity of the information (Paul & Elder, 2019). As social workers, we may be tempted to share misinformation if it supports values such as social justice. To maintain honesty and integrity, we need to avoid temptations to spread false information (Smith et al., 2021). Pursuing social justice does not justify spreading false information. If we demonstrate lack of integrity, we squander trust and we make it more difficult to advance social justice and other core values. In addition, when helping others use social media, we may encourage them to consider the accuracy of information that they are reading before deciding whether to share it. We can educate ourselves and others about ways of searching for reliable sources of information, using critical thinking while reading, making conscious choices about sharing information that is accurate and reliable, and citing sources of information so others can check the veracity of our postings.

MORAL DISTRESS AND MORAL COURAGE

In many instances, *doing the right thing* is relatively easy. If you provide a client with honest and accurate information to make informed decisions about treatment options, for instance, you are fulfilling your ethical obligations (NASW Code, S. 1.03) and you are doing good for your client and your agency. Everyone is morally comfortable.

In situations of **moral distress**, doing the right thing is not so easy (Golden et al., 2019). You know how to act with integrity but you are experiencing pressure from your client, employer, or others to act in a manner inconsistent with your ethical obligations (Janssen, 2016). Assume you are working in an agency that is expected to serve 400 clients per day. The agency has just 10 social workers and you cannot possibly do your job effectively with so many clients. You and your colleagues feel pressure to see 400 clients per day even though you know the quality of your services is suffering. As Chapter 2 notes, **moral courage** is the strength to do what is right even when it is difficult to do so (Papouli, 2019). To maintain the integrity of your services, you and your colleague could advocate for additional social workers or fewer clients. If you are concerned about how agency administration will react, you may experience moral distress. Your concerns are valid but this does not mean that you should simply abide by rules that are compromising your services. You may need to consult with your supervisor, colleagues, and other sources of support to determine the best way to proceed.

Research suggests that some helping professionals cope with moral distress by rationalizing their actions. Some professionals simply deny that their ethics are being compromised, allowing them to avoid dealing with the ethical conflict (Shdaimah & Strier, 2020). Others may justify their participation in ethically questionable situations by suggesting they are just following agency policies or their supervisor's orders. They may rationalize their actions (or inaction) by saying that they are not responsible for making the decisions (Hultman et al., 2018). Although it may be true that others are making rules or giving directions, we are still responsible for the integrity of our conduct (Frennert, 2020). We should summon our moral courage and speak up in an assertive, respectful manner. To build moral and tangible support, we can identify allies within and outside our agencies. Ideally, we can use our conflict resolution skills to advocate for change, listen to one another, and work toward joint solutions that satisfy everyone's interests (Fisher et al., 2011). In some situations, we may not be able effect change and resolve the situation of moral distress. We may leave the organization and look for work in an organization that is more supportive of our integrity. If we remain in the organization and continue to experience moral distress, we may experience anxiety, gastrointestinal issues, insomnia, headaches, and nightmares (Health Nurse, Healthy Nation, n.d.). To cope with ongoing moral distress, we can make use of peer consultation, supervision, therapy, and other support systems (Jannsen, 2016; Shdaimah & Strier, 2020). Even if we cannot ultimately rectify the ethical issues, we can strive to maintain our emotional and social well-being.

ETHICAL EXCEPTIONS TO HONESTY AND FULL DISCLOSURE?

Standard 4.04 of the NASW Code clearly states, "Social workers should not participate in, condone, or be associated with dishonesty, fraud, or deception." So, is dishonesty or lack of full disclosure ever ethically justified? We need to be cautious about deviating from the truth, even if we feel morally justified. If we start deviating from the truth in one situation, then what is to stop us from deviating from the truth in others? Even little lies or well-intentioned mistruths could lead us down a path of more and more mistruths. If we start justifying lack of truth and full disclosure, then how can clients, research participants, or others trust us? How can we expect them to be fully honest with us if we are not fully honest with them? Being honest should be our default position. If we are to stray from honesty and full disclosure, then we need very strong justifications for doing so (Churchill, 2020).

According to Dolgoff et al., 2012, we should ordinarily resolve ethical issues by following the law, agency policy, and the NASW Code of Ethics. They further suggest that if these guidelines provide unclear or conflicting guidance, then we should resolve the issues by weighing seven core ethical principles: **protection of life**, **equality and inequality**, **autonomy and freedom**, **least harm**, **quality of life**, **privacy** and **confidentiality**, and **truthfulness and full disclosure**. Dolgoff et al. suggest that these principles are ranked in order of importance, with protection of life being the highest principle. This model suggests that we can justify breaching truthfulness to protect life or to advance the other values. Assume that a client's spouse asks whether you know where she is. Although your client has given you permission to speak with her spouse, you are concerned that he is drunk, angry, and planning to kill her. You would be justified in refusing to disclose where your client is because you are concerned about protecting her life.

Although Dolgoff et al.'s ranking of ethical principles may be useful in some situations, it might lead us to justify lying or deception in more dubious situations. Assume that your agency is hiring new social workers. The agency has a history of hiring white social workers. You want to advance equality by ensuring that the agency hires people of color. Dolgoff et al. rank equality above honesty. Are you, therefore, justified in hiding the applications of anyone who is not a person of color? Although your intention may be to advance equality, your proposed means for doing so is unethical. Rather than being deceitful (hiding applications), you could work with your agency to ensure more equitable hiring practices. In this situation, you do not have a strong justification for breaching the principles of honesty and integrity.

Some people try to justify dishonesty or deception by noting, "Everyone else is doing it." This argument is not a valid ethical justification. The fact that other people are acting in an unethical manner does not mean that it is ethical for us to do so. As the saying goes, "Two wrongs don't make a right." We may need to be the ones to operate on higher ethical principles, breaking patterns of unethical behavior and acting as models of integrity. Consider working in an agency where your coworkers exaggerate the effectiveness of the program to foster positive expectations among clients. Given the culture of the agency, you may feel that it is appropriate for you to exaggerate in a similar fashion. Although exaggeration may be the norm within the agency, it is still unethical. Exaggeration may be giving clients false expectations about the program. Further, if clients discover that you and your colleagues are exaggerating, they may lose trust in you, your program, and your profession. Even when exaggeration, lying, or deception is common, truth is valuable (Churchill, 2020).

The ethical principle of beneficence suggests that we should do good for the people we serve (Cottone et al., 2022). We act out of kindness, caring, altruism, and respect for others (Stanford Encyclopedia of Philosophy, 2019). So, does the principle of beneficence justify holding back on the truth to benefit our clients or others? As noted earlier, we need to be careful about deviating from the truth because the people we serve generally expect the truth and deserve the truth. Consider a client who tests positive for a fatal disease that has no cure. You and the medical team are concerned that the client cannot handle the truth, so you are considering withholding this information. From a teleological perspective, you believe that telling the client would do more harm than good. Telling the client might lead to high levels of anxiety and stress. You believe the client could be overwhelmed and contemplate suicide. You believe the client's quality of life might be better if the client does not know about the diagnosis. Considering the principles of *respect for the dignity of all people* and informed consent, however, we should also consider the client's right to full and accurate information (Churchill, 2020). How else can the client make fully informed decisions? We should be careful not to substitute our decisions for the client's. Further, we need to be aware of our internal motivations and feelings (Reamer,

2021e). When I am thinking about withholding information from the client, am I actually doing so for the client's best interests? What if I am uncomfortable sharing the truth with the client? What if the client can deal with the truth and I am not giving the client enough credit for having the intelligence, resilience, and coping skills to handle it? Once again, when dealing with challenging ethical situations, consulting with supervisors, peers, ethicists, or others may be helpful in ensuring that our decision making is based on a full and fair assessment of the relevant considerations.

ETHICAL DILEMMAS INVOLVING HONESTY AND FULL DISCLOSURE

In the previous section, we explored whether there are certain exceptions to our ethical obligations regarding honesty and full disclosure. Rather than carving out specific exceptions for honesty and full disclosure, it may be better to think about how to manage ethical dilemmas that arise when honesty and full disclosure conflict with other ethical duties. Remember, when we experience true ethical dilemmas there is no singular, perfect solution. Reasonable people may come to different conclusions about the most prudent way to manage the ethical dilemma. Regardless of which course of action we take, we may not be able to fulfill all our ethical duties and certain people may be put at risk of harm. Because there is no perfect solution, we may feel anguish about how to act. Feeling anguish can be a sign that we truly appreciate the tension between conflicting obligations.

Assume that you are assisting Zelda, a 20-year-old client who is pregnant and wants to make her child available for adoption. She does not feel that she is ready, emotionally or financially, to take care of the child. She believes it is in the best interests of the child to be adopted. According to the policies of your adoption agency, you ask Zelda for the name and contact information of the baby's biological father so you can request his consent to the adoption. Zelda says the father, Charles, does not know about her pregnancy and she does not want any further contact with him. She says he is emotionally abusive and telling him about the baby would cause more harm than good. When reflecting on how to respond, you identify your ethical obligations and how they apply to this situation:

- You believe in honesty and full disclosure, suggesting that Charles should know about the pregnancy and Zelda's plans for adoption.
- You believe in client self-determination and your primary obligation to Zelda as your client.
- You believe in nonmaleficence and thus in protecting Zelda and the baby from the possible harm that may arise if Charles finds out about the planned adoption.

How should you manage these conflicting ethical obligations and interests?

One option is to proceed with the adoption without informing Charles about the baby or the adoptions plans. This course of action fits with Standards 1.01 and 1.02 of the NASW Code in terms of prioritizing the client's interests and self-determination. When considering the risks of proceeding with the adoption without notifying Charles, you and Zelda should consider agency policies and state laws. Assume that they require parental notification. If you and Zelda do not disclose that you know the father, you could incur sanctions for violating agency policies and the law. Further, if Charles later becomes aware of the adoption, he could contest it. Having a contest over adoption and moving the baby from the adoptive parents to the biological father could be difficult for the baby (e.g., abrupt changes in parenting could negatively affect the baby's psychosocial development and ability to develop secure attachment).

A second option is to let the adoption agency and court know about Charles and request an exception to notification given his history of mistreating Zelda. With this option, you could advance Zelda's wishes in an open and honest manner. Let's assume in this case that Zelda does not have strong evidence about the history of emotional abuse and her attorney advises that the court would likely require Charles to be notified.

A third option is to notify Charles, but to try to do so in a way that minimizes the risks to Zelda and the baby. You and Zelda could discuss various options for letting Charles know about the baby: you meet with Charles, Zelda meets with Charles, and Zelda asks her attorney, a friend, or a family member to meet with Charles. Whoever is chosen to speak with Charles could practice having a conversation to increase the chances that he will offer consent. You could also develop a safety plan with Zelda to reduce the risks of Charles re-establishing contact and making life difficult for Zelda.

A fourth option would be for you to tell Zelda that you cannot facilitate the adoption for her without notifying Charles and asking for his consent. You could also let Zelda know that she could go to another adoption agency and simply tell them that she does not know the father. The other agency might facilitate the adoption without taking further steps to identify the father; however, they might take further steps to identify and locate the father. Although you are not directly participating in fraud with the second adoption agency, you have encouraged the client to act in a fraudulent manner. Zelda may be willing to withhold information at the second agency. Zelda's intent (to do what is best for the baby) may be good (Reamer, 2021e); however, honesty and disclosure are still being compromised.

So, what would you do in this situation? How would you try to fulfill your ethical obligations? How would you manage the risks related to the choices that you and Zelda make?

Let us consider a different situation, one that invites us to think about honesty in connection with self-disclosure. Assume that I am working with a community organization mandated to raise public awareness of mental illness. Members of my organization ask me whether I have experienced mental illness. I am a very private person. I have bipolar disorder. With the aid of medication and talk therapy, my mental condition is currently under control. I know that disclosing my disorder to the community organization (and to the public) could be beneficial. I could gain trust and I could use my story to help others understand mental illness. Still, I fear that some people may discriminate against me if I disclose that I have bipolar disorder. So, when analyzing the ethical dilemma, what ethical obligations should I consider? Honesty and full disclosure, beneficence, nonmaleficence, and social justice. Nothing in the NASW Code of Ethics requires me to self-disclose. Still, to promote social justice, should I be willing to take certain risks? The NASW Code also reminds me to engage in self-care. Self-care includes establishing appropriate boundaries between my personal and professional life. In this situation, discussions with my therapist may be valuable. My therapist can help me work through my personal issues and make a decision that addresses both my personal and professional concerns. Further, I may not need to make a final decision today. I may require time to process my concerns and then decide whether or not to self-disclose. If I do self-disclose, I could also benefit from a follow-up plan (e.g., to monitor the reaction of my community organization, to ensure that I have appropriate support, and to take additional steps to address any problems that arise).

Box 11.3 provides another situation that raises issues related to honesty and full disclosure. As you explore this situation, consider how baseline ethical obligations and aspirational ethics may apply.

BOX 11.3

NAMESAKE

Benno and Akira are social workers in a nonprofit organization that provides support to individuals and families affected by violent crimes. They have recently discovered that the namesake for the organization was a strong proponent of Jim Crow laws in the 1950s. As a real estate agent, he used redlining (systematically refusing to sell properties in certain neighborhoods to people of color). Benno believes that the organization should change the name of the organization to take a clear stance against segregation and racism. Akira thinks that the organization should keep the same name because nobody remembers the namesake or his association with segregation. She believes that telling people about the namesake's history will do more harm than good for the organization and its reputation (including the loss of donations and volunteers).

How would you advise Akira and Benno about how to manage the issues raised by this situation? Does the agency have an ethical duty to disclose the racist history of its namesake? Note that the organization serves a racially and ethnically diverse community.

Throughout our professional careers we may be faced with situations in which honesty and full disclosure conflict with other ethical obligations. Sometimes, we have to make difficult choices. Ideally, we are not making these choices alone. Ideally, we are working collaboratively with our clients, supervisors, attorneys, or others who can help us analyze situations from different perspectives and choose the best path forward.

RESEARCH INTEGRITY AND ETHICALLY QUESTIONABLE PRACTICES

Research integrity refers to conducting all aspects of research in an honest and ethically responsible manner. The National Institutes of Health (n.d.) suggests that research integrity is based on four values: honesty, accuracy, efficiency, and objectivity.

- *Honesty* refers to acting openly and truthfully in all stages of the research process (including proposing, performing, and reporting research). Being honest also means honoring commitments to research participants, funding bodies, scholarly publications, and others involved in or affected by the research process.
- *Accuracy* includes reporting findings precisely, using rigorous research methods, and taking care to avoid errors.
- *Efficiency* means being good stewards of research funding and other resources, avoiding waste, and ensuring that resources are used in a cost-effective manner.
- *Objectivity* means being fair and impartial in all stages of the research process. We need to ask unbiased questions, use robust research methods, analyze data in an honest and accurate manner, and let the data and research findings speak for themselves in our research publications and presentations.

Research integrity works best when we internalize and live these values rather than simply adhering to externally imposed rules and regulations (Berling et al., 2019).

Research integrity is not the sole responsibility of individual researchers. It requires the support of the social agencies, research institutions, or other organizations where we work (Bouter, 2020). Our organizations can promote a culture of integrity by developing and following ethics guidelines and procedures supporting the aforementioned values. Ethics protocols should include guidance for informed consent, managing risk, avoiding conflicts of interest, and complying with federal and state laws pertaining to research endeavors. To foster a culture of research integrity, organizations can facilitate supervision, peer consultation, and mentoring. Some organizations have Institutional Review Boards or ethics committees designed to review research proposals and monitor for compliance with research standards and regulations. In organizations without these formal structures, you may seek out supervision and peer support to ensure that you are carrying out your research functions in an ethically responsible manner.

Assume that you are developing a research proposal as an assignment for your social work research course. You inform your professor that you would like to study the experiences of first-generation college students (students who do not have any parents or other close relatives who have attended college). You are interested in learning about the challenges that first-generation students experience, as well as what types of support or strategies help with these challenges. This is an exploratory study, so you plan to use qualitative methods. Your professor tells you to use a survey because qualitative methods will take too long and you will not be able to complete your research within the allotted time. You are concerned that there is not enough prior research to determine what questions to ask on the survey. You want your study to be meaningful. You believe that using a survey that has not been tested for validity and reliability would be a waste of time. What ethical issues arise from this situation? How might you and your professor manage them?

In terms of honesty, it is important be open with your professor about your concerns. At the same time, you do not want to anger your professor or do something that could hurt your grades. Think of ways to speak with your professor in an empathic and collaborative manner. "I understand that you're concerned about my ability to complete this project within the allotted time. I'm concerned about that, too. I also want to make sure that I am learning how to use the best methods to answer my research question." The professor might then be able to describe how you can use a survey effectively to answer the research question. In terms of efficiency, you might raise concerns about whether the survey research will be credible. "I would like to be able to publish my research. I'm concerned that I won't be able to construct a valid and reliable survey. I think I have a better chance of publishing my research if I conduct a rigorous qualitative study." Your professor might say that this course is not designed for students to implement publishable research, but rather, to practice certain skills and develop competence for future research. Your professor might further explain how qualitative research can take much more time than a survey study. This honest exchange of concerns allows the two of you to better understand one another's perspectives. You could then move into problem-solving by considering different options. For instance, if you wanted to develop competence in qualitative research, is there a way to construct the research in manner that you could complete the research within the time frame of the course (e.g., limiting the number of people interviewed and keeping the interviews very focused to limit the size of the data set)? If you were to use a survey design, how could you do so in a way that the results would be valid, reliable, and publishable? Rather than using a survey that has not been tested for validity and reliability, for instance, your research project could focus on how to construct and pilot test a survey. You might then conduct a larger, publishable study after the course ends. Ideally, you and your professor can develop a plan that meets both of your interests. If you do not reach a mutually acceptable agreement, as least you have had an honest exchange and can understand where your differences lie.

For a situation related to honesty when conducting online research, see Box 11.4.

BOX 11.4

ALTERNATIVE FACTS

Noella is studying what motivates people to spread false information over the Internet. She joins two social media groups, one that identifies with conservative ideology and one that identifies with liberal ideology. She posts clearly false information on each website and documents which members share the information with others. She then invites people who share the misinformation to participate in qualitative research interviews. She informs prospective participants that they were randomly chosen. She withholds telling them that they were chosen because they had shared false information with others. She justifies withholding information about the research because she does not want this information to sway their answers. She believes the research poses no harm to the research participants because they are simply answering questions about why they decided to share information that is blatantly false.

To what extent has Noella's research violated the principles of informed consent (as described in Chapter 4) and the principles of integrity? What are the ethical justifications, if any, for withholding information from research participants? How could Noella's research methods affect how people view social work researchers?

The following list illustrates how violations of integrity may arise at various stages of the research process.

- Asking research questions that violate social work ethics (e.g., "Which types of extreme pressure tactics during criminal interrogations are most effective at producing confessions").
- Selecting research designs and data gathering methods that are not capable of answering the primary research question (e.g., when studying the effectiveness of a support group for caretakers of people with dementia, asking group members whether they liked the facilitator; National Institutes of Health, n.d.).
- Fabricating data (e.g., researchers have identified 80 research participants; the study requires at least 100, so the researchers make up answers for 20 fictitious participants; Bouter, 2020).
- Plagiarizing (e.g., during a literature review, the researcher copies and pastes information from other articles without giving credit to the original authors; Bouter, 2020).

- Engaging in conflicts of interest without full disclosure (e.g., researchers include 11 family members as research participants without letting their institution or funding sponsor know about the dual relationships, and without taking steps to manage potential risks to the integrity of the research; Bouter, 2020).
- Conducting research without informed consent of participants (e.g., telling research participants that the risks of participating in a study are negligible when there are significant risks of emotional harm).
- Falsifying the results of a study (e.g., modifying statistics so that it appears that there is a significant correlation between the dependent and independent variables when the true data showed no significant correlation; Bouter, 2020).
- Withholding important information from the funding body, scientific community, or broader public (e.g., a social worker finds that her agency's outreach services for people with depression are not effective; the agency asks her to bury the study so that nobody will know and they will continue to receive funding for their program).

In addition to knowing how to conduct research with integrity, it is important to know how to communicate with others when we feel pressured into practices that violate our ethical responsibilities. As the earlier section on moral courage suggests, we should consult with others and seek support in order to stand up for what is right.

As researchers, we rely on other researchers to be trustworthy, and they rely on us to be the same. We also need to nurture the support of the public, our funding sponsors, and future research participants (National Institutes of Health, n.d.). When we violate their trust, we may lose their support—not just for our current research endeavors, but for future research.

CONCLUSION

Whether we are working with individuals, families, organizations, communities, or research participants, honesty and integrity are the cornerstones of our professional relationships. Building trust may take time, particularly with people who have felt that their trust has been violated in the past by social workers or other helping professionals. We strive to act with the highest levels of integrity and honesty so that our professional conduct is above reproach. When we fall short of acting with integrity and honesty, we need to be accountable for our actions. As Chapter 12 describes, we do not need to wait until others discover our missteps and file formal grievances or lawsuits. We can accept responsibility, consult with others, and determine the best steps forward. By taking corrective actions, we not only repair the immediate harm. We also repair the trust in our relationships and character.

When working with clients, we want them to act with honesty and integrity. We understand that being open and honest with us may be challenging. They may feel embarrassed about sharing certain information, for instance, if they have been involved in abusive, illegal, or dishonest behavior. They may also feel embarrassed if family members, friends, or others have abused or mistreated them. If we want clients to be frank with us, we need to be frank with them. Our honesty and integrity not only shows clients that they can trust us; it also models how to be honest and open, even when discussing challenging or embarrassing issues.

DISCUSSION QUESTIONS AND EXERCISES

1. *Integrity Reflection*: Identify a time in your life when you did not act with integrity. What was going on in your life that might have led to the lapse in integrity? What could you have done differently to enhance your ability to act with integrity? What types of personal and professional self-care help you to maintain your integrity?

2. *Family Secret*: During family counseling, Obie and Leya tell you that their 13-year-old son, Artie, was conceived through sperm donation. They are concerned that Artie will discover this family secret one day, because he is already talking about genetic testing to learn more about his biological heritage (Landers & Parrish, 2021). They say that they do not want Artie to know that Obie is not his biological father so that Artie will continue to treat Obie as his "real father." They are also concerned that Artie may be very angry that they kept his parentage a secret for so long. Use the first three steps in the Framework for Managing Ethical Issues (in Chapter 2) to analyze this situation. Consider your ethical responsibilities, including honesty, full disclosure, nonmaleficence and self-determination?

3. *False Impression*: You are working with Toni, a teenager referred to you by a school guidance counselor due to recent fighting with classmates. Toni thinks she has to see you or she will be expelled from school. The guidance counselor told you that Toni was not at risk of expulsion, but that she needed help with personal issues that may have led to the fighting. You are concerned that if you tell Toni that she is not at risk of expulsion then she will stop seeing you. According to the principles of honesty and integrity, do you have a positive obligation to tell her that the school is not requiring her to engage in social work services? If informing Toni is morally good but not ethically required, are there any ethical justifications for not informing her? What would you say (or not say) to Toni, and why?

4. *Violation, Dilemma, or Distress*: Consider each of the following situations from the social worker's perspective. Identify whether each situation involves a violation of integrity, an ethical dilemma involving ethical

integrity, a situation of moral distress, or a situation with no significant ethical concerns. If you were the social worker, how would you manage the ethical issue?

a. Lereece, a client, asks whether everything they discuss in counseling is confidential. Kayla wants to encourage Lereece to trust her, so she explains confidentiality in broad terms. She downplays the exceptions to confidentiality. She explains that there are rare exceptions related to child abuse and neglect. Kayla does not explain exceptions related to serious, imminent risks to the client or others.

b. Yakob is planning research into the effects of positive encouragement on public speaking. He plans to provide positive encouragement to the experimental group, but not to the control group. He will then compare the levels of stress experienced by members of each group during public speaking. To avoid biasing the results by telling research participants the true purpose of the research, Yakob plans to tell them that the purpose of the study is to compare different styles of public speaking. Yakob asks for your advice about the ethics of the proposed study.

c. Alby comes into his social worker's office wearing a purple shirt, white belt, and green and orange striped pants. Alby says, "I'm going for a job interview today. How you like my new outfit?" The worker thinks the outfit is ugly and embarrassing but does not want to hurt Alby's feelings. The worker replies, "I love it. You look very debonair."

d. Viola is an outreach worker in a public library. Her job is to connect with people who may need shelter, food, addiction treatment, or mental health services. Viola tries to dress as an "ordinary person" so that she does not look like a social worker. When she initially strikes up conversations with people in the library, she does not identify herself as a social worker. She wants people to connect with her first. She fears that some people will not speak with her if they know she is a social worker.

e. Leland works in a school for children with special needs. His program director, Anita, tells him to ask parents to volunteer to help teachers at least one day per week because volunteering will help their children's academic success. Leland knows that Anita's true reason for wanting more volunteers is to reduce the cost of hiring teachers' aides. Leland worries that if he does not comply, he may face negative treatment from Anita.

f. Ariana works for a career counseling agency that boast a 97% success rate in terms of securing jobs for clients within 60 days. When screening clients for intake, Ariana excludes people who have felony convictions. It is difficult to find jobs for people with criminal records and she does not want to harm they agency's success rate. She believes that she is following agency policy and precedent.

5. *Subpoena*: You have been providing case management services to Sydnee, a client who has been charged with assaulting a police officer. Sydnee's attorney sends you a subpoena requiring you to testify in the upcoming hearing. Although Sydnee thinks that you have only positive information to share with the court, you also have information that is potentially embarrassing. If you go to court, you are legally required to tell the truth and respond honestly to all questions. You are thinking of discouraging Sydnee and her attorney from calling you as a witness. What are your ethical responsibilities and how should you respond?

6. *Influencer*: You and a coworker, Lionel, are fundraising for an agency that serves people with disabilities. Lionel sees himself as an "influencer" who has been able to attract lots of traffic for his social media by including exaggerations and misinformation in his posts. He has found that various social media use algorithms which spread information faster, farther, and more broadly if it is divisive and provocative. He suggests posting fabricated stories and photos of people with disabilities being exploited and suffering great indignities. He believes these posts will incite controversy, thus leading to more clicks and more donations to the agency's good cause. How would you respond to Lionel? In your discussion with Lionel, consider ethical issues in relation to honesty, beneficence (doing good), nonmaleficence, respect, deontology, teleology, and virtue ethics.

7. *Informed Consent*: Jasper is studying the spread of disease within an assisted living facility. He informs residents that he is placing a device in their toilets to help sanitize them. In fact, the device does not disinfect. The device will be used to measure bacteria and viruses in the toilet water. How does this plan violate informed consent? What are the possible ethical justifications for deception in research. Do they apply in this situation? You may refer back to Chapter 4 regarding deception in research.

8. *Cherry Picking*: You are working for a school district that is trying to reduce students' use of screen time and social media. You come across research suggesting that excessive use of social media negatively affects self-esteem in adolescents. Upon closer look at the research, you note that the research has limitations. In particular, it was conducted with a culturally homogenous sample that does not reflect the diversity of your school district. You believe that citing the research would be very helpful to your campaign; however, you are concerned that citing limitations of the research will detract from the main message. Would it be ethical to use this research to support your campaign to reduce screen time? If you cite this research, do you need to disclose its limitations? Provide your reasoning.

9. *Comparing Values*: Imagine that you have a client named Cloé. She tells you she exaggerated on her résumé to get a job. Without exaggerating,

she would not have met the minimum requirements that were advertised for the job. She claims she was unemployed for 3 months and was about to be evicted from her apartment. She needed money desperately for food and rent. What does this scenario tell you about how Cloé prioritizes values such as honesty, shelter, security, and survival? How are your values and priorities similar to or different from Cloé's?

10. *Family in Transition*: You are facilitating a families-in-transition group for parents going through separation and divorce. Some group members start discussing how they contrive stories about how their former partners were abusive so the court will deny or limit visitation with their children. How would you respond to this discussion? Would you allow members to make their own decisions about what to share with the court? Would you actively discourage members from fabricating stories of abuse? Would you let the court know that certain people are not telling the truth about their former partners? Provide your reasoning, including how concerns about honesty, confidentiality, nonmaleficence, and client self-determination factor into your reasoning.

11. *Roommates*: You provide supportive counseling to freshman students at a state college. One client, Scott, says that he is planning to live together with Eric next year. They do not know that you are serving both of them. Until Scott's disclosure, you did not know that Eric and Scott were friends. Eric has schizophrenia. Although this condition is currently under control, Eric has engaged in violent behavior stemming from hallucinations within the past year. You think it would be helpful for Scott to know about Eric's mental health situation. You recognize that you have an unintentional dual relationship. You believe in honesty and full disclosure. At the same time, you want to honor their confidentiality and trust. Would you raise your concerns with either client? If so, how?

12. *Moral Support*: Who would you consult for assistance in the situation of moral distress arising in each of the following situations?
    a. In your field placement, your field instructor asks you to falsify records to make it look as though a particular client meet's the agency's eligibility requirements for services.
    b. In one of your social work classes, you believe that a professor is discriminating against students on the basis of their sexuality. You and everyone else in the class are afraid to raise concerns because it may negatively affect your grades.
    c. On a group presentation assignment for a social work class, other students in your group are plagiarizing from a presentation they found online. You are concerned that they will call you a snitch (or worse) if you tell anyone.

12

Social Work Accountability and Regulation

LEARNING OBJECTIVES

Upon successful completion of this introduction, you will be able to

- describe how social workers may be held accountable for professional misconduct through various systems, including complaints within their agencies, malpractice lawsuits, professional review processes, licensing complaints, and criminal charges;
- identify laws and standards of practice to which you may be held accountable as a social worker;
- assess which avenues of redress are most appropriate when pursuing compensation for damages, protection of clients, protection of the public, contract enforcement, or promotion of ethical practice; and
- appreciate the aspirational role that virtues play in promoting moral behavior and ethical practice.

The concept of *professional accountability* means that we are answerable for our conduct to the people we serve, including clients, employers, communities, research participants, and the profession of social work itself. We may be held accountable for our conduct through a variety of systems: criminal law, civil (tort) law, professional regulatory laws, professional codes of ethics, agency policies, legally enforceable contracts with clients, administrative laws, community norms, and personal conscience. Each of these sources provides rules or standards of conduct, delineating what types of behavior are appropriate and inappropriate. Some sources are mandatory, prescribing certain types of behavior and prohibiting other types of behavior. Some sources are quasi-mandatory, meaning that they provide general standards of behavior but leave room for interpretation and applicability given the specific context of the behavior. When we breach a **mandatory** rule or quasi-mandatory standard, we may be held accountable for our actions. Consequences for breaching rules or standards range from punishments (imprisonment, fines) to compensation (paying for damages) to protecting the public (prohibiting further practice, rehabilitating the professional through education or counseling) to restoration (making right the wrong through healing processes or restitution).

Before delving into this chapter, please review the Adult Protection Investigation situation described in Box 12.1. As you read through this chapter, consider how the social worker, Dakota, could be held accountable for her actions through the criminal justice system, civil court, her agency, the NASW National Ethics Committee, or any regulatory systems governing her practice.

As we consider various sources of professional accountability throughout this chapter, note the difference between *minimum ethical standards* and *aspirational ethics*. Minimum (baseline) standards[1] refer to the most basic ethical expectations or obligations of social workers (Cottone et al., 2022). In other words, what types of professional conduct should clients, agencies, and society be able to expect of social workers—at the very least? Aspirational (or maximal) ethics refer to the highest ideals of professional practice that social workers should pursue (Street, n.d.). Minimum ethical standards are sometimes called the floor, the level of practice beneath which social workers should not fall. Aspirational ethics are sometimes called the ceiling or the sky, the level to which we should strive, even though the ceiling may always rise above our reach (Kirkland & Kirkland, 2006). Aspirational ethics do not dictate what types of behaviors are required, but rather what types of behaviors are broadly praised for their goodness (Beauchamp & Childress, 2019). As social workers, we should pay heed to both types of standards. In terms of minimum standards, for instance, we should practice in a manner demonstrating basic competence (NASW Code, 2021, S.1.04), we should respect client confidentiality (S.1.07), and we should ask clients for consent rather than imposing interventions on clients (S.1.03). In terms of aspirational ethics, we should strive for practice excellence (rather than mere competence), we should strive to enhance client confidentiality (rather than merely respect it), and we should broaden clients' choices (rather than simply asking clients for consent to a single intervention). In terms of accountability, we may be held **responsible** for falling below the floor or minimum standards. For instance, you may become subject to discipline from your agency, you may be sued by an injured client for malpractice, or you may be held to account by your professional association or regulatory body (e.g., the NASW or your state licensing board). Although we are expected to strive for the ceiling, there are typically no penalties or disciplinary actions for failing to reach the ceiling (Street, n.d.). We may be motivated to avoid discipline for falling beneath the floor. Ideally, we should be motivated to aspire much higher, based on deeply held values rather than fear of punishment. From a practical perspective, we are less likely to be exposed to

---

1. Some authors refer to minimum standards as "mandatory ethics," suggesting that social workers are required to follow these rules. The NASW Code of Ethics, however, expresses most of its standards in terms of "should" rather than "must." The term "should" suggests that these standards are not mandatory, even though they are offered as general expectations of social workers.

BOX 12.1

ADULT PROTECTION INVESTIGATION

Dakota recently graduated with a BSW degree. She is a proud member in good standing with the NASW. She works for a state agency that investigates allegations of elder abuse and neglect. As you will see in the following scenario, Dakota makes a number of missteps during a particular investigation. When reviewing this situation, consider how Dakota may have violated various state laws or standards in the NASW (2021) Code of Ethics. Note that Dakota is not a licensed social worker.

One morning, Dakota's supervisor asks her to investigate an anonymous report that Mr. Rokaw, 87, is at risk due to neglect. According to the report, Mr. Rokaw lives with his daughter, Alayna. The report suggests that Alayna is not taking care of his basic needs, including food, hygiene, and healthcare. Mr. Rokaw has dementia and cannot take care of himself. Dakota plans to meet Mr. Rokaw and Alayna at their house. On her way, Dakota's car breaks down and she is unable to meet them in person. While waiting in the car repair shop, Dakota calls Alayna and conducts her investigation over the telephone. Alayna reassures Dakota that everything is okay and that she is able to take care of Mr. Rokaw's needs without further assistance. After the telephone conversation, a man in the waiting room approaches Dakota. He confides that he overheard her conversation. He says that he knows Mr. Rokaw and Alayna as his neighbors. He reassures Dakota that Alayna is taking good care of her father, whom she loves very much. Dakota feels relieved by this confirmation that Mr. Rokaw is not at risk.

In her agency's electronic records, Dakota documents her meeting with Alayna. She feels embarrassed that her car broke down, so she simply writes that she met Alayna and Mr. Rokaw in-person. State law requires adult protection investigations to be conducted in-person. Dakota does not document anything about her telephone call with Alayna or her conversation with the man who said Alayna is taking good care of her father.

A week later, Mr. Rokaw's other daughter, Vicki, calls the adult protection agency to report that Mr. Rokaw died of pneumonia. Vicki is furious when she discovers that the agency knew her father was at risk but did nothing to help. Vicki claims that the agency could have saved his life by ensuring that he had proper food and medical care. She says that she will do whatever it takes to ensure that the social worker, Dakota, is held fully accountable for the wrongful death of her father.

Consider, what laws did Dakota violate? What ethical standards did she breach? How did Dakota's **standard of care** fall below that expected of an adult protection investigator with a BSW degree? What avenues of redress should Vicki consider in order to hold Dakota accountable?

malpractice lawsuits and professional disciplinary complaints if we strive toward aspirational standards, rather than settling for mere observance of minimal standards (Kirkland & Kirkland, 2006).

The following sections explore each source of accountability, starting with criminal law. For each source of accountability, you will learn who may initiate an action for misconduct, what types of rules or standards apply, and what types of consequences may result from a successful action. Most of this chapter focuses on accountability for social workers. Toward the end of this chapter, a section on "Interprofessional Practice" explores how professional accountability extends to physicians, attorneys, nurses, psychologists, and other allied professionals.

CRIMINAL LAW—ACCOUNTABILITY TO THE STATE

Criminal law refers to the system of laws enacted by state or federal governments to protect the public from specific types of harm, for instance, theft, assault, rape, and trespass.[2] Crimes are defined as wrongs against the state, even if there is a specific individual or group that is the target of the crime. Thus, the state is primarily responsible for enforcing criminal laws.[3] The criminal justice system includes police, judges, prosecuting attorneys, defense attorneys, courts, forensic mental health practitioners, probation, parole, jails, and prisons. Traditionally, the primary focuses of the criminal justice system were punishment, retribution, and deterrence. The state imposes fines, incarceration, or other punishments as retribution (or payback) for committing a wrongful act and to deter people from recommitting similar offences. Thus, the criminal justice system seeks to prevent harm to individuals and maintain social order (Patterson, 2018). Although public safety, punishment, retribution, and deterrence remain as primary goals of the criminal justice system, greater emphasis has been placed on rehabilitation and restorative justice since the 1970s. Thus, the criminal justice system has been expanded to include programs such as rehabilitative therapy, mediation, problem-solving courts, therapeutic jurisprudence, community services, family group conferences, healing circles, victim assistance, and other interventions that divert cases from court and prison (Restorative Justice Network, n.d.).

As social workers, we are subject to the same criminal laws as members of the general public. Thus, if you murder, steal, or assault, you are subject to the same criminal laws and consequences as non–social workers. Criminal offenses that relate

---

2. For federal crimes see https://www.law.cornell.edu/uscode/text/18. To locate the criminal code of your state, see Legal Information Institute (n.d.) at https://www.law.cornell.edu/wex/table_criminal_code.

3. Although the vast majority of criminal cases are initiated by state officials, some types of cases may be initiated by private persons.

specifically to acts that social workers may commit in their professional capacities include fraud and unlawful confinement of clients. We may be convicted of fraud for intentionally overcharging clients, forging documents, stealing directly from clients, receiving kickbacks for referring clients to certain service providers, and billing clients, Medicare, Medicaid, or private insurance providers for services never rendered (Mackey et al., 2020). We may also be convicted of unlawful confinement for restricting a person's movement without that person's consent. Thus, we should be cautious about preventing clients from leaving their facilities. Although we may be justified in restricting the movement of clients with urgent risks of suicide or homicide,[4] we are not generally permitted to restrain clients against their will.

To convict someone of a crime, the prosecution must prove all the elements of the crime *beyond a reasonable doubt.* This high standard of proof is required because the state does not want to take away a person's rights and freedoms unless there is a high degree of certainty that the allegations are true. The elements of a crime include the *actus reus* (guilty act) and *mens rea* (guilty state of mind). Accordingly, to convict a person of murder, the state must prove not only that the alleged criminal killed, but also intended to kill.[5]

Although social workers may be criminally charged for acts that infringe the NASW Code of Ethics, the basis for charging them would have to be a violation of a criminal law, not merely a violation of the Code. Thus, stealing from a client would not only be a violation of the Code (S.4.04). It would also be a criminal offense for which the worker could be charged. In contrast, failure to promote client self-determination would amount to an ethical violation (S.1.02), but it would not amount to a criminal offense. Although social workers may be held accountable through the criminal justice system, most criminal laws do not focus on professional standards of conduct. Social workers are more likely to be held accountable for professional misconduct under other systems.

CIVIL LAW—ACCOUNTABILITY TO INDIVIDUALS

Civil law refers to the branch of law that regulates relations between individuals.[6] Civil wrongs (torts) include assault, defamation, nuisance, and unlawful confinement. Generally, civil lawsuits are initiated by the person harmed by the tort

---

4. We must abide by the provisions of our state's mental health laws regarding how to manage clients posing serious, imminent risks to themselves or others.

5. Different offenses require different types of mental states. For a more detailed description of criminal law, see Bartol & Bartol (2018).

6. Civil law has different meanings, including a codified system of law used by most continental European countries, the state of Louisiana, and the province of Quebec. The rest of the United States and Canada base their legal systems on English common law (in which law developed through cases and legal principles determined by judges, in contrast to the Roman civil code). For the purposes of this chapter, civil law will refer only to the branch of law that regulates relations between individuals (Bartol & Bartol, 2018).

(exceptions include cases brought by parents on behalf of a child). Whereas the most common criminal law sentences are fines, incarceration, house arrest, and probation (intended for punishment, deterrence, and incapacitation), the most common legal remedy for torts is a court order for the wrongdoer (or tortfeasor) to compensate the victim of the tort for the harm caused (Bartol & Bartol, 2018). In some cases, courts may order other remedies, such as restitution or doing something that puts the person back in a position as if the tort was never committed (e.g., rebuilding a house that the tortfeasor burned down).[7]

A person may be charged in criminal court and sued in civil court for the same act. Thus, the State of California charged former football star O. J. Simpson in criminal court for murdering Nicole Brown Simpson and Ronald Goldman. Goldman's parents also sued Simpson for wrongful death.[8] The prosecutors in the criminal case were not able to prove the murder beyond a reasonable doubt, so the court acquitted Simpson. In the subsequent civil trial, the parents did not have to prove their case beyond a reasonable doubt, but to the lesser standard of "on the preponderance of the evidence" (essentially, greater than a 50–50 chance). Although the criminal court did not find Simpson guilty of murder, the civil court found Simpson liable, and he was ordered to pay **damages** to Goldman's parents for wrongful death of their son (*Rufo* et al. v. Simpson, 1997).

The primary tort related to professional accountability is malpractice (sometimes called professional negligence). **Malpractice** refers to "bad practice" or providing services in a manner that falls below standards reasonably expected of a prudent professional (Reamer, 2018a). Clients may sue for malpractice if they believe you have not acted in accordance with relevant professional standards of practice and this breach of standards results in damages experienced by the client. To win compensation for malpractice, a client must prove

- you owed the client a *duty of care*;
- you *breached* that duty;
- the breach of the duty *caused harm* to the client; and
- the breach was the *proximate cause* of the harm.

The four criteria may be summarized as the four d's: "dereliction of duty directly causing damages" (Polychronis & Brown, 2016, p. 140). To illustrate how these criteria are applied, consider the following vignette.

Smadar is a school social worker, working with a 7-year-old student named Clyde. Clyde's teachers referred him for an assessment at the beginning of

---

7. Another civil remedy is an "injunction," a court order stating that the perpetrator must desist a certain behavior (e.g., causing a specific type of harassment or nuisance).

8. Nicole Brown Simpson's family sued for battery rather than wrongful death.

the school year because he was having difficulties in class. Smadar performs a biopsychosocial assessment. She concludes Clyde's problems are related to inappropriate discipline used by his parents. She engages them in family counseling to redress this problem. Clyde's school performance does not improve and he fails second grade. Clyde's parents, frustrated with lack of progress, take Clyde to another social worker for an assessment. This social worker discovers that Clyde has a learning disability. Clyde's parents sue Smadar for malpractice.

Duty of care: A duty of care refers to the acceptance of responsibility to act in a reasonable manner toward another person or class of persons. For social workers, a duty of care is established whenever they engage clients in services. When Smadar offers services to Clyde's family, she implicitly agrees to provide services in a professional manner. According to this criterion, we do not owe a duty of care to nonclients; for instance, if you pass a person on the street who needs assistance finding a safe place to sleep that night, you are not legally obliged to provide such assistance (even if you believe, morally, you should help). If you offer your professional services, however, you will owe the person a duty of care.

Breach of duty: A breach of duty refers to acting in a manner inconsistent with what would reasonably be expected of a similar professional, acting prudently. The specific duty of care that social workers assume depends on their background and the context of practice. A worker with a BSW providing community organization services would be expected to perform services at a level reasonably expected of a competent BSW practitioner who is providing community organization services. A worker with an MSW and specialized training in sexuality therapy would be expected to perform at a level reasonably expected of a competent MSW practitioner with specialized training in sexuality therapy. Smadar is a school social worker with a BSW, so she would be expected to maintain the standards reasonably expected of a competent school social worker with a BSW.

Courts may refer to a variety of sources to establish the standards to which the practitioner should be held accountable. One of the primary sources is the NASW Code of Ethics, given that this code is comprehensive and nationally recognized. Although courts may consider whether a social worker violated the NASW Code, breaching this code does not automatically indicate liability for malpractice (NASW Code, Purpose Section).

In addition to the general Code of Ethics, the NASW has standards for specific fields of practice, for instance, substance use disorders, school social work, palliative care, long-term care, health, and case management (see https://www.social workers.org/Practice/Practice-Standards-Guidelines). Even if a social worker is not a member of the NASW, the court may use NASW standards to establish what types of behavior are appropriate. As a sexuality therapist, the MSW practitioner noted above could be judged according to standards and ethical guidelines established for sexuality therapists (American Association of Sexuality Educators, Counselors, and Therapists, 2020). Courts may also use standards of practice established through research, theory, and best practices (Moffett & Moore, 2011). In other words, social workers should base their assessments and information on the best evidence available in their field. Failure to do so may result in a breach of the duty of care. As a school social worker, Smadar would probably be expected to be able to make a proper assessment for learning disabilities. Even if she is not responsible for making a specific diagnosis, she should have screened for disabilities as part of her assessment and referred Clyde for a more specific diagnosis from a specialist. Arguably, her shoddy assessment resulted in offering Clyde's family an intervention that was inappropriate, not dealing with the primary cause of Clyde's school problems.[9] Malpractice law does not require social workers to be perfect, but rather to act in good faith and make professional judgments to the best of their ability (Moffett & Moore, 2011). If it is reasonable for a school social worker to miss the learning disability and offer family counseling, then Smadar has not breached her duty. If no reasonable school social worker would have overlooked the learning disability, then Smadar has breached her duty.

Caused harm: To establish malpractice, clients must also prove that the social worker's breach of duty resulted in specific harm to the client (whether that client is an individual, family, group, organization, or community). In other words, there must be a causal link between the worker's inappropriate actions (or inactions) and the damages suffered by the client. Damages to clients may include biological, psychological, social, financial, and spiritual damages. As a practical matter, it is much easier to prove damages that are physical or financial in nature. It is harder to prove less concrete harm, such as anxiety and loss of friendship. Clyde's family could argue that by not properly assessing Clyde's learning disability, Smadar caused Clyde to fail second grade. They could also argue that her breach caused the family mental anguish and that ultimately, Clyde would be financially dependent on his family for an extra year as a result of being held back one grade. Proving that a breach of duty resulted in specific harms is one of the most difficult parts of establishing malpractice claims against social workers. The specific impact of social work interventions may be difficult to prove because of many possible intervening variables: Did Clyde fail because he did not receive a proper assessment, or because of ineffective teaching, improper parenting, or other problems not associated with Smadar's breach? How could the parents prove that Smadar's breach caused them anguish, and how can the court place a value on this breach? Assume that the family is able to prove the breach caused them financial loss, specifically, the cost of maintaining Clyde at home one more year plus one year of lost income for Clyde.

9. In court, Smadar could argue that parenting problems were the most important issue, so the court would have to judge whether her assessment and intervention were appropriate, given Clyde's overall situation and what a competent school social worker would reasonably be expected to do.

Proximate cause: Clients must not only prove a factual causal link between the breach and the resulting harm; they must also prove that the harm was a reasonably direct or foreseeable consequence of the breach. To determine whether there is proximate cause, consider the chain of causality and whether there was a close connection between the original breach and the harm that resulted. Was it reasonably foreseeable that missing a learning disability could result in Clyde's failing second grade, being financially dependent on his parents for an extra year, and losing one year's income over the course of his life? In this situation, the link between the breach and the claimed damages seems relatively direct and foreseeable. Suppose Clyde's parents claimed that they suffered additional losses because Clyde's younger sister suffered by receiving less parental attention. As a result, she might be at higher risk of developing a drug addiction. These additional losses would not be sufficiently direct or foreseeable to satisfy the criterion of proximate cause. As this example illustrates, determining whether a particular social worker's conduct constitutes malpractice is a complex task. As social workers, we should be aware of the elements of malpractice and should be able to recognize potential examples of malpractice. We should not give legal opinions on whether malpractice has occurred. When legal opinions are needed, we should seek the advice of an attorney who specializes in malpractice lawsuits.

Some of the more common claims of malpractice against social workers include allegations involving incorrect treatment, improper referrals, and boundary violations, including sexual relations with clients (Barsky et al., 2021; Reamer, 2015). Other possible bases for malpractice lawsuits include failure to obtain informed consent, not explaining the risks of an intervention, failure to consult or refer to a specialist, false imprisonment, breach of confidentiality, failure to report suspected child abuse or elder abuse, violating parental rights, client abandonment, practicing beyond scope of competency, inadequate record keeping, and failure to control a dangerous client (Boland-Prom et al., 2015; Reamer, 2018a). Risks of malpractice lawsuits may also be higher for interventions that engender higher risks of harm (Halfond et al., 2021). Examples of riskier interventions include the use of hypnosis to recover unconscious memories of childhood sexual abuse or the use of pharmacotherapy to treat people with substance use disorders. The relatively low fees for malpractice insurance for social workers suggest that malpractice lawsuits against social workers are not as prevalent as for higher risk professions, such as law and medicine.

Qualified immunity refers to a law shielding certain professionals and government officials from civil liability provided they act in good faith and within the scope of their employment (King & Pinals, 2017; Montin v. Moore, 2017). Qualified immunity laws are most common for social workers in fields such as child protection, in which workers assume a quasi-judicial role, having to make judgments that balance potentially conflicting public and private interests (e.g., parents' rights versus protecting the welfare of children). People performing adjudication functions should have the freedom and confidence to assess situations and make judicial decisions without having to fear that either party might try to manipulate their judgments by threatening an arbitrary lawsuit if they are not happy with the professional's determinations (*Butz v. Economou*, 1978; Kirkland & Kirkland, 2006).

Qualified immunity laws try to strike a balance between holding professionals accountable for their actions and ensuring that professionals are not subjected to unreasonable expectations and risks of liability (American Bar Association, 2020). Unrealistic expectations and undue risks of liability may lead to restricted services because social workers will avoid practicing in those fields (Collins et al., 2002). Different jurisdictions have different immunity laws, so you should consult relevant legislation and case law in your state to determine whether you are covered by immunity laws and what types of immunity are provided.[10] Qualified immunity laws do not protect us from intentionally inflicting harm on clients (e.g., physically assaulting a client; intentionally misdiagnosing someone with a mental disorder to have the person detained in a psychiatric facility). These laws are more likely to protect us when we make honest but questionable practice decisions. Qualified immunity laws have been criticized in light of various situations in which police officers have been granted immunity despite using excessive or fatal force with BIPOC people who police pursued or detained for suspected crimes. Accordingly, some states have enacted laws limiting the scope of qualified immunity (National Conference of State Legislatures, 2021).

PROFESSIONAL REGULATION—ACCOUNTABILITY TO CLIENTS AND THE PROFESSION

Whereas criminal and civil laws create systems of accountability for all people, professional regulations are designed specifically to ensure accountability for social workers and other professionals. By definition, professionals hold themselves to higher standards of conduct than the general public. As professionals, we have specialized knowledge, skills, education, and training. We also agree to practice according to our profession's values and ethics (NASW Code of Ethics, Purpose). The following sections describes three approaches to professional regulation: government-regulated professions, self-regulating professions, and unregulated professions.

Government-Regulated Professions

Government-regulated professions are established by laws designed to promote public health and welfare and protect clients from unethical and substandard

---

10. For a federal qualified immunity statute, see Civil action for deprivation of rights (2007).

practice by creating specialized systems of accountability (Association of Social Work Boards, n.d.). Models of government regulation include licensure, certification, title protection, and registration.

Licensure is the highest level of regulation because it restricts which occupational groups can perform certain functions or services (U.S. Department of Education, n.d.). By law, only licensed physicians may perform surgery. Only licensed attorneys may represent clients in court and draft legal contracts. If a social worker performs surgery (or drafts a legal contract), that worker may be incarcerated, fined, or otherwise punished for unauthorized practice of medicine (or law). Laws governing professional licensure vary from state to state (Association of Social Work Boards, n.d.; U.S. Department of Education, n.d.). Some states provide licensure for clinical social workers, meaning that we must be licensed in order to perform clinical functions such as psychiatric diagnoses, psychotherapy, supervision of other clinical workers, and initiating proceedings to commit clients with suicidal ideation to a psychiatric facility. These functions overlap with functions provided by other types of professionals. Thus, mental health counselors, family and marriage therapists, psychiatrists, and psychologists may also be licensed to perform these functions. To obtain licensure, we must comply with the requirements of the specific laws that establish licensure. Licensure laws require us to meet certain qualifications, for instance, an MSW degree, supervised practice experience, passing a licensure exam, maintaining professional liability insurance, and taking a certain number of hours of continuing education credits each year. Some states have a tiered system of licensure, granting different licenses to social workers with different levels of education (e.g., BSW versus MSW). Each tier of licensure permits social workers to perform different types of functions; for instance, generalist practice versus specialized clinical practice (Association of Social Work Boards, n.d.). Licensed social workers must adhere to the specific laws that regulate them. Failure to comply may result in fines, temporary suspensions or restrictions on practice (e.g., restricted from practicing with children), conditions on practice (e.g., must attend weekly supervision), or revocation of licensure. Revoking licensure is a powerful legal consequence because it prevents affected individuals from practicing their profession. To invoke consequences such as suspension or revocation of licensure, the licensing body must establish "clear and convincing evidence" that the licensee violated a licensing law. The precise standard of proof varies from state to state; the standard of proof for licensing violations is less strict than the criminal law standard, "beyond a reasonable doubt." To substantiate a licensing violation, the licensing board does not require proof of harm to the client others (Gricus & Wysiekiersky, 2021). The board only needs evidence that the licensee's behavior violated a licensing law.

If you decide to practice with clients in different states, then you may need to obtain licensure in each state where you practice. When using videoconferencing or other technology to serve clients in different locations, note that the location of practice is generally deemed to be where the client is located, rather than where you live or practice (NASW et al., 2017). Accordingly, if you live in New York and want to provide clinical social work services via videoconferencing to clients in Texas, then you would need to be licensed to practice in Texas. Some states have reciprocal arrangements, recognizing one another's licensure or where they make it easier for social workers in one state to become licensed in another. Check the Association of Social Work Board's website at https://www.aswb.org/licenses for information on how to obtain licensure in various states. The NASW and ASWB have been advocating for states to recognize one another's licensure in order to allow social workers to practice across state boundaries.

The most common licensing violations are dual relationships and issues in maintaining licenses such as not meeting continuing education requirements or not submitting appropriate documentation to renew licenses (Gricus & Wysiekiersky, 2021). Other common licensing problems include violations of standards of care, client-social worker boundaries, confidentiality, and fraud (Magiste, 2020).

Certification, the second highest level of regulation, refers to a regulatory system that establishes certain professional credentials and provides the public with information on who has met these credentials. Certification and accreditation are synonymous terms. Unlike licensure, certification does not restrict who can perform certain functions. Still, employers, clients, and referral sources may use certification status to determine which social workers to hire or engage (e.g., some substance use disorder treatment programs hire only people who qualify as a Certified Addiction Professional). Certification credentials may include the same types of credentials as licensing—advanced professional degrees, knowledge, skill, supervised practice, and acceptance of a particular code of ethics. Sometimes, certification requirements are less onerous than licensing requirements because licensing suggests a higher level of professional expertise and expectations.[11] When professionals fail to comply with the terms of certification, the regulatory body can suspend or revoke their certification. Unlike licensing bodies, however, they cannot completely stop a person from practicing. Thus, if you have your accreditation revoked for breaching client confidentiality, you could still offer services as a nonaccredited social worker. Informed employers, clients, and referral sources, however, may refuse to hire you given your loss of accreditation.

---

11. Newly developing professions go through an evolutionary process (Grise-Owens et al., 2016; Kirkpatrick et al., 2021). Typically, they start out as unregulated professions and then develop voluntary associations with standards of practice. If they are able to secure government support for legislative regulation, they often receive registration or accreditation systems, which are less onerous and less expensive to operate than licensing systems. Also, since licensing systems restrict practice, other professional groups are more likely to challenge licensure for a new profession. In 1915, physician Abraham Flexner suggested that social work was not a true profession, but rather an amateur occupation (Prescott, 2019). Although social work has advanced as a profession through higher levels of education, a body of evidence-based practice, development of a code of ethics and national professional association, and government-recognized regulation, some people still question the status of social work as a profession.

Title protection[12] refers to laws restricting who can call themselves by a particular professional title. Historically, people were able to call themselves social workers whether or not they had specific training, knowledge, skills, or accreditation as social workers. In some jurisdictions this is still true. Licensing laws automatically protect title. For instance, only licensed attorneys may represent themselves to the public as attorneys. Only social workers with clinical licensure may call themselves clinical social workers. In some jurisdictions, social workers have advocated for title protection so that agencies, referral sources, and clients will know that they are working with a "real social worker" when the person calls themself a social worker. The question remains as to who is a "real social worker." Typically, title is granted to those with a particular diploma or degree. Some jurisdictions grant social work title only to people with MSW degrees. Others use the BSW degree as the minimum requirement. Still others permit people with social work-related college diplomas to call themselves social workers (Collins et al., 2002). Title protection does not include mechanisms for holding social workers accountable to any professional standards. It merely prevents others from calling themselves social workers. The penalty for violating a title protection law is typically a fine. The person may be able to continue to offer services but use a title other than social work to describe their line of work.

Registration refers to a system in which a governmental or nongovernmental body provides a list of people who practice in a particular field of professional work; for instance, addictions counseling, gerontology, or crisis intervention. Some people use the term *registration* interchangeably with certification or accreditation. Technically, registration does not require the regulating body to attest to the registrant's having met any special criteria. Often, registration systems do require professionals to comply with certain credentials, resulting in the overlap between regulation and certification (and confusion about how each term is used by different laws and different practitioners). When registration does not require credentialing, registration is the weakest form of regulation. It merely lists those people who say they practice in a particular field. Clients who want to ensure that social workers have certain credentials should check whether workers must meet such credentials in order to be registered.

Grievances against government-regulated professionals should be directed toward the government body that has been assigned by statute to enforce the professional regulations and standards (e.g., the state's department of health, a social work regulatory board, or another department responsible for regulating health professionals). Although professionals and referral sources may initiate complaints, clients are often in the best position to initiate them. Clients are most likely to have first-hand knowledge of the concerns. If another professional or referral source initiates a claim and only possesses second-hand (hearsay) evidence, the regulatory body may not have sufficient evidence to prosecute the grievance.

---

12. Sometimes called protection or ownership of title.

Self-Regulating Professions

Self-regulating professions are professional groups that establish their own standards and enforcement procedures. Some, like the NASW, are voluntary associations that offer various types of membership levels and credentialing.[13] When you join the NASW, you are voluntarily agreeing to abide by its code of ethics. Schools of social work and agencies may require you to be an NASW member, but most jurisdictions do not actually require NASW membership for people to practice social work. Some jurisdictions adopt the NASW Code of Ethics in their licensing or accreditation legislation, making their licensed or accredited social workers legally accountable to the standards enunciated in the NASW Code. If state laws do not specifically adopt the NASW Code, then social workers may be held accountable by the NASW but not by the government-run regulatory bodies. If a state mandates NASW membership and adherence to NASW standards, then the state-run regulatory body is responsible for monitoring and enforcing compliance with these standards.

The NASW National Ethics Committee (NEC) is responsible for promoting ethical practice among NASW members. It develops ethics policies and procedures, helps members interpret them, oversees development of ethics education and training, and hears complaints against members alleged to have violated the NASW Code of Ethics (NASW, n.d.-b). When clients or others initiate complaints against NASW members, the NEC intake committee reviews the written "Request for Professional Review" to determine whether it alleges specific misconduct that violates the NASW Code. If the complaint meets the basic eligibility requirements for review, the NEC refers the case for mediation or an adjudication hearing.[14] When mediation is authorized, an NEC-appointed mediator brings the complainant and social worker together to try to work out an amicable solution for the grievance. When adjudication is authorized, a panel appointed by the National Ethics Committee hears the case. Each party has an opportunity to provide evidence in a trial-like process. When a panel finds an NASW member has violated the Code of Ethics, it may order various corrective actions and sanctions: compensation for damages; participation in a prescribed number of hours of professional consultation, supervision, or training; private or public censures; suspension of or expulsion from NASW membership; and notification to state regulatory boards or credentialing bodies (NASW, 2012; Reamer, 2021c). If the violations

---

13. See https://www.socialworkers.org/Careers/Credentials/Apply-for-NASW-Social-Work-Credentials for the various types of credentialing offered by the NASW (e.g., certifications for generalists, clinical social workers, gerontology, school social work, healthcare practice, case management, military social work, and addiction counseling).

14. Adjudication is typically required for cases involving sexual relationships, sexual harassment, physical contact, violence, and safety concerns (NASW, 2012). Mediation is generally preferred for other types of violations because it may lead the parties to creative, collaborative, future-oriented solutions. The NASW National Ethics Committee may also refer allegations of severe and repetitive violations to adjudication.

are related to underlying mental health issues, then the social worker may also benefit from psychotherapy. In many cases, the impact of revoking NASW membership is not as strong as revoking a license to practice. Most social workers may continue to practice even without NASW membership. Still, revoking NASW membership may have serious impacts on a social worker's ability to practice because

- some social agencies require NASW membership as a condition of employment;
- some BSW and MSW programs require students to be NASW members;
- some referral sources and clients may avoid social workers who have had their NASW membership revoked; and
- professional liability insurance companies may require NASW membership or provide members with a reduced fee for insurance.

In these circumstances, revoking NASW membership severely restricts the worker's ability to practice. Although the NASW National Ethics Committee may impose disciplinary consequences, its primary efforts are to prevent ethics violations and take corrective actions in response to violations that do arise. Corrective actions are strategies used to improve the social worker's professional behavior and to reduce the risk of future ethical violations. Revocation of NASW membership is only used for serious violations or ongoing patterns of violations when corrective actions are insufficient means of protecting clients and the public.

Unregulated Practitioners

Unregulated practitioners have no profession-specific laws, regulations, or professionally enforced codes of ethics. Anyone can perform the functions of the practitioner without legal or professional restrictions. Although many social workers are members of professional associations or are accredited by governmental regulations, many functions performed by social workers do not require the service provider to be a social worker or to hold any form of accreditation—for instance, facilitating a task group, assisting with policy development, organizing community members to advocate on their own behalf, teaching basic life skills, facilitating clients through the generalist problem-solving model, and providing instrumental help (e.g., assisting clients with budgeting, making doctors' appointments, and helping them arrange transportation to job interviews). Unless state laws provide otherwise, social workers who graduate with BSWs or MSWs may also offer such services without being members of NASW and without obtaining government-sponsored accreditation. Some social workers call themselves "personal coaches" or "life coaches" specifically to avoid the higher levels of scrutiny that accredited social workers or other mental health professionals endure.

In states with social work licensing, social workers without licensure cannot perform the functions that the laws restrict to licensed professionals. Although enforcement officials may consider the titles social workers use to describe their roles and work, the primary issue is whether the functions they perform fall within the purview of the restricted activities. If an unlicensed social worker calls themself a personal coach but provides psychotherapy, that person could still be held accountable for practicing without a license. The term *paraprofessional* is sometimes used to describe practitioners who perform certain social work functions but are not regulated by professional associations, licensure, or accreditation. Social service workers and case managers, for instance, are sometimes called paraprofessionals because they perform some of the same functions as social workers, but they are not accountable to the same professional code of ethics or regulatory bodies as social workers.

So, why should social workers bother with NASW membership or professional regulation? Career and financial opportunities may be the primary source of motivation for some workers. Certain agencies will not hire social workers unless they are NASW members or meet particular standards of professional regulation. Some agencies pay higher salaries for credentialed social workers. Some professionals will not refer clients to social workers unless they are licensed or accredited. Some clients will not accept services from social workers unless they are licensed or accredited. Further, health insurance companies typically require licensure in order for social workers to be eligible for insurance reimbursement for mental health services. Ideally, financial factors are not the only motivation for obtaining credentials. Social workers can promote important social work values (e.g., competence, respect for clients, accountability, and integrity) by becoming NASW members and qualifying with the relevant professional regulatory bodies.[15]

AGENCY POLICIES—ACCOUNTABILITY
TO CLIENTS AND THE EMPLOYING AGENCY

When clients[16] have concerns about our professional conduct, the most accessible avenue of recourse is typically within the agency that employs us. Most agency grievance processes are less formal and less costly than civil lawsuits and professional review processes. Typically, **agency policies** specify that aggrieved clients should first discuss

---

15. The names of professional regulatory bodies vary from jurisdiction to jurisdiction. Some states have bodies specific to social work, but many regulatory bodies cover social work within general health or mental health regulatory bodies. See the Association of Social Work Boards website for specific information on professional regulation in your own state—https://www.aswb.org/regulation/laws-and-regulations-database.

16. Although nonclients may also initiate grievances within an agency, agencies may not be able to deal with such grievances if doing so would involve disclosure of confidential client information. If a client's family member, for instance, initiates a grievance, the agency may not be able to address the grievance because the client has not given the family member permission to access the client's confidential information.

their concerns with us, the person with whom they have the concern. We may not have been aware of the concern and we may be able to negotiate a solution directly with the clients (e.g., acknowledging the problem and agreeing to act differently in the future).[17] When clients are unable to achieve a successful resolution at this stage, they can pursue concerns up the agency's chain of responsibility, for instance, with our supervisor, the program director, a regional director, an ombudsperson, and a state oversight committee (Children's Bureau, n.d.). Our agencies may have specific conflict resolution or grievance procedures, including mediation, arbitration, and appeals processes (Barsky, 2017a). Most hospitals and some social agencies have ethics committees that review ethics complaints. Ethics committees also provide consultation to provide timely ethics guidance (Baker et al., 2020), preventing ethical concerns from escalating. Agencies may use various corrective actions and sanctions, for instance, assigning a different social worker to work with the client, providing additional social work supervision or training, suspending us, reassigning us to different functions, putting us on agency probation, or terminating our employment (if the agency has just cause to terminate).

When employers review our conduct, they hold us accountable to the laws and policies governing our particular agency. Laws that regulate healthcare facilities, for instance, include special provisions for protecting patient confidentiality (Health Insurance Portability and Accountability Act, 1996). Agencies may have policies that supplement these legal rules, such as using specific forms of technology to safeguard client information. If a social worker does not comply with these laws and policies, the agency may take corrective action or impose sanctions.[18] Unless the agency adopts the NASW Code of Ethics as a source of ethical guidance for its social workers, the agency cannot hold us accountable to this Code. Some agencies require their social workers to be NASW members, suggesting that the agency does expect us to abide by the NASW Code. Even when agencies do not compel their workers to abide by the NASW Code, agency policies may include many of the same ethical standards as the Code (e.g., informed consent, confidentiality, and respect for clients).

In sum, social workers may be held accountable according to the laws and policies that govern the agency. In many instances, these laws and policies promote the same types of ethical behaviors as the NASW Code or other professional standards. Thus, clients may choose whether to pursue grievances with the agencies, with other relevant professional regulatory bodies, or with a combination of venues. If agency policies and laws do not cover the aggrieved behavior, the client should consider taking the grievance to a venue that does cover such behavior.[19]

---

17. If a client feels too threatened to approach the practitioner directly, agency policy may specify others with whom the client may consult (e.g., a client advocate, an ombudsperson, or the practitioner's supervisor).

18. If the agency itself is not complying with applicable laws, then the governmental body that regulates the agency may impose its own corrective actions and sanctions.

19. E.g., an agency may not have policies that prohibit social workers from having sex with former clients. Former clients may need to pursue such grievances with the NASW or a licensing body rather than with the agency.

CONTRACTS—ACCOUNTABILITY TO
THE CONTRACTING PARTIES

When two or more people or organizational entities exchange promises, they enter into a contract (Eisenberg, 2018). Contracts are enforceable by civil courts, providing the parties have appropriate mental capacity to enter contracts and both parties enter the contract voluntarily (without coercion). When agencies hire us as social workers, we are entering into contractual relationships. Terms of contracts may be written, oral, or implied. For legal purposes, written contracts offer the benefit of providing tangible evidence of the contract.[20] We are accountable for performing our duties as provided in our contracts. Thus, if we breach the terms of the contract, we may be sued in civil court (similar to a malpractice lawsuit as described earlier). Some employment contracts include provisions for confidentiality, informed consent, and other ethical standards, similar to those in the NASW Code. Employment contracts may impose additional duties, such as noncompetition clauses. Noncompetition clauses state that we will not engage in practice outside the agency that compete with services offered by the agency. If we accept a client in private practice rather than as an agency client, the agency can sue for damages. Employment contracts may also prohibit taking clients with us when we move from one agency to another. The standard of proof for breach of contract is the *preponderance of evidence.*

As social workers, we may enter into various types of contracts with clients. Confidentiality agreements are essentially contracts that say we will maintain confidentiality of client information except as otherwise agreed. Service agreements are contracts stating which services we will provide, as well as the obligations that we and our clients have in carrying out the assessment and intervention. Thus, if we violate the contract, the client may sue for damages. Consider a service agreement stating that you will ensure 24-hour, 7-day-per-week access to crisis intervention counseling. If you fail to provide such services and the client sustains injuries as a result, you (and your agency) may be liable to compensate the client. Thus, you may be held accountable for provisions in your agreements with clients that go above and beyond the standards expressed in the NASW Code. Given the potential legal consequences for breach of contract, we (and our agencies) should consider obtaining legal advice before entering into legally binding agreements with clients or others. Attorneys can help us clarify our contractual obligations, as well as specifying what happens if either party breaches the contract.

In terms of enforceability, some contracts state that contract-related disputes must be handled in mediation or arbitration rather than court. With social work services now being offered through technology across state boundaries, some contracts also indicate which state's laws apply in relation to enforcing the contract (often, the state where the social worker and agency are physically located).

---

20. For oral or implied contracts, it may be difficult to prove who agreed to what.

Some contracts with clients are not intended to be legally enforceable agreements. Assume you are working with a client who has experienced intimate partner abuse. The client agrees to a safety plan, including a provision that the client will go to a neighbor's house if their partner makes threats. Although this agreement is intended to solidify the client's commitment to the contract, it is not intended to be enforced by the courts. When developing these types of agreements with clients, you could include a statement that the document is not intended to be a legally enforceable contract. Also, rather than calling the agreement a "contract," you could use terms such as "safety plan," "intervention plan," or "client guidelines."

ADMINISTRATIVE LAWS—ACCOUNTABILITY TO GOVERNMENT AGENCIES AND THE PUBLIC

Administrative laws comprise statutes and regulations prescribing how government agencies operate and how services should be provided. Social workers practice in an array of federal- and state-regulated agencies including schools, child protection agencies, foster care, assisted living facilities for older adults, jails, prisons, and probation departments. When working these contexts, we need to abide by the laws regulating them. If we violate an administrative law, then actions may be taken against us (individually), our agency, or both. The consequences for breaching administrative laws are prescribed by the particular laws. Consequences for violating administrative laws include fines and injunctions (orders to cease conduct that violates the law). Typically, breaching an administrative law does not lead to criminal charges or incarceration. If an administrative agency discovers that someone has violated criminal laws, then it may provide information to state or federal criminal prosecutors to determine whether to press charges.

Sometimes, administrative laws conflict with our general ethical obligations as social workers. For instance, we have a general obligation to maintain the confidentiality of information shared with us by clients. When working within the child protection system, however, we may have an overriding responsibility to share information with courts during child protection proceedings. When regulatory laws provide different obligations than our general ethical duties, we should clarify these differences with our clients. "Although I have a general duty to maintain your privacy, as a child protection worker I may need to share certain information with the court so that the judge can make informed decisions about your child's welfare." As part of the informed consent processes (NASW Code, S.1.03), we need to be honest with clients about the nature of our services, including our obligations under pertinent administrative laws.

Examples of federal laws that may be relevant to our practice as social workers include the following:

- Health Insurance Portability and Accountability Act (1996): HIPAA covers healthcare providers such as hospitals, physicians, nurses, psychologists, and social workers who work in healthcare (including physical and mental health). HIPAA states that healthcare providers need to take certain precautions to protect their patient's private health information. When transmitting client information through technology, for instance, the information needs to be encrypted. To protect electronic patient records from unauthorized access, we need to use strong passwords or other methods of verification. HIPAA also requires specific forms for transmitting information to health insurance providers and obtaining a client's consent to release confidential information to other agencies.

• Family Educational Rights and Privacy Act (1974): FERPA governs all elementary, middle, and high schools that receive funding from the U.S. Department of Education. FERPA includes privacy protections for student records. It also identifies who may have access to student records (e.g., school officials with legitimate educational interests, school auditors, and financial aid providers).

• Confidentiality of Substance Use Disorder Records (2017): These regulations protect the confidentiality of the patient records maintained by any substance use disorder treatment program that receives federal assistance. In addition, courts may only order disclosure of patient records under limited circumstances (e.g., disclosure is necessary to protect someone from life-threatening or serious bodily harm).

Most social agencies and services providers are governed primarily by state laws and regulations. When working in a child protection agency, for instance, it is important to understand state laws governing child protection services. When working in a hospital, it is important to understand state laws governing hospitals. Some agencies are governed by both state and federal regulations (e.g., treatment programs for people with substance use disorders).

COMMUNITY NORMS AND PERSONAL CONSCIENCE— ACCOUNTABILITY TO COMMUNITY AND SELF

The final areas of social work accountability are related to community norms and personal conscience. Although the term *professional accountability* suggests that we are accountable to professional bodies (e.g., the NASW and licensing boards), we should also consider accountability to our communities and personal belief systems. In addition to our professional organizations, we operate within a social context that may include our neighbors, friends, family, cultural community, and faith or spiritual communities. Thus, we are, to varying extents, accountable to these additional systems. In many instances, our work is confidential. These systems may never know whether we are acting ethically in our private dealings with clients. Still, some professional conduct is open to the public and other conduct may become open to the public if a case proceeds to court or a client takes a grievance to the media.[21]

In some instances, accountability to nonprofessional sources is very powerful. Assume you are working in a boarding school. You discover that certain teachers are abusing children, but you take no action to protect the children. Because child abuse goes against community norms, friends and neighbors may become angry or disgusted when news of your complicity in the abuse comes to light. The court of public opinion may be particularly harsh when professional misconduct is picked up by media that sensationalize malpractice cases. Media often ignore our stories of good, competent work. Good, competent practice may not be considered newsworthy because it is expected, commonplace, and perhaps boring. A worker with a glowing professional record of 25 years could become media fodder for a single breach (or alleged breach) of professional ethics. Even family members may turn on a social worker who has been tainted by accusations of unethical or **illegal** behavior. One method of determining the ethicality of your professional conduct is to consider how you would feel if the media, your parents, and community discovered what you were doing. If you would feel embarrassed or ashamed, it may be because you know that your conduct would not be considered ethical by these audiences.

For some social workers, spirituality and religion are very powerful sources of moral guidance and accountability (Loue, 2017). Each religion has its own rules and belief systems, including beliefs about the consequences for disobeying the tenets of the religion (Scales & Kelly, 2016). We need to be aware of how our religious or spiritual convictions affect our professional judgments and behaviors. As a matter of respect for the dignity and worth of all people, we should not impose our religious beliefs on clients. If, while serving clients, a conflict arises between our professional responsibilities and our religious belief systems, we should prioritize our professional ethical obligations. Thus, a secular, professional code of ethics may suggest that it is ethical for social workers to facilitate divorces, yet the social worker's religious beliefs may suggest that facilitating divorces contravenes divine laws. To prioritize the client's interests while still taking the worker's religious beliefs into account, the worker might refer the client to another professional who can help facilitate the divorce.

In terms of accountability to ourselves, Aristotle suggests that eudaimonia, the flourishing life, is a life where we embrace moral virtues (Aristotle, 2013). We live with the intent to do good. We may not be perfect in living our virtues,

---

21. Professional disciplinary hearings and agency grievances are typically confidential to protect both client and practitioner. The results of such hearings and grievances could be made public if the decision makers determine that publicizing the results is in the best interests of clients and the public (e.g., publishing names of professionals who have lost licenses so the public knows not to hire them).

but we can continuously strive to do good. Our conscience serves as a moral compass (Kaldjian, 2019). When we engage in immoral or unethical conduct, we may have trouble sleeping, aware that we have violated principles that we hold dear. We may feel pain or shame. We can use awareness of these feelings as signals to hold ourselves accountable. One of the primary means of holding ourselves accountable is own up to our misbehavior and make right the wrong. We may apologize to those we have hurt. We may compensate them for damages. Finally, we may correct our behavior, ensuring that we do not repeat past misconduct.

To nurture our **virtues**, we practice what is virtuous, making virtue a habit. When we treat our clients with respect, we make respect a habit. When we practice honesty and integrity, we incorporate these virtues into our being. When we are true to our moral virtues, we take delight in what is fine and noble. Whereas licensing boards and professional associations hold us accountable when our conduct falls below certain standards, virtues are aspirational, inspiring us to live moral, flourishing lives (Aristotle, 2013).

INTERPROFESSIONAL PRACTICE

When we work with physicians, nurses, attorneys, psychologists, or other professionals, we should be aware that we may each be held accountable to different regulatory laws and different codes of ethics. Although we may have similar professional obligations concerning matters such as self-determination, informed consent, and documentation of services, we need to appreciate differences pertaining to each of our roles. In terms of physical boundaries, for instance, physicians and nurses may engage in physical examinations of clients, whereas social workers are not generally authorized to provide physical examinations. In terms of sexual boundaries, some professional codes permit their members to engage in sexual relations with former clients, whereas the NASW Code explicitly prohibits such relationships (S.1.09[c]).

When clients sue for malpractice, they may sue multiple professionals (and their agency) at the same time. If the case proceeds to trial, the court will consider different standards of practice for each professional involved in the case. For social workers, the standard of practice relates to what a reasonable social worker, acting prudently, would do in similar circumstances. For licensed family counselors, the standard of practice relates to what a reasonable licensed family counselor, acting prudently, would do in similar circumstances. Each professional should stay within their own scope of practice and area of competence. Each professional should also be aware of the scope of practice and ethical standards of their professional colleagues.

CONCLUSION

As social workers, we are accountable to our clients, our profession, our regulatory bodies, our communities, and ourselves. From an ethics perspective, we should do what is right because it is right. Still it is important to understand how we and our professional colleagues may be held accountable if we violate relevant laws or codes of ethics.

If you, a colleague, or a client has concerns about a social worker's conduct, consider the following guidelines for how to address these concerns:

- Generally, the first course of action should involve the person most directly affected by the concern should try to resolve the concern through conversations with the social worker (NASW Code, S.2.10[c]). Often, the person most directly affected by the concern is the client. By taking the concern directly to the social worker, the grievance may be resolved in a timely, efficient, informal, and collaborative manner (Barsky, 2017a).
- If speaking directly with the social worker does not sufficiently resolve the issues, then the person affected by the concern should consider addressing the issue through the agency's grievance processes, for instance, speaking informally with a supervisor or program director, filing a formal grievance, or appealing a decision to an administrator (NASW Code, S.2.10[d]). These avenues of redress are generally less formal and less costly than taking an issue to court or to a professional regulatory body, as described below.
- If you, the client, or other persons have questions about your legal rights or avenues of redress, prudent practice suggests speaking with an attorney. When speaking with an attorney, discuss all options for resolving the concern, including collaborative approaches such as mediation and informal conflict discussions.
- If a social worker may have engaged in criminal offences, anyone may report the allegations to the police for prosecution. The alleged victim of the crime may be in the best position to report a crime, given that the victim is likely to have the most direct evidence. The police will investigate the case and the state or federal attorneys will determine whether or not to press charges. Note that criminal proceedings can be long and protracted, sometimes taking years until a case is finally resolved. To convict someone of a crime, the prosecution must prove all the elements of the crime (the acts and the mental state) "beyond a reasonable doubt." If the prosecution does not think that it has sufficient evidence to prove a crime, it may decide not to press charges (see Table 12.1 for a comparison of what types of proof are required for different systems of accountability).

Table 12.1. Comparing Proof Required for Systems of Accountability

	Burden of Proof	Standard of Proof	Proof of Intent Required?	Proof of Harm Required?
Criminal Charges	Prosecution	Beyond a reasonable doubt	Yes	No
Malpractice Lawsuit	Plaintiff	Preponderance of evidence	Must prove negligence (not intent to harm)	Yes
Licensing Complaint	Regulatory Body	Clear and convincing evidence or equivalent (varies by state)	No	No
Professional Review Process	Professional Association	Preponderance of evidence or equivalent (varies by professional body)	No	No

- If a client has experienced harm due to negligence of a social worker, the client may sue for damages in civil court. To be successful in a civil lawsuit, the client must prove that the social worker owed the client a duty of care, the worker breached the duty, and the client suffered damages as a relatively direct result of the worker's breach (Polychronis & Brown, 2016). The client (with the aid of an attorney) must prove all the elements of malpractice on "the preponderance of evidence." Although hiring an attorney can be expensive, some litigation attorneys charge fees on a contingency basis (i.e., they charge only if the lawsuit is successful and their fee is based on a percentage of the damages awarded).
- If someone believes that a social worker has violated state licensing laws, then they may report the alleged violation to the state licensing board. Ideally, a client or other person with direct knowledge of the violation makes the report. The board is responsible for investigating whether the social worker has violated any licensing laws. The main function of the licensing board is to protect the public (ASWB, n.d.), not to reimburse clients who have been harmed by social workers. The consequences for a positive finding of a licensing violation include reprimands, suspensions, conditions put upon the types of cases that a licensee may handle,

supervision requirements, or revocation of a license (Barsky et al., 2021). To prove a licensing violation, the licensing board does not have to prove intent to violate a law. Further, the licensing board does not have to prove that the client suffered damages. The licensing board needs evidence that the social worker's conduct violated a particular licensing law (e.g., breaching confidentiality or engaging in a sexual relationship with a client). Each state's licensing law may state the degree of proof required for a violation, for instance "the preponderance of evidence" or "clear and convincing evidence." The degree of proof for licensing violations is typically less than the degree of proof required to prove criminal charges.

- The NASW has a process for reviewing allegations that NASW members have violated the NASW Code of Ethics (NASW, 2012). The person requesting professional review must be the client or someone with direct information about the violation. The alleged misconduct needs to have occurred within the past year. Most professional review processes go to mediation. For those cases that proceed to a hearing, the hearing committee focuses on whether the social worker has violated any specific standards in the NASW Code. To substantiate a violation, the committee does not require evidence of harm or evidence of intent to violate an ethical standard. When a violation is substantiated, the focus of the committee's disposition is corrective action, including how to redress problems, promote ethical practice, and protect clients from harm (e.g., requiring the NASW member to be supervised, to take a specific continuing education course, or to restrict their practice to avoid future violations; Barsky, 2020a).

- When the concern about the social worker is related to violating an administrative law or regulations, then the process pursuing grievances are specified by the relevant administrative laws. If the social worker has allegedly violated human rights laws, then the person with the grievance should take the concern to the designated human rights board. If the social worker has allegedly violated laws governing group foster homes, then the grievance should be taken to the government entity that oversees foster homes. Administrative bodies are generally responsible for ensuring compliance with specific administrative laws. The most common consequence for violating an administrative law is a fine. Administrative bodies may also order injunctions, orders requiring a person or agency to stop acting in a manner that violates a particular law.

Although we aspire to ethical practice, we may experience situations throughout our professional lives in which we fall below the standards prescribed by relevant laws, agency policies, professional codes of ethics, community norms, and personal conscience. As professionals, we should recognize the value of various systems of professional accountability. Acting with integrity includes taking responsibility for situations in which we have erred.

DISCUSSION QUESTIONS AND EXERCISES

1. *Contrasting Regulatory Approaches*: Compare and contrast two of the following approaches to regulating social workers: licensure, accreditation, registration, title protection, self-regulated, or completely unregulated. What are their respective advantages and disadvantages? Given your assessment, what would you recommend as the preferred approach to regulating social workers in your state? Does your answer depend on whether the social workers' areas of practice (e.g., generalist social work, clinical social work, macro social work, or practice in a specialized area such as forensic social work, family mediation, or sexuality therapy)?

2. *Professional Accountability*: For each of the following scenarios, identify which forums clients may use to pursue their complaints: criminal justice system, civil court, voluntary professional association, government-mandated licensing or accrediting body, or agency. Which of these forums should the client try to use first? Provide your reasoning in terms of accessibility, costs, timeliness of remedial action, available remedies, protection of the public, and chances of success.

   a. Simeon has a BSW and is an NASW member. He provides case management services in an assisted living facility for people with physical disabilities. He has been engaging in sexual relations with a client, Cindylou, an adult who has full mental capacity. Although Cindylou originally felt the sexual relationship was consensual, she now believes Simeon manipulated her into having sex. She now feels very ashamed because of it.

   b. Shayla is a Licensed Independent Social Worker who provides counseling as a private practitioner. Chandra is a client experiencing sleep problems. Shayla uses dream analysis to help Chandra. Chandra believes Shayla's counseling has made her problems worse, as she now experiences horrible nightmares.

   c. Steffi has an MSW, but no licensure or accreditation. She works for a health maintenance organization that puts pressure on social workers to decrease their number of billable sessions with clients. One of her clients, Consuela, believes that Steffi terminated work prematurely. Consuela now feels abandoned. She cannot identify specific damages that she has suffered as a result.

   d. Herb is a human service provider at a social assistance office. He has no social work degrees, but he calls himself a social worker. The state does not have laws protecting social work title. A client named Cait finds out Herb has been depositing some of her social assistance checks into Herb's own bank account.

   e. Shahar is a state-accredited social worker with an MSW and NASW membership. He advises the Campbell family (former clients) to re-arrange their retirement savings so they can take advantage of certain tax credits. Years later, the Campbells discover this was bad advice, costing them thousands of dollars. When they contact Shahar's agency, they learn he no longer works there. The agency claims it is not responsible for his misconduct because he was not authorized to provide tax or investment advice (functions regulated by other professions).

f. As part of his work with the state health department, Horatio develops a public awareness campaign to discourage women from drinking alcohol while pregnant. Although there are significant risks of harm from drinking while pregnant, Horatio vastly overstates the risks to ensure that women heed the warnings from his campaign. You work in the same department as Horatio. You discover the exaggerated claims on social media. You are concerned about Horatio's lack of honesty and its impact on the credibility of social workers, researchers, and the health department.

3. *State Regulation*: Identify which body(ies) regulate social workers in your state (http://www.aswb.org/members_reglinks.shtml). Locate the primary website for each of these bodies. What type(s) of regulation are available in your state: licensure, accreditation, registration, or title protection? Describe what types of grievances clients may submit to each of the bodies that regulate social work in your state. What are the first steps that a client should take when submitting a grievance to each of these bodies?

4. *Regulation Debates*: Choose one of the following debate issues. Select a position, pro or con, and write an advocacy brief in support of your position.

a. Some people argue that professional regulation is motivated by self-interest; it does not protect the public so much as create elitist groups and erect inequitable and discriminatory barriers against professional status for minority groups (Collins et al., 2002; cf., Grise-Owens et al., 2016, for an article supporting professional regulation).

b. In some states, the only type of social work licensure available is a license for clinical practice. Critics argue that too many social workers are attracted to financially lucrative private practice, providing psychotherapy to middle-class clients and neglecting their historic roles of promoting community empowerment, challenging discrimination, and fostering social justice (Specht & Courtney, 1994). Social workers should advocate for regulatory laws that promote generalist practice, inclusive of community practice, and resist being lumped together with psychologists and other mental health professionals.

c. Some social workers believe that social work accreditation should be available for social workers with either a BSW or MSW degree (not just for those with MSWs). Including either degree will increase the pool of accredited social workers and the larger numbers will give social workers more political clout in comparison with other professions.

5. *Regulatory Accountability*: Identify regulatory or administrative laws that govern practice in your agency (either your current field agency, your employer, or an agency that you would like to work with when you graduate). What do these laws say, if anything, about client self-determination, confidentiality, informed consent, conflicts of interest, and record keeping? If a client had concerns about your conduct as a social worker in this agency, what is the appropriate administrative body for issuing a complaint?

6. *Malpractice*: For each of the following scenarios, use these questions to analyze whether the situation satisfies the criteria for a successful malpractice lawsuit: *(i)* Did the social worker owe the client a duty of care? *(ii)* What professional standards, if any, did the social worker breach? *(iii)* Was there a causal connection between the breach and the harm experienced by the client? *(iv)* Was the causal connection between the breach and damages incurred by the client reasonably foreseeable (or proximate)? If you require further information to answer these questions, state what information you would need.

   a. Salwa (an NASW member) asks Carlton if it is okay to talk with him about past traumas. Salwa explains the benefits of talking about trauma, but does not tell him about her model of intervention or its risks. After the counseling session, Carlton becomes agitated and obsessed, recalling memories of the trauma over and over. He engages in cutting and other self-harmful behaviors. His sibling advises him to sue Salwa for malpractice.

   b. Two Cuban American community organizations hire Skip to help them advocate for better social services in their neighborhood. Skip uses appropriate advocacy skills and strategies, but his efforts are unsuccessful. The community organizations consider suing for return of their payments to Skip because he did not actually help them achieve anything.

   c. Selda receives a phone call from a boy, Brady, asking for help. Selda says she does not work with children, so she gives him the name and phone number of another social worker. Brady is too distraught to call another worker and attempts suicide by jumping out a window. He breaks both legs. When Brady tells his parents that he called Selda prior to the suicide attempt, they wonder whether they can sue or lay criminal charges.

   d. Shadé told Chaïm that she is a trained psychoanalytic therapist. In fact, she has only generalist social work training. After four months of intensive therapy, Chaïm loses his job (including his $120,000 per year salary). He blames Shadé because her psychoanalysis surfaced abandonment issues from his childhood. He became so obsessed with these issues that he could not concentrate at work. He also became rude to customers who bore any resemblance to his parents.

When he told his boss that he was undergoing psychoanalysis and he was not feeling emotionally secure, his boss fired him.

e. Sandeesh works in a corrections department. As part of a diversity training, Sandeesh invites all probation officers to take a test for implicit bias. Many probation officers become upset when the test indicates that they have significant racial biases. They believe the test is invalid and Sandeesh has jeopardized their jobs by suggesting that they are prone to discriminating. Sandeesh responds that knowing about their biases will help ensure that they do not allow their biases to interfere with their work with clients from diverse backgrounds. Sandeesh offers to provide them with strategies to minimize or avoid the effects of implicit bias; however, the probation officers refuse to participate in this training. Research on the reliability and validity of the implicit bias test suggests that it is a sound and accurate assessment tool. The probation officers would like Sandeesh to lose his job and to be prohibited from practicing social work ever again.

7. *Interprofessional Ethics and Accountability*: Sienna (a social worker) and Neal (a nurse) are cofacilitating a psychoeducational group for people with Parkinson's disease. Neal starts socializing with group members, meeting them for dinner or drinks, visiting their homes, and taking them shopping. Sienna tells Neal that he should not engage in friendships with clients because Standard 1.06 of the NASW Code of Ethics prohibits dual relationships with clients. Neal says that this standard does not apply to him because he is a nurse, not a social worker. How should Sienna and Neal determine which professional standards apply when cofacilitating this group?

8. *Interstate Accountability*: Malissa provides parenting skills training to new parents. She uses videoconferencing with most of her clients. Malissa is not licensed as a social worker. She is an NASW member. Malissa lives in Nevada, but her office and agency are based in Utah. She is currently working with a Mary and Alvin Rhodes, a couple located in California. The couple is not satisfied with Malissa's work because she misses scheduled meetings, provides parenting suggestions that are not evidence-based, and makes value judgments about their religion. If the Rhodes want to sue Malissa for malpractice, in what state should they bring the lawsuit? Which state's laws apply? What would the Rhodes need to prove to win the lawsuit?

9. *Aspirational Ethics*: What is the difference between aspirational ethics and baseline ethics? Are aspirational ethics enforceable by professional associations, licensing boards, or civil courts? Which of the following professional guidelines are examples of aspirational ethics?

a. Social workers should challenge racism and discrimination.

b. Social workers should not sleep with clients.

c. Social workers should respect the dignity and worth of all clients.

d. Social workers should obtain a client's informed consent in order to provide services.

10. *Conflicting Ethical Codes*: Lois is a social worker who is also licensed as a massage therapist. As a member of both the NASW and the National Certification Board for Therapeutic Massage & Bodywork (NCBTMB), she has two different codes of ethics to guide her professional practice. Under Standards 1.06 and 1.10 of the NASW Code, Lois is supposed to maintain appropriate boundaries with clients, including physical boundaries. Ordinarily, social workers do not provide clients with massages. Under her NCBTMB Code (2017), she is certainly authorized to provide massages. Lois wonders, given her dual professional background, whether it is ethical to provide social work clients with massages (e.g., to help them with anxiety). How should Lois deal with the potential conflict between her two codes of ethics regarding whether it is ethical to provide massages for clients?

11. *Community Organizers*: The NASW Code of Ethics provides similar ethical guidelines to social workers, regardless of whether their clients are individuals, families, groups, organizations, or communities. Unfortunately, some provisions are written primarily for individual, family, and group work, leading to challenges when social workers are involved in macro practice, including community organization. For each of the following scenarios, identify the primary ethical issue, which of the standards in Part 1 of the NASW Code of Ethics apply, and what special concerns community organizers may have in trying to apply these standards to their work.

   a. Shamus is a community organizer for his town of 15,000 people. He is helping the town develop recreational activities for youth. When Shamus hires his neighbor to help build a new recreational center, others accuse Shamus of favoritism. Shamus does not believe he violated any rules. The town is small and he hired the best builder available. Shamus claims everyone in the town knows one another.

   b. Mrs. Smith is working with a Vietnamese American community to help bring better resources for older adults. Initially, Mrs. Smith had the support of key members from the community. Recently, the community has become disenchanted with Mrs. Smith, finding her tactics for advocacy are too aggressive, thus shaming the community. Community leaders do not think that they consented to these rude tactics.

   c. Mr. Santana is organizing a group of citizens who do not want a toxic waste dump to be built in their community. Mr. Santana recommends that the group initiate a series of negative advertisements to embarrass the politicians who are currently in favor of building the dump. The proposed ads would include embellished facts and exaggerations about the politicians' motivations and integrity. Some citizens raise questions about the ethics of these negative ads. Mr. Santana says that the means (stretching the truth a bit) is justified by the ends (protecting the community from exposure to toxic waste).

13

Risk-Benefit Management

LEARNING OBJECTIVES

Upon successful completion of this introduction, you will be able to

- describe exemplary practice in relation to compliance with relevant laws, agency policies, ethical standards, and evidence-based practice;
- identify common forms of professional misconduct;
- recognize and manage high-risk practice situations; and
- develop and implement risk-benefit management strategies, including documentation, use of supervision and consultation, responding constructively to complaints, self-reporting, and self-care.

For the purposes of this chapter, *risk* refers to the likelihood that particular harms may arise as a result of a particular situation or course of conduct. The practice of social work entails many risks, for instance, the risk that clients become angry, depressed, or anxious; the risk that clients initiate malpractice lawsuits or agency-based grievances; or the risk that someone dies by suicide or violence toward others (Reamer, 2015). When assessing possible risks in social work practice, we should consider risks across a broad spectrum of people who could be affected by our actions: our clients, family members and other people with whom our clients interact, ourselves, our agencies, our profession, and the public or society as a whole. Risks may include the possibility of various types of harm, including physical, psychological, social, spiritual, legal, and financial harm (Card, 2020). Some risks are avoidable (Reamer, 2015). For instance, if I do not want to get into trouble for having sexual relationships with my clients, I can avoid having sexual relationships with my clients. Other risks are unavoidable. For instance, if you work in child protective services, there are risks if you decide to allow a child to remain in the custody of their biological parents; there are also risks if you decide to place the child in foster care. When risks are unavoidable, we can use **risk-benefit manage-ment** (RBM) strategies—as described throughout this chapter—to advance the wellbeing of the people we serve and to minimize the risks of harm (Sicora, 2017).

The point of discussing risks in social work practice is not to encourage us to oper-ate out of fear, but rather, to operate out of prudence (Whittaker & Havard, 2016; Zur, 2021). *Prudence* refers to the moral virtue of using good judgment. Good judgment entails gathering relevant information, considering our possible courses of action, assessing risks and benefits of each course of action, engaging with others who can help us think through the situation, and selecting the best course of action based on a comprehensive analysis of the situation. To assess risk we may use decision-making aids, such as the Framework for Managing Issues described in Chapter 2 or tools designed to assess for particular risks (e.g., a suicide risk assessment tool or an elder abuse assessment instrument). We may also use informal assessment and reflection to monitor for possible risks on an ongoing basis (Hardy, 2017).

As social workers, our goals for work may include promoting **social justice**, helping clients address biopsychosocial issues, and empowering clients to maxi-mize their potentials and reach their own goals (International Federation of Social Workers, 2018 National Association of Social Workers Code of Ethics, 2021, Preamble). If our only ethical commitment is to eliminate risks arising from prac-tice, then we should all retire; however, we do have other commitments and goals for work. To promote good for the people and communities we serve, we need to balance benefits and risk (Zur, 2021). In terms of **deontology**, this means weigh-ing the ethical principles of *beneficence* ("do good") and *nonmaleficence* ("do no harm"; Card, 2020). In other words, when making practice decisions, we should factor in both the benefits and the risks of the courses of conduct that we are con-sidering. As the strengths perspective of social work suggests, we should focus on promoting good ethical conduct, building on strengths, and taking corrective actions when needed (Cottone et al., 2022). Although we need to take risk avoid-ance into account, we also need to keep sight on the good we are trying to achieve.

Assume you work in a halfway house where you are helping a client recently released from prison after serving a long sentence for armed robbery. From many perspectives, helping the client reintegrate in society is a good thing. You may help the client learn job skills and other social skills that will improve the client's wellbe-ing and quality of life. Serving this client also benefits the community to the extent that the client remains a law-abiding, constructive member of society. At the same time, you need to be aware of potential risks, both to the client and to others who may be affected by the client. You do not want to do anything that puts the client at risk of harassment, discrimination, or undue stress. You also do not want to do anything that increases the risk of the client committing another armed robbery or crime. To enhance the chances of positive outcomes and to reduce the risks of negative ones, it is important to be guided by evidence-based practice (Gambrill, 2019). What does the theory and research say about helping people transition from prison to community life? What do you know about this particular client in terms of what types of help may be helpful and what types of help may be risky? When making decisions about helping this client, you can weigh the benefits and risks of each option. Under Standard 1.01 of the NASW Code, our primary obligation is to serve our clients, considering both their wishes and wellbeing. If we focus only on avoiding risks, we are not properly serving our clients (Sicora, 2017).

Using the strengths perspective, this chapter begins by exploring exemplary practice. To the extent that we practice in accordance with the highest principles and standards of social work practice, we can maximize benefits and reduce risks of harm to the people we serve. The second section describes common forms of misconduct, behaviors that social workers should avoid. The third section details how to manage risky situations such as worker stress. The fourth section highlights the role of agency policies and procedures in maximizing benefits and minimizing risks for the people we serve. Policies and procedures should be designed to promote exemplary practice. They should also help social workers and clients navigate challenging practice issues, providing ethical guidance and decision-making support. The fifth section delves into the roles of supervision and consultation in risk-benefit management. Prudent people do not assume they have all the answers. They solicit help from others who can help them make prudent decisions. The sixth section examines how to use documentation to manage risks. Documentation helps us keep track of the concerns arising in practice so that we can manage them in a strategic manner. Documentation also provides evidence that may be useful to defend ourselves in response to client grievances, malpractice lawsuits, or licensing investigations. The following sections, "Responding to Complaints" and "Self-Reporting," provide strategies for responding when problems are brought to our attention. None of us is perfect. We are likely to run into ethical issues and other problems at some point in our careers. Just as kindergarten children are taught to clean up after themselves, we also need to take responsibility for any messes that we create. The section on "Self-Care" provides strategies for fostering our own biological, psychological, social, and spiritual wellbeing. If we do not take good care of ourselves, then how can we take good care of our clients, and how can we meet our other ethical obligations? Self-care includes engaging in continuing professional education and development, helping us remain current on best practices, relevant research, legal and ethical issues, and skill development. Finally, the conclusion notes the importance of aspirational ethics, going above and beyond our baseline responsibilities. Rather than simply minimizing the risks of practice, we should boldly pursue client wellbeing, social justice, and other ideals of the social work profession.

To start thinking about how risks may arise in practice, please reflect on the scenario in Box 13.1. In this scenario, the social worker makes a number of questionable choices. As you learn more about risk-benefit management throughout this chapter, consider how the worker might have made more prudent choices.

BOX 13.1

BAD HAIR DAY

Review the following situation. Consider each of Kelly's decision points throughout the day. Identify the potential benefits and risks of each decision. As you read this chapter, identify which RBM strategies might have been helpful to Kelly, their agency, and the people they serve.

Kelly B., a social work intern, gets up on the wrong side of their bed. Literally. Kelly, not fully awake and unaware of where they were walking, bumps into a lamp, causing a gash above their left eye. As the day proceeds, Kelly wonders why they ever got out of bed. Kelly works as an advocate at an LGBTQ+ community center. They know that they had to get out of bed and go to work, despite the horrendous start to the day. They have a full schedule of clients to meet, as well as an important staff meeting to attend.

Upon meeting with their first client, Asta, Kelly apologizes. "I'm so sorry that I'm late. As you can see, I had a little catastrophe this morning." Asta sees that Kelly had a large bandage on their forehead with some blood seeping through. Kelly explains the details of what happened. Asta feels sorry for Kelly. "It looks like you need to see a doctor. Why don't we reschedule." Kelly responds, "No, that's ok. You're my first priority. Last time we met, you said that you were being harassed at work and that you wanted to know your legal options. I did some research and I found out that you should file a grievance with the county human rights board. I can help you draft this grievance and then represent you at the hearing." Feeling relieved that someone could finally help her, Asta affirms that she wants Kelly to help her with the grievance.

Kelly's second appointment of the day is a staff meeting. Colleagues greet Kelly with questions about what was wrong with their head and offer to help them go to a hospital for medical care. Kelly says, "I'll be ok. Please don't worry about me." During the meeting, it becomes clear that Kelly is not okay. They start to feel dizzy and nauseous. Kelly vomits on the floor. "Wow, I wasn't expecting that. It must have been something I ate. I'm not contagious or anything like that." Kelly's supervisor responds, "We'll clean up. Please take the rest of the day off. You're in no shape to be working today. We need you to be healthy." Although Kelly thinks they could manage at work, they acquiesce to the supervisor's request. "Ok, I'll just take a few client files home so that I can work on them for the rest of the day. I promise that I'll stay out of trouble."

Kelly asks one of the support staff to call her clients and cancel the rest of their appointments. The support staff asks, "What should I tell the clients if they ask about you? Should I refer them to another social worker?" Kelly replies, "Just tell them that I have a mild concussion. Nothing to worry about. I'll be back tomorrow and I can meet them then." Kelly packs their files and goes home. Once home, Kelly takes codeine to ease their headache. Feeling a bit better, Kelly starts writing progress notes for work with clients over the past few days. Writing becomes more and more challenging as their vision starts to blur. After struggling through writing two progress notes, Kelly sighs aloud, "That's enough. I am going back to bed."

EXEMPLARY PRACTICE

A fundamental strategy for maximizing benefits and managing risks is to practice in an exemplary manner. Act in accordance with the highest standards of social work ethics. Engage in competent, ethically conscientious, client-centered practice (Reamer, 2021c). Take care of the little things that can go a long way in terms of serving clients and others. Be on time. Be courteous. Build positive rapport by demonstrating empathy, unconditional positive regard, and genuineness (Rogers, 1957). Ensure that your practice conforms to agency policy, the NASW Code of Ethics, and professional standards appropriate to your field of practice. Listen carefully to clients and explain the basis of options for intervention (Gambrill, 2017). Respect client self-determination (NASW Code, S.1.02) and informed consent (S.1.03), allowing clients to make choices based on relevant information and understanding the benefits and risks of various options. When family members have an influence on the clients' decision making, consider asking clients whether it would be appropriate to discuss the intervention plan with family members (Hagihara & Tarumi, 2007). Ensure that you have current and appropriate education, training, and supervision. Do not accept work that goes beyond your level and areas of competence (S. 1.04). If you are unable to competently serve the needs of a particular client, consult with an expert or refer the client to someone who can provide competent services. Do not simply give the client the name of a referral; ensure that the client has access and connects with the referral. Otherwise, the client may claim abandonment (S.1.17[b]). Maintain clear records regarding assessments, professional recommendations, and client decisions, particularly for situations involving higher levels of risk (e.g., suicidal ideation, suspicions of child abuse, and clients presenting with hallucinations or drug-induced impairments; Kanani et al., 2002).

Exemplary practice includes following the principles of evidence-based practice. Our work should be informed by current theory and research, including research into the effectiveness of various social work interventions (NASW Code, n.d.-a). We should keep attuned to generally accepted standards for competent practice in whatever field we are practicing (Caudill, n.d.). We should be able to enunciate the theoretical orientation and research basis for our work, particularly for complex or risky interventions. Systemic reviews provided by organizations such as the Campbell Collaborative (https://www.campbellcollaboration.org) and the Cochrane Library (www.theCochraneLibrary.com) may be particularly useful for determining the best evidence on specific forms of intervention. Manualized interventions can help us identify specific strategies and skills to ensure we are following proper protocols for specific interventions. We may also use checklists to ensure that we are following appropriate steps, as well as documenting that we are practicing in a competent manner (Gawande, 2011). When we do not use theory or research to inform our practice, we may be putting our clients at greater risk of harm and ourselves at greater risk of malpractice lawsuits, agency grievances, and complaints with our professional organizations.

We have been studying respect, honesty, self-determination, confidentiality and other ethical principles throughout this volume. Simply knowing these principles, however, is not sufficient. We need to embrace them as virtues, making them habits that we incorporate into our everyday practice (Berling et al., 2019). As the maxim says, "Always behave as if someone is watching." In addition, we should always be watching ourselves. We should be aware of the people we are serving. We should be aware of our roles. We should be aware of our legal and ethical responsibilities. We should be aware of how our choices are affecting our clients, research participants, colleagues, and others. We should not let down our guard.

On days when we feel stressed, achy, rushed, or out of sorts for other reasons, we might be tempted to take shortcuts. For instance, we might rush through an assessment, ask a client to sign a consent form without ensuring that they know what they are signing, or skip a step in an intervention process. Often, these types of shortcuts may not lead to significant problems. Still, we should be aware of the slippery slope of sloppy practice. One false step along a slippery slope could lead to a drastic fall (Cottone et al., 2022). Assume that you allow certain clients to connect with you on your personal social media accounts, thinking "What is the harm of letting certain clients see cute photos of me, my family, and my dog?" Although nothing untoward may happen with most clients, what happens if maintaining inappropriate digital boundaries leads to unintentional breaches of client confidentiality? What if your clients start seeing you as more of a friend or romantic partner than as a professional social worker? Certainly, not all shortcuts lead to major problems. Still, staying on a safer path may be prudent in the long run.

Note that risks may arise even when we practice in an exemplary manner. You might facilitate a group session in accordance with the best theory and research available; still, some group members may experience negative effects (e.g., stress or trauma). Further, clients may initiate lawsuits or grievances even in situations where your service was exemplary. Although exemplary practice can enhance the chances of good outcomes, it does not eliminate all risks. Accordingly, we should consider other RBM strategies, as discussed in the following sections.

COMMON FORMS OF MISCONDUCT

Identifying the most common forms of social worker misconduct is challenging because there is relatively little research on the prevalence of grievances against social workers. Many grievances are handled informally (e.g., through discussions between clients and social workers or informal complaints through supervisors or others within agencies). It is also challenging to gather data and conduct research on professional review and licensing review processes because these processes are confidential (Barsky & Spadola, 2022). The bulk of recent research on the prevalence of social worker misconduct is based on the frequency of complaints and sanctions against licensed social workers. Across the United States, approximately 1 to 2% of all licensed social workers have received licensing complaints (Gricus & Wysiekiersky, 2021); however, Magiste (2020) suggests that as many as 10% of social workers have engaged in unprofessional conduct. The most common licensing violations and professional complaints against social workers include substandard practice (practicing below the duty of care expected of the social worker), problems in record keeping, sexual boundary violations, nonsexual boundary violations, incompetence, lack of informed consent, dishonesty, infractions with colleagues, reimbursement violations, conflicts of interest, criminal behavior, continuing education non-compliance, and not submitting sufficient information to renew licenses (Boland-Prom, 2009; Boland-Prom et al., 2015; Daley & Doughty, 2007; Strom-Gottfried, 2000).

Certain types of misconduct may be more common in some contexts of practice than in others. For instance, *Medicare fraud* may be more common in agencies providing health and mental health services to older adults, whereas *conflicts of interest* may arise more frequently in small communities. You could ask your supervisors about the most common forms of professional misconduct or risky behavior within your agency. By understanding the common risks, you can take specific precautions to reduce them.

The basic steps of a traditional risk-management approach are to detect, monitor, assess, mitigate, and prevent risks (NEJM Catalyst, 2018). Consider an alcohol detoxification program. One risk that the program should consider is that patients may experience seizures. Accordingly, it is important for staff to be trained in how to detect, monitor, and assess for risks of seizures. To mitigate or prevent risks of seizure, the program should have medical staff who can intervene as needed (e.g., administering antiseizure medication). Although physicians and nurses may take a primary role in identifying and managing these risks, all staff (including social workers) can play important risk-management roles.

As social workers, we may get into trouble either when we actively engage in misconduct or when we fail to perform our duties (Reamer, 2021c). Misconduct is called *malfeasance* or an *error of commission*. Failure to perform duties is called *nonfeasance* or an *error of omission* (Rodziewicz et al., 2022). An example of malfeasance is lying to a client about the benefits of a particular intervention. In this context, lying constitutes a breach of two ethical standards: informed consent (NASW Code, S.1.03) and our duty to be honest (S.4.05). An example of nonfeasance is failing to conduct a suicidal ideation assessment for a client expressing plans of suicide. A competent social worker should recognize when clients are at risk of suicide and should take appropriate steps, such as assessing the level of risk. In this instance, *doing nothing* constitutes nonfeasance.

MANAGING RISKY SITUATIONS

Often, when social workers breach ethical standards, they had no intention to violate their ethical obligations or hurt their clients. This section explores risky situations that may lead to unintended ethical violations or harm to clients or others. By detecting these risks early, we can avoid ethical violations and harm, or at least reduce these risks. Risky situations include lack of knowledge of ethical and legal standards, high stress experienced by the worker, inappropriate worker-client boundaries, clients with risk of violent behavior, novel or high-risk interventions, and emergency situations.

Lack of Knowledge

One of the riskier situations in social work practice is not knowing what we are supposed to know. Consider the following scenario: A man calls your agency asking for the time of his wife's next appointment so he can ensure that she comes to the appointment on time. You give him the time. Later, your supervisor censures you for breaching your client's right to confidentiality. You explain that you were just trying to help your client. You thought confidentiality did not apply between a husband and wife. Even though your intent was good, you were mistaken due to lack of information.

As the maxim goes, ignorance of the law is no excuse. Similarly, ignorance of agency policies or social work ethics is no excuse. As professional social workers, we are expected to know the legal rules, agency policies, and ethical standards that govern our practice. For beginning social workers, knowing all the laws, policies, and standards may seem daunting. It is vital, therefore, to be prepared with sufficient knowledge before you see your first client. It is also imperative to know where to access help should any questions quickly arise when you are seeing clients.

Your coursework should provide you with a foundational understanding of social work ethics. When you begin working at an agency, however, you need to know the specific laws and policies that govern the agency and your work there. If you feel overwhelmed by the agency's enormous policy statement or by the jargon used in the laws governing your agency, ask your supervisor for help: What do I need to know right away? What do I need to learn in the next few months of work? When I have questions, whom should I consult (e.g., my supervisor, the program director, the ethics committee, the agency's attorney)? Do not be afraid to admit ignorance by asking questions. It is better to risk embarrassment that you are lacking certain knowledge than to risk breaking laws, policies, or ethics because you were afraid to ask.

In addition to learning the about agency-specific laws, policies, and ethics, we also need to identify which theories, research, and models of practice that we need to know to serve clients in a competent manner. If I were a child protection worker, for instance, I should know how to assess for risk of child abuse and neglect. Applying the principles of evidence-based practice, my supervisor and I could identify valid and reliable risk assessment tools (Gambrill, 2017). Assume that you are developing a recreational program for an agency serving young adults with developmental disabilities. To provide competent services, what knowledge bases would you require? What would you need to know about developing recreational programs and what would you need to know about serving people with developmental disabilities? Once we identify what we need to learn, we can then use readings, trainings, supervision, consultation, and reflection to build our competence.

Worker Stress

When experiencing high stress, we may act in ways that we would never consider under ordinary situations. A social worker with a high caseload may fall behind on writing progress notes, thereby breaching requirements to maintain proper client records. A worker with high financial debts might consider absconding with client funds, breaching ethical standards of integrity and criminal laws related to theft. A worker who becomes depressed might resort to drug abuse, making it difficult to provide services in a competent manner. A social worker experiencing a tough divorce may unintentionally impose personal feelings about marriage on an unsuspecting client. As social worker, we are human, with human vulnerabilities in response to stress.

Although high stress may help explain why we violated a law or ethical standard, experiencing stress does not excuse us from accountability. As professionals, we should not allow personal problems interfere with our work (NASW Code, S.4.05). To prevent stress and personal problems from adversely affecting our practice, we should

- strive for early awareness of stress and personal problems through self-reflection, journaling, or clinical supervision.
- take steps to deal with the stress or personal problems as soon as possible (e.g., seeking help from a therapist or other professional from outside the agency; ask the agency to develop a less stressful, more supportive work environment).
- develop strategies to ensure that work is not adversely affected by the stress or personal problems (e.g., take a leave of absence from work; ask your supervisor if you can focus on certain tasks or clients that you can manage effectively; use meditation and stress reduction techniques at home or prior to seeing clients).

In some situations, stress may affect the nature of our relationships with clients, putting us and our clients at risk. Problematic social worker–client relationships are the topic of the next section.

Inappropriate Worker–Client Boundaries

If I were to ask why you decided to become a social worker, you might say, "I want to help people." Wanting to help people is altruistic and admirable. Wanting to help people may also lead to possible boundary violations. As social workers, we might ponder the following:

What type of help do my clients need? Why can't I provide all the types of help that my clients need?

Consider a client who is crying. Wouldn't it be helpful to put your arms around the client to comfort them? Consider an unemployed client who needs $50 to buy clothes for upcoming job interviews. Wouldn't it be helpful to give the client the money to help her gain employment? Consider a client who says she has committed an adulterous sin. Wouldn't it be helpful to join the client in prayer for forgiveness? Although crossing professional boundaries with clients may offer certain benefits (Zur, 2021), we also need to take risks into account.

We are much more likely to get into ethical and legal trouble when our relationships with clients start to look more like relationships between close friends, family members, or romantic partners. As Chapter 8 suggests, we can reduce ethical and legal risks by maintaining appropriate professional boundaries. To understand and maintain professional boundaries, consider the following strategies.

- Develop a clear explanation of your role as a social worker, including how that role is different from that of friend or family member.
- Discuss your role with clients at the beginning of your social work relationship; remind them of the appropriate boundaries of your relationship should any boundary issues arise.
- Check your feelings toward the client—before, during, and after each session—to see if they may be getting in the way of effective, appropriate social work practice.
- Consider how you would feel if you were in the client's position (e.g., what type of boundaries would you expect, and how you would respond to the types of boundaries you plan to establish with the client?).
- Use supervision to help distinguish behaviors and roles that fit within your professional boundaries, and those that do not.

As Standard 1.06 suggests, we should generally avoid engaging in dual relationships with clients, particularly in situations where engaging in dual relationships puts client at risk. If we do engage in dual relationships, then we are responsible for establishing appropriate boundaries to minimize the risks (Reamer, 2015). Assume you are working in a residential treatment center, providing clients with both individual and group counseling services. The fact that you are seeing the same clients as an individual counselor and as a group facilitator means that you are engaging in dual relationships. Ideally, each client has a separate social worker for individual versus group work; however, many agencies require their social workers to serve both functions. There may even be some benefits to serving in both functions; for instance, if you identify a client concern in group work but the concern goes beyond the purposes of the group, you could assist the client with the concern during individual work. Still, there are potential downsides to these types of dual relationships. Assume that a client discloses embarrassing information in individual work but does not want you to share the information with the group. Although the group might benefit from the client sharing this information, your duty of confidentiality means that you should not disclose it or pressure the client to disclose it. When serving many clients at the same time, it may also be challenging to remember which information was shared by each client during group versus individual sessions.

When boundary violations arise, they are often related to some element of intimacy with clients, including (in extreme situations) sexual intimacy (Reamer, 2021d). We need to be aware of early signs that a professional relationship with a client may be slipping into an intimate one. Consider, for instance, a client who buys gifts, invites you to a social get-together, or expresses strong affection for you. Consider, also, situations in which you might feel sexually attracted or personally connected with a client. In each of these situations, you could use supervision to determine the best way to ensure appropriate professional boundaries. You might also discuss the possibility of referring the client to another professional, should maintaining appropriate boundaries become too difficult.

Remember that maintaining appropriate boundaries includes relationships with clients through social media and other communication technology (NASW et al., 2017). Although we have constitutionally recognized freedoms of speech and association, we should be aware that what we post online could lead to boundary confusion, dual relationships, and potential harm to our clients (NASW Code, S.1.06[f]). Be mindful about what types of personal information that you share in public online forums. Know that clients may conduct online searches and delve into personal information that you may not have intended to share with clients. Know also that allowing clients to connect with your personal social networking sites may lead to boundary confusion. To manage risks, it may be useful periodically to review your social media sites, checking your privacy settings, reviewing with whom you are connected, and reviewing content to determine whether there is information that you should remove because it may incur negative repercussions for your clients or your practice. A meme or joke that you once thought funny might be viewed as stereotyping or bigoted. Moving forward, you might also want to proofread your postings before submitting them—not just proofreading for grammar and spelling, but also considering how the substance of what you post might be perceived by employers, clients, or others involved in your professional life.

Risk of Violence

Certain clients may be at risk of engaging in violent behavior, including clients with suicidal or homicidal ideation. Whenever we interact with clients, we should use our assessment skills and knowledge to screen for risks. When potentially risky situations arise, we may also use risk assessment tools designed to assess for specific risks based on prior research and actuarial predictions (Hardy, 2017). When we identify significant risks, we may consider involving specialized mental health professionals to provide second-level assessments and crisis intervention. Even if we do not specialize in crisis intervention, we should be prepared with a range of interventions designed to help clients deal with underlying issues, such as anger, depression, or impulse control issues. In addition, we should be familiar with de-escalation techniques to diffuse risky situations: crisis intervention counseling, safety plans, taking the person to a safe room (away from others and away from items that could be used as weapons), or calling in a specialized mobile crisis intervention team for assistance (Occupational Health and Safety Administration, n.d.). We should avoid calling law enforcement or initiating proceedings for involuntary psychiatric admissions unless they are truly necessary to protect the client or others. Although involving law enforcement and involuntary committals may be needed in some situations, they can also escalate volatile situations or generate further trauma (Crisis Intervention Team International, 2019).

To eliminate risks of violence, some might suggest that we should simply lock up everyone who poses such risks. Although locking up anyone who poses risks to others may prevent violence, mass confinement or incarceration is not ethical, legal, or practical (Sicora, 2017). From an ethics perspective, locking up people without sufficient justification means that we are violating the principles of client self-determination, autonomy, and respect for the dignity and worth of all people. From a legal perspective, criminal prosecutions and convictions are intended for people who have committed crimes, not for people posing a risk of violence. Mental health laws that regulate when a person can be involuntarily committed to a psychiatric institution typically require evidence that the person is at imminent, serious risk of bodily harm to themself or others. If a person poses some risk of violence, but the risk is not high within the next 24 to 48 hours, involuntary psychiatric admission may be inappropriate. In terms of practicality, we are much better maintaining people with mental health issues in the community, rather than locking them up for indefinite periods of time. We can provide them with mental health services in the community, building in supports to ensure that they and those around them are safe.

When assessing risk, we should consider relevant risk factors while also ensuring that we do not stereotype or overgeneralize. Some people who experience mental illness, substance abuse, and hallucinations are at high risk of engaging in violence. This does not mean that all people with these concerns are automatically at high risk. Many people with these concerns may be at no greater risk of violent behavior than the general population (Mannarini & Rossi, 2019). We should assess each particular person and note the risks for that person at a particular moment in time. Just because a client has a prior history of aggression does not mean that the client is currently at risk. We should assess all relevant factors, including the client's current mental state, motivation, and plans.

Some social workers may be tempted to avoid working with clients who they believe to be at high risk of engaging in violent behavior (Whittaker & Havard, 2016). Although it is certainly prudent to take steps to protect ourselves from harm, we also have a duty to serve the most vulnerable populations in society (NASW Code, Preamble). Sometimes, the most vulnerable in society include people at risk of engaging in violence. Rather than refusing service to clients in need, we may bring in additional resources to ensure that we can provide services in a safe and effective manner (e.g., asking a supervisor to cofacilitate a group session in which you have concerns about potential violence; bringing a professional colleague to assist with a home visit; or alerting a colleague with specialized crisis-intervention training that you may need help de-escalating a particular situation).

Review the situation in Box 13.2 involving an adolescent who may be at risk of engaging in violent behavior. Consider the client's current and future levels of risk.

BOX 13.2

ALDO

You are working with Aldo, a 15-year-old boy, in a community-based family counseling center. His parents brought him for help, concerned that he is self-isolating and spending a lot of time on his computer. At the outset of services, Aldo and his parents agree that whatever Aldo says during counseling will remain between you and Aldo. They also agree that you may share information with the parents if it becomes necessary to protect Aldo or another person from a "serious, imminent risk of harm."

While working with Aldo, you learn that he has connected online with a domestic terrorist organization called MUTO-Q. The organization espouses racist, anti-Muslim, and anti-Semitic beliefs, encouraging supporters "to engage in violent acts in support of preserving America as a White and Christian society." When you assess Aldo's risk of engaging in violent acts, he says he has no plans to engage in violence. He denies having any weapons or access to weapons. He is vague about what he truly believes concerning Muslims, Jews, and People of Color. You sense that he does not want you to judge him or report him to authorities. Although you do not think he poses a risk of immediate harm to himself or others, you are concerned that he may one day become radicalized and engage in violence toward people from religious or racial minority groups. When you ask whether his parents know anything about his involvement with MUTO-Q, he asks you to respect his confidentiality and say nothing to them.

What RBM strategies should you consider? What are the risks and benefits of each strategy?

Consider, also, your options for managing the risks, while also promoting the client's rights to self-determination, autonomy, and dignity.

Novel and High-Risk Interventions

For some fields of practice and models of intervention, research is limited or just emerging. When new models of intervention are being developed, standards of competence may be nonexistent or imprecise. In such instances, we should be particularly careful to protect clients from risks of harm (S.1.04[c]). Consider when a previously unknown communicable disease emerges in a community. At first, researchers and helping professionals may not know how the disease is spread and the best ways to prevent transmission. Initial guidance for helping individuals and communities prevent transmission may be tentative. As new research emerges, the standards for what constitutes competent, effective practice may change. As social workers, we need to remain current on the latest research, including best practices and the risks and benefits of various interventions.

The prior example highlights the need to develop interventions for newly identified problems. Sometimes, we need to develop new interventions for problems that are not new to us. Consider, for instance, how to help a family with codependency issues. We may have models of intervention that are moderately helpful, but they may not be as effective as we and our clients would like. To "stay safe," we might continue practicing with existing models of intervention, refusing to explore novel ones (Whittaker & Havard, 2016). "Staying safe," however, means that we do not advance social work practice and learn new ways to help people with codependency issues (or whatever other concerns they have).

When planning to use novel interventions with clients, consider the following strategies to manage the risks and benefits.

- Even if there is no direct research on the efficacy of the proposed intervention, review the best available theory and research that is related to the proposed intervention (e.g., research on an intervention which is similar or been used to help clients with related concerns).
- Prior to implementing the intervention, develop your competence to implement the intervention through study, consultation, role-play training, or supervision (NASW Code, S.1.04[b]).
- Involve clients in the decision making, helping them understand the potential benefits and risks of the new intervention, as well as the uncertainties given that this is a novel intervention or a novel application of an existing intervention (Cottone et al., 2022; Gambrill, 2017).
- Closely monitor the implementation and impacts of the intervention, gathering feedback from our clients and using critical reflection to learn as we practice the intervention (Sicora, 2017).

Emergency Situations

risk benefit Management

An essential aspect of RBM is being prepared for emergency situations. Rather than waiting until urgent situations arise, we should have backup plans and procedures in place. We can then respond in a timely and effective manner when emergency situations do arise. Examples of emergencies include

- earthquakes, hurricanes, tornadoes, fires, floods, pandemics, and other natural disasters;
- mass shootings, terrorist attacks, wars, accidental explosions, large-scale hazardous-waste exposure, or other human-caused disasters; and
- power outages, technology failures, bridge or building collapses, and other major infrastructure calamities.

At a personal level, we should have plans for taking care of ourselves, our family members, and others who depend on us. If you were called on short notice to help with a large-scale emergency, for instance, who could care for your children so that you would be free to work? If your home were destroyed or at risk because of the disaster, where could you and your family take up temporary residence? If your phones, computers, electricity, or other technology were inoperable due to the disaster, what types of backup technology could you use? The precise type of disaster preparedness that we need depends on our location and the type of disasters that are more likely to arise. If you live in an area prone to wildfires, for instance, then you could develop precautions and emergency responses specifically for wildfires.

At an organizational level, your agency should have policies and procedures for various types of emergencies or disasters. When the COVID-19 pandemic spread worldwide in 2020, many agencies quickly changed their methods of practice. Some agencies equipped their social workers and other staff with masks and other protective equipment. Some instituted policies of physical distancing or limited service to only those who needed urgent attention. Others switched from in-person to online services using videoconferencing. As vaccinations became available, some agencies mandated vaccinations for employees, not only to protect them, but also to protect clients and other vulnerable populations (Camper & Felton, 2021). During emergency situations, we should not abandon clients in need (NASW Code, S.1.17[b]). By having emergency preparedness plans, we can ensure that clients have continuity of services (S.1.15).

On a client-by-client basis, we can prepare for emergencies by helping clients identify individualized backup plans. If you are unable to contact a client during an emergency situation, for instance, whom would the client like you to contact? If a client experiences problems in connecting with you by videoconferencing or other technology, what other means should they use to contact you (NASW et al., 2017)? If you are not available to serve a client due to a natural disaster or other emergency, what other services could the client access? If your clients need emergency shelter, food, transportation, or other resources, where could they go for help?

At a community level, identify organizations that you and your colleagues could partner with as part of your emergency preparedness plans. Should you be working with police, the fire department, Red Cross, or other organizations that assist with emergency responses? How can your agency assist first responders? How could you use cell phones, artificial intelligence, social media, and other technology to ensure that community members are safe and informed, and their needs are being addressed (Augusterfer et al., 2018)? Note that social workers can play a key role in how people respond to trauma by providing services in the immediate aftermath of a disaster or emergency situation. In addition to being prepared to help our existing clients, we should be ready to help with other community needs and response efforts (S.6.03).

See Box 13.3 for an illustration of why emergency preparedness and response plans are vital.

BOX 13.3

School Shooting

It was a beautiful sunny morning. Sandy Park's day as a high school social worker began the same way as any other. As students departed the buses and made their way into the school, Sandy greeted them, saying hello and checking in with students that might need extra attention. Everyone seemed okay. Nothing seemed out of the ordinary.

While meeting with her first student of the day, an announcement came over the intercom. "Code Red. Active shooter. Everyone, please shelter in place. Stay in your classrooms and follow the directions of your teacher and staff." In accordance with Code Red policies, Sandy and her client stayed in her office with the door locked and the lights off. They heard shooting from somewhere down the hall and screams from classrooms nearby. Still, they sheltered in place for what seemed like an eternity. After 40 minutes, a second announcement was heard. "A shooter has been apprehended. The Code Red is over." The school dismissed students early, allowing them to go home to be with their families.

Faculty and staff met to debrief with the principal. Although the principal asked Sandy to help with the debriefing, she was in a state of shock. She was not sure what to say or do. She was still feeling a sense of fear and panic. Sandy was the only school social worker. She had nobody to talk with, making her feel very isolated and embarrassed. The principal facilitated the debriefing as well as he could. Still, he did not seem to have sufficient preparation or training to handle the situation. The next day, Sandy was afraid to return to the school. She called in sick, knowing that she would not be in any shape to carry out her professional duties. She did not want to abandon her students and the school in a time of need, but she did not know what other choices she had.

What types of disaster preparedness and response did Sandy and the school have in place for this emergency? What additional forms of disaster preparedness and response should Sandy and the school have had in place?

AGENCY POLICIES AND PROCEDURES

RBM is not an individual endeavor. As the previous section highlights, we need the support of our agencies and colleagues to put effective RBM strategies in place. In this section, we explore how agency policies and procedures can help us maximize benefits and manage risks for our clients, agencies, communities, and ourselves. Specifically, agency policies and procedures can promote RBM by fostering a culture of ethics, providing guidance for managing issues, and giving us concrete tools to put policy into practice.

Promoting a Culture of Ethics

Having a culture of ethics means that an agency has a shared purpose and values (Martinez et al., 2021). When an agency develops vision, mission, and goal statements, it is proclaiming its values, principles, and preferred outcomes. These statements promote a culture of ethics within the agency, providing employees with common philosophies, language, norms, and expectations (Cottone et al., 2022). When an agency states its mission is to promote social justice, mental health, social wellbeing, and so on, it is motivating everyone to work toward these common purposes (Alegre et al., 2018). When an agency describes itself as a caring organization, it is inspiring everyone to attend to the needs and wishes of the people it serves (Tronto, 2010). In addition to using these statements for motivational purposes, we may use them to hold our agencies accountable to the values and ethics that they are espousing. If our agency's policies and practices do not align with its values and principles, we can advocate for changes to ensure consistency and moral integrity.

Agency policies and procedures build on the agency's stated values and principles. To promote ethical conduct, an agency's policies and procedures should promote a culture of responsibility rather than a culture of blame (Sicora, 2017). Although we strive for exemplary ethical practice at all times, we acknowledge that we are all fallible. When we make mistakes, agency policies should encourage us to acknowledge what went wrong and take responsibility for taking corrective action. Agencies should not make people feel afraid or embarrassed to discuss risks or errors. We are more likely to foster safe and effective practices when we encourage everyone to come forward with any issues or problems.

Rather than issuing formal grievances or complaints against our colleagues, our first step should be to consult with them directly, providing constructive feedback and offering to assist with remedial action (S. 2.08[a]). If we can resolve issues on an informal and collaborative basis, there may be no need for more formal or more adversarial actions (Barsky, 2017a). Sometimes, we may find it difficult to confront colleagues who have acted inappropriately (Reamer, 2021c). We may not want to embarrass our colleagues and we may not want to instigate conflict. Some agencies provide anonymous mechanisms for reporting ethical violations or harms experienced by clients or others. By offering anonymity, more people may be willing to come forward. Ideally, we should raise concerns without anonymity. When supervisors, human resources, **risk management** teams, or others receive anonymous concerns, it may be harder to address these concerns. When we let our names be known when we raise concerns, we can help the agency follow up (e.g., providing additional information; offering support in responding to the concern).

Guidance on Managing Particular Issues

Although the NASW Code of Ethics provides general guidance on how to implement client self-determination, informed consent, confidentiality, and other ethical standards, agency policies and procedures provide specific guidance on how to implement these standards in relation to the agency's particular context of practice. Consider the issue of receiving gifts from clients. Standard 1.06 says that we should maintain appropriate boundaries with clients. However, the notion of an appropriate boundary in one agency may be different from that in another agency. Some agencies permit receiving gifts under certain circumstances; others prohibit gifts outright. Different agencies may have different calculations about the risks and benefits of allowing social workers to receive gifts. Similarly, they may have different calculations about whether it is appropriate to hug clients, barter for services, or self-disclose to clients. Although each of these forms of conduct entail risks, they may also entail benefits to the people we serve (Zur, 2021). Make sure you understand your agency's policies regarding each of these issues, including their rationale and limits. In a 12-step addiction treatment program, for instance, agency policies may allow social workers to self-disclose about their own addictions and recovery processes. However, these policies may limit self-disclosure to information that is likely to help the clients with their recovery processes. In contrast, an agency that provides forensic assessments may prohibit self-disclosure outright so that social workers will be seen as independent, unbiased assessors.

Agency policies are proactive in the sense that they help everyone pre-empt problems rather than wait until they arise. Consider problems such as worker impairment due to burnout, compassion fatigue, or vicarious trauma. By acknowledging these risks up front, agencies can implement policies to support self-care and reduce these risks (Grise-Owens et al., 2022). For instance, agencies can implement policies to ensure that we have appropriate supervision, training, and time off for mental health concerns. Agencies should also ensure that we have sufficient resources to perform our duties in an ethical manner (Gambrill, 2017). No amount of self-care can prevent burnout, compassion fatigue, or vicarious trauma if we are overwhelmed by serving large numbers of clients experiencing severe trauma, without proper training and agency support.

If you come across gaps in agency policies, consult your supervisor for guidance. Assume, for instance, that you have been receiving requests from former clients to connect with them on social media and your agency has no policy on this matter. What are the potential benefits and risks of connecting online with former clients? Under what circumstances, if any, is it appropriate to connect online with former clients? What should you do if you accidentally connect with a client online (e.g., you join an online group that promotes mental health, not knowing that former clients are also members). If your agency does not have a social media policy, then you might suggest that it develops one (Reamer, 2021c). Having a social media policy not only informs practitioners about how to maintain appropriate digital boundaries with clients; it also informs clients about the agency's expectations.

In addition to having good policies and procedures, RBM requires agencies to have appropriate mechanisms for putting these policies and procedures into practice. When people begin work at an agency, they should receive training about how to implement informed consent, confidentiality, respect, honesty, and other ethical guidelines and policies (Cottone et al., 2022). For instance, what are the agency's protocols for ensuring that electronic records are safeguarded from unauthorized access? What precautions should you take at intake to ensure that you are not accepting new clients with whom you have a conflict of interest?

Some agencies conduct periodic ethics audits to review the agency's policies, procedures, and practices (Agheorghiesei et al., 2014; Reamer, 2021b). Audits can be used to ensure that the agency's policies, procedures, and practices are consistent with legal requirements, professional ethics, and best practices (as supported by the most current research). Consider a new law that requires social workers to engage in specialized training in order to provide counseling or therapy through videoconferencing or other communication technology. If the agency does not update its policies and practices, it could be putting clients, workers, and the agency at risk. Although agency administration may take primary responsibility for updating its policies and procedures, all of us can play a role. If we see something that can use updating, we should say something to our supervisors or others who are responsible for the upkeep of our agency's policies and procedures.

Consider something as mundane as the layout of your offices. Some offices are designed with aesthetics in mind; for example, how attractive are the offices in terms of color, texture, shape, and size; how comfortable are the chairs and workstations? But how well are the offices designed in terms of ethical issues such as confidentiality and respect for people from diverse backgrounds? Do social work offices have sufficient soundproofing to offer clients a confidential environment to meet? Are offices sufficiently lit to assist people with visual challenges? Are offices and restrooms accessible to people who use wheelchairs or have various physical disabilities? Does the artwork on the walls include images that may be triggering for people with a history of trauma? I remember conducting groups for people with addictions in a room with posters intended to demonstrate risks of sharing needles. Some clients complained that the images of needles triggered cravings to use drugs. We jointly decided to remove the posters. As frontline workers, we may be in a good position to identify ethical issues and bring them to the administration's attention. All of us can play important roles in ensuring that agency policies and procedures align with social work values and ethics.

Concrete Procedures and Tools

Whereas agency *policies* provide general directions for how employees should conduct themselves, *procedures* provide specific steps to implement those policies. Consider an agency policy allowing clients to have access to their records. Agency procedures indicate how clients may access their records. For instance, do clients have automatic access to their electronic records by logging into their agency account? Do clients need to ask their social workers to release specific records to them? Or do clients need to come into the agency and meet with their workers in order to review the records together? Each procedure has different risks and benefits. Providing clients with automatic access saves time and empowers clients to determine whether and when to access their records. However, they could misinterpret or overreact to certain information if they do not have a social worker reviewing the records with them.

Consent forms are useful tools for putting informed consent into practice. By having comprehensive consent forms, we can ensure that clients are familiar with

- the purpose and nature of services offered, including different options for services;
- benefits and risks of specific interventions; rights and responsibilities of the client (e.g., time, fees, participation in particular activities, ability to withdraw from services); and
- what the client can expect of the social worker (NASW Code, S.1.03; Reamer, 2018a).

Consent forms should be easy to read and understand. To ensure that clients truly understand and agree to the terms of the informed consent, we should review consent forms with our client, explaining terms that may be more difficult to understand and being open to answering questions. When we ensure that clients understand and agree to services up front, we lessen the likelihood of future disappointments, conflicts, grievances, and lawsuits.

Agencies should have specific protocols for handling risky situations (e.g., a client with suicidal or homicidal ideation, a client who threatens a lawsuit, a client who leaves a residential treatment program against professional advice, or a situation raising conflicts of interests). For each type of risk, you should know whom to contact within your agency and what steps to take. For threats of lawsuits, for instance, should you inform your supervisor, a risk management officer, or the agency attorney? Should you continue to see the client, and if not, how can you guard against abandonment (i.e., ensuring the client has access to services)? When in doubt about how to respond, consulting with your supervisor is often a prudent first step.

SUPERVISION AND CONSULTATION

In our endeavors to practice ethically, safely, and effectively, we are not alone. Just as clients can benefit from the assistance of others, so can we. In particular, we should make use of supervision and consultation to help us deal with challenging ethical decisions (NASW Code, Purpose Section). We can use supervision and consultation as proactive measures, helping us practice in a competent manner and helping us make well-informed decisions when faced with ethical dilemmas (Reamer, 2021b). We can also use supervision and consultation after problems arise, helping us assess the problems and develop appropriate responses.

A *supervisor* is a professional within our agency who is responsible for overseeing our work. Supervisors provide us with work-related training, oversight, feedback, guidance, and moral support (Corey et al., 2019; Shulman, 2020). As educators, supervisors foster safe places to explore how we are interacting with clients, how we are using ourselves, and how to manage ethical issues as they arise in practice (Falender & Shafranske, 2014). They can help us raise awareness of any thoughts and feelings impeding our ability to practice ethically. They can provide us with guidance on how to focus on the needs of our clients. They can also help us develop professional competencies, including the ability to assess clients, conceptualize cases, think critically, and translate theory into evidence-based practice (Watkins & Milne, 2014). In some instances, supervisors act as gatekeepers for the profession (Calden, 2020), determining which social workers meet expectations for graduation and/or licensure. As agency representatives, supervisors ensure accountability and compliance with agency policies, norms, and expectations (Wong & Lee, 2015). As mentors, they help us develop professional identities, including our alliance with social work values and ethics. Ideally, we have trusting relationships with our supervisors so that we feel free to ask for help even when we have made mistakes or feel embarrassed that we do not know how to handle a challenging practice situation (Mo et al., 2021).

A *consultant* is a professional who assists with making prudent practice decisions by providing information, feedback, and a supportive environment to reflect upon how to handle challenging practice situations. We may seek help from different types of consultants depending on the type of expertise that we could use, for instance, clinical, legal, or ethical expertise. In some instances, we may access expertise within our agencies (e.g., a colleague with expertise trauma who can help us with a client experiencing trauma or an ethics committee mandated to help us with ethical concerns). In other instances, we may seek consultation from outside sources (e.g., the NASW's ethics consultants or attorneys that provide legal information or advice). Sometimes, we may benefit from consultation with another social worker; other times, we may benefit from consultation with a physician, psychologist, social policy expert, or another type of professional (Cottone et al., 2022). Although there is overlap between the roles of consultants and a supervisors, consultants do not have oversight responsibility and do not have authority to prescribe how we should practice.

If you are unsure of how to act or you feel something might be wrong, slow down the process of thinking and acting (Kahneman, 2011). Access help before making important decisions or wading deeper into troubled waters. You, your clients, and your agency will benefit. Supervisors and consultants can help ensure that you are using effective critical thinking rather than relying on assumptions, stereotypes, or other mental shortcuts (Gricus & Wysiekiersky, 2021). Although you may feel nervous about accessing help and getting into more trouble, it is generally wiser and safer to access help (Whittaker & Havard, 2016). If you are worried about being fired or incurring other negative consequences from your agency, you could first consult with an attorney or ethics expert from outside your agency. Rather than ignoring errors or avoiding accountability, face up to these concerns and take appropriate steps to manage them (Sicora, 2017).

Box 13.4 presents a situation in which a social worker runs into trouble while trying to manage a client with mental health concerns. As you read this situation, identify potential risks and how the worker could have used supervision or consultation to assist with the ethics, safety, and effectiveness of his interventions.

DOCUMENTATION

Documentation plays a key role in managing the risks and benefits of practice. From a practice perspective, documentation is prudent because it helps us keep track of our work with clients: what concerns our clients have, what goals they want to work on, what they agreed to do as part of the informed-consent process, and how they are progressing under our care. When serving many clients, documentation

BOX 13.4

TOKLO

Toklo is a relatively new child protection worker in a rural county where almost everyone knows everyone else. On three evenings per week, Toklo is on call to handle emergencies that arise after regular working hours. One evening, while having dinner in a café, Toklo receives a call from local law enforcement. They ask him to meet at Ms. Saini's house. They want help taking Ms. Saini's children into protective custody because she is "having a mental health issue." Several people in the café overhear the call. They ask Toklo if they can come to help. Not wanting to exacerbate the problems, Toklo discourages them from coming. They ignore his pleas and follow him to Ms. Saini's house. Upon arriving at the house, police escort Toklo to the front door. Toklo knocks. Ms. Saini opens the door and starts yelling profanities at Toklo and the police. Toklo tries to de-escalate, offering to take Ms. Saini for a walk outside. Her face is flushed and she is obviously feeling distressed. Toklo knows that she has bipolar disorder. Although he does not have much training in work with people with bipolar disorder, he knows the importance of being supportive and calm, avoiding arguments and confrontation.

Initially, going for a walk seems helpful. Unfortunately, some neighbors who followed Toklo start to yell at Ms. Saini: "What's wrong? Are you having another one of those episodes? Are the police here to take away your kids?" The yelling seems to trigger Ms. Saini. She attacks an onlooker. Police intervene, trying to subdue Ms. Saini. Although they are able to restrain her, Ms. Saini suffers a concussion, broken ribs, and emotional trauma during the altercation.

What types of RBM strategies could Toklo have used in this situation? How could he have used supervision or consultation prior to the incident with Ms. Saini? How could he use supervision or consultation after the incident? What factors may make it challenging for Toklo to access supervision in this situation?

---

helps us remember important information for work with each client. For instance, if I document concerns about the risk of elder abuse or neglect, I can make sure to follow through on these issues. If a client asks for help applying for Medicaid, documentation reminds me to complete this task. If I miss work due to illness, my supervisor can follow up with my clients based on my documentation. If my agency wants to evaluate the effectiveness of my work, it can use my documentation to determine the extent of my success with clients (Wilkins, 2017).

From a legal perspective, documentation provides a source of evidence that can be used to defend our professional decisions and conduct in malpractice cases, licensing complaints investigations, professional review processes, and other legal processes (Reamer, 2015). Informed consent forms, for instance, can provide key evidence about whether we provided clients with sufficient information about the risks and benefits of services. Given the importance of documentation in legal processes, some attorneys joke, "If it's not in writing, it didn't happen." If a legal process that comes down to your word versus the client's, the deciding factor may be your documentary evidence. When people give oral testimony, their evidence may be questioned because the events transpired long ago. Memories may be inaccurate due to the passage of time. Accordingly, documentation at the time of client contact tends to be given greater weight than oral testimony. Documentary evidence may also be given stronger weight because the documents were created in the course of our usual practice; in contrast, live oral testimony may be tainted by the legal process itself (i.e., people providing oral testimony may be tempted to stray from the truth to influence the court's decision).

In terms of managing risks, it is particularly important to document ethical issues, practice errors, and client complaints (NEJM Catalyst, 2018; Reamer, 2015). Such documentation should answer the following questions.

1. What is the nature of the issue, error, or complaint and how did it come to our attention?
2. How did we reflect upon and analyze the issue (including who we consulted, what factors we considered, and what process did we use to analyze the issue)?
3. What decision did we make and what was our rationale?
4. How did we implement and monitor the decision?
5. What were the outcomes of the decision?
6. What types of follow-up were planned and implemented?

Box 13.5 provides an example of how to document an ethical issue using this six-question framework.

Note that documenting ethical issues, errors, or harms demonstrates professional integrity and accountability. Rather than trying to hide these concerns, we should document them and how we took responsibility for addressing them. By documenting our decision-making processes, we are demonstrating prudent practice, that is, how our conduct fits with what would reasonably be expected of a social worker in a similar situation (Reamer, 2015). Documentation can be used to enhance reflective practice. By reflecting on issues and our decision-making processes, we are in a better position to learn from past decisions and make better informed decisions moving forward (Sicora, 2017).

RESPONDING TO COMPLAINTS

Most of this chapter has focused on how to avoid risks, including complaints that could lead to malpractice lawsuits, professional grievances, or licensing investigations. If you do receive a complaint, it is important to continue to use RBM

BOX 13.5

Group Harassment

The following points demonstrate how to document how a worker handled a client complaint. In this scenario, a client named Connie reported that she was verbally attacked by other members of a psychoeducational group.

1. Issue: Following a group session on January 11, Connie met with me to express concerns that she felt others were harassing her during today's session. She felt that I did not protect her. She wanted me to take appropriate action to ensure that she would not be subjected to abuse in future sessions.

2. Assessment: Connie said she felt harassed because others suggested that the way she dressed was sexually provocative. Although she felt hurt by these comments, she said she was willing to return to the group if I could ensure the group would treat her with respect. I met with my supervisor, Benita Lloyd, to discuss Connie's concerns. We agreed that Connie raised valid concerns and that I needed to address them before the next group session. Connie seemed to be coping well, so the main concern was ensuring that she would be free from harassment moving forward.

3. Decision: Connie, Benita, and I agreed that that Benita would cofacilitate the next group session with me. I would begin the session by reviewing the group's ground rules, including the importance of treating one another with respect. Connie would have an opportunity to discuss how she felt harassed during the prior session. We would give the group time to process their reactions to Connie's concerns. We decided it was important for Benita to participate in the group to ensure that everyone felt emotionally safe to discuss these issues. We considered other options, such as meeting with group members individually or having Benita express Connie's concerns to the group. Connie said she wanted to speak on her own behalf, as long as Benita and I would be there for support. Initially, Connie asked whether certain group members could be expelled from the group. We decided that expulsion from the group was a harsh measure and would not be necessary if everyone could commit to treating one another with respect.

4. Implementation and Monitoring: Prior to the next group session, Connie and I role-played what each of us would say. During the meeting, we discussed group ground rules and Connie's concerns as planned. Some group members said they did not think that they were being mean or disrespectful. We discussed the importance of the impact and not just the intent of what people say to one another. Some group members offered apologies. Others remained silent. After the meeting, Benita and I met with Connie to debrief. Connie said she was satisfied with the meeting. She had some concerns about group members who said little, but said she was feeling safer about participating in the group.

5. Evaluation: The discussion about treating one another with respect seemed to be successful. No further concerns about harassment or disrespect have been raised by Connie or other group members.
6. Follow-Up: Connie and I agreed to meet individually after future group meetings to assess whether further concerns about harassment or disrespect require attention.

---

strategies, including consultation with your supervisor and anyone else in your agency responsible for responding to complaints. If you are faced with a lawsuit or licensing complaint, you may also need to hire an attorney. An attorney can help you assess the seriousness of the complaint and the best way to respond. Remember that an agency's attorney represents the agency. Although the agency's interests and yours may be similar, it is often useful to have your own attorney who specifically represents you and your interests. Malpractice insurance typically covers legal costs to defend against malpractice lawsuits and licensing complaints. At the very least, you should consider having an initial consultation with an attorney to determine whether you can benefit from ongoing representation.

Clients sometimes sue or file grievances because they are unhappy, stressed, or angry, whether or not you have actually violated professional ethics or committed malpractice. Even if you successfully defend a malpractice suit or grievance process, defending can take a huge toll, emotionally and financially. Whenever possible, pre-empt escalation of disputes with clients by using your best conflict resolution skills when clients initially express concerns about your practice (Barsky, 2017a). If you can work through concerns on an informal basis, you can avoid having to defend an actual lawsuit. Consider consulting an attorney even before an actual lawsuit is initiated. Attorneys can help you strategize the best ways to respond to grievances. Attorneys may advise against providing apologies for improper care, as they could be used in court as admissions of malpractice. On the other hand, providing apologies could be the best way to avoid being sued, facilitating mutual understanding and conflict resolution (McMichael et al., 2017). In some situations, you can listen and validate client concerns without admitting guilt. You could also offer corrective action that averts going to court. Many jurisdictions have "apology laws" that allow health care professionals to offer apologies to patients without fear that the apologies can be used against them in malpractice lawsuits. These laws encourage health care professionals and organizations to resolve issues with patients through informal discussions rather than through adversarial court processes.

Whether and how you contest a complaint or allegation depends on the particular situation, including the nature of the evidence supporting or disproving the client's case. Some topics to discuss with your supervisor and attorney include

- whether you should have any further direct communication with the client pending the results of the complaint or lawsuit;

- whether you should refer the client to another social worker or agency to ensure continuity of care;
- what types of evidence that you should gather or maintain (e.g., electronic communications, progress notes, and other documentation); and
- your alternatives for resolving the issues in a collaborative manner (e.g., attorney-led negotiations, mediation, or settlement conferences).

Note that although you have a right to defend yourself against a client's allegations, you should maintain client confidentiality as much as is reasonably possible (NASW Code, 1.07[j]). In other words, limit your disclosures in court or other proceedings to that which is necessary to defend yourself. Note also that even if you are upset with the client's behavior or allegations, you still have a duty to treat the client with dignity and respect.

SELF-REPORTING

Sometimes, we may realize that we have violated our ethical obligations, breached agency policy, or caused harm to a client even if the client or others have not raised any complaints. We should consider reporting these concerns to our supervisor, professional association, licensing board, or liability insurance company (NASW Assurance Services, 2021; Reamer, 2015). By self-reporting, we are being proactive, enabling us to initiate corrective action in a timely manner. Although it may sound counterintuitive to report ourselves, it could lessen the severity of the consequences (e.g., an agency may be less likely to dismiss us if we accept responsibility and initiate corrective action). To help decide whether to self-report, it may be prudent to consult an attorney. If we decide to self-report, our attorney can help us determine the best way to issue the report (e.g., in-person, in writing, or through attorney-initiated communications).

SELF-CARE

As Chapter 11 notes, it is important that we engage in self-care, not only to ensure our own personal wellbeing, but to ensure that we can serve clients as effectively as possible. By supporting our physical, psychological, social, and spiritual wellbeing, self-care helps us reduce risks and maximize the benefits of our practice. When we neglect our own wellbeing, we may be putting clients at risk (Grise-Owens et al., 2022; Raines, 2021).

Self-care includes monitoring our wellness and any threats to our wellbeing. When we start to experience personal problems, psychological distress, substance abuse, or mental health difficulties, we should gauge their impact on our ability to practice. We do not want personal issues to impair our professional judgment or ability to serve clients (Reamer, 2021c). When we become aware that personal problems are affecting our ability to practice, we should take remedial actions (e.g., consulting a supervisor, accessing professional help, adjusting our workload, requesting a leave of absence, or referring clients to other professionals (Cottone et al., 2022).

As social workers, we have a duty to develop and enhance our competence (NASW Code, S.1.04). Self-care includes engaging in continuing professional education and development. In terms of RBM, we should periodically assess our particular educational needs. Topics for continuing education and development include

- recent updates in laws, ethics, or social policies affecting our areas of practice;
- current research on social work interventions, including interventions that we currently use and new ones that we might consider using; and
- enhancing specific assessment and intervention skills.

We can pursue continuing professional education and development through a combination of readings, online and in-person trainings, conferences, and consultation with relevant experts.

CONCLUSION

At its best, risk-benefit management is about good ethical practice, putting the principles of respect, autonomy, social justice, human relationships, integrity, and competence into action. Although some literature focuses on how to practice in a manner that reduces the risk of malpractice, licensing violations, or other types of legal liability (Rodziewicz et al., 2021), reducing errors and legal risks is just part of the equation (Gambrill, 2017). Rather than focusing on our baseline ethical requirements and avoiding errors, we should strive for moral excellence in our practice (Beauchamp & Childress, 2019). As the notion of aspirational ethics suggests, we should reach high, pursuing the highest values and ideals of our profession: serving clients in a proficient manner, promoting social justice, acting with integrity, enhancing human relationships, and advancing the dignity and worth of all people.

DISCUSSION QUESTIONS AND EXERCISES

1. *Contrasting*: What is the difference between acting ethically, managing risks, and maximizing benefits? What is the relationship between "good ethical practice" and "risk-benefit management"?
2. *Litigious Client*: Veronique calls to request social work counseling services. She says she needs help because she is going through a nasty divorce. During intake, you discover that she has a history of suing professionals for malpractice. She has fired two attorneys and three mental health professionals. She describes each of them as incompetent and corrupt. Given her litigation history, you are concerned about

accepting Veronique as a client. If you decide to work with Veronique, what RBM strategies could you use to limit the risks of being sued? Would it be ethical to refuse service to Veronique? What ethical principles and standards should you consider?

3. *Documentation Error*: You are helping a client, Balki, apply for social assistance using an online application system. You accidentally submit inaccurate income information. Balki starts receiving much more social assistance than he is entitled. When you ask Balki to return the excess funding and amend his social assistance application, he tells you he is entitled to the money. He instructs you to respect his confidentiality, stating, "Do not say anything to anyone." What RBM strategies should you use? Who, if anyone, would you consult for assistance on how to manage this situation: your agency supervisor, your attorney, the police, the social assistance office, your psychic, the NASW Office of Ethics and Professional Review, your liability insurance company, or some other organization? What is your rationale? How could you consult others without breaching your duty of confidentiality?

4. *Non-Imminent Risk*: You are working with a client, Fernanda, who has been diagnosed with bipolar disorder. While conducting a home visit, you discover that Fernanda has stopped taking her antipsychotic medications. She says she no longer needs them. You are concerned because she has been experiencing auditory hallucinations. She is an adult who understands the benefits and risks of taking medications. You do not think she is at immediate risk of harming herself or others, but she may be in the future. You consult with her psychiatrist who says that Fernanda should resume taking her medications, but there is no way to force her to do so. What legal and ethical risks arise in this situation? What RBM strategies should you use? How do these strategies fit with your ethical obligations regarding client self-determination, informed consent, safety, beneficence, and nonmaleficence?

5. *Risk Assessment Tools*: Select one of the following risks and conduct a literature search to identify an evidence-based risk assessment tool that you could use to assess for this risk: suicide, homicide, child abuse and neglect, elder abuse and neglect, intimate partner abuse, or overdosing (on opiates or another specific psychoactive substance). How would you determine whether the tool is valid, reliable, and normed for the particular cultural group with whom you are working?

6. *RBM Strategies*: Which RBM strategies would you suggest for each of the following situations? Provide your reasoning. If you suggest consultation as part of the risk management plan, include the type of professional with whom you would consult and the purpose of the consultation. If you suggest documentation, what specifically would you document?

   a. You provide post-test counseling for people who test positive for sexually transmitted infections. You are meeting with a client, Joylynn, who has just tested positive for herpes. She has recently engaged in unprotected sexual activities with several partners. Joylynn knows how to contact some of her partners; however, other sexual partners were anonymous.

b. Hailee, a social work colleague at your agency, tells you that her supervisor has been "sexting," sending messages with sexualized jokes and pictures. Although Hailee seems distressed, she asks you not to tell anyone because she fears for her job.

c. You are working with Mr. Omaña, an 81-year-old client who has early-stage dementia. He does not want his children to know about his condition because he does not want to lose his independence. You are concerned that Mr. Omaña is at risk. He has described a number of concerning incidents, such as forgetting his oven was on (leading to a small fire in the kitchen) and forgetting to take medications that lower his blood pressure.

d. You are conducting a study on the effectiveness of a support group for children with impulse control challenges. One of the research participants, Akosh, is your child's best friend.

e. You are working with Ophelia, a client who recently experienced hearing loss due to meningitis. You are concerned that her sibling, Vern, is taking advantage of her emotionally and financially. Ophelia has full mental capacity. You discuss the possibility of a referral to adult protective services (APS). Ophelia asks you not to contact APS. She does not want to embarrass or upset Vern, her primary source of support.

f. You are in recovery and you attend the only Alcoholics Anonymous self-help group in your small town. One of your clients, Anders, starts attending the same AA group.

g. You are facilitating a social action group for people interested in pursuing antiracist advocacy. During one session, some group members start accusing one member, Bernard, of trying to sabotage the group by sidetracking them with extraneous issues. Bernard reports feeling intimidated and afraid.

h. You are cofacilitating family counseling sessions with another social worker, Mimi. You are concerned that Mimi is not competent to cofacilitate. She frequently self-discloses and does not respect clients' personal boundaries. You do not want to get Mimi in trouble; also, you do not want to put your clients or yourself at risk.

i. You work in hospice care. Ordinarily, you do not have difficulty working with people who have terminal illnesses. Recently, however, your oldest son, Chaoxiang, has been diagnosed with a brain tumor. His physicians advise that the tumor is inoperable and he has less than six months to live. You have overwhelming feelings of anguish and despair, making it very difficult to go to work and focus on your clients' needs.

j. You work in a residential treatment program for teenagers with eating disorders. The agency is considering a new program of activities for the psychoeducational group sessions that you facilitate. The program has never been used before, so you are concerned about whether the program is effective and whether there are any risks that you need to consider.

14

Conclusion

LEARNING OBJECTIVES

Upon successful completion of this introduction, you will be able to

- compare and contrast five approaches to integrating ethics in practice: legalism, deontology, teleology, virtue ethics, and narrative ethics;
- Apply futurism to anticipate and envision ethical opportunities as social work practice evolves **CONCLUSIONVIDEO** (including changes related to increased use of technology, practice across state and national borders, and interprofessional practice); and
- engage social workers and others in aspirational discussions about the future of social work practice and ethics.

Throughout this volume, we have explored how to integrate ethics in various contexts of social work practice, including practice with individuals, families, groups, organizations, and communities, as well as social work research and policy practice. Ethics is not merely about making decisions when faced with distinct ethical issues. Rather, ethics is embedded in our everyday practice (Banks, 2016). The first half of this chapter recaps five approaches to ethics: legalism, deontology, deontology, virtue ethics, and narrative ethics. Although we may have one or two preferred ways of incorporating ethics into practice, it is useful to understand how each approach works, including how we can integrate various models. By integrating various models, we are in a better position to strive for the highest ethical aspirations of the profession. The second half of this chapter introduces the concept of ethical futurism, an approach to envisioning opportunities and challenges for social work ethics in the coming years. Rather than simply focusing on the state of ethics and social work practice in the current moment, futurism encourages us to be proactive by imagining possible transformations in social work ethics. To advance social work ethics, we need to consider how social work is currently evolving and how it may continue to evolve. Rather than being satisfied with the status quo, we should think about a future of social work ethics that strives for even higher levels of ethical analysis, conversational engagement, and management of ethical issues.

APPROACHES TO ETHICS

The manner in which we define ethics affects how we think about ethical issues, how we evaluate what is morally right or appropriate, how we engage in ethics conversations with others, how we define who we are as moral beings, and how values and ethics shape our professional identities. When faced with ethical issues, we may desire clear, definitive answers about what to do and how to do it. Some ethical issues deserve clear, definitive answers. For instance, if a colleague asks whether it is ethical to lie to a client to benefit ourselves, we should respond clearly that this type of behavior is unethical because it is dishonest and self-serving. It also breaches our fiduciary commitment to our clients. Other ethical issues may not warrant singular, absolute answers. When faced with competing ethical principles such as client safety and client self-determination, for instance, we need to use professional judgment to prioritize these principles. When faced with **ethical dilemmas**, prudent social workers may have reasonable disagreements about the best way to proceed (Reamer, 2018a). One reason that we may reach different conclusions about how to proceed is because we are using different approaches to thinking about and managing ethical issues. Accordingly, to engage in ethical analysis and collaborative conversations with others, it is advantageous to understand, compare, and apply various approaches to ethics. It is also important to remain flexible, relinquishing the need for moral certainty and being open to others' perspectives (Churchill, 2020).

Moral intuition refers to our sense of right and wrong without thinking—or at least without taking time to think deliberately, consciously, or strategically (Haidt, 2013). When we rely on instincts, intuitions, feelings, or automatic thinking, we may be basing decisions on unconscious biases and cognitive distortions (Kahneman, 2011). As professionals, we should approach ethical issues with a more strategic, deliberative process. In other words, we need to slow down our thinking (Broadley, 2021). The approaches to ethics described throughout this volume (and summarized below) are designed to help us make better decisions, promoting ethics in all our interactions with clients, colleagues, research participants, and others with whom we engage in our professional practice.

A *legalistic approach* to ethics suggests that if there is a clear rule telling us how to act, then we should follow it (Dolgoff et al., 2012). These rules could stem from laws, agency policies, or ethical codes. As long as these laws, policies, and codes are based on good ethics, then following them should lead to ethical outcomes. Challenges arise, however, when these rules are not based on good ethics or when they provide conflicting guidance. Consider practicing under a law that requires us to discriminate against a particular class of people, while also operating under an ethical code that prohibits discrimination (NASW Code of Ethics, 2021, S.4.02). To resolve this type of issue, we need to go beyond simply following laws, agency policies, or ethical codes. We need to apply additional approaches to ethics to determine the best course of action.

Deontology and **teleology** are rational approaches to ethical decision making. These approaches ask us to put aside our feelings, faith beliefs, assumptions, and biases, so that we can apply principles, facts, and critical thinking in an unbiased manner. Deontology invites us to identify and apply universal ethical principles (Kant, 1779/1979). Within social work practice, these principles include showing respect for the dignity and worth of all people, acting with integrity, practicing within our areas of competence, fostering social justice, elevating service above self-interest, and promoting human relationships (NASW Code, Principles section). Other guiding principles include beneficence (doing good), nonmaleficence (do no harm), autonomy, and justice (Beauchamp & Childress, 2019).

Whereas deontology prioritizes *acting* ethically, teleology prioritizes the *conse-quences* of the act. According to teleology, we should consider various options for responding to an ethical issue and choose the option that creates the greatest good. When determining which option is best, we should consider both the potential benefits and the risks of each option. We should also consider who is most likely to experience the benefits and risks (e.g., our clients, ourselves, our agencies, or others). Classical teleologists suggest that we should choose the option that produces the greatest good for the greatest number (Bentham, 1823; Mill, 1863). From a social work perspective, however, our primary ethical obligation is to our client (NASW Code, S.1.01). We also have special obligations to serve the needs of people from vulnerable or disadvantaged groups (NASW Code, S.6.02[b]).

Although deontology and teleology lead to similar conclusions for some ethical issues, they can lead to significantly different conclusions for others. Consider the question of whether to be fully honest with a client who you believe is acting in a self-harmful manner. The client is sensitive to criticism and does not think she is engaging in self-harmful behavior. Applying deontology, you might decide that the primary guiding principle is to be honest, meaning that you should tell the client that you think she is engaging in self-harmful behavior. Applying teleology, you might decide that the consequences would be better if you withhold your honest opinion at this point. If you are fully honest, the client might respond in a defensive manner, perhaps terminating service and engaging in more severe self-harmful behavior. As this example demonstrates, different ethical approaches may lead to different decisions.

One criticism of deontology and teleology is that they can be manipulated to support predetermined decisions based on our initial intuitions, impulses, biases, or feelings (Anderson & Klamm, 2018). If we simply choose an ethics approach that justifies what we have already decided, then we are not truly engaging in rational decision making. Rather, we are cherry-picking arguments to support conclusions based on nonrational factors. Accordingly, we should strive for awareness of our intuitions, impulses, biases, and feelings at the outset of the decision-making process (Anderson & Klamm, 2018; Broadley, 2021). We can then engage in deliberate ethical reasoning, deciding which ethical principles, standards, or rules should be factored into our decision-making.

In contrast to the principle-based approaches of deontology and teleology, **virtue ethics** and **narrative ethics** embrace more holistic approaches. Rather than starting from the premise that we should make ethical decisions based impartial and rational analysis, virtue ethics and narrative ethics suggest that we should immerse ourselves in the situation. By immersing ourselves in the situation, we are not limited to applying universal principles in a dispassionate manner. Rather, we take our values, virtues, feelings, convictions, relationships, and social context into account. We also consider the values, virtues, feelings, and convictions of clients, family members, and others affected by the issue (Broadley, 2021). Although this approach takes feelings and intuition into account, it goes well beyond moral intuition. Virtue ethics and narrative ethics require us to raise awareness of the full range of factors affecting our perception and analysis of the ethical issues. By doing so, we can then make deliberate choices about what it means to respond in an ethical manner.

Virtue ethics suggests that we should identify and nurture virtues so that we can live true to them (Aristotle, 2013; Fowers et al, 2021). Virtues are enduring moral qualities, such as care, compassion, practice wisdom, generosity, integrity, and moral courage. Assume that you are working with an older adult who discloses that he is being abused by a neighbor, but does not want you to tell anyone. Virtue ethics suggests that you should be aware of your relationship with the client and contemplate what living your virtues means in this situation. As a caring social worker, you may respect the client's wishes—not because you are following prescribed laws, agency policies, ethical codes, or universal principles—but because respecting the client's wishes is an expression of caring. Further, because you are a caring professional, you offer the client additional forms of support (e.g., counseling, advocacy, or access to resources). Virtue ethics encourages us to be aware of our intuitions and feelings, using reflection, practice experience, and emotional intelligence to determine what we can learn from them (Broadley, 2021). Virtue ethics suggests that we go beyond our basic ethical obligations, integrating morality and aspirational ethics throughout our professional and personal lives.

Narrative ethics encourages us to approach ethical concerns by listening, interpreting, and responding to stories told by clients, coworkers, or others affected by the situation (Barsky, 2019b; Charon, 2007). Stories help us understand what others embrace as valuable and right, as well as what they deem contemptible and unethical (Brody & Clark, 2014). In the example of a client asking you not to report that he is being abused, listening to his full story helps you understand the context of his request. Assume that he shares stories about the cultural importance of keeping family matters private. Attending to his stories provides you with better understanding of the types of help deemed appropriate or inappropriate within his culture. You may also help him reconstruct his story, perhaps helping him see new ways of moving the family story forward and addressing his need for safety.

Remember that ethical issues exist within a social context. Accordingly, it is vital to engage our clients, colleagues, supervisors, and others in effective ethics conversations and conflict resolution processes. When faced with challenging ethical issues, we are not alone. Supervisors and consultants can help us apply various approaches to critical thinking. Further, they can help us raise awareness of our thoughts, feelings, and perspectives, as well as tuning into the thoughts, feelings, and perspectives of others affected by the ethical issue. Consulting with others not only helps us manage ethical issues more effectively, but also lends credence to our decisions.

FUTURIST ETHICS

Futurism refers to studying the future in order to anticipate, analyze, and prepare for coming changes (Nissen, 2014b). Futurists do not make predictions about *what will happen* in the future, but rather, explore *what might happen*. They use foresight strategies to consider and describe how particular phenomena may change or evolve (Association of Futurist Professionals, n.d.). Within the profession of social work, futurist ethics means exploring how social work practice and ethics might evolve and, perhaps, should evolve. Rather than assuming social work ethics will remain the same, futurism asks, "What do we want the future of social work ethics to be?" and "How can we move the theory and practice of social work forward with moral goodness?" Futurist ethics can help social work practitioners, agencies, and associations to be proactive in promoting ethical visions and addressing ethical issues on the horizon. By engaging various stakeholders in explorations about the future of social work practice and ethics, we can envision preferred futures and develop ideas about how to bring such futures to fruition; we can also anticipate unwanted futures and imagine ways of preventing them (Nissen, 2020a). By using moral imagination, we lay the groundwork for a future that aspires us to the highest values, virtues, and ethical principles of the profession.

One process for engaging in futurism is scanning the current situation and recent trends (Association of Futurist Professionals, n.d.). We can then extrapolate to consider various possibilities, opportunities, and challenges that we may encounter in future years. In terms of the future of social work ethics, consider the following trends:

- greater use of technology in social work practice, including the use of social robots, chatbots, virtual reality, and artificial intelligence (AI) (NASW et al., 2017; Persson et al., 2021);
- greater emphasis on interprofessional practice (Interprofessional Education Collaborative, 2016; Schot et al., 2020);
- increased backlash and opposition to social justice and antioppressive education and practice (Patterson et al., 2021; Pettit, 2021); and
- more opportunities for social work practice across state and national borders (Association of Social Work Boards, 2020).

In the following sections, we explore both challenges and opportunities for social work ethics in connection with each of these trends.

Technology in Social Work Practice

For many social workers, technology in practice means using electronic records, videoconferencing, secured email, or other communication technology to communicate with clients and professional colleagues. Increasingly, we see the use of social robots, chatbots (automated conversational agents), and apps employing artificial intelligence to engage clients in intakes, assessments, counseling, education, problem solving, advocacy, research, and other functions associated with social work practice. Proponents of technology suggest that technology can help us provide services more efficiently. Although some people question the ability of technology to provide human connection, emotion, compassion, and spontaneity, recent and emerging technologies are incorporating these qualities; research indicates that people can engage in meaningful communications and helping relationships with social robots, augmented reality, and chatbots (Darcy et al., 2021; Feng et al., 2020; Liu & Shyam, 2018).

When we envision how AI will be used in practice, we might imagine it taking over social work and putting social workers out of jobs. We can imagine, however, how AI and other new technology could instead foster new jobs for social workers (Mathiyazhagan, 2021). Consider, for instance, how tech social workers could help program social robots, how they could personalize social robots to work with particular individuals or diversity groups, and how they could ensure that social robot programming and design incorporate social work values and ethics.

The following list identifies particular risks of using technology in social work practice; as you review each risk, ponder ways that they could be prevented and how new opportunities for ethical practice could be enhanced.

- How can we ensure that technology does not dehumanize people? Critics of technology suggest that it can take away human agency and self-determination through processes such as covert surveillance, restricting communication, and indoctrinating people through repetitive conditioning of human behavior (Oviatt, 2021). To prevent dehumanization, we may work together with computer scientists and other developers to promote technology that enhances rather than detracts from human agency and self-determination (Leonhard, 2016). We may also advocate for agency and social policies that foster respect for the dignity and worth of all people, including their right to autonomy and their needs for human connection. Technology may be viewed as a tool for social work practice, not a replacement for it.

- How can we guard against disruption of services when technology fails? The more we depend on technology to provide social work services, the greater the risks of service interruption and abandoning clients in need when the technology fails. When implementing new technology to provide services, we should evaluate the stability and security of the technology. We should also have good backup plans should the technology fail. Consider a client who depends on a social robot for companionship, counseling, and guidance for managing depression or anxiety. What plans can be implemented to ensure that the client's needs are met if the social robot glitches or crashes (NASW et al., 2017)?
- When using technology to serve individuals, families, and small groups, how do we ensure the connection between the personal and political is not lost? Social work has a historic dual mission of enhancing individual well-being and promoting social justice (Hepworth et al., 2023). If a particular technology is designed solely for one purpose but not the other, then we may lose opportunities to integrate both purposes in our practice. For example, if a chatbot just helps clients on an individual basis, how would we ever know that significant numbers of clients are experiencing discrimination, trauma, or other phenomena that need addressing at an organizational, community, or national level. Accordingly, we could design technology to enhance the dual mission of social work rather than detract from it. Consider, for instance, the use of metadata, particularly using data collected for one purpose for additional purposes. Upon consent of clients, data collected in the course of their interactions with technology could be used to identify trends, problems, and challenges. Social workers could then use this data to promote social justice through advocacy, community organization, and other macro strategies. One advantage of using metadata is that it can be collected on an aggregate and anonymous basis, protecting clients' privacy while also allowing us to use this information to promote social justice and other social changes.

When envisioning the future of technology in social work, we should consider not only what ethical challenges might arise, but also opportunities that can enhance ethical practice and moral societies.

- How can technology promote greater privacy and confidentiality for clients? Some clients might feel safer conversing with a social robot than with a person, particularly if they know that the technology has secure privacy protections and that they are in control of what information is shared and with whom. We could ensure, for instance, that technology providers and government agencies are not mining, exploiting, or selling confidential information (Goldkind et al, 2020). We could also explore new forms of security precautions, going beyond current practices such as strong passwords and encrypted data to guard against unauthorized access to client information (Cottone et al., 2022). For clients who feel safer conversing with a person rather than a robot, we could continue to offer social work services without robots or other technology.

- How can technology promote greater access to social work services? One opportunity to enhance access to social work services is to make use of technology to manage some of the more mundane and repetitive tasks, freeing up social workers to have more time to serve clients and focus on higher-level tasks and functions. Another opportunity to promote access to social work services is to ensure access to technology, particularly among groups experiencing poverty, discrimination, and other barriers to access (NASW Code, S.1.05[e]).

- How can we use technology to screen for risks such as suicide, homicide, child abuse, or intimate partner abuse? If we make greater use of technology to engage clients in various helping processes, one concern is that the technology may miss risks that a social worker may have identified. Alternatively, we could program chatbots or other technology to incorporate risk screening so the concerns are identified and managed in a timely manner (Barsky, 2020b). Technology can make use of algorithms based on evidence-based risk and resilience factors. One concern about using algorithms to identify risk is that they may be based on biases against particular racial, ethnic, or other diversity groups (Gillingham, 2019). Thus, it will be important for risk-screening technology and algorithms to take culture and diversity into account. Further, rather than allowing technology to take full responsibility for assessing risk, we could have social workers and other professionals use the technology as just one of their tools for assessing risk.

These questions are not meant to provide an exhaustive list for envisioning how technology can promote ethical practice, but rather, to provide some examples of how we might think about technology in an aspirational manner. Note that technology should be seen as a tool that people use, not as a replacement for humans (Leonhard, 2016). Rather than allowing technology to make ethics decisions for us, we may use technology to help us make good ethical decisions.

Some of these issues and possibilities may seem vast, complicated, or distant from our day-to-day practice and the ethical issues that we are likely to face in the immediate future. Still, if we want to have a say in whether and how particular technologies are going to be used with our clients and communities, then it is vital that we participate in these thought processes and conversations. As anthropologist Margaret Mead is often quoted as saying, "Never doubt that a small group of thoughtful, committed people can change the world." As a social work student, you are being taught to question the status quo and seek new ways of improving practice. Accordingly, you are in a great position to consider new ways for technology to promote ethical practice.

Interprofessional Practice

Social work values human relationships (NASW Code, Principles Section), including relationships with other professionals. Although we have long worked with other professionals for the benefit of our clients, there is a trend toward greater integration of the professions in various fields of practice, including health and mental health (Pakkanen et al., 2021). When working with people from other professions, we may experience ethical conflicts related to the different functions, ethical and legal requirements, and power dynamics between professionals. Although interprofessional practice may give rise to many ethical challenges, it may also spawn many ethical opportunities. During interprofessional practice, we can learn from one another, including different ways that our ethical obligations can be put into practice. With the growth of interprofessional education, we are being socialized to appreciate the contributions of each profession. We are also learning how to communicate and resolve conflicts more effectively (Interprofessional Education Collaborative, 2016). Moving forward, it may be helpful to develop interprofessional codes of ethics or practice standards, providing guidance on how to manage ethics in an interprofessional context (Neal et al., 2021). An interprofessional code of ethics could highlight the values, ethical principles, and standards that various professionals have in common, as well as identifying areas in which each of the professions differ. Interprofessional practice standards could provide guidance on how the interprofessional team (including the client and family members) can communicate and engage in problem solving to manage ethical conflicts that may arise.

Social Justice and Antioppressive Social Work

In the 2021 revisions to the NASW Code of Ethics, the following language was added in Standard 1.05(b) to strengthen social work's commitment to challenge oppression and promote social justice.

> Social workers must take action against oppression, racism, discrimination, and inequities, and acknowledge personal privilege.

This language reflects other trends in social work education and practice, including greater emphasis on diversity, **equity**, inclusion, and antiracist practice (Council on Social Work Education, 2022; Finn, 2021). At the same time that social work is formulating stronger commitments to challenge racism, sexism, homophobia, ablism, and other forms of oppression and discrimination, there is also a backlash against these efforts, particularly from political conservatives (Patterson et al., 2021). Some states have passed laws prohibiting teaching or trainings related to critical race theory, systemic racism, unconscious bias, privilege, discrimination, or oppression (Pettit, 2021; Ray & Gibbons, 2021). This backlash could affect social work programs and jobs. Governments opposed to anti-oppression practice could defund social work programs that incorporate anti-oppression training and practice (Lauer, 2021); governments and other funding bodies that oppose anti-oppression training and practice could also refuse to hire social workers who embrace these frameworks. From an ethics perspective, we have an ethical obligation to confront oppression, but our programs and jobs may be endangered if we engage in anti-oppression training or practice.

So, where are the opportunities for enhancing social work ethics in this social and political environment? The fact that society is talking about racism and other forms of oppression is a good thing. Sometimes, having backlash against a social movement means that the movement is making progress. If we want to make fundamental change, then backlash may be part of the process. To advance the ethical principles of **social justice** and anti-oppression, we will need to understand the nature of political backlash and how to work through it (della Porta, 2020). Doing what is right ethically is not necessarily easy (Papouli, 2019). We will need moral courage, allies, and long-term strategies to see the processes of social reform through to fruition.

Practice Across State and National Borders

With the advent of videoconferencing and other communication technologies, more and more social workers are practicing across state and national borders (Mathiyazhagan, 2021; NASW et al., 2017). In terms of clinical practice, more social workers have licensure in more than one state so they can provide services to clients in different locations (ASWB, 2020). Along with the increased opportunities for interstate and international social work come a number of ethics challenges. For instance, how can we ensure against social work colonizing (Mathiyazhagan, 2021), exploiting other countries by having foreign social workers take control of social work services and imposing their own practices, ethics, and values?

Assume that I am designing an international crisis intervention service, using videoconferencing and other technology to provide services around the globe. I could train all the service providers based on a single practice model supported by current research. Given economies of scale from serving such a large catchment area, I could offer services at lower prices than local service providers. Although my plan promotes a key social work principle—access to services—it ignores other ethical principles. Particularly, my plan infringes the principle of respect for the dignity and worth of all people. I have not incorporated **cultural humility** and I have not considered the impact on local service providers and social justice. I need to rethink whether a global crisis intervention service can be implemented in an ethical manner, taking the views of other countries and cultures into account. I could also consider partnering with people and programs in other countries rather than imposing services from the outside.

In terms of ethics opportunities, we have national codes of ethics and an international statement of ethical principles (IFSW, 2018). We could build on these documents, adding more specific guidance on the ethics of cross-border practice: how can we ensure that our practices are welcomed and culturally informed; how can we deal with conflicts that may arise between the laws, norms, and ethical codes of different countries; and how can we promote social justice when expanding services into different countries or regions?

In terms of the interface between legal and ethical issues, social workers practicing across state or national boundaries may run into conflicts in the laws of the jurisdiction where they are located and the jurisdiction where the client is located. What may be reportable as child or elder abuse in one jurisdiction may not be considered child or elder abuse in another. The age of consent to services in one jurisdiction may be different from that in another. With the growth of cross-border practice, various states and countries may be motivated to harmonize their laws. As social workers, we can help identify how conflicting law inhibit good practice and promote law reforms designed to enhance ethical practice.

CLOSING ASPIRATIONS

As you have worked through this volume and your ethics course, I hope you have learned many tools that can help you identify, analyze, discuss, and manage a broad range of ethical situations and challenges that may arise in practice. When deciding how to manage particular ethical issues, use the skills that you have been developing in all your courses: self-awareness, empathy, genuineness, respect, flexibility, active listening, communicating clearly, building trust, collaborating, problem-solving, being creative, and building on strengths (Churchill, 2020).

As we have discovered throughout this volume, ethical practice is not simply about finding the right answers to particular ethical issues. Often, ethical practice starts with being aware of potential ethical issues and asking good questions. I sincerely hope that you will continue to ask good ethics questions throughout your professional career. I hope you will ponder how social work values, virtues, and ethical principles apply in all your interactions with clients, research participants, supervisors, coworkers, and others with whom you practice. And finally, I hope that you will inspire others to strive for what is good and moral, however they define these terms.

The following points summarize six perspectives that you may take into account as you ponder what ethical practice means in a particular situation.

- From a legalistic perspective, we should follow laws, agency policies, and ethical codes that are intended to promote good practice.

- From a deontological perspective, we should identify universal principles or ethical imperatives and act in accordance with them.
- From a teleological perspective, we should explore various courses of action and choose the course of action that produces the best consequences.
- From the virtue ethics perspective, the flourishing life[1] is one in which we embrace and live our moral virtues.
- From a narrative ethics perspective, we should listen closely to one another's stories, demonstrating understanding, identifying ethical issues, and determining how to construct the next steps of the story in an ethical manner.

An integrated approach to ethical practice requires not only critical thinking, but also critical reflection, self-awareness, humility, consultation, and collaboration with others (McAuliffe & Chenoweth, 2008). We may not always agree about which ethics approaches to use or how to apply them when managing a particular ethical issue. Still, we can engage with one another with respect, honesty, compassion, joy, and the will to be guided by our core values, virtues, and ethics.

DISCUSSION QUESTIONS AND EXERCISES

1. *Preference*: Which of the following approaches to ethics do you think that you will rely upon most as a professional social worker: legalism, deontology, teleology, virtue ethics, or narrative ethics? Why do you think this approach will be most useful? What are the advantages and disadvantages of this approach?

2. *Remember*: What are three key points that you have learned about social work ethics from this textbook and your coursework? Describe why these points are important and give examples of how they will affect you as a professional social worker.

3. *Questions*: What are two key questions that you still have regarding social work ethics? Your questions may be related to information from this textbook that could use further clarification, specific ethical issues that you are still pondering, or additional strategies that you would like to learn in order to enhance your ability to manage ethical issues.

4. *Using Foresight*: Select one of the following topics: dual relationships, cultural humility, self-care, honesty in social media, end-of-life decision making, genome editing, abortion, children's rights, global climate change, or religious freedom. Identify current trends and future possibilities for how that topic may evolve, particularly in relation to social work practice and ethics. What are some of the future ethical risks

---

1. Or as decluttering expert Maria Kondo might suggest, the life that "sparks joy."

for which social work should be planning? Envision and describe how the profession of social work could promote ethical practice in relation to this issue.

5. *Envisioning a New Code*: Select a particular section of the NASW Code of Ethics (e.g., 1.01 on primary commitment to clients, 1.03 on informed consent, 1.05 on cultural competence, 1.07 on confidentiality, 6.04 on social and political action). Brainstorm ways in which this section of the code might be revised. Consider recent trends and how social work could be practiced differently in the future. Using your moral imagination, develop a revised version of your section. As you compose your revised section, do not be concerned about whether your revision is worded perfectly. Focus on writing a standard that is inspiring and creative.

6. *Imagine*: Imagine a just future—for your community, for your country, or for the world. What would be different? How would we know the future is more just? What is one novel action that you could take to help facilitate a just future?

7. *Self-Efficacy Assessment*: Consider the following ethics competencies. Rate your ability to put each competency into practice: (1) could use improvement; (2): moderately competent; (3) very competent.
   a. Identify ethical issues and ask good questions
   b. Engage with supervisors or others for consultation
   c. Practice critical thinking (applying various approaches to managing ethical issues: legalism, deontology, teleology, virtue ethics, and narrative ethics)
   d. Raise awareness of your own intuitions, thoughts, feelings, values, and perspectives
   e. Demonstrate empathy for the thoughts, feelings, values, and perspectives of others
   f. Ask probing questions
   g. Engage with others in constructive communication and conflict resolution
   h. Be flexible in situations of ethical uncertainty
   i. Use creativity and imagination in problem solving
   j. Listen to stories and deconstruct them
   k. Implement decisions and follow through on commitments
   l. Monitor implementation and identify needs for follow-up on ethical concerns

For each of the competencies that you rated as a (1), describe what you can do to enhance your ability to demonstrate this competency.

absolutism an approach to ethical analysis based on applying fixed rules to all cases, regardless of the circumstances (cf. relativism)

agency policies behavioral guidelines created by an agency and enforced by an agency. In some situations, agency policies can be enforced through court proceedings.

autonomy and freedom the ethical principle of promoting liberty, choice, self-determination, or independence; uninhibited by restriction or control from the state or others

beneficence ethical principle of doing good (cf. nonmaleficence)

boundary crossing an act of a professional that departs from the usual norms or expectations of the professional–client relationship, whether or not the client is harmed by the deviation from standard practice (e.g., offering a client money in an emergency situation to pay for food)

boundary violation an act of a professional that deviates from the usual or normal expectations of the professional–client relationship and harms the client or puts the client at significant risk of harm (e.g., pressuring a client to lend money)

case law the body of legal principles that develop over time through the decisions of judges in individual cases (also called "common law")

certification a form of accrediting professionals by officially stating that the professional has met certain standards of education, training, or competence

communitarianism a philosophy emphasizing the social rights and responsibilities that people owe one another within a community, family, culture, or other group, recognizing that individual rights and interests need to be balanced with those of the larger group

confidentiality the ethical principle of protecting a client's privacy, keeping personal information private unless the client consents to disclosure

conflict of interest situation in which a social worker or other person in a position of trust is perceived to have contradictory or competing obligations, often as a result of dual or multiple relationships (e.g., competing professional and personal interests)

conflict resolution any process aimed at helping two or more parties manage differences between them (e.g., negotiation, mediation, or advocacy)

consequentialism theory of moral decision-making by weighing the consequences of various options; teleology (cf., deontology, virtue ethics)

cultural competence possessing skills, knowledge, self-awareness, respect, and commitment to serve clients from diverse backgrounds in an appropriate and effective manner (taking the client's background, language, values, beliefs, worldviews, rituals, norms, and experiences of discrimination or oppression into account)

cultural humility an approach to working with people from diverse backgrounds by treating them as experts in their own lives and cultures, learning from them, critically reflecting on one's own beliefs and cultural identities, engaging in self-correction for biases, and committing to lifelong learning

damages harm experienced; in civil lawsuits, damages also refer to compensation for harm suffered

deontology an approach to analyzing ethical issues by applying fixed duties (moral principles or categorical imperatives), as opposed to looking at specific situations and the consequences of various options (cf. teleology, virtue ethics)

dual (multiple) relationships having two (or more) types of affiliations with a client (e.g., a social worker who is also a friend or customer of the client)

duty an obligation to act in a particular manner (e.g., to follow particular laws, ethical obligations, agency policies, social norms, or family customs)

egalitarianism a social philosophy by which people are treated equally, without discriminating on the basis of age, gender, socioeconomic status, or other factors

equality and inequality the principle of treating people equally or the same if they come from similar situations, and also allowing for differential treatment when people come from different situations, to ensure fairness or equal opportunity for all (e.g., affirmative action programs at universities for applicants from certain groups that have been deprived of a good primary education)

equity the principle of treating everyone in a fair or socially just manner

ethic a principle, guideline, or standard that indicates whether certain types of behaviors are right or wrong

ethical breach contravention or infringement of an ethical standard

ethical decision making a problem-solving process in which one or more decision makers identify ethical issues and work through a strategic process of analyzing the issues in order to reach a decision concerning the best way to respond (may be based on an analysis of laws, rules, principles, ethics, duties, values, beliefs, virtues, or other factors)

ethical dilemma a situation marked by a difficult choice in how to respond, given that there are conflicting ethical standards, no completely satisfactory option for resolving the ethical concerns, or a lack of clear direction about what is ethically appropriate

ethical issue a situation in which stakeholders need to make decisions about how to respond in light of their ethical obligations (may include questions about how to deal with ethical breaches or ethical dilemmas)

ethical standards guidelines for ethical behavior that are based upon more general ethical principles

ethics a system of principles and standards that guide judgments and behavior based upon a set of morals and values (cf. values, morals); the study of the right conduct, moral duties, good character, and the good life

ethics of care an approach to ethics based on the virtue of caring, emphasizing the importance of relationships and emotional responses in how professionals or others make moral and ethical decisions

fiduciary a relationship based on trust in which professionals with power or control over others have special ethical obligations or higher standards of care in order to respect their positions of trust

gray area a situation in which there is no single, clear, and right way of responding to an ethical issue; a matter in which there is ethical uncertainty or ambiguity

honesty the quality of being forthright, truthful, and law abiding

illegal or illicit unlawful, against the law, in contravention of criminal law

immunity legal protection against being sued (e.g., social workers who report suspicions of child abuse are protected from litigation as long as their decisions to report were made in good faith)

integrity the quality of being honest, responsible, reliable, true, transparent, and consistent in relation to one's primary values and ethics

jurisdiction a legally defined geographic area such as a city, county, state, or country within which a government is empowered to pass laws over certain types of issues (e.g., in the United States, states have primary authority to pass laws regulating the health and mental health professions)

justice the quality of fair treatment of individuals; an equitable sharing of rights, responsibility, resources, costs, benefits, and risks; conforming to legal rules or moral standards (cf. social justice)

justifiable an act that may be accepted as right or ethical based upon sound reasoning and judgments

law a system of rules that is passed by the state and enforced by the state (cf. ethics, morals, values)

least harm the ethical principle of choosing a course of action that poses the least damage or injury, particularly when there is no choice that eliminates the risk of harm altogether

legalism an approach to dealing with ethical concerns by following relevant laws, agency policies, or codes of ethics (cf., deontology, teleology, narrative ethics)

liable responsible; subject to criminal charges or civil lawsuits to recover damages for harm caused

libertarianism a social philosophy emphasizing individual liberty and seeking to diminish or abolish control by the state or other social forces (cf. egalitarianism, communitarianism)

licensure a method of regulating professionals by limiting the right to practice to people who have completed certain courses and tests, or who have demonstrated certain types of competence

malpractice poor or shoddy practice; professional negligence; failure of a professional to exercise a reasonable standard of care or perform services in a manner reasonably expected of a prudent professional of similar background in similar circumstances, resulting in harm to the client

mandatory compulsory (e.g., required by law or agency policy)

mental capacity the ability of a person to think, reason, and remember; used by professionals to assess the ability of clients to provide informed consent (cf. mental competence)

mental competence a legal status, determined by the judge, that a person is able to enter into contracts or provide informed consent (antonym: mental incompetence)

moral courage the internal strength to do what is ethical or right, even when there are pressures that make it difficult to do so

moral distress a situation in which a person knows how to act ethically, but there is pressure on the person to act unethically

354 ESSENTIAL ETHICS FOR SOCIAL WORK PRACTICE

morals a system of rules and principles that defines appropriate and inappropriate behavior for an individual, family, community, or other social unit (cf. ethics, values)

narrative ethics an approach to dealing with ethical concerns by listening, interpreting, and responding to the stories told by clients, coworkers, other people affected by the situation (cf., deontology, teleology, legalism)

nonmaleficence the ethical principle of not causing harm; avoiding actions that may hurt others (cf., beneficence, least harm)

principle a general guide for conduct, such as a professional's ethical principles or an individual's moral principles (cf. rule; standard)

privacy the right to control over one's own personal information, including what is shared or not shared with others

privilege a legal principle suggesting that information gathered within a confidential relationship should not be compellable in court (to determine when privilege arises, refer to applicable case law and legislation)

professional an individual who, through education and training, possesses specialized knowledge and skills, and agrees to abide by a code of ethics and standards of practice established by the profession

proportionality an ethical principle used to promote egalitarianism by ensuring that policy makers strike a balance between the benefits, costs, and risks experienced by different groups in an organization, community, or society

protection of life the ethical principle promoting preservation of all human beings, shielding people from acts or conditions that may cause death or put their lives at risk; preserving and prolonging life, regardless of the economic cost or resulting quality of life (cf. quality of life)

qualified immunity legal protection from being sued or held legally liable for conduct performed within specific governmental positions (e.g., child protection workers, judges, police)

quality of life the ethical principle of promoting the general welfare of people, including physical and mental health, happiness, spiritual fulfillment, family and social support, job satisfaction, clean environment, and so on (cf. protection of life)

records progress notes, psychosocial assessments, psychosocial test results, videos, drawings, or any other documentation of the practitioner's work or professional interactions with a client (including paper and digital records)

registration a voluntary system of professional regulation in which people may file their names and list their professional training, skills, or other credentials so that employers, clients, or other service users are aware of their stated professional backgrounds

relativism an approach to ethical analysis that explores the consequences of actions in particular circumstances, rather than applying fixed duties (or moral rules) that apply to all situations (cf. absolutism)

responsible having a legal, moral, or ethical obligation; accountable for one's actions or the consequences of one's actions

restorative justice a system of responding to crime or misbehavior by repairing harm, restoring people to their prior situations, and fostering healing rather than punishment and retribution

risk-benefit management making decisions and plans based on a strategic assessment of the potential benefits and risks of various courses of action (cf. risk management)

risk management making strategic decisions and plans to pre-empt harm, to reduce harm, or to reduce the negative consequences of a harmful event (cf. risk-benefit management)

rule a specific behavioral guideline, often with consequences for violations (cf., principle, standard)

rule of law legally defined mandates, requirements, or prohibitions regulating behavior in a nation or society

self-awareness consciousness of one's own thoughts, feelings, attitudes, beliefs, morals, motivations, social identities, and behaviors; internal reflection

social justice equity and fair treatment in society, including equitable division of resources, access to the necessities of life, freedom from discrimination, social and political inclusion, and maximizing opportunities for people to fulfill their potentials

standard a guideline for appropriate behavior; general expectations of behavior for professionals (as in a code of ethics; cf, rule, principle)

standard of care the expected behavior of a particular practitioner based upon what would usually be expected of a similar professional acting prudently, under similar circumstances

subpoena a written mandate requiring a person to testify in court and/or to turn over records and other documents to be used as evidence in court

teleology an approach to analyzing ethical issues by looking at the situation and consequences of various options, rather than simply applying fixed rules or moral duties to all situations (cf. consequentialism, deontology, virtue ethics)

title protection a method of regulating professions by mandating that only people with certain educational backgrounds may use a specific professional name (e.g., in some jurisdictions, only people with an MSW or BSW may call themselves social workers)

transparency the principle of openness (e.g., by providing clients or the public with access to relevant information about decisions made, including the decision-maker's reasoning)

truthfulness and full disclosure an ethical principle promoting an honest and open sharing of information; candor (e.g., providing a client with complete, accurate information about the client's condition and intervention choices)

utilitarianism a consequentialist approach to ethical analysis by comparing the potential benefits and costs of different courses of action, and prioritizing the greatest good for the greatest number of people (cf. deontology, absolutism, teleology)

values core preferences or ideals about what is good or important (cf. ethics, morals)

virtue ethics an approach to ethics emphasizing character traits for leading the good life, for instance, honesty, moderation, and generosity (cf. deontology, teleology, ethics of care, narrative ethics)

virtues enduring moral qualities such as caring, temperance, honesty, and respect

voluntary decisions or choices made without undue influence from friends, family, employers, or other sources, and without coercion by the law or legal systems

BIBLIOGRAPHY

Abe, J. (2020). Beyond cultural competence, toward social transformation: Liberation psychologies and the practice of cultural humility. *Journal of Social Work Education*, 56(4), 696-707. https://doi.org/10.1080/10437797.2019.1661911

Agheorghiesei, T., Dabija, M., & Copoeru, I. (2014). An ethical approach to accreditation standards for hospitals in Romania: The need for ethics audit to improve the quality of care for patients. *Revista Romana de Bioetica*, 1(2), 70–83.

Ahmed, A., Ali, N., Azis, S., Abd-alrazaq, A., Hassan, A., Khalifa, M., Elhusein, B., Ahmed, M., Ahmed, M., & Househ, M. (2021). A review of mobile chatbot apps for anxiety and depression and their self-care features. *Computer Methods and Programs in Biomedicine Update*. https://doi.org/10.1016/j.cmpbup.2021.100012

Alegre, I., Berbegal-Mirabent, J., Guerrero, A., & Mas-Machuca, M. (2018). The real mission of the mission statement: A systematic review of the literature. *Journal of Management & Organization*, 24(4), 456–473. https://doi.org/10.1017/jmo.2017.82

Alonso, D. (2016). Social work and technology: Acceptance and use among professionals in training. Doctoral dissertation (translated from Spanish). Universidad Complutense de Madrid.

Alston, M., Hazeleger, T., & Hargreaves, D. (2019). *Social work and disasters: A handbook for practice*. Routledge.

American Association for People with Disabilities. (n.d.). https://www.aapd.com

American Association of Sexuality Educators, Counselors, and Therapists. (2020). *Code of ethics for AASECT certified members*. https://www.aasect.org/sites/default/files/documents/Code%20of%20Conduct%2011.2020.pdf

American Bar Association. (2020). Qualified immunity. https://www.americanbar.org/groups/public_education/publications/insights-on-law-and-society/volume-21/issue-1/qualified-immunity

Americans with Disabilities Act (ADA). (1990). Pub. L. No. 101–336, 104 Stat. 328.

Andersen, M., & Klamm, B. (2018). Haidt's social intuitionist model: What are the implications for accounting ethics education? *Journal of Accounting Education*, 44, 35–46. https://doi.org/10.1016/j.jaccedu.2018.05.001

Anderson, K. (2015). Victims' voices and victims' choices in three IPV courts. *Violence Against Women*, 21(1), 105–124.

Appleton, C. (2010). *Integrity matters: An inquiry into social workers' understandings* (unpublished master's thesis). School of Health and Social Services, Massey University, Palmerston North, New Zealand.

Arczynski, A., & Morrow, S. (2017). The complexities of power in feminist multicultural psychotherapy supervision. *Journal of Counseling Psychology, 64*(2), 192–205.

Aristotle. (2013). *Eudemian ethics.* Cambridge University Press.

Asakura, K., & Maurer, K, (2018). Attending to justice in clinical social work: Supervision as a pedagogical space. *Clinical Social Work Journal, 46*, 289–297.

Ash, A. (2016). *Whistleblowing and ethics in health and social care.* Jessica Kingsley.

Association of Futurist Professionals. (n.d.) Vision. https://www.apf.org/page/MissionVision

Association of Social Work Boards (ASWB). (2020). Social work practice mobility by the numbers. https://www.aswb.org/social-work-practice-mobility-by-the-numbers

Association of Social Work Boards (ASWB). (n.d.). Licenses. https://www.aswb.org/licenses

Assor, Y., & Goodman, Y. (2020). Beyond ethics: Professionalism and social belonging in social workers' moral deliberations, *Ethnos, 85*(1), 168–187. https://doi.org/10.1080/00141844.2019.1575889

Augusterfer, E., Mollica, R., & Lavelle, J. (2018). Leveraging technology in post-disaster settings: The role of digital health/telemental health. *Current Psychiatry Reports, 20*, 88–96. https://doi.org/10.1007/s11920-018-0953-4

Baker, E., Geiderman, J., Kraus, C., & Goett, R. (2020). The role of hospital ethics committees in emergency medicine practice. *Journal of Medical Ethics and History of Medicine, 9*. https://doi.org/10.1002/emp2.12136

Banks, S. (2012). *Ethics and values in social work* (4th ed.). Palgrave Macmillan.

Banks, S. (2016). Everyday ethics in professional life: Social work as ethics work. *Ethics and Social Welfare, 10*(1), 35–52. https://doi.org/10.1080/17496535.2015.1126623

Barsky, A. E. (2012). *Clinicians in court: A guide to subpoenas, depositions, testifying, and everything else you need to know* (2nd ed.). Guilford Press.

Barsky, A. E. (2017a). *Conflict resolution for the helping professions* (3rd ed.). Oxford University Press.

Barsky, A. E. (2017b). Social work practice and technology: Ethical issues and policy responses. *Journal of Technology in Human Services, 35*(1), 1–12.

Barsky, A. E. (2019a). *Ethics and values in social work: An integrated approach for a comprehensive curriculum* (2nd ed.). Oxford University Press.

Barsky, A. E. (2019b). Narrative ethics in social work practice. In S. Marson and McKinney, R. (Eds.). *The Routledge handbook of social work ethics and values* (pp.51–57). Routledge.

Barsky, A. E. (2020a). Ethics alive! Responding to NASW's professional review process. *The New Social Worker, 27*(1), 4–6. http://www.socialworker.com/topics/allan_barsky

Barsky, A. E. (2020b). Reporting and other ethical obligations of automated clinical interventions. *Journal of Social Work Values and Ethics, 17*(2), 78–84. https://jswve.org/download/2020-2/2020-2-articles/78-Automated-clinical-interventions-17-2-Fall-2020-JSWVE.pdf

Barsky, A. E. (2020c). Serious imminent harm to non-identifiable others: Updated exceptions to confidentiality. *Journal of Baccalaureate Social Work, 23*, 342–353. https://doi.org/10.18084/1084-7219.23.1.341

Barsky, A. E. (2020d). Sexuality-and gender-inclusive genograms: Avoiding heteronormativity and cisnormativity. *Journal of Social Work Education, 56*(4), 1–11. https://doi.org/10.1080/10437797.2020.1852637

Barsky, A. E., Carnahan, B., & Spadola, C. (2021). Licensing complaints: Experiences of social workers in investigation processes. *Journal of Social Work Values and Ethics, 18*(2),

29–42. https://jswve.org/download/2021-2/8-Licensing-Complaints-Experiences-of-Social-Workers-in-Investigation-Processes-JSWVE-18-2-2021.pdf

Barsky, A. E., & Northen, H. (2017). Ethical challenges and opportunities in social work with groups. In C. D. Garvin, L. M. Gutiérrez, & M. J. Galinsky (Eds.), *Handbook of social work with groups* (pp. 74–92). Guilford Press.

Barsky, A. E., & Spadola, C. (2022). "Don't shame me; Walk with me:" The impact of sanctions for social work licensing violations. *Advances in Social Work, 21*(4). 1300–1315. https://doi.org/10.18060/25190.

Bartol, C., & Bartol, A. (2018). *Psychology and law, research and practice* (2nd ed.). SAGE.

Beauchamp, T. L., & Childress, J. F. (2022). *Principles of biomedical ethics* (8th ed.). Oxford University Press.

Beer, M. (2021). *Civil resistance tactics in the 21st century*. International Center for Nonviolent Conflict. https://www.nonviolent-conflict.org/icnc-publications

Bentham, J. (1823). *An introduction to the principles of morals and legislation*. http://www.laits.utexas.edu/poltheory/bentham/ipml/ipml.c01.html

Berger, J., & Miller, D. (2021). Health disparities, systemic racism, and failures of cultural competence. *American Journal of Bioethics, 21*(9), 4–10. https://doi.org10.1080/15265161.2021.1915411

Berling, E., McLeskey, C., O'Rourke, M., & Pennock, R. (2019). Internalized values rather than externally imposed rules: A new method for a virtue-based responsible conduct of research curriculum. *Science & Engineering Ethics, 25*(3), 899–910. https://doi.org/10.1007/s11948-017-9991-2

Bertram, B. (2017). How Jane Addams expands our view of education as an ethical enterprise. *Educational Theory, 67,* 677–692.

Bharara, P. (2019). *Doing justice: A prosecutor's thoughts on crime, punishment, and the rule of law*. Alfred A. Knopf.

Bibus, A. (2015). Supererogation in social work: Deciding whether to go beyond the call of duty. *Journal of Social Work Values and Ethics, 12*(2), 27–40.

Bloor, M. (2010). The researcher's obligation to bring about good. *Qualitative Social Work, 9*(1), 17–20.

Boaz, D. (2015). *The libertarian mind*. Simon & Schuster.

Boland-Prom, K. (2009). Results from a national study of social workers sanctioned by state licensing boards. *Social Work, 54*(4), 351–360. https://doi.org/10.1093/sw/54.4.351

Boland-Prom, K., Johnson, J., & Gunaganti, G. (2015). Sanctioning patterns of social work licensing boards, 2000 to 2009. *Journal of Human Behavior in the Social Environment, 25*(2), 126–136.

Borkosky, B. G. (2020). Responding to subpoenas: Written objections. *Professional Psychology: Research and Practice, 51*(4), 352–361.

Bouter, L. (2020). What research institutions can do to foster research integrity. *Science and Engineering Ethics, 26,* 2363–2369. https://doi.org/10.1007/s11948-020-00178-5

Boyd, C., & Timpe, K. (2021). *The virtues: A very short introduction*. Oxford University Press.

Bragg, N. (2022). Social justice in social work: A foundational understanding. In L. Rapp-McCall, K. Corcoran, & A. Roberts (Eds.), *Social workers' desk reference* (pp. 84–90). Oxford University Press.

Bright, C. (2021). Social work and environmental justice. *Social Work Research, 45*(4), 227–220. https://doi.org/10.1093/swr/svab024

Broadley, K. (2021). Applied ethics for child protection: What would Aristotle say? *Ethics and Social Welfare*, *15*(2), 135–150. https://doi.org/10.1080/17496535.2020.1859578

Brody, H., & Clark, M. (2014). Narrative ethics: A narrative. *Hastings Center Report*, *44*(1), S7–11.

Bryan, V., Sanders, S., & Kaplan, L. (2022). *The helping professional's guide to ethics*. Oxford University Press.

Buddhist Centre. (n.d.). What is meditation? Retrieved March 23, 2022. https://thebuddhistcentre.com/text/what-meditation

Butz v. Economou. (1978). 438 U.S. 478, 512–13 (United States Supreme Court).

Calden, D. (2020). Social work supervisors as gatekeepers (doctoral dissertation). Walden University. https://scholarworks.waldenu.edu/cgi/viewcontent.cgi?article=10138&context=dissertations

Caldwell, B. (2017). *Preparing for the California clinical social work law and ethics exam*. Ben Caldwell Labs.

Camper, A. (2020). Social worker's disclosure responsibilities during the pandemic. *National Association of Social Workers*. https://www.socialworkers.org/LinkClick.aspx?fileticket=6KIPl8ArqZ8%3d&portalid=0

Camper, A., & Felton, E. (2021). COVID-19: Legal considerations for resuming in-person services: What about vaccination requirements. *National Association of Social Workers*. https://www.socialworkers.org/About/Legal/COVID-19-Legal-Resources/COVID-19-Legal-Considerations-for-Resuming-In-Person-Services

Canda, E., Furman, L., & Canda, H. (2020). *Spiritual diversity in social work practice: The heart of helping* (3rd ed.). Oxford University Press.

Card, A.J. (2020). What is ethically informed risk management? *American Medical Association Journal of Ethics*, *22*(11), E965–975. https://doi.org/10.1001/amajethics.2020.965

Carey, M., & Bell, S. (2021). Universal credit, lone mothers, and poverty: Some ethical challenges for social work with children and families. *Ethics and Social Welfare*, *16*(1), 3–18. https://doi.org/10.1080/17496535.2021.1939756

Carlson, J., Nguyen, H., & Reinardy, J. (2016). Social justice and the capabilities approach: Seeking a global blueprint for the EPAS. *Journal of Social Work Education*, *52*(3), 269–282. http://doi.org/10.1080/10437797.2016.1174635

Caron, R., Lee, E., & Sansfacon, A. (2020). Transformative disruptions and collective knowledge building: Social work professors building anti-oppressive ethical frameworks for research, reaching, practice and activism. *Ethics & Social Welfare*, *14*, 298–314.

Casebeer, W. D. (2003). *Natural ethical facts: Evolution, connectionism, and moral cognition*. MIT Press.

Caudill, B. (n.d.). Malpractice & licensing pitfalls for therapists: A defense attorney's list. http://www.kspope.com/ethics/malpractice.php

Chafee, Z. (1919). Freedom of speech in war time. *Harvard Law Review*, *32*(8), 932–973. https://www.jstor.org/stable/pdf/1327107.pdf

Chang, J., Lai, A., Yuanhong, A., Gupta, A., Nguyen, A., Berry, C., & Shelley, D. (2021). Rapid transition to telehealth and the digital divide: Implications for primary care access and equity in a post-COVID era. *Milbank Quarterly*, *26*(11), 1–29.

Charon R. (2007). What to do with stories: The sciences of narrative medicine. *Canadian Family Physician*, *53*(8), 1265–1267.

Chechak, D. (2015). Social work as a value-based profession: Value conflicts and implications for practitioners' self-concepts. *Journal of Social Work Values and Ethics*, *12*(2), 41–48.

Children's Bureau. (n.d.). From complaint to resolution: Understanding the child welfare grievance process. https://www.childwelfare.gov/pubPDFs/cw_grievance.pdf

Churchill, L. (2020). *Ethics for everyone: A skills-based approach*. Oxford University Press.

Civil action for deprivation of rights (2007). 42 U.S.C. §1983 at https://www.law.cornell.edu/uscode/text/42/1983

Civil Rights Act. (1964). §7, 42 U.S.C. §2000e et seq.

Cole, H. (2021). Intersecting social work practice, education, and spirituality: A conceptual model. *Journal of Religion & Spirituality in Social Work: Social Thought, 40*(1), 68–91. https://doi.org/10.1080/15426432.2020.1831420

Collins, D., Coleman, H., & Miller, P. (2002). Regulation of social workers: A confusing landscape. *Canadian Social Work Review, 19*(2), 205–225.

Common Rule. (1991/2018). United States Code of Federal Regulations, Title 45, §46 (Authority: National Research Act [1974]. 5 U.S.C. 301; 42 U.S.C. 289[a]). https://www.hhs.gov/ohrp/regulations-and-policy/regulations/finalized-revisions-common-rule/index.html

Confidentiality of Substance Use Disorder Records. (2017). 42 CFR §2.13. https://www.law.cornell.edu/cfr/text/42/part-2

Corey, G., Corey, M. S., & Corey, C. (2019). *Issues and ethics in the helping professions* (10th ed.). Cengage.

Cottone, R., Tarvydas, V., & Hartley, M. (2022). *Ethics and decision making in counseling and psychotherapy* (5th ed). Springer.

Council on Social Work Education (CSWE). (2022). Educational policy and accreditation standards. Author. http://www.cswe.org

Craig, H. (2020). 10 ways to build trust in a relationship. *Positive Psychology*. https://positivepsychology.com/build-trust

Crisis Intervention Team International. (2019). Crisis intervention team (CIT) programs: A best practice guide for transforming community responses to mental health crises. https://www.citinternational.org/resources/Best%20Practice%20Guide/CIT%20guide%20desktop%20printing%202019_08_16%20(1).pdf

Daley, M. (2021). *Rural social work in the 21st century* (2nd ed.). Oxford University Press.

Daley, M., & Doughty, M. O. (2007). Preparing BSWs for ethical practice: Lessons from licensing data. *Journal of Social Work Values & Ethics, 4*(2), 3–9. https://jswve.org/download/2007-2/4-Preparing-BSWs-for-Ethical-PracticeLessons-from-Licensing-Data-JSWVE-4-2-2007.pdf

Darcy, A., Daniels, J., Salinger, D., Wicks, P., & Robinson A. (2021). Evidence of human-level bonds established with a digital conversational agent: Cross-sectional, retrospective observational study. *JMIR Formative Research, 5*(5). https://formative.jmir.org/2021/5/e27868; http://doi.org/10.2196/27868

Dayton, A. K. (2014). *Comparative perspectives on adult guardianship*. Carolina Academic Press.

Dean, H. (2020). A radical humanist approach to social welfare. *Ethics and Social Welfare, 14*(4), 353–368. https://doi.org/10.1080/17496535.2020.1777454

della Porta, D. (2020). Conceptualising backlash movements: A (patch-worked) perspective from social movement studies. *British Journal of Politics and International Relations, 22*(4). 585–597. https://doi.org/10.1177/1369148120947360

Delmas, C., & Brownlee, K. (2021). Civil disobedience. *The Stanford Encyclopedia of Philosophy*. https://plato.stanford.edu/archives/sum2021/entries/civil-disobedience

Denzin, N. K., & Lincoln, Y. S. (2017). *The SAGE handbook of qualitative research* (5th ed.). SAGE.

den Braber, C. (2013). The introduction of the capability approach in social work across a neoliberal Europe. *Journal of Social Intervention: Theory and Practice, 22*(4), 61–77.

DePergola, P. A. (2018). The ethical justification of equal candidacy for organ transplantation in alcoholic patients. *Online Journal of Health Ethics, 14*(1). https://doi.org//10.18785/ojhe.1401.03

Dolgoff, R., Harrington, D., & Loewenberg, F. M. (2012). *Ethical issues for social work practice* (9th ed.). Cengage.

Doran, J., & Bagdasaryan, S. (2018). Infusing financial capability and asset building content into a community organizing class. *Journal of Social Work Education, 54*(1), 122–134.

Doss, B., Feinberg, L., Rothman, K., Roddy, M., & Comer, J. (2017). Using technology to enhance and expand interventions for couples and families: Conceptual and methodological considerations. *Journal of Family Psychology, 31*(8), 983–993.

Eisenberg, M. (2018). *Foundational principles of contract law.* Oxford University Press.

Elässer, L., Hense, S., & Schäfer, A. (2020). Not just money: Unequal responsiveness in egalitarian democracies. *Journal of European Public Policy, 28*(12), 1890–1908. https://doi.org/10.1080/13501763.2020.1801804

Enabling Guide. (n.d.). Sensory disability. https://www.enablingguide.sg/disability-info/sensory-disability

Environmental Justice. (n.d.). United States Environmental Protection Agency. https://www.epa.gov/environmentaljustice

Falender, C. A., & Shafranske, E. P. (2014). Clinical supervision: The state of the art. *Journal of Clinical Psychology, 70*(11), 1030–1041.

Fairchild, R., Ferng-Kuo, S., Rahmouni, H., & Hardesty, D. (2019). Affiliations expand: Telehealth increases access to care for children dealing with suicidality, depression, and anxiety in rural emergency departments. *Telemedicine & e-Health, 26*(11), 1353–1362. http://doi.org/10.1089/tmj.2019.0253

Family Educational Rights and Privacy Act (FERPA). (1974). 20 U.S.C. §1232g; 34 CFR Part 99. https://www.law.cornell.edu/cfr/text/34/part-99

Family Violence and Prevention Services Act. (1994). 42 U.S.C.10, §10401. https://www.law.cornell.edu/uscode/text/42/chapter-110

Feng, Y., Barakova, E., Yu, S., Hu, J., & Rauterberg, G. (2020). Effects of the level of interactivity of a social robot and the response of the augmented reality display in contextual interactions of people with dementia. *Sensors 20*(13), 3771–3783. https://doi.org/10.3390/s20133771

Fine, A. D., & van Rooij, B. (2021). Legal socialization: Understanding the obligation to obey the law. *Journal of Social Issues, 77,* 367–391. https://doi.org/10.1111/josi.12440

Fine, M. D. (2019). Care and caring. In M. Payne & E. Reith-Hall. (Eds.). *The Routledge handbook of social work theory* (pp. 83–94). Routledge.

Finn, J. (2021). *Just practice: A social justice approach to social work* (4th ed.). Oxford University Press.

Fisher, A. (2016). *Confidentiality limits in psychotherapy: Ethics checklists for mental health professionals.* American Psychological Association.

Fisher, R., Ury, W., & Patton, B. (2011). *Getting to yes: Negotiating agreement without giving in* (3rd ed.). Penguin.

Fowers, B., Carroll, J., Leonhardt, N., & Cokelet, B. (2021). The emerging science of virtue. *Perspectives on Psychological Science, 16*(1), 118–147. https://doi.org/10.1177/1745691620924473

Freire, P. (1994). *Pedagogy of hope: Reliving pedagogy of the oppressed.* Continuum.

Frennert, S. (2020). Moral distress and ethical decision-making of eldercare professionals involved in digital service transformation. *Disability & Rehabilitation: Assistive Technology,* 1-10. https://doi.org/10.1080/17483107.2020.1839579

Frunză, A., & Sandu, A. (2016). Updating ethics expertise: Supervision of ethics as a communicative action. *Journal of Social Work Values and Ethics, 13*(1), 73–84.

Gambrill, E. (2017). Avoidable ignorance and the ethics of risk in child welfare. *Journal of Social Work Practice, 31*(4), 379–393. https://doi.org/10.1080/02650533.2017.1394824

Gambrill, E. (2019). *Critical thinking and the process of evidence-based practice.* Oxford University Press.

Ganzini, L., Volicer, L., Nelson, W., Fox, E., & Derse, A. R. (2005). Ten myths about decision-making capacity. *Journal of the American Medical Directors Association, 6*(3), S100–S104.

Gao, F., Foster, M., & Liu, Y. (2019). Disability concentration and access to rehabilitation services: A pilot spatial assessment applying geographic information system analysis. *Disability & Rehabilitation, 41*(20), 2468–2476.

Gawande, A. (2011). *The checklist manifesto: How to get things done right.* Metropolitan Books.

Gillingham, P. (2019). Decision support systems, social justice and algorithmic accountability in social work: A new challenge, *Practice, 31*(4), 277–290. https://doi.org/10.1080/09503153.2019.1575954

Golden, R., Swidzinski, J., Baylor, M., Broyles. D., & Deloney, J. (2019). Integrity for the 21st Century Social Worker. *New Social Worker.* https://www.socialworker.com/extras/social-work-month-2019/integrity-for-the-21st-century-social-worker

Goldkind, L., LaMendola, W., & Taylor-Beswick, A. (2020). Tackling COVID-19 is a crucible for privacy. *Journal of Technology in Human Services, 38*(2), 89–90.

Gottlieb, M. (2020). The case for a cultural humility framework in social work practice. *Journal of Ethnic & Cultural Diversity in Social Work, 30*(6), 463–481. https://doi.org/10.1080/15313204.2020.1753615

Government Accountability Project. (n.d.). Government accountability. Retrieved April 11, 2022 from https://whistleblower.org/government-accountability

Green, A. D., & Latting, J. K. (2004). Whistleblowing as a form of advocacy: Guidelines for the practitioner and organization. *Social Work, 49*(2), 219–230.

Gricus, M., & Wysiekiersky, L. (2021). Social workers' perceptions of their peers' unprofessional behavior. *Journal of Social Work,* 1–23. https://doi.org/10.1177/14680173211012576

Grimwood, T. (2019). Autonomy and dependence. In M. Payne & E. Reith-Hall. (Eds.). *The Routledge handbook of social work theory* (pp. 95–108). Routledge.

Grinnell, R. M. (2021). *Foundations of research methods for social workers: A critical thinking approach.* Pair Bond.

Grinnell, R. M., Williams, M., & Unrau, Y. A. (2018). *Research methods for social workers: An introduction* (12th ed.). Pair Bond.

Grise-Owens, E., Owens, L., & Miller, J. (2016). Recasting licensing in social work: Something more for professionalism. *Journal of Social Work Education, 52*(Supp.1), 126–133.

Grise-Owens, E., Owens, L., & Miller, J. (2022). Self-care for social workers. In L. Rapp-McCall, K. Corcoran, & A. Roberts (Eds.), *Social workers' desk reference* (pp. 30–37). Oxford University Press.

Groessl, J. (2017). Leadership in the field: Fostering moral courage. *Journal of Social Work Values and Ethics*, 14(1), 72–79. http://jswve.org/download/2017-1/14-1-articles/72-Leadership-in-the-Field-.pdf

Gutheil, T. G., & Brodsky, A. (2011). *Preventing boundary violations in clinical practice.* Guilford Press.

Hacker, J., & Pierson, P. (2016). Making America great again. *Foreign Affairs*, 95(3), 69–90.

Hafford-Letchfield, T., & Engelbrecht, L. (2020). *Contemporary practices in social work supervision.* Taylor & Francis.

Hagihara, A., & Tarumi, K. (2007). Association between physicians' communicative behaviors and judges' decisions in lawsuits on negligent care. *Health Policy*, 83(1/2), 213–222.

Haidt, J. (2013). Moral psychology for the twenty-first century. *Journal of Moral Education*, 42(3), 281–297. https://doi.org/10.1080/03057240.2013.817327

Halfond, R. W., Wright, C. V., & Bufka, L. F. (2021). The role of harms and burdens in clinical practice guidelines: Lessons learned from the American Psychological Association's guideline development. *Clinical Psychology: Science and Practice*, 28(1), 19–28. https://doi.org/10.1111/cpsp.12343

Halverson, G., & Brownlee, K. (2010). Managing ethical considerations around dual relationships in small rural and remote Canadian communities. *International Social Work*, 53(2) 247–260. https://doi.org/10.1177/0020872809355386

Hammersley, M., & Traianou, A. (2011). Moralism and research ethics: A Machiavellian perspective. *International Journal of Social Research Methodology*. 14, 379–390.

Hardy, M. (2017). In defence of actuarialism: Interrogating the logic of risk in social work practice. *Journal of Social Work Practice*, 31(4), 395–410. https://doi.org/10.1080/02650533.2017.1394828

Hayden, C. (2020). Remembering John Lewis: The power of 'good trouble.' Library of Congress. https://blogs.loc.gov/loc/2020/07/remembering-john-lewis-the-power-of-good-trouble

Hayes, C. M. (2016). Social work at the crossroads: How to resist the politics of a Donald Trump presidency: Social work is not nor should it be a neutral profession. https://www.huffpost.com/entry/social-work-at-the-crossroads-how-to-resist-the-politics_b_583f22ade4b0cf3f6455863a

Health Insurance Portability and Accountability Act (HIPAA). (1996). Pub. L. 104–191, 110 Stat. 1936. https://www.gpo.gov/fdsys/pkg/PLAW-104publ191/pdf/PLAW-104publ191.pdf (see also, https://www.hhs.gov/hipaa/for-professionals/compliance-enforcement/examples/by-issue/index.htmldisclosurestoavert for case examples)

Health Nurse, Healthy Nation. (n.d.). Moral distress: What it is and what to do about it. Retrieved April 12, 2022, from https://engage.healthynursehealthynation.org/blogs/8/531

Hepworth, D. H., Der Vang, P., Blakey, J. M., Schwalbe, C., Evans, C., Rooney, R., Dewberry Rooney, G., & Strom, K. (2023). *Direct social work practice: Theory and skills* (11th ed.). Cengage.

Hermann, J. (2019). Technological justice. *Justice everywhere*. http://justice-everywhere.org/international/technological-justice

Higgins, M. (2021). Virtue epistemology and epistemic humility: Implications for social work. *Journal of Practice Teaching & Learning*, 18(1), 64–79. https://doi.org/10.1921/jpts.v18i1-2.1339

Hinman, L. M. (n.d.). *Glossary of ethical terms.* https://www.scribd.com/document/109786657/Glossary-of-Ethical-Terms-Hinman

Howard, D. (2017). The medical surrogate as fiduciary agent. *Journal of Law, Medicine, & Ethics, 45*(3), 402–420.

Hultman, L., Forinder, U., Fugl-Meyer, K., & Pergert, P. (2018). Maintaining professional integrity: Experiences of case workers performing the assessments that determine children's access to personal assistance. *Disability & Society, 33*(6), 909–931. https://www.doi.org/10.1080/09687599.2018.1466691

Institute for the Study of Conflict Transformation. (n.d.). *About transformative.* http://www.transformativemediation.org/about-transformative

International Federation of Social Workers. (2016). *The role of social work in social protection systems: The universal right to social protection.* https://www.ifsw.org/the-role-of-social-work-in-social-protection-systems-the-universal-right-to-social-protection

International Federation of Social Workers (IFSW). (2018). *Global social work statement of ethical principles.* https://www.ifsw.org/global-social-work-statement-of-ethical-principles

Interprofessional Education Collaborative. (2016). *Core competencies for interprofessional collaborative practice.* https://ipec.memberclicks.net/assets/2016-Update.pdf

Jacobsen, J., & Levy, D. (2018). Letter to the editor (re: LGBTQ Topics and Christianity in Social Work). *Social Work & Christianity, 45*(4), 132–135.

Jaffee v. Redmond. (1996). 518 U.S. 1 (U.S. SC). https://www.oyez.org/cases/1995/95-266

James, A. G., Coard, S., Fine, M., & Rudy, D. (2018). *Journal of Family Theory & Review, 10*(2), 419–433. https://doi.org/10.1111/jftr.12262.

Janebová, R. (2012). Dilemmas between law and ethics in Czech social work. *European Journal of Social Work, 15*(3), 331–344. https://doi.org/10.1080/13691457.2010.545769

Janssen, J. S. (2016). Moral distress in social work practice: When workplace and conscience collied. *Social Work Today, 16*(3), 18. https://www.socialworktoday.com/archive/052416p18.shtml

Johns, R. (2016). *Ethics and law for social workers.* SAGE.

Johnson, K. (2019). *SOGIE: Sexual orientation, gender identity, and expression affirming approach and expansive practices.* New York State Department of Health. https://www.health.ny.gov/prevention/sexual_violence/docs/sogie_handbook.pdf

Johnson, R. A., & Karlawish, J. (2015). A review of ethical issues in dementia. *International Psychogeriatrics, 27*(10), 1635–1647. https://doi.org/10.1017/s1041610215000848

Kahneman, D. (2011). *Thinking, fast and slow.* Farrar, Straus, and Giroux.

Kaldjian, L. (2019). Understanding conscience as integrity: Why some physicians will not refer patients for ethically controversial practices. *Perspectives in Biology & Medicine, 62*(3), 383–400. https://doi.org/10.1353/pbm.2019.0022

Kalichman, S. C. (1999). *Mandated reporting of suspected child abuse: Ethics, law, and policy* (2nd ed.). American Psychological Association.

Kanani, K., Regehr, C., & Bernstein, M. (2002). Liability considerations in child welfare: Lessons from Canada. *Child Abuse & Neglect, 26*(10), 1029–1043.

Kant, I. ([1785] 1964). *Groundwork of the metaphysic of morals.* Harper-Collins.

Kant, I. (1779/1979). *Lectures on ethics* (L. Infield, Trans.). Methuen.

Kaushik, A. (2017). Use of self in social work: Rhetoric or reality. *Journal of Social Work Values and Ethics, 14*(1), 21–29. http://jswve.org/download/2017-1/14-1-articles/21-Use-of-Self-in-Social-Work-.pdf

King, I. G., & Pinals, D. A. (2017). Clinician immunity against claims of malpractice and constitutional violations. *Journal of the American Academy of Psychiatry and the Law, 45*(4), 495–497. https://dx.doi.org/10.1093%2Fjlb%2Flsaa018

Kirkland, K., & Kirkland, K. E. (2006). Risk management and aspirational ethics for parenting coordinators. *Journal of Child Custody, 3*(2), 23–43.

Kirkpatrick, I., Aulakh, S., & Muzio, D. (2021). The evolution of professionalism as a mode of regulation: Evidence from the United States. *Work, Employment, and Society.* https://doi.org/10.1177/09500170211035297

Kirschenbaum, H. (2013). *Values clarification in counseling and psychotherapy: Practical strategies for individual and group settings.* Oxford University Press.

Kirst-Ashman, K. K., & Hull, G. H. (2018a). *Generalist practice with organizations and communities* (7th ed.). Cengage.

Kirst-Ashman, K. K., & Hull, G. H. (2018b). *Understanding generalist practice* (8th ed.). Cengage.

Kölbel, R., & Herold, N. (2019). Whistle-blowing from the perspective of general strain theory. *Deviant Behavior, 40*(2), 139–155. https://doi.org/10.1080/01639625.2017.1411054

Koocher, G. P., & Keith-Spiegel, P. (2016). *Ethics in psychology and the mental health professions: Standards and cases* (4th ed.). Oxford University Press.

Lambek, B. D. (1987). Necessity and international law: Arguments for the legality of civil disobedience. *Yale Law & Policy Review, 5*(2), 472–402.

Landers, J., & Parrish, D. (2021). The rise of genetic genealogy and the need for social work's voices. *Social Work* (electronic publication). https://doi.org/10.1093/sw/swab018

Lauer, C. (2021). PA Christian college ends program citing gender, sex guidelines. NBC Philadelphia. https://www.nbcphiladelphia.com/news/local/pa-christian-college-ends-program-citing-gender-sex-guidelines/2837511

Lavoie, R. (2021). Illuminating moral distress in social work: A grounded theory study informed by critical realism (Thesis). *University of Manitoba.* https://mspace.lib.umanitoba.ca/bitstream/handle/1993/35396/Lavoie_Richard%20thesis.pdf?sequence=1

Legal Information Institute. (n.d.). Accessory after the fact: https://www.law.cornell.edu/wex/accessory_after_the_fact; Obstruction of Justice: https://www.law.cornell.edu/wex/obstruction_of_justice

Lens, V. (2004). Social work and the Supreme Court: A clash of values; a time for action. *Social Work, 49*(2), 327–330.

Leonhard, G. (2016). *Technology vs. human: The coming clash between man and machine.* Fast Future Publishing (https://www.futuristgerd.com).

Levy, C. (1993). *Social work ethics on the line.* Haworth Press.

Liu, B., & Shyam, S. (2018). Should machines express sympathy and empathy? Experiments with a health advice chatbot. *Cyberpsychology, Behavior, and Social Networking, 5*, 2152–2715. https://doi.org/10.1089/cyber.2018.0110

Locke, J. (1689). *Two treatises of government.* https://www.yorku.ca/comninel/courses/3025pdf/Locke.pdf

Loue, S. (2017). Social work values, ethics, and spirituality. In *Handbook of Religion and Spirituality in Social Work Practice and Research* (pp. 17–35). Springer. https://doi.org/10.1007/978-1-4939-7039-1_2

Mackenzie, J. (2018). Knowing yourself and being worth knowing. *Journal of the American Philosophical Association, 4*(2), 243–261. https://doi.org/10.1017/apa.2018.19

Mackey, T. K., Miyachi, K., Fung, D., Qian, S., & Short, J. (2020). Combating health care fraud and abuse: Conceptualization and prototyping study of a blockchain antifraud framework. *Journal of Medical Internet research, 22*(9). e18623. https://doi.org/10.2196/18623

Madura, T. L. (2018). *The role of power in counseling psychology faculty and student relationships: Differentiating perceptions of nonsexual boundary crossings* (Doctoral dissertation). Dissertation Abstracts International: Section B: The Sciences and Engineering 78 (11-B(E)).

Magiste, E. J. (2020). Prevalence rates of substantiated and adjudicated ethics violations. *Journal of Social Work, 20*(6), 751–774. https://doi.org/10.1177/1468017319837521

Mannarini, S., & Rossi, A. (2019). Assessing mental illness stigma: A complex issue. *Frontiers in Psychology, 9*, 2722. https://doi.org/10.3389/fpsyg.2018.02722

Marley, R. (2019). Indigenous data sovereignty: University Institutional Review Board policies and guidelines and research with American Indian and Alaska Native Communities, *American Behavioral Scientist, 63*(6), 722–742.

Maslow, A., Frager, R., & Fadiman, J. (1987). *Motivation and personality* (3rd ed.). Addison-Wesley.

Martínez, C., Skeet, A. G., & Sasia, P. M. (2021). Managing organizational ethics: How ethics becomes pervasive within organizations. *Business Horizons, 64*(1), 83–92. https://doi.org/10.1016/j.bushor.2020.09.008

Marx, K. (1875). Critique of the Gotha program. *Marx/Engels Selected Works, 3*, 13–30. http://www.marxists.org/archive/marx/works/sw/index.htm

Maschi, R., & Leibowitz, G. S. (Eds.). (2018). *Forensic social work: Psychosocial and legal issues across diverse populations and settings.* Springer.

Mason, K., Cocker, C., & Hafford-Letchfield, T. (2022). Sexuality and religion: From the court of appeal to the social work classroom. *Social Work Education, 41*(1), 77–89. https://doi.org/10.1080/02615479.2020.1805426

Mathiyazhagan, S. (2021). Field practice, emerging technologies, and human rights: The emergence of tech social workers. *Journal of Human Rights and Social Work* (online). https://doi.org/10.1007/s41134-021-00190-0

McAuliffe, D. (2014). *Interprofessional ethics: Collaboration in the social, health, and human services.* Cambridge University Press.

McAuliffe, D., & Chenoweth, L. (2008). Leave no stone unturned: The inclusive model of ethical decision making. *Ethics and Social Welfare, 2*(1), 38–49. https://doi.org/10.1080/17496530801948739

McMichael, B., Van Horn, R., & Viscusi, W. (2019). "Sorry" is never enough: How state apology laws fail to reduce medical malpractice liability risk. *Stanford Law Review, 71*(2). 341–409.

McMillan, N. (2020). Moral distress in residential child care. *Ethics & Social Welfare, 14*(1), 52–64.

McNutt, J. (2019). Data justice and international development. In S. Marson and McKinney, R. (Eds.). *The Routledge handbook of social work ethics and values* (pp. 280–286). Routledge.

Mill, J. S. (1863). *Utilitarianism.* https://www.utilitarianism.com/mill1.htm

Miller, J.J., Lee, J., Niu, C., Grise-Owens, E., & Bode, M. (2019). Self-compassion as a predictor of self-care: A study of social work clinicians. *Clinical Social Work Journal, 47*, 321–331. https://doi.org/10.1007/s10615-019-00710-6

Mishna, F., Sanders, J., Sewell, K., & Milne, E. (2021). Teaching note: Preparing social workers for the digital future of social work practice. *Journal of Social Work Education, 57*(Sup.1), 19–26. https://doi.org/10.1080/10437797.2021.1912676

Mo, K., Tsang, W., Wong, E., Sing, L., & Cheung, J. (2021). Golden opportunities for resolving students' emotional disturbance in learning social work values: A

3Ps approach in fieldwork practicum. *International Social Work*, 1–10. https://doi.org/10.1177/0020872820985914

Moffett, P., & Moore, G. (2011). The standard of care: legal history and definitions: The bad and good news. *The Western Journal of Emergency Medicine, 12*(1), 109–112.

Montin v. Moore. (2017). 846 F.3d 289 (Eighth Circuit) https://casetext.com/case/montin-v-moore-2

Moore, B. (2019). Ethically permissible inequity in access to experimental therapies. *Clinical Ethics, 14*(1), 1–8. https://journals.sagepub.com/doi/pdf/10.1177/1477750919839920

Moore, C. W. (2014). *The mediation process: Practical strategies for resolving conflict* (4th ed.). Jossey-Bass.

Morain, S., & Joffe, S. (2019). When is it ethical for physician-investigators to seek consent from their own patients? *American Journal of Bioethics, 19*(4), 11–18.

Morgaine, K., & Capous-Desyllas, M. (2020). *Putting theory into action*. Cognella.

Morrison, E. (2016). *Ethics in health administration: A practical approach for decision makers.* Jones and Bartlett Learning.

Musgrove, P., & Fox-Rushby, J. (2006). Cost-effectiveness analysis for priority setting. In D. Jamison, J. Breman J, A. Measham AR, et al. (Eds), *Disease control priorities in developing countries* (2nd ed.). The International Bank for Reconstruction and Development. https://www.ncbi.nlm.nih.gov/books/NBK11780/?report=reader

National Alliance on Mental Illness. (n.d.). *People with disabilities.* https://www.nami.org/Your-Journey/Identity-and-Cultural-Dimensions/People-with-Disabilities

NASW Assurance Services. (2021). Episode 10: Duty to bear witness. https://policyholder.naswassurance.org/social-work-risky-business-podcast/transcript-episode-10-your-duty-to-bear-witness

National Association of Social Workers (NASW). (n.d.-a). History of the NASW Code of Ethics. https://www.socialworkers.org/About/Ethics/Code-of-Ethics/History

National Association of Social Workers (NASW). (n.d.-b). Professional review. https://www.socialworkers.org/About/Ethics/Professional-Review

National Association of Social Workers (NASW). (2012). *NASW procedures for professional review* (6th ed.). Author. https://www.socialworkers.org/LinkClick.aspx?fileticket=E6Gsz89w0rw%3D&portalid=0

National Association of Social Workers (NASW). (2013). Best practice standards in social work supervision. Author. https://www.socialworkers.org/LinkClick.aspx?fileticket=GBrLbl4BuwI%3D&portalid=0

National Association of Social Workers (NASW). (2015). *Standards and indictors for cultural competence in social work practice.* Author. https://www.socialworkers.org/LinkClick.aspx?fileticket=PonPTDEBrn4%3D&portalid=0

National Association of Social Workers (NASW). (2021). *Code of ethics.* Author. https://www.socialworkers.org/About/Ethics/Code-of-Ethics/Code-of-Ethics-English

National Association of Social Workers (NASW), Council on Social Work Education, Association of Social Work Boards, & Clinical Social Work Association. (2017). *Practice standards on social work and technology.* National Association of Social Workers. https://www.socialworkers.org/Practice/Practice-Standards-Guidelines

National Center on Elder Abuse. (n.d.). *State resources.* https://ncea.acl.gov/Resources/State.aspx

National Conference of State Legislatures. (2018). *Mental health professionals' duty to warn.* https://www.ncsl.org/research/health/mental-health-professionals-duty-to-warn.aspx

National Conference of State Legislatures. (2021). Qualified immunity. https://www.ncsl.
org/research/civil-and-criminal-justice/qualified-immunity.aspx

National Institutes of Health. (n.d.). What is research integrity? https://grants.nih.gov/
policy/research_integrity/what-is.htm

National Lawyers Guild. (n.d.). Questions and answers about civil disobedience and the
legal process. Retrieved April 11, 2022 from http://old.vcnv.org/files/NLG-LA.pdf

Neal, S., Travers, M., & Brastow, I. (2021). When X shouldn't mark the spot: A crosswalk
to a unified code of ethics for collaboration in the COVID-19 Era. *Public Integrity, 23*(4),
349–368. http://doi.org/10.1080/10999922.2020.1869407

Neilson, G., Chaimowitz, G., & Zuckerberg, J. (2015). Informed consent to treatment in
psychiatry. *Canadian Journal of Psychiatry, 60*(4), 1–11.

NEJM Catalyst. (2018). What is risk management in healthcare? https://catalyst.nejm.
org/doi/full/10.1056/CAT.18.0197

Nicotera, A. (2019). Social justice and social work, a fierce urgency: Recommendations for
social work social justice pedagogy. *Journal of Social Work Education, 55*(3), 460–475.
https://doi.org/10.1080/10437797.2019.1600443

Nissen, L. (2020a) Social work and the future in a post-covid 19 world: A foresight lens
and a call to action for the profession. *Journal of Technology in Human Services, 38*(4),
309–330. https://doi.org/10.1080/15228835.2020.1796892

Nissen, L. (2020b) —Social work education and practice in post-normal times:
Using futures thinking to move the field and the world forward. Council on Social
Work Education (Conference Presentation). https://drive.google.com/file/d/
1eQh-27DnRdce4HrziMw_otN-XIQsRwzG/view

Nissen, M. A., & Engen, M. (2021). Power and care in statutory social work with vulnerable
families. *Ethics and Social Welfare, 15*(3), 279–293. https://doi.org10.1080/17496535.
2021.1924814

Nozick, R. (1974/2013). *Anarchy, state, and utopia.* Basic Books.

Nuffield Council on Bioethics. (2007). *Public health: Ethical issues.* http://nuffieldbioethics.
org/wp-content/uploads/2014/07/Public-health-ethical-issues.pdf

Nussbaum, M. (2011). *Creating capabilities.* Harvard University Press.

Occupational Health and Safety Administration (n.d.). Guidelines for preventing
workplace violence for healthcare and social service workers. https://www.osha.gov/
sites/default/files/publications/osha3148.pdf

Office of Juvenile Justice and Delinquency Prevention. (n.d.). Guide for implementing the
balanced and restorative justice model. http://www.ojjdp.gov/pubs/implementing/
balanced.html#principles

Olmstead v. United States. (1928). 277 U.S. 438 (United States Supreme Court).

Ordway, A., & Casasnovas, A. (2019). A subpoena: The other exception to confidentiality.
The Family Journal: Counseling and Therapy for Couples and Families, 27(4), 352–358.
https://doi.org/10.1177%2F1066480719868701

Ortega, A., Pérez, F., & Turianskyi, Y. (2018). Technological justice: A G20 agenda. Kiel
Institute for the World Economy. http://www.economics-ejournal.org/economics/
discussionpapers/2018-58

Orwell, G. (2019). *Orwell on truth.* Mariner Books.

Osmo, R., & Landau, R. (2006). The role of ethical theories in decision making by social
workers. *Social Work Education, 25*(8), 863–876.

Oviatt, S. (2021). Technology as infrastructure for dehumanization: Three hundred million people with the same face. Proceedings of the 2021 International Conference on Multimodal Interaction (pp. 278–287). https://doi.org/10.1145/3462244.3482855

Pakkanen, P., Häggman-Laitila, A., & Kangasniemi, M. (2021). Ethical issues identified in nurses´ interprofessional collaboration in clinical practice: a meta-synthesis. Journal of Interprofessional Care. 1–10. https://doi.org/10.1080/13561820.2021.1892612

Papouli, P. (2018). Aristotle's virtue ethics as a conceptual framework for the study and practice of social work in modern times. European Journal of Social Work (online), 2018, 1–14.

Papouli, P. (2019). Moral courage and moral distress. In S. Marson and McKinney, R. (Eds.). The Routledge handbook of social work ethics and values (pp. 225–232). Routledge.

Patterson, K., Santiago, A., & Silverman, R. (2021). The enduring backlash against racial justice in the United States: Mobilizing strategies for institutional change. Journal of Community Practice, 29(4), 334–344. https://doi.org/10.1080/10705422.2021.1998875

Patterson, T. (2018). Clinical outcomes for clinical justice populations. In G. Patterson and W. Graham, Clinical Interventions in Criminal Justice Settings (pp. 49–68). Academic Press. https://doi.org/10.1016/B978-0-12-811381-3.00004-4

Paul, R., & Elder, L. (2016). The thinker's guide to Socratic thinking. Foundation for Critical Thinking.

Paul, R., & Elder, L. (2019). A thinker's guide to ethical reasoning. Foundation for Critical Thinking. http://www.criticalthinking.org/store/get_file.php?inventories_id=169

Pennycook, G., Epstein, Z., Mosleh, M., Arechar, D., Eckles, D., & Rand, D. (2021). Shifting attention to accuracy can reduce misinformation online. Nature, 592, 590–595. https://doi.org/10.1038/s41586-021-03344-2

Persson, M., Redmalm, S., & Iversen, C. (2021). Caregivers' use of robots and their effect on work environment: A scoping review. Journal of Technology in Human Services, https://doi.org/10.1080/15228835.2021.2000554

Pettit, E. (2021). The academic concept conservative lawmakers love to hate: How critical race theory became enemy no. 1 in the battle against higher ed. Chronicle of Higher Education, 67(19), 1.

Piggott, D., & Cariaga-Lo, L. (2019). Promoting inclusion, access, and equity through enhanced institutional culture and climate. Journal of Infectious Diseases, 220, S74–S81.

Pineda, E. (2021). Seeing like an activist: Civil disobedience and the civil rights movement. Oxford University Press.

Pollock, J. M. (2017). Ethical dilemmas and decisions in criminal justice (9th ed.). Cengage.

Polowy, C. I, & Felton, E. (2008). School social workers and confidentiality. https://www.socialworkers.org/assets/secured/documents/sections/school/newsletters/2015%20School%20Social%20Work%20-%20Fall%20issue.pdf

Polowy, C. I., & Gorenberg, C. (2004). Client confidentiality and privileged communication. NASW Legal Defense Fund.

Polowy, C. I., & Morgan, S. (2004). Social workers and clinical notes. NASW Legal Defense Fund.

Polychronis, P. D., & Brown, S. G. (2016). The strict liability standard and clinical supervision. Professional Psychology: Research and Practice, 47(2), 139–146. http://dx.doi.org/10.1037/pro0000073

Pope, K. S. (2015). Steps to strengthen ethics in organizations: Research findings, ethics placebos, and what works. Journal of Trauma & Dissociation, 16(2), 139–152.

Prescott, D. (2019). Flexner's thesis was prescient: Ethical practices for social workers "in the trenches" requires forensic knowledge. *Journal of Social Work Values & Ethics*, *16*(2), 40–52. https://jswve.org/download/fall_2019_volume_16_no._2/articles/40-Flexners-thesis-was-prescient-16-2-Fall-2019-JSWVE.pdf

Prochaska, J. O., & Norcross, J. C. (2018). *Systems of psychotherapy: A transtheoretical analysis* (9th ed.). Cengage.

Puschel, K., Furlan, E., & Dekkers, W. (2017). Social health disparities in clinical care: A new approach to medical fairness. *Public Health Ethics*, *10*(1), 78–85.

Raines, J. C. (2021). Ethics in an epidemic: Nine issues to consider. *Children & Schools*, *43*(2), 89–96. https://doi.org/10.1093/cs/cdab011

Rawls, J. (1971). *A theory of justice*. Harvard University Press.

Ray, R., & Gibbons, A. (2021). Why are states banning critical race theory? https://www.brookings.edu/blog/fixgov/2021/07/02/why-are-states-banning-critical-race-theory

Raymond, S., Beddoe, L, & Staniforth, B. (2017). Social workers' experiences with whistleblowing: To speak or not to speak. *Aotearoa New Zealand Social Work*, *29*(3), 13–29.

Reamer, F. G. (2015). *Risk management in social work: Preventing professional malpractice, liability, and disciplinary action*. Columbia University Press.

Reamer, F. G. (2018a). *Social work values and ethics* (5th ed.). Columbia

Reamer, F. G. (2018b). Pursuing social work's mission: The philosophical foundations of social justice. *Journal of Social Work Values and Ethics*, *15*(1), 34–42. https://jswve.org/download/15-2/bookreviews15-2/15-1-Articles/34-Pursuing-SW-Mission-15-1-rev.pdf

Reamer, F. G. (2019c). Ethical theories and social work practice. In S. Marson and McKinney, R. (Eds.). *The Routledge handbook of social work ethics and values* (pp.15–21). Routledge.

Reamer, F. G. (2021a). *Boundary issues and dual relationships in the human services* (3rd ed.). Columbia University Press.

Reamer, F. G. (2021b). Ethical issues in supervision. *The Routledge international handbook of social work supervision* (Chapter 24). Routledge.

Reamer, F. G. (2021c). *Ethics & risk management in online and distance social work*. Cognella.

Reamer, F. G. (2021d). Sexual boundary violations in the digital age: New frontiers and emerging challenges. In A. Steinberg, J. L. Alpert, & C. A. Courtois (Eds.), *Sexual boundary violations in psychotherapy: Facing therapist indiscretions, transgressions, and misconduct* (pp. 185–204). American Psychological Association. https://doi.org/10.1037/0000247-011

Reamer, F. G. (2021e). The trolley problem and the nature of intention: Implications for social work ethics. *Journal of Social Work Values and Ethics*, *18*(1), 43–54. https://jswve.org/download/2021-2/9-The-Trolley-Problem-and-the-Nature-of-Intention-JSWVE-18-2-2021.pdf

Reamer, F. G. (2022). Ethical issues in social work. In L. Rapp-McCall, K. Corcoran, & A. Roberts (Eds.), *Social workers' desk reference* (pp. 111–118). Oxford University Press.

Reisch, M., & Garvin, C. (2016). *Social work and social justice*. Oxford University Press

Reporters' Committee for Freedom of the Press. (n.d.). *Open government guide*. https://www.rcfp.org/open-government-guide

Restorative Justice Network. (n.d.). *What is restorative justice?* http://www.restorativejustice.org

Reyes Mason, L., & Rigg, J. (Eds.). (2019). *People and climate change: Vulnerability, adaptation, and social justice*. Oxford University Press.

Richardson, H., & Chowns, G. (2020). *Social work practice and end-of-life care.* Routledge.

Rhoads, S., & Rakes, A. (2020). Telehealth technology: Reducing barriers for rural residents seeking genetic counseling. *Journal of the American Association of Nurse Practitioners, 32*(3), 190–192. https://doi.org/10.1097/JXX.0000000000000373

Rodziewicz, T.L., Houseman, B., & Hipskind, J. E. (2021). Medical error reduction and prevention. *StatPearls.* https://pubmed.ncbi.nlm.nih.gov/29763131

Rogers, C. (1957). The necessary and sufficient conditions of therapeutic personality change. *Journal of Counseling Psychology, 21,* 95–103.

Rogers, S., & Jacobowitz, J. (2015). Mindful ethics and cultivation of concentration. *University of Las Vegas.* https://scholars.law.unlv.edu/cgi/viewcontent.cgi?article=1595&context=nlj

Rogerson, C., Prescott, D., & Howard, H. (2021). Teaching social work students the influence of explicit and implicit bias: Promoting ethical reflection in practice, *Social Work Education,* 1–12. https://doi.org/10.1080/02615479.2021.1910652

Rooney, R. H. (2018). Legal and ethical foundations for work with involuntary clients. In R. H. Rooney & R. G. Mirick (Eds.), *Strategies for work with involuntary clients* (pp. 19–46). Columbia University Press.

Rufo et al. v. Simpson. (2001). Superior Court Numbers SC031947, SC035340, and SC036876 (California Court of Appeal). https://caselaw.findlaw.com/ca-court-of-appeal/1211279.html

Rural Health Information Hub. (n.d.). Healthcare access in rural communities. https://www.ruralhealthinfo.org/topics/healthcare-access

Sabatello, M., Burke, T., McDonald, K., & Appelbaum, P. (2020). Disability, ethics, and health care in the COVID-19 pandemic. *American Journal of Public Health, 110*(10), 1523–1527.

Senger, P., & Wiest, C. (2022). Professionalism in the field of social work. In L. Rapp-McCall, K. Corcoran, & A. Roberts (Eds.), *Social workers' desk reference* (pp. 12–20). Oxford University Press.

Scales, T. L., & Kelly, M. (Eds.). (2016). *Christianity and social work: Readings on the integration of Christian faith and social work practice* (5th ed.). North American Association of Christians in Social Work.

Schot, E., Tummers, L., & Noordegraaf, M. (2020). Working on working together. A systematic review on how healthcare professionals contribute to interprofessional collaboration. *Journal of Interprofessional Care, 34*(3), 332–342. https://doi.org/10.1080/13561820.2019.1636007

Schroeder D., Chatfield K., Singh M., Chennells R., & Herissone-Kelly P. (2019). The four values framework: Fairness, respect, care and honesty. In: *Equitable Research Partnerships. Springer Briefs in Research and Innovation Governance.* Springer. https://doi.org/10.1007/978-3-030-15745-6_3 https://link.springer.com/chapter/10.1007/978-3-030-15745-6_3#citeas

Schulman, L. (2021). *Let the records show: A political history of ACT UP New York, 1987–1993.* Farrar, Straus, & Giroux.

Schur, M. (2022). *How to be perfect: The correct answer to every moral question.* Simon & Schuster.

Sen, A. (2010). *The idea of justice.* Penguin.

Shafer-Landau, R. (2018). *The fundamentals of ethics.* Oxford University Press.

Shah, A., Anderson, K., Li, X., Meadows, J., & Breitsprecher, T. (2019). Clinical social work scope of practice related to diagnosis. *Clinical Social Work Journal, 47*(4), 332–342. https://doi.org/10.1007/s10615-018-0693-2

Shah, P., Thornton, I., Turrin, D., & Hipskind, J. (2020). Informed consent. https://www.ncbi.nlm.nih.gov/books/NBK430827

Shaw, E. (2015). Ethical practice in couple and family therapy: Negotiating rocky terrain. *Australian & New Zealand Journal of Family Therapy, 36*(4), 504–517. https://doi.org/10.1002/anzf.1129

Shdaimah, C., & Strier, R. (2020). Ethical conflicts in social work practice: Challenges and opportunities. *Ethics and Social Welfare, 14*(1), 1–5. https://www.doi.org/10.1080/17496535.2020.1718848

Shulman, L. (2020). *Interactional supervision* (4th ed.). NASW Press.

Sicora, A. (2017). Reflective practice, risk and mistakes in social work. *Journal of Social Work Practice, 31*(4), 491–502. https://doi.org/10.1080/02650533.2017.1394823

Sissoko, D. R. G., & Nadal, K. L. (2021). *Microaggressions toward racial minority immigrants in the United States.* In P. Tummala-Narra (Ed.), *Cultural, racial, and ethnic psychology. Trauma and racial minority immigrants: Turmoil, uncertainty, and resistance* (p. 85–102). American Psychological Association. https://doi.org/10.1037/0000214-006

Smith, K., Jones, A., & Hunter, E. (2021). Navigating the multidimensionality of social media presence: Ethical considerations and recommendations for psychologists, *Ethics & Behavior.* https://doi.org/10.1080/10508422.2021.1977935

Sobočan, A., Banks, S., Bertotti, T., Strom, K., de Jonge, E., & Weinberg, M. (2020). *Ethics & Social Welfare, 14*(3), 331–346. https://www.doi.org/10.1080/17496535.2020.1726982

Specht, H., & Courtney, M. E. (1994). *Unfaithful angels: How social work has abandoned its mission.* Free Press.

Stanford Encyclopedia of Philosophy. (2019). The principle of beneficence in applied ethics. https://plato.stanford.edu/entries/principle-beneficence/

Stein, G. L. (2007). *Advance directives and advance care planning for people with intellectual and physical disabilities.* U.S. Department of Health and Human Services. http://aspe.hhs.gov/daltcp/reports/2007/adacp.htm

Steiner, O. (2020). Social work in the digital era: Theoretical, ethical, and practical considerations. *British Journal of Social Work, 51*, 1–19. https://doi.org/10.1093/bjsw/bcaa16/0

Stephan, A., Bieber, A., Hopper, L. et al. (2018). Barriers and facilitators to the access to and use of formal dementia care: Findings of a focus group study with people with dementia, informal carers and health and social care professionals in eight European countries. *BMC Geriatrics, 18*, 131. https://doi.org/10.1186/s12877-018-0816-1

Strait, J., Strait, G., McClain, M., Cassillas, L., Streich, K., Harper, K., & Gomez, J. (2020). Classroom mindfulness: Education effects on meditation frequency, stress, and self-regulation. *Teaching of Psychology, 47*(2), 162–168. https://doi.org/10.1177%2F0098628320901386

Street, R. (n.d.). Counseling ethics. http://psychology.iresearchnet.com/counseling-psychology/counseling-ethics

Strom-Gottfried, K. (2000). Ensuring ethical practice: An examination of NASW Code violations, 1986-1997, *Social Work, 45*(3), 251–261. https://doi.org/10.1093/sw/45.3.251

Substance Abuse and Mental Health Services Administration (SAMHSA). (n.d.-a). Substance abuse confidentiality regulations. https://www.samhsa.gov/about-us/who-we-are/laws-regulations/confidentiality-regulations-faqs

Substance Abuse and Mental Health Services Administration. (2022). Disaster technical assistance center. https://www.samhsa.gov/disaster-preparedness/samhsas-efforts

Sue, D. W., Rasheed, M., & Rasheed, J. (2016). *Multicultural social work practice: A competency-based approach to diversity and social justice* (2nd ed.). Wiley.

Sunstein, C. R. (2016). *The ethics of influence: Government in the age of behavioral science.* Cambridge University Press.

Tabaac, A., Solazzo, A., Gordon, A., Austin, S., Guss, C., & Charlton, B. (2020). Sexual orientation-related disparities in healthcare access in three cohorts of U.S. adults. *Preventive Medicine*, https://doi.org/10.1016/j.ypmed.2020.105999

Tarasoff v. Regents of the University of California. (1976). 17 Cal. 3d 425 (Supreme Court CA). https://caselaw.findlaw.com/ca-supreme-court/1829929.html

Thomas, R. R. (1999). *Building a house for diversity: A fable about a giraffe and an elephant for today's workforce.* Thomas.

Thomas, R. V., & Pender, D. A. (2008). Association for specialists in group work: Best practice guidelines 2007 revisions. *Journal for Specialists in Group Work*, 33(2), 111–117.

Thurber, A. (2020). Cultural humility in community practice: Reflections from the neighborhood story project. *Reflections: Narratives of Professional Helping*, 26(2), 75–88. https://reflectionsnarrativesofprofessionalhelping.org/index.php/Reflections/article/view/1744

Torda, A. (2006). Ethical issues in pandemic planning. *Medical Journal of Australia*, 185(10), 73–76.

Toseland, R. W., & Rivas, R. F. (2017). *An introduction to group work practice* (8th ed.). Pearson.

Tronto, J. C. (2010). Creating caring institutions: Politics, plurality, and purpose. *Ethics and Social Welfare*, 4(2), 158–171. https://doi.org/10.1080/17496535.2010.484259

United Nations. (1948). *Universal declaration of human rights.* https://www.un.org/en/about-us/universal-declaration-of-human-rights

U.S. Constitution. 1st Amendment (1791); 11th Amendment (1795); 14th Amendment (1868); 19th Amendment (1920). http://www.usconstitution.net/const.html

U.S. Declaration of Independence. (1776). https://www.ushistory.org/declaration/document

U.S. Department of Education. (n.d.). Professional licensure. https://sites.ed.gov/international/professional-licensure

U.S. Department of Health and Human Services. (n.d.). *Health information privacy.* https://www.hhs.gov/hipaa/index.html

Valutis, S., & Rubin, D. (2016). Value conflicts in social work: Categories and correlates. *Journal of Social Work Values and Ethics*, 13(1), 11–24. https://jswve.org/download/2016-1/articles/13-1-2016-11-Value-Conflicts-in-Social-Work-Categories-and-Correlates.pdf

van der Tier, M., Hermans, K., & Potting, M. (2021). Social workers as state and citizen-agents. How social workers in a German, Dutch, and Flemish public welfare organization manage this dual responsibility in practice. *Journal of Social Work*, 22(3), 595–614. https://doi.org/10.1177/14680173211009724

Vieille, S. (2013). Frenemies: Restorative justice and customary mechanisms of justice. *Contemporary Justice Review*, 16(2), 174–192.

Watkins, C. E., & Milne, D. L. (Eds.). (2014). *The Wiley international handbook of clinical supervision.* Wiley.

Weiss, D. C. (2021). How Florida's new anti-riot law could run afoul of the First Amendment. *American Bar Association Journal.* https://www.abajournal.com/news/article/how-floridas-new-anti-riot-law-could-run-afoul-of-the-first-amendment

Wendler, D., Wesley, R., Pavlick, M., & Rid, A. (2016). Do patients want their families or their doctors to make treatment decisions in the event of incapacity, and why? *AJOV Empirical Bioethics, 7*(1), 251–259. https://doi.org/10.1080/23294515.2016.1182235

Whistleblower Protection Act. (1989, as amended). 5 U.S.C. §2302.

Whittaker, A., & Havard, T. (2016). Defensive practice as "fear-based" practice: Social work's open secret? *British Journal of Social Work, 46*(5), 1158–1174. https://doi.org/10.1093/bjsw/bcv048

Whitaker, J., & Smith, D. (2018). Ethics, meditation, and wisdom. In D. Cozort & J. Shields, *Oxford handbook of Buddhist ethics* (pp. 51–74). Oxford University Press. https://www.academia.edu/35070174/Ethics_Meditation_and_Wisdom

Whittle, E., Fisher, K., Reppermund, S., & Trollor, J. (2019). Access to mental health services: The experiences of people with intellectual disabilities. *Journal of Applied Res Intellectual Disabilities, 32*(2), 368–379. https://doi.org/10.1111/jar.12533

Wiebe, E., Shaw, J., Green, S., Trouton, K., & Kelly, M. (2018). Reasons for requesting medical assistance in dying. *Canadian Family Physician, 64*(9), 674–679.

Wilkins, D. (2017). How is supervision recorded in child and family social work: An analysis of 244 written records of formal supervision. *Child & Family Social Work, 22*(1), 1130–1140.

Wong, P. Y. J., & Lee, A. E. Y. (2015). Dual roles of social work supervisors: Strain and strengths as managers and clinical supervisors. *China Journal of Social Work, 8*(2), 164–181.

Yanow, D., & Schwartz-Shea, P. (2018). Framing "deception" and "covertness" in research: Do Milgram, Humphreys, and Zimbardo justify regulating social science research ethics? *Forum: Quality Social Research, 19*(3), Art.15.

Zastrow, C. H., & Hessenauer, S. L. (2021). *Generalist social work practice: A worktext* (12th ed.). Oxford University Press.

Zehr, H. (2015). *The little book of restorative justice.* Good Books.

Zieff, G., Kerr, Z. Y., Moore, J. B., & Stoner, L. (2020). Universal healthcare in the United States of America: A healthy debate. *Medicina (Kaunas, Lithuania), 56*(11), 580. https://doi.org/10.3390/medicina56110580 (https://www.ncbi.nlm.nih.gov/pmc/articles/PMC7692272/pdf/medicina-56-00580.pdf)

Zlodre, J., Yiend, J., Burns, T., & Fazel, S. (2016). Coercion, competence, and consent in offenders with personality disorder. *Psychology, Crime & Law, 22*(4), 315–330.

Zur, O. (2021). The risky business of risk management: How risk management guidelines can increase risk and decrease clinical effectiveness. https://www.zurinstitute.com/risk-management

Zur, O. (n.d.). Dual relationships, multiple relationships, boundaries, boundary crossings & boundary violations in psychotherapy, counseling & mental Health. https://www.zurinstitute.com/boundaries-dual-relationships/

ADDITIONAL RESOURCES AND WEBSITES

Alden March Bioethics Institute: https://www.bioethicstoday.org

American Medical Association: https://www.ama-assn.org/delivering-care/ama-code-medical-ethics

American Nursing Association: https://www.nursingworld.org/practice-policy/nursing-excellence/ethics/code-of-ethics-for-nurses

American Society for Bioethics and Humanities: https://asbh.org

Association of Family and Conciliation Courts (Standards of practice for family mediators, parenting coordinators, and custody evaluators): http://www.afccnet.org/Resource-Center/Practice-Guidelines

Association for Practical and Professional Ethics: https://appe-ethics.org

Association of Social Work Boards: https://www.aswb.org

Association for Specialists in Group Work (Group Work Standards): https://www.asgw.org

Canadian Association of Social Workers: https://www.casw-acts.ca

Clinical Social Work Association: https://www.clinicalsocialworkassociation.org

Council on Social Work Education (CSWE) (accreditation for social work schools in USA): https://www.cswe.org

Ethics and Malpractice: https://www.kspope.com/ethics/malpractice.php

Ethics of Care: https://ethicsofcare.org

Foundations of Critical Thinking: https://www.criticalthinking.org

Ethics Codes Collection (links to codes from around the globe): https://ethicscodescollection.org

International Journal of Social Work Values and Ethics: https://jswve.org

Joint Centre for Bioethics: https://jcb.utoronto.ca

Journal of Law, Medicine, and Ethics: https://onlinelibrary.wiley.com/journal/1748720x

Journal of Moral Education: https://www.tandfonline.com/loi/cjme20

Jubilee Centre for Character and Virtues: https://www.jubileecentre.ac.uk

Kennedy Institute of Ethics: https://kennedyinstitute.georgetown.edu

National Association of Black Social Workers Code of Ethics: https://www.nabsw.org/page/CodeofEthics

National Association of Social Workers: https://www.socialworkers.org

National Institutes of Health—Human Subjects Review Training: https://humansubjects.nih.gov

Stanford Encyclopedia of Philosophy: https://plato.stanford.edu (including entries on St. Thomas Aquinas, Immanuel Kant, Martin Buber, and other social philosophers and ethicists)

Tuskegee University, National Center for Bioethics in Research and Health Care (including concerns specific to African Americans and other underserved people): https://www.tuskegee.edu/bioethics

INDEX